11/5/14

For Chuck and Roberta,

With fond memories of
the old days — and glad
we've stayed connected —

Warmly,
Michael

On The Front Lines In A Changing Jewish World

Michael C. Kotzin

Collected Writings
1988-2013

Foreword by
Steven B. Nasatir

Preface by
Yossi Klein Halevi

 **JUF PRESS**

ISBN 978-0-9907128-0-0

 JUF PRESS

JUF Press
30 South Wells Street
Chicago, IL
www.JUF.org

Permission to reprint the following pieces, all by the author, is acknowledged with appreciation:

"Confronting the Holocaust Fifty Years Later," in *Criterion* (Spring/Summer, 1997).

"Louis Farrakhan's Anti-Semitism," in *Christian Century* (March 2, 1994).

"The Language of the New Anti-Semitism," in *Global Antisemitism: A Crisis of Modernity,* ed. Charles
Asher Small. New York: Institute for the Study of Global Antisemitism and Policy (ISGAP), 2013.

"Pictures at an Exhibition," in *Anti-Semitism International* (Nos. 5-6, 2010).

"The State of Israel Studies," with Elie Rekhess, in *The Bloomsbury Companion to Jewish Studies,* ed.
Dean Phillip Bell. London: Bloomsbury, 2013.

"Afterword" in *A Legacy of Catholic-Jewish Dialogue: The Joseph Cardinal Bernardin Jerusalem Lectures,* ed.
Thomas Baima. Chicago: Archdiocese of Chicago Liturgy Training Publications, 2012.

"Local Community Relations Councils and Their National Body," in *Jewish Polity and American Civil
Society,"* ed. Alan Mittleman, Jonathan D. Sarna, and Robert Licht. New York: Rowman & Littlefield, 2002.

"Words to Remember Him By," in *University of Chicago Magazine* (March-April, 2013).

"A Look from the Left," in *The Book: An Online Review at The New Republic* (February 14, 2012).

"From Chicago to the Yishuv," forthcoming in Hebrew translation in
Iyunim Bitkumat Israel: Studies in Israeli and Modern Jewish Society.

Book design by Susan Marx

Printed in the United States of America
First Printing, 2014

Publisher's Cataloging-In-Publication Data
(Prepared by The Donohue Group, Inc.)

Kotzin, Michael C.
    On the front lines in a changing Jewish world : collected writings, 1988-2013 / Michael C. Kotzin ;
foreword by Steven B. Nasatir ; preface by Yossi Klein Halevi.

        pages : illustrations ; cm

    Issued also as an ebook.
    Includes bibliographical references.
    ISBN: 978-0-9907128-0-0 (hardcover)
    ISBN: 978-0-9907128-1-7 (softcover)

    1. United States--Ethnic relations. 2. Jews--United States--Social conditions--20th century. 3. Jews-
-United States--Social conditions--21st century. 4. United States--Foreign relations--20th century. 5.
United States--Foreign relations--21st century. 6. Antisemitism--United States. 7. Essays. I. Nasatir,
Steven B. II. Klein Halevi, Yossi, 1953- III. Title.

E184.36.S65 K68 2014
305.8924073

For Judy

•　•　•

CONTENTS

Defending Israel in the Community, in the Media, and on Campus 167

Foreword

by Steven B. Nasatir

• • •

I first met Michael Kotzin in 1983, when he returned to Chicago after living in Israel with his family for eleven years while teaching at Tel Aviv University and then working in two other American Jewish communities for the ADL. His return to his hometown came when he was tapped to assume ADL's top position in Chicago, a post long held by the legendary Ab Rosen. Historically ADL and this Federation enjoyed a good cooperative relationship and my first impressions of Michael were of a smart, experienced, Jewishly knowledgeable and committed colleague. I immediately liked and respected him.

I learned early that he too was a "Chicago guy." In Chicago, when someone asks where you went to school, they aren't asking about college. As it happens, Michael has his undergraduate degree from the University of Chicago and a Ph.D. from University of Minnesota. But to the question of what high school did you attend—Michael went to Sullivan and I Von Steuben. Back in the day, the north side Chicago public high schools of choice were Sullivan, Von Steuben, Roosevelt and Senn, with Mather added in 1959. There was a familiar bond among the Jewish students attending those schools. There were no six degrees of separation. One degree was more like it. We pretty much grew up the same way, had been taught similar values by our parents, knew one another's geographical turf, spoke with a Chicago accent, and competed academically, athletically, and in every other way. The added ingredient in the familiarity between Michael and me was our unusual devotion to the major league baseball team located south on 35th and Shields. This overall Chicago context was not incidental to our rapport or our shared Jewish world view.

Thus, in 1988, when Federation's Jewish Community Relations Council (JCRC) Executive Director, Peggy Norton, z"l, informed me of her desire to retire, I set my sights on Michael Kotzin as the perfect fit to set our public affairs agenda going forward.

In reading this compendium of Michael's insightful, motivating articles, it is helpful to be aware of Chicago's unique Jewish public affairs scene in the decades before he came to work at Federation. As it happens,

Chicago and New York were the last two major Jewish communities to establish a JCRC. That is rather ironic, since in many other ways Chicago and New York are more often among the first to move in important new directions. But for Chicago, the reason a JCRC wasn't established earlier (some communities had JCRCs as early as the 1930s), and the reason why we started it in 1972 with more limited goals and budget as compared to other JCRCs, was because a lot of good work was already being done by ADL, American Jewish Committee, the Jewish Labor Committee and (back then) American Jewish Congress, among others.

Overall, before the 1967 Six Day War the need to coordinate community relations advocacy and community action among all Jewish organizations working on the local level was not as clear as it eventually became. Furthermore, some of the Federation leadership in Chicago had to be convinced that the organization's agenda needed further expansion and that Federation itself should be the direct provider of this type of service. Those questioning that assumption thought it was challenging enough to raise funds for local human service and Jewish educational needs and, of course, for the ongoing need to help Israel and to address all the other national and international Jewish needs. They also asked, since Federation is a community-wide, consensus driven body, why take the risk of becoming involved in policy differences that do and will forever exist within the community, thereby placing Federation exactly where it needs to avoid being: at the very center of internal communal strife?

Over time, the leadership began to realize that in fact the long standing agenda (fundraising and helping people at home and abroad) and community relations were deeply entwined. The Jewish community was strong and involvement in the great events in Jewish life such as the struggle for Soviet Jewry and supporting the people of Israel required funds but also public advocacy, coordination and action. In short, leadership from the community's leading institution in a new arena was called for.

When we talked about his coming to the Federation, Michael and I discussed that shared vision. He himself brought extraordinary creativity and intellectual prowess to bear in advancing it, and the timing was perfect: the new public affairs approach Federation sought to follow was to be led by a professional who could both imagine and implement that new reality. Michael and I wanted to see our Federation ramp up its advocacy agenda and more closely connect our community to those great events and major issues in Jewish life, and in assuming the helm of the JCRC he was the one to help take us there.

Furthermore, as Yossi Klein Halevi observes in his Preface to this volume, Michael sought to more vigorously project this expanded public affairs agenda within and beyond the Jewish community. In addition to producing the written words re-printed here, which first appeared in impressive, diverse venues, Michael also emerged as our community's leading spokesperson in the key electronic media outlets of those days – radio and television. In short, Michael's coming to Federation was b'sheret – perfect timing for him, the Federation's new directions, and the challenges and opportunities that the next 25 plus years would present to our community.

Michael is the recipient of numerous awards and honors. Having added other federation responsibilities to his portfolio beyond the JCRC, he has been a mentor and a role model for other professionals and a trusted friend and advisor to generations of key volunteer leadership. He is my friend and confidante, and the community and I are indebted to him for the major contribution he has made to our collective work.

As I reread Michael's flowing prose, I am reminded of the times, places and circumstances where his experience, passion and clarity of thought have made such a difference. The pages of this book speak to Michael's express convictions of how communities, institutions and governments have distinct but connected roles in developing policy and action agendas. The articles also represent Michael's belief in the central role of Federation in organizing, invigorating, and activating the Jewish people.

Together, these pieces reflect a particular period in American Jewish and global Jewish history. They constitute an authoritative, first-person account of where this community and this federation have been, and they provide important bottom lines on directions that the Federation and the community should continue going. We have all been enriched by Michael's life work and touched by his writings.

Kol hakavod, my dear Chaver.

Steven B. Nasatir is President of the Jewish United Fund / Jewish Federation of Metropolitan Chicago

Preface

Michael Kotzin and the
Struggle for Jewish Legitimacy
by Yossi Klein Halevi

• • •

The post-Holocaust alliance that emerged between the American Jewish community and the state of Israel was based on a shared vision of Jewish life. The most dignified and effective response to the Holocaust, most Israelis and American Jews believed, required Jews to find their place as equals in the non-Jewish world – but together, as a Jewish collective. The mainstream of the two communities rejected both assimilation and self-ghettoziation. Each community devised its own strategy for entering the non-Jewish world as a collective. For Israel, that meant becoming a nation among nations; for American Jews, an increasingly self-confident minority defending its ethical commitments and political agenda in the public space of the world's most powerful nation.

The practical message of the Final Solution was that Jewish powerlessness had become literally untenable. The philosophical message of the Final Solution was that the Jews were entirely Other, outside a shared humanity. By creating collectives committed to restoring Jewish power and comfortable functioning in non-Jewish arenas, Israelis and American Jews joined together to define and defend a new model of Jewish life.

The result was the simultaneous rise of the two most powerful Jewish communities in history, a renaissance all the more astonishing given its proximity to the Holocaust.

But that achievement has come under growing assault. The movement to delegitimize Israel and banish it to a diplomatic ghetto, along with challenging the legitimacy of American Jewish political clout, aims at reversing the post-Holocaust Jewish success story and returning us to an era of vulnerability and demoralization.

The first major victory of the delegitimizers occurred on November 9, 1975, with the UN vote to equate Zionism with racism. Since then, their efforts have known varied success. The delegitimization campaign waned in the 1990s, with the collapse of the Soviet Union and the launching of the Oslo process. But with the emergence of the Boycott, Divestment and

Sanctions movement (BDS), the war against the post-Holocaust Jewish renaissance has become an even greater threat than in the past.

As a result, the agenda of the organized American Jewish community has been increasingly focused on defending the legitimacy of Jewish political and military power. A subtle but historic transformation has occurred in Jewish life: The American Jewish "establishment," once reviled by activist critics for lack of will in defending Jewish rights, has emerged in recent decades as the carrier of the activist ethos. At once confident as Americans and as Jews, inspired by Israel's achievements and tormented by American Jewry's failure to effectively respond to the Shoah, a generation of Jewish leaders and professionals has reshaped the community into the extraordinarily effective instrument for Jewish interests that it is today. It is in that context that Michael Kotzin's life work should be understood. Michael, who grew up in a family of lovers of Zion, moved to Israel in 1968. His three children were all born there, and he served in the IDF. Since moving back to his native Chicago, he has been a leading force, both locally and nationally, in strengthening ties between American Jewry and Israel, and defending Israel's good name against the demonizers.

Michael's emergence as a preeminent advocate for Israel parallelled the emergence of an assertive American Jewish community, championing the state of Israel along with endangered Diaspora communities.

Michael took as his starting point Zionism's two great promises to the Jewish people: to restore us as a sovereign nation in our homeland, and to restore us as a nation among nations, respected in the international community. Michael's passionate commitment to both those goals helped him become one of the first in the Jewish community to clearly perceive and effectively respond to the threat of anti-Zionism. Recognizing that the greatest danger to Israel in academia was not Israel Apartheid Week but what was being taught and not taught in Middle Eastern studies classes, Michael pioneered Israel Studies programs that were among the first in the country. Working with university presidents, Christian clergy, newspaper editorial boards, Michael pressed Israel's case and challenged those who would criminalize the Jewish state. Michael's very demeanor -- dignified, persistent, unapologetic – has embodied the post-Holocaust transformation of American Jewish life.

Michael is that rare activist who is also a powerful writer. The essays and op-eds collected here are at once passionate and restrained, a literary sensibility reflecting Michael's background in English literature. (He taught literature at Tel Aviv University.) There is no empty rhetoric in these pages. Michael chooses his words carefully, makes his points in the same refined way with which he conducts his advocacy efforts.

Reading these essays, one senses that Michael is drawn to Jewish identity at least in part because of his love for a good story. The Jews are, after all, a story that we tell ourselves about who we think we are. That is why the seminal ritual uniting Jews across time and space is the Passover seder, the retelling of our origins.

Michael knows that Jewish survival depends on a coherent Jewish narrative. And so the war for the legitimacy of Zionism and Israel is an existential struggle – no less, ultimately, than the war Israel must periodically fight along its borders. The attempt to delegitimize Israel is ultimately aimed against Jewish history. In the Muslim world, that war takes the form of an assault on the most basic facts of our story, from the existence of the Temple to the Holocaust. In the West the assault is more subtle but no less devastating: an attempt to invert the Jewish story by relativizing the Holocaust and transforming Israelis into colonialists and even Nazis – turning the Holocaust itself against the Jews. ("How could you, after all you've suffered, do the same thing to another people?")

Michael's writings are dispatches from the front in the war for Jewish legitimacy. Here, in one powerful essay, is Michael resurrecting a long-forgotten book about the pre-state Zionist struggle by leftwing journalist I.F.Stone, reminding us that Zionism was once a liberal cause. And here, in numerous op-eds, is Michael taking on the enemies of the Jewish people – personally, in the ring against Farrakhan and Butz and Ahmadinejad. One can feel Michael's outrage at the cunning persistence of anti-semitism after the Holocaust – in its way as astonishing a phenomenon as the ability of the Jews to survive the Holocaust. Yet even as he takes on the new would-be genocidal enemies of the Jews, Michael fights like a gentleman, arguing rationally, never hitting below the belt.

Some of his most evocative writing is about traveling the Jewish world. In Michael's literary/historical consciousness, Jewish time is elastic. Even as he writes of the past – from seeking collective roots in Andalucia to family roots in Odessa – Michael's thoughts are never far from contemporary Jewish reality. Nor is the personal ever entirely personal. Retracing his family's steps in early 20th century Odessa, he discovers the homes of Babel and Shalom Aleichem – and of the great Zionist writers and poets, Bialik and Pinsker and Ahad Ha'am. He savours a novel about Jewish life in Odessa written by another of its notable sons, Jabotinsky. The state of Israel, he reminds us, is a story that began in the tracts and poems and novels of Jewish writers. In Odessa's streets, the literary, the historical and the personal converge – the ultimate Michael Kotzin moment.

These essays, written with deep love for the Jewish people, offer many such moments. They provide a compelling glimpse into the motivations and inner life of an American Jewish leader in the post-Holocaust era, revealing the struggles and joys of being a 21st century Jew.

Yossi Klein Halevi is a senior fellow of the Shalom Hartman Institute in Jerusalem. He is the author of Like Dreamers: The Story of the Israeli Paratroopers Who Reunited Jerusalem and Divided a Nation, which won the 2013 Everett Family Jewish Book of the Year Award of the Jewish Book Council.

The Past As Prologue:
By Way of Introduction

The foxglove blossom – a third part bud, a third part past,
a third part in full bloom – is a type of the life of this world.
John Ruskin, *The Stones of Venice, 1851-53*

• • •

Growing Up Jewish in Chicago

This book is a collection of pieces written during my years of employment at the Jewish Federation of Metropolitan Chicago, which
began in the fall of 1988. In selecting the items to include and in thinking
back over the developments and experiences that led me to write them, I
have come to recognize the extent to which my work at the Federation integrated key elements of my personal background, experience, interests,
and values. I touch on aspects of that background and on some of those
experiences from time to time within these pieces, but this Introduction
provides a more extended opportunity for me to look inward and to pull
together several details about myself. And it also provides the occasion
for observing how extensively variations on the theme of change recur in
one of the collected pieces after another and how that theme informs the
book as a whole.

Like Saul Bellow's Augie March, I am an American, Chicago born.
But there the likeness mostly ends. Still, my family background is of a
sort that Bellow was very familiar with. My paternal grandfather left
Poland for Canada shortly before World War I but was not able to go
back for the rest of his immediate family until the war had ended. My
father, the youngest of four brothers, thus spent the first 13 years of his
life in Poland, and the family's Eastern European Jewish background
had an impact on the conditions in which I grew up. My grandmother's
Chicago apartment, shared with an unmarried uncle and family cousin,
had an "old world" ambiance. Relatives who had remained in Europe
still longer – some of whom survived the Holocaust by making their way
into Russia – added to the flavor.

My grandfather, who died nearly two decades before I was born,
brought a collection of Hebrew language books to the New World,
among them volumes that currently reside on my bookshelves. Some

were prayer books or other religious texts, others history books or novels. And while the family had maintained a level of religious observance in Poland, they were very much part of the enlightened urban world there as well. The family's primary language then was Polish, and in fact my father used to joke that he didn't learn Yiddish until coming to Chicago as a young man and becoming active in Zionist affairs. His brothers had preceded him in that realm of activism back in Europe, and the family was so Zionistic that the album they brought with them to North America, filled mostly with photos of relatives taken while still in Europe, had a picture of Theodor Herzl on its first page.

When my grandfather was able to go back to get his family and bring them to Canada – along with a cousin who had lived with them and a stranger he met on a train and "adopted" so he could come with as well – they went to Edmonton, Alberta, where my father spent his high school years. The family moved to Chicago in 1923 and settled in the Humboldt Park neighborhood. While working during the day, my father attended DePaul University, then Kent Law School in the evening. He practiced law for a while, then joined two of his brothers in a manufacturing business. But beyond family life it always was his involvement in Zionist activity that engaged his passions most deeply. In the '20s, he founded a city-wide Labor Zionist youth group, and in the years after that he was one of the key Labor Zionist leaders in Chicago, until he retired and he and my mother made Aliyah to Israel in 1971.

My mother's background (which I talk about more extensively in the piece in this volume based on a visit to Odessa, where she was born and where her father died) was somewhat different but had key similarities. In her case the family was able to leave Eastern Europe right before World War I, when she was a small child, and she and her family also first went to Canada. In Winnipeg, Manitoba, she attended the I.L. Peretz Folk School, which the Jewish Encyclopedia identifies as the first Yiddish day school in North America, and then went to a public high school.

My mother and members of her family also moved to Chicago in the '20s, and she and my father were married in 1932. I was born in 1941, and when I was a year old, we moved into the house I grew up in, in West Rogers Park. The neighborhood at first was "mixed," which in our part of the North Side of Chicago in those years meant that there were Jews and Catholics, along with some Protestants. The area was not yet very heavily built-up, and in fact, the streets were hardly paved, and I remember passing a farm field while walking to the bus with my mother. In the '50s there was considerable construction in the neighborhood, which became heavily Jewish.

Our family was Jewishly involved in many ways. Like many members of Conservative synagogues in that time, we kept a kosher home and maintained an annual calendar marked by observing the holidays with our extended family, but we did not observe all of the traditional rituals or regularly attend synagogue on the Sabbath. Education was emphasized in our house, and my Jewish education started even before I was old enough to attend our synagogue's Hebrew School, when my parents arranged for another Hebrew School's principal to come to our home to tutor my sister, three years older than me, and I participated as well.

After attending Hebrew School at Ner Tamid Congregation and having my Bar Mitzvah there, I continued in the Communal Division of the Hebrew High School maintained in those days by Chicago's Board of Jewish Education. Classes, held at the College of Jewish Studies building at 72 East 11th Street after the first couple of years, took place after our public school days had finished on two weekdays and on Sundays. Many of our teachers were refugees from Europe or Holocaust survivors who, I came to realize much later, were probably trained to instruct a very different sort of student from our group of young Americans, who, when all is said and done, cared more about having a good time than being serious scholars.

A goodly number of my classmates were children of rabbis and Jewish educators, but there I was too, getting an education in tune with the values my parents wanted to inculcate in me. Many of us knew one another from Camp Ramah, the Conservative movement's overnight camp in northern Wisconsin, where I started going the summer after my Bar Mitzvah. I continued going there for four more summers, the last of them in a "work-study" group, and in later years I came to recognize how profoundly those Ramah summers shaped my Jewish identity.

A central aspect of that identity, in this case influenced most directly by my home life, included connecting with Israel. As far back as I can remember, Israel was a key part of our family's existence, driven in great part by my father's Zionist activities and by my mother's participation as well. I remember the pieces of mail that would be set out on a hall table until my father would come home from work, mail which included Yiddish newspapers from New York, early issues of I.L. Kenen's biweekly Near East Report, and the Jewish Frontier, the monthly publication of the Labor Zionist movement, with its frequent articles by notable figures like Ben Halpern and Marie Syrkin – articles that I started reading myself as I grew older. I also frequently turned to the family bookshelves, reading short stories I found in a massive, wonderful collection, and novels, but also selections from such works as the collected essays of Hayim Greenberg, a major Labor Zionist thinker.

My parents first visited Israel right after the Sinai Campaign of 1956. My sister, who was more active than I in Habonim, the Labor Zionist youth movement, went to Israel on their year-long Workshop after graduating high school, and she made Aliyah in 1961. My own first visit to the country was for her wedding, in the summer of 1962 right after I graduated from college. My touring the country and seeing the Jewish state for the first time, just 14 years after independence, had a lasting impact.

My undergraduate years were spent at the University of Chicago, which had attracted me in part because of the impression made on me by several U of C students who were on the staff at Ramah. Along with Ramah, I've always considered the university the greatest formative intellectual influence on me outside of my home. Before that, however, came high school.

Our neighborhood had been redistricted shortly before I graduated Rogers Elementary School, and so although my sister and others of her generation had attended Senn High School, I went to Sullivan in East Rogers Park. That neighborhood also had a sizable Jewish population, but not as great as that of West Rogers Park, so going to Sullivan gave me greater opportunity to connect with classmates from different religious backgrounds than had been the case in my earlier school years. At the same time, once the kids from our neighborhood started going to Sullivan, that school became more "Jewish" than it had been – something that apparently bothered a couple of the old-time teachers, who provided me with my first personal introductions to anti-Semitism. One of those teachers repeatedly – and surely deliberately – mispronounced the name of a Jewish student, while another insisted on giving exams on Jewish holidays and did not allow those of us who missed school to observe the holidays to make them up.

The most memorable aspects of the high school years for me were of a non-curricular sort. One was being on the freshman-sophomore basketball team, whose schedule included games at high schools throughout the city. Another was being a member of an honors service group, which enabled a handful of fellow students and me to spend our study hall time on our own and allowed us to leave school on various errands. And finally there was the pleasure of writing a column for the school newspaper while serving as one of its editors. And then I was off to college.

Setting Out

For me the University of Chicago was a place of intellectual excitement where I had scintillating teachers while being exposed – to use the cliché – to great ideas and great books. Those teachers were scholars of the first order who treated my classmates and me as initiates into their community. Despite the image of the school, those years were also fun. A couple of my classmates had been friends of mine in high school, while others came from very different sorts of backgrounds, broadening my world on the one hand and inclining me to appreciate my own background and the values with which I had grown up on the other.

During my high school years, I worked in a neighborhood grocery store (along with a friend I have remained close with since fourth grade), but most of my subsequent part-time jobs through college and the early graduate school years were in the Jewish community. After graduating high school, I spent two summers working at a synagogue day camp, and while in college, I spent another summer working at the Chicago Jewish Community Center's overnight facility, Camp Chi. During the school year I directed JCC activities in South Shore and staffed a United Synagogue Youth group in that neighborhood. Then, during my early years in graduate school in Minneapolis, before I began teaching Freshman English as a teaching assistant, I taught in a synagogue Sunday School and was a swimming instructor for the local JCC. And in the summer after my first year there I worked at the overnight camp operated by the Rochester, New York, equivalent of the JCCs, Camp Seneca Lake, where I met my future wife, Judy, also a native Chicagoan.

Despite that continuous connection to the Jewish community and the urging of my own rabbi and one of the rabbis I worked for, I never thought at that time that I would end up having a career in Jewish communal service. Instead, enchanted by books and inspired by some of the teachers I had at the University of Chicago (foremost among them Norman Maclean), I chose a career studying and teaching literature, and I became a graduate student in English at the University of Minnesota. I remember, in my first quarter there, taking a class in the Metaphysical Poets from Leonard Unger (one of the few Jewish professors in that department, as I recall) and going to see him to ask what I had gotten myself into. Most of the texts we began with were Christian in purpose, language, and imagery, and I couldn't help wondering how much the literature I would now be studying, writing about, and teaching, was an expression of that faith tradition. He told me that was only part of the story, and in the long run I benefitted from broadening my range of knowledge and understanding – as I discovered in this case, especially, when I later became involved in interfaith activities.

When, in my fifth year at Minnesota, Israel was threatened with destruction and then had its amazing victory in the Six Day War of June 1967, I inevitably was emotionally engaged. I vividly remember the dread induced by the Israel-hating slogans that emanated from Arab countries during the build-up to the war, and the television images of the massive crowds that took to the streets of Cairo and Alexandria calling on Nasser to rescind the resignation he announced after Egypt's initial reverses. As the war was about to break out, I was approached by a friend of mine from my Ramah and college days who was working in the local Anti-Defamation League office. At his request, I prepared what I suppose was my first bit of writing of its sort, an informational background piece about Israel and its neighbors which my friend then distributed. (I had, during those Minnesota years, already been writing film and theater reviews for the university newspaper.)

Though Israel was already a significant aspect of my being, along with much of the American Jewish community I was galvanized by the impact of that war. And then, a year later, when I began my search for the first job I would hold after receiving my Ph.D. and I learned that the Chairman of the English Department at Tel Aviv University would be interviewing at that year's Modern Language Association meeting in Chicago, I made an appointment, spoke to him, and accepted his offer. And so, at the end of August 1968, one day after a walk through Grant Park, which was still suffused with an acrid stench from the tear gassing of Democratic Convention protesters the night before, my wife and I said goodbye to our parents in Chicago and were on our way to Israel.

Our plan was to stay in Israel two or three years, but we ended up remaining for eleven, with all three of our children born there. These were, in many ways, wonderful and deeply meaningful years, though they were at times challenging as well. Needless to say, there is much I could talk about regarding that time, especially referencing the events we experienced, the friends we made, and the delightful students I had. But a good deal of that is recollected in various pieces in this collection, and the primary purpose of this introduction is to describe the forces that led me to the Federation, that strengthened me as I have played my role there, and that enabled me to write the kinds of pieces that are collected in this volume, so I will keep those remembrances short here. Suffice it to say that living in Israel greatly enriched my understanding of the reality of that country, intensely strengthened my own ties to it, and profoundly deepened my belief in the importance of ensuring the safety of the state and its people.

Living in Israel during those years and especially serving in the Israel Defense Forces during the 1973 Yom Kippur War and for several months afterwards, while also sharing experiences like the exhilaration of learning about the rescue of the Israeli hostages in Entebbe, Uganda, on July 4, 1976, left me, I believe, with a reset internal gyroscope, enabling me to be better able to keep the extremes that life presents in perspective. And it also gave me the sense of how it feels to be part of something bigger than oneself.

In 1979 I returned to the States with my wife and our three children feeling that, if I was not going to live in Israel, it was important to somehow serve the Jewish people. I went to work for the Anti-Defamation League, first in their Atlanta office; then as Director of their Ohio-Kentucky-Indiana regional office, based in Columbus, Ohio; and then, beginning in 1983, as Director of their Chicago regional office.

The ADL was a perfect transition between Israel and the Chicago Federation. I learned the ropes from superb mentors in Atlanta, and then in Columbus I became familiar with what it means to be a part of American Jewish organizational life. And then came the move to Chicago. The city had changed in many ways since I'd left 21 years before, and so had I. But it was still the city I knew, with a Jewish community whose history, demographics, and characteristics were familiar to me.

The ADL years gave me the experience of dealing with some of the issues confronted by America's Jewish community. But the subsequent move up the street to the Federation, first as Director of its Jewish Community Relations Council, later also as supervisor of the Communications Department, then as Executive Vice President, gave me broader scope and placed me in the city's main locally-based Jewish community organization. Coming to work at the Federation – an institution originally founded primarily to raise funds for functional agencies in the community – at a time when it was increasingly moving into programmatic territory of its own enabled me to grow further professionally, with greater responsibilities and a greater chance to determine my own, and the institution's, directions.

For more than 25 years – during the past three of which I have served as Senior Counselor to the President – the Federation has provided me with many extraordinary experiences. Much of that has involved travel, which has included visiting the Soviet Union with a Jewish United Fund mission; visiting Lithuania and Poland with Dick Durbin shortly after he was elected to the Senate; and going to Israel on numerous trips, several for members of the Illinois Congressional Delegation and others for Christian clergy and leaders in Chicago's academic and intergroup worlds. It also meant joining with an American Jewish Committee counterpart and two representatives of the Archdiocese in planning and participating in an unprecedented trip to Israel with Joseph Cardinal Bernardin and a Catholic-Jewish delegation from Chicago. And it meant planning and participating in a high visibility Federation trip there with Chicago Mayor Richard M. Daley; accompanying then-Senator Barack Obama during his first trip to Israel; and traveling there with Illinois Governor Pat Quinn.

With a guest pass from Senator Obama, I was able to be present when Prime Minister Ehud Olmert addressed a joint session of the U.S. Congress. Later, back in Chicago, I was able to be up close in Grant Park on the election night which marked a breakthrough in the history of race in America. (The inauguration didn't work out as well since, along with thousands of other holders of purple tickets, I was shunted into a tunnel underneath the Washington Mall from whence we were not to emerge until it was too late to get on the Mall itself.)

As I once said to the Federation staff when we gathered at a time when Israel's people were suffering from a wave of suicide bombings, we were fortunate enough to not just feel the anguish but to be able to do something to address the situation in a meaningful way. I have had the opportunity to guide communal responses in arenas of concern ranging from Iran's attempt to obtain a nuclear weapon capability to the rise of the new anti-Semitism to the attempts to deny Israel's right to exist. Much of that has meant participating in national and international structures while also helping to spearhead local responses to such challenges. I was able to participate in efforts such as the Israel Foreign Ministry's "Brand Israel" endeavor. And I had the opportunity to draw upon my academic background in establishing an innovative Israel Studies Project supported by the Federation while also pulling together a Federation Faculty Advisory Group and forming relationships with administrators at many of the main universities in the Chicago area.

I have had the opportunity to serve as a spokesman of the Federation and of the community in dealing with a range of critical issues. For a dozen years I had the chance to stretch myself creatively in making the videos produced annually by the JUF. And I have had the opportunity to give the speeches and to write the articles, columns, and reviews that are collected in this volume.

Some of the pieces included here have an advocacy thrust, while others are more analytic and contemplative. While each of them reflects the time in which they were written, I believe that they have continuing relevance as well. Put together as they are, they demonstrate the ebbing and flowing of history through a quarter-century of dramatic change which has taken the Jewish community through evolving challenges and circumstances.

About Change

Looking back, friends and I have often remarked that ours was a particularly fortunate generation. Spending our childhood in the years following World War II and then our teen years in the '50s, we benefited greatly from that era's social stability, when life for young people was simpler, less pressured, and less uncertain than is the case today, and when we had greater freedom to simply get about on our own, without fear. For Jews, anti-Semitism was lessening, and it soon entered into what we now can see as a temporary lull. Overall acceptance was up and discrimination was down. This was the era when Jews assumed the status of the third religious community in America, encapsulated in the title of Will Herberg's famous book of 1960, Protestant-Catholic-Jew.

For a young person, life was easier and looser than it had been for earlier generations or than it is for today's youth. When, as young neighborhood kids, we wanted to go out to play in an empty lot on a long, hot summer evening, or when my friends and I got a bit older and wanted to play ball after school or during the weekend, we simply did it, on our own, without adult supervision. When we wanted to go ice skating on the frozen-over Touhy Beach or to head to Wrigley Field to see the Cubs (though I was a White Sox fan and more often went to their games, frequently with my father), or to go downtown to the public library, or to a movie theater, we simply got on the bus or the "L" by ourselves and did it. This began even when we were in elementary school.

When it came time to go to college, there was none of the stress of making an impression or the pressure of making a choice like our lives depended on it. I applied to one college, via a fairly simple form, got accepted, and went there. When it came time to make a career choice, we realized that the possibilities were far greater than they had been for our parents' generation. And unlike the generations that have followed, we did not, at the time, think it was likely that the career we had chosen might become defunct and that we would probably be making multiple career changes through our working lives.

Needless to say, that era has also merited criticism and mockery for being stultifying and conformist. And not everything turned out the way we had anticipated it would in those early years. With my wife and me playing our part through involvement in the anti-Vietnam War movement, through campaigning for Eugene McCarthy in the Presidential primaries, and in other ways, our generation created the '60s, the decade when, to cite our folk singer-poet laureate, the times they were a-changing. And since then the times have kept changing in American society, in the world at large, in the Jewish world, and in many personal lives.

To illustrate with just one set of details, from the age of one until the age of 18, I lived in just one home. During my college years, I lived with friends in different apartments for three straight years, and I had two residences during my first two years of graduate school. That kind of nomadic life could have been expected for a student. But from the time my wife and I were married in 1964 until we moved to Chicago in 1983, we had eight different residences (two of them when I had sabbatical leaves), giving our children a very different set of experiences from those I had grown up with. Furthermore, while I had begun to sense the ground shifting during my youth, and with change being a fact of life during the '60s in America, during the 11 years I then spent in Israel I lived in circumstances in which the unexpected always lurked just around the corner, and often presented itself. Experiencing the Yom Kippur War of 1973 – and serving in the Israel Defense Forces for six of the eight months following its outbreak, on three separate tours of Reserve duty, with a child being born two-thirds of the way through all of that – made me feel like I existed in a crucible of change and uncertainty.

At the same time, the focus of my primary academic endeavors connected me with writers and thinkers from an age when life was seen as greatly defined by the process of change. My major field of study was Victorian Literature (I specialized in the works of Charles Dickens), which I gravitated to while in graduate school given the greatness of some of that era's literary output and its anticipation of our own time. What I learned was that it was an age which saw profound changes wrought by industrialism, the coming of the railroad, urbanization, evolutionary thought, and other forces, with writers who powerfully portrayed and analyzed those conditions.

Tuned in, thus, to the dynamics of change, it has struck me how much change has become a prevailing circumstance in the life of our time, and in the issues in which I have been involved and have written about. While it has been common over the past 200 years or so for citizens of the Western industrialized world to feel themselves living in transitional conditions, and while that certainly has been the case for the Jewish people, at the same time, these last 25 years have without question been marked by great, accelerating changes of particular kinds. Driving that sense of change has been the collapse of the Soviet Union and the reshaping of international relations (a reshaping which continues to evolve in sometimes unpredictable ways, as the events taking place in Ukraine as I write this have reminded us); the intensification of globalization; the rise of radical Islamism; the development of new technologies leading to a communications revolution; cultural, economic, and climate changes; and more. Many of these changes have been interlinked, and all of them, in one way or another, have implications for Jewish interests and the Jewish communal agenda, while the Jewish community has also experienced internal changes of its own. And practically all of this has come into play in events I have experienced and subjects I have dealt with and written about over this past quarter-century.

Rather than proceeding chronologically, this collection of pieces is divided into thematically-framed sections, with each of those sections proceeding more or less in a chronological fashion. Given the overlapping nature of some of the topics dealt with in these sections, several pieces might have been placed in different sections from those in which they appear. Hopefully, though, the way the material is organized will make sense to the book's readers.

The book begins with reflections based on visits to countries in the "Old World" and the Jewish communities there, many of them places directly affected by the fall of the Soviet Union and by other changes connected with that transformative event. The next section focuses on the rise of international terrorism, an issue which became central in America following the 9/11 attacks and which has had great impact on the Jewish people. Following that come analyses of trends surrounding anti-Semitism – both expressions of traditional forms of it (which in Chicago has repeatedly emanated from Louis Farrakhan) and the development of a new form, one which at its core involves attitudes toward Israel and the attempted delegitimization of that country. That leads into a section that focuses on the defense of Israel, the need for which intensified in the new century as the hopes for peace generated by the Oslo process were dashed by the escalating terror against Israeli civilians, by the growth of

Hezbollah and Hamas, and by blatant assaults on Israel's right to exist –
not to mention the threat of a nuclear Iran.

A notable development regarding perspectives on Israel among
American Jewry in this period has involved the fact that, to a great extent,
the new generations of Jews – often with a reduced sense of Jewish identity to start with – have inevitably been less directly connected with the
Israel of its inspirational founding years and of the Six Day War period
than were their predecessors. Accordingly, the creation of new ways to
understand and connect with the Israeli reality has become necessary,
and the next section of the book deals with responses to that need. From
there the book moves on to talk about evolving relationships between
Jews and others, especially as that has played out in Chicago, with the
focus being on intergroup relations with African Americans and on interreligious relations with Catholics. From there the subject matter of the
collection becomes more internal to the Jewish community, with pieces
that reflect on shifts that have transpired in the communal agenda.

The final section of the volume is something different – not really
about a single subject but instead an accumulation of pieces I have written through these 25 years about books, films, and plays, along with several pieces that discuss the authors of such works. That section ends with
two pieces on books by writers with whom I first became acquainted in
scanning my parents' bookshelves, books which, in the spring of 2013,
I taught as a Visiting Professor at the University of Illinois in a seminar
with students not too much older than I was when I first discovered their
authors more than half a century before. While a number of these pieces
themselves talk about various kinds of change, I suppose it can be said
that the form of change that is most relevant in reference to this section is
not as much a change in the outer world as something internal, reflecting
the ways I have absorbed the changes that have transpired over the years
since I grew up in the circumstances I have described.

Lessons Learned

And what is it that, through these years and decades, what is it that I
have learned, particularly in these last 25 years? What am I left believing
about the best ways to deal with the issues that the Jewish community
faces today?

A most basic lesson, to be sure, is that, living in this world of change,
we who serve the Jewish community need to stay on our toes, ready to

adjust. And as tuned in as we need to be to the prevailing gestalt, we must try to take things in the directions we want to go rather than simply putting ourselves at the mercy of forces outside of ourselves. Despite the suffering the Jewish people have undergone in the past, the difficulties Jews are encountering in many places today, and the threats that Israel faces, we must not, I believe, allow ourselves to wallow in a paralyzing sense of victimhood. What the Zionist thinkers and the Zionist project have taught us is that, for our survival and our well-being, we must regard ourselves as having our destiny in our own hands and act accordingly. And we must attempt to realize that potential with wisdom and strength, acting with purpose and keeping our eyes on our goals.

Going along with that set of principles, I have come to witness and admire the resilience of the Jewish people as they have withstood attack and lived up to the Biblical injunction to choose life. And I have learned that while virulent anti-Semitism may have returned to the world's stage and while we must protect ourselves with sound, solution-oriented tactics based on an understanding of things as they really are, not everyone is our enemy and we are not alone in this world. Besides being important as we frame our communal strategies, this realization also means that we have obligations to others in addition to ourselves.

A conclusion I came to shortly after I started working at the Federation, as I tried to account for its success on many fronts, was that it was at once attached to earlier ways of doing things and at the same time committed to exploring new approaches. In both cases its agenda and style were driven by what needed to be done. I elaborate on that formula in a piece in this volume in which I challenge the call for innovation alone as the route which will solve all of the Jewish community's current problems. As I say there, while we indeed need to take innovative steps, we also need to maintain those traditional steps which continue to work, with our goal not being to simply throw out the old and bring in the new, but rather to draw upon what is both old and new, using whichever approach (or combination of them) best satisfies the needs we are trying to address.

Overall, I have learned to what an extent my thinking as a whole moved as it did in reference to the two points I have just developed, where I talked about the need to care for both ourselves and others and the need to value both tradition and innovation. That approach reflects a dialectical frame of mind, one which involves attaching value to two seemingly alternative perspectives and often coming down with a merger of the two. In following this kind of approach, I recall how the late Joseph Cardinal

Bernardin, whom I write about in several pieces in this volume, was described as a "radical centrist," a label which implies that while it is easy to automatically take positions at either end of the spectrum, gravitating to the center means that you have to thoughtfully work your way toward a position that makes the most sense under the prevailing circumstances.

The kind of dialectical approach I am talking about is especially important in relating to the apparent dualism that is rendered in the opposition between particularism and universalism, a tension that has greatly affected Jewish life in the two centuries since the European Emancipation. While some Jews of that time held to strict observance, shunning modern developments, others welcomed their liberation and apparent acceptance into general society. But when the sense of being like everyone else while continuing to be Jewish proved a chimera and anti-Semitism intensified in the late nineteenth century, different paths were taken. Some Jews denied their Jewishness altogether and pursued assimilation into the society around them; others chose the path of revolutionary universalism; and still others were drawn to Zionism, a nationalistic force which in the long run proved the most far-sighted of those options in the European context. But as particularist as it is, Zionism also contains universalistic values within it, and the tensions between those two modes of thought and behavior can continue to be seen in modern Israel and Jewish life elsewhere today.

Here in America, we are finding the tug of universalism creating one of our most serious communal problems, since that attraction can overwhelm the particularistic approach which, it can be argued, is essential for a meaningful Jewish identity. The pull of universalism, which is especially strong for today's young people, makes an argument for particularistic values in Jewish life countercultural in contemporary America. But a merged reconciliation of these two poles is necessary, I believe, if Jewish life is going to be sustained in the years to come.

Similarly, there is an acute tension between the individualistic pull which is so strong in America today and the value of communal attachments. We want our young people to think for themselves and to choose their own paths and ways of doing things, while at the same time, Jewish life has always played out in a community framework. As a minority, we have needed community both to protect ourselves and to sustain ourselves, while attachment to communal life can provide meaning in today's atomistic world. Furthermore, community at large becomes the principle of peoplehood, a factor which makes Jews more than the mere religious group that we have sometimes been seen as – and have seen

ourselves – in certain Western societies, including America. Our founding narrative as a people begins with the story of the exodus from Egypt,
a story told yearly at our Passover Seders, and to continue to be what we
have been, I believe the attachment to community needs to be maintained
and the sense of peoplehood needs to be sustained. How we do that with
a younger generation which is inclined to go other ways and is impacted
by strong countervailing influences is a key challenge of our time.

In my view, personal connections with Israel – where Jewish peoplehood takes shape in a national polity – can both enrich those young peoples' sense of Jewish identity and can help enable them to forge their own
dialectical answers, merging individualism with peoplehood, as it does
particularism with universalism. I well know, however, that as history has
unfolded over the past few decades, the naturalness of ties with peoplehood in Israel that was experienced by many of my generation no longer
automatically applies and cannot be taken for granted. I touch on that in
one or two pieces in this volume, and in this Introduction I would merely
observe that the issues I have been discussing here are essential factors in
the world of change that I have been talking about overall, while adding
that the emergence of strong "next generation" community leaders at the
Federation as well as the addition to our staff of bright, talented, committed young people certainly offers hope for a promising future.

So what am I left with looking forward? If the admission that we
live in a world of change and uncertainty has taught me anything it is
that nothing can be predicted for sure except that change will continue.
Still, it is my hope that even in today's world of change and uncertainty,
America's Jewish community and Jews worldwide will continue to find
themselves rooted in contemporary variants of the basic values and principles that have sustained the Jewish people during previous centuries of
change, and that we will embrace the new – indeed, will play a leading
role in creating what is to come – while holding to aspects of our identity
and heritage as touchstones that have kept us what we have been. I am
thus left with the hope that, even as I was shaped by my background in
the time in which I came of age, but then made my own way as I determined to do, without losing sight of the values with which I was raised,
so too for today's generation of Jews and those which will follow.

In sum, the pieces in this volume provide a record of certain aspects
of some of the central conditions and situations faced in the Jewish world
during 25 years of change, rendered through the eyes of one whose perspective was forged in ways I have tried to describe in this Introduction,
who found himself on the front lines of communal activity and who is

grateful for having had the opportunity to serve the Jewish community of Chicago and the Jewish people during this dramatic time.

April 2014

Visiting the Old World
in a Time of Flux

In April of 1989, six months after I came to work at the Federation, I staffed a Jewish United Fund mission to the Soviet Union for JUF lay leaders and donors. It was an auspicious time to make the trip, which included visits to Moscow and Leningrad and a stop in Romania after that. The Iron Curtain had not yet come down and, while change was in the air, we had the distinct feeling of visiting countries with oppressive regimes. In Russia, our agenda, along with touring, included visits to Refuseniks and their families – people whom Soviet authorities had prevented from leaving and whose right to leave had been strenuously advocated for by the Federation and other Jewish organizations. We came to make direct connections and to provide what support we could.

During the visit there was a powerful personal moment for me as well. Drawing upon information I was given by relatives living in the States, I was able to connect with cousins in Moscow. And so one evening, hoping that the rudimentary Russian I had acquired during one year of study at the University of Chicago and had practiced on Chicago relatives from time to time would suffice, I headed out, took the Moscow subway, and made my way to my destination. There, in one of the large, ugly building blocs with small apartments common in that country, I for the first time met and visited with a cousin and her adult son. He had participated in Samizdat activity and was a student in the Yeshiva established in Moscow by Adin Steinsaltz. His great-grandfather and my grandfather were brothers, and he and I were named after those respective ancestors. Strikingly, in this reconnection of Jewish relatives whose progenitors had gone in different directions three quarters of a century before, the language in which we conversed was Hebrew.

Not long after that visit the Berlin Wall came down, the Soviet Union collapsed, and millions of Soviet Jews came streaming out. The majority (including the cousins I had met with) left for Israel, another sizable number went to the U.S., and some ended up in other destinations.

The end of the Cold War was one of the most significant turning points in the world in the period of time that this book covers. It led to dramatic changes in the satellites and former republics of the Soviet Union, changes which among other things had major impact on the Jews who remained in those countries and who attempted to rediscover their Jewish identities and rebuild their communities. The changes also brought new attention to the Holocaust, knowledge of which had been attenuated in many of those countries with the coming of the Cold War. But those changes at the same time gave space to the revival of nation-alistic right-wing anti-Semitism. Meanwhile, changes came to Western Europe as well, in part in connection with an influx of immigrants, refu-gees, and foreign workers, including radical Islamists who brought with them hostility to Israel and the Jewish people. These issues and more are dealt with in the articles in this section, all of them based on my travels, some of which were work-connected, some personal.

As the Floodgates Open:
A Visit to the Soviet Union, Poland, and Hungary,
September 4-16, 1990

An edited version of this piece appeared
in the October 1990 JUF News as part of a Soviet Jewry Update

• • •

Near the end of the Kabbalat Shabbat service at the Dohany Street Synagogue in Budapest, the entire congregation is called upon to say kaddish in memory of the community's victims of the Holocaust. Out of a pre-War population of about 650,000 around 450,000 Hungarians were killed in the Shoah, and at least 6,000 of them were buried in a mass grave in an area immediately adjacent to that synagogue.

Joining in that service on Friday evening, September 14, were members of a Chicago mission organized by the Jewish United Fund on which I served as Scholar in Residence. The following night, after a briefing from the Jewish Agency for Israel's station manager in Hungary, a colleague, the incoming chair of the JUF campaign, and I were able to go to the Budapest airport to observe first-hand the transit of Jews from the Soviet Union en route to Israel. And suddenly, in the final hours of a 12-day trip, the pieces of our mission, with its stops in Moscow, Leningrad, Warsaw, Krakow, and Budapest, came together in a revelation with great emotional force.

Suddenly we knew how privileged we were to be witness to a human drama of historic magnitude. In what is, very probably, the most important Jewish story of the second half of this century, Jews are on the move in huge numbers. The facts are awe-inspiring. The context is haunting.

It was in 1944, as the war approached its ending, that mass deportations of Hungarian Jews took place, via crowded train cars on railway lines funneling into Auschwitz, which we had visited only days before our stop in Budapest. At Auschwitz we saw where Hungarian Jews and others from throughout Europe had met their horrifying fate at the hands of the Nazis and their henchmen. We saw that vast graveyard for multitudes of Jewish individuals and, symbolically, for the Jewish civilization of Eastern Europe, where synagogues have become museums and monuments to the past. We saw graffiti in Krakow reading "Jews out: Poland for Poles" and the now-cleaned spot on the new memorial in the Umschlagplatz in Warsaw which had recently had painted on it the slogan, "A good Jew is a dead Jew," verifying that hatreds of the past remain alive and that a country doesn't need many Jews to have anti-Semitism.

In Hungary too we heard of the resurgence of pre-War nationalistic anti-Semitism, being rendered in a political context. But in that community, which has the largest number of Jews in Eastern Europe outside of the USSR, we also learned of a revival of Jewish identity and Jewish communal life, much of it assisted by the efforts of the Joint Distribution Committee. And at the same time as we saw signs of resurgent anti-Semitism we learned of official steps being taken to acknowledge realities of the Holocaust: at Auschwitz and Birkenau we saw evidence of an increasing readiness to acknowledge that Jews were primary victims of those death camps; in Budapest we saw the first government-sponsored memorial to Jewish martyrs of the Holocaust in Eastern Europe, which had been dedicated only two months earlier.

Despite the possible maintenance of vibrant Jewish life in Hungary in the post-Communist era, though, it is obvious that even that community is but a remnant of what it once was and that, as demonstrated by the memorial we saw and the kaddish we joined in saying, its affairs are carried out in the shadow of the Shoah. Meanwhile, the Jewish community of the Soviet Union, which had been afflicted by the horrors of the Holocaust in its own way, is only now emerging from its decades of suffering under Soviet Communist rule when, denied the opportunity for expression or even knowledge of Jewishness, members of the community nevertheless continued to pay a price for their Jewish identity. And while its long-term viability as a community remains even more in doubt, most of the Jews in that country seem to be making fundamental decisions about their own futures.

When I was in the Soviet Union nearly a year-and-a-half ago with another JUF mission, the signs of the rebirth in Jewish religious and cultural life were thrilling. Such signs can continue to be seen, and our group was particularly touched by the beautiful singing of a recently trained men's choir during Friday evening services in Moscow's Choral Synagogue and by the opportunity to be present at the heavily attended opening of a museum exhibit in Leningrad consisting of photos, paintings, and artifacts from the area's Jewish communities.

Unlike the last time, though, these changes seemed practically incidental to the overall impact of the visit. The Soviet Union is in severe transition, and the changes experienced by the Jewish community thanks to the success of glasnost continue to be tied up as well with the failure of perestroika and the collapse of the Communist system and possible dismantling of the Soviet empire. Seeing the lines of people hoping to be able to buy the meager remaining foodstuffs and wondering what will happen next economically and politically in their country, sensing the seething emotion of a Russian nationalist mob about to begin a Pamyat rally, talking to experts on the scene and to ordinary people, we confirmed the observation that life in the Soviet Union is now utterly unpredictable. With anti-Semitism resurgent in that country too, and seemingly with greater potential of getting out of hand, Jews are especially concerned about what the future will bring.

Thus there was a striking difference between the impressions rendered by my previous visit to the USSR and this one. If then too it was clearly a moment of transition, at that point the referent for responding to the current changes was in the past. What was exceptional about what was happening then was how it compared to what had been happening before, when there had been extremely limited opportunities for Jewish cultural and religious expression as well as for emigration. But now, even with continued improvement in those areas, as one wonders what will be, the major referent for relating to the latest change is not the past but the future.

With the future so uncertain and of great concern, the prevailing mood is thus one of anxiety, not celebration, and most Jews are doing what they can, not so much to build a new communal infrastructure as to get out. Those with relatives or other connections in the United States are hoping to be among the 40,000 processed annually through the U.S. Embassy. And multitudes of others are making their plans to join the mass exodus to Israel, learning Hebrew from visiting Israelis and from one another as they do.

In the gloom and doom of Moscow we entered, one afternoon, a veritable oasis – a brightly lit room within one of the city's main libraries, full of video screens, computers, books, earnest young people with glowing faces, and more serious older ones. It is an educational center which Israel opened some ten weeks before we came, where hundreds of Jews come daily, eager to learn about Israel. In Leningrad we had dinner with the leadership of a recently formed Jewish communal association, including the editors of a bi-weekly newspaper. The head of the association, who directs Hebrew studies, told us that as many as 90 percent of the 120,000 members of that community would like to get out. The lines we saw outside of the Dutch Embassy in Moscow, which houses the Israeli Consular officials processing applications, demonstrated too that what was happening now is that a whole community, given the chance at last, is doing what it can to go.

Going they are, with 17,494 of them making their way to Israel in August, around 20,000 expected in September, and even larger numbers anticipated in October and beyond. To get some perspective on the magnitude of these numbers, it is useful to note that back in 1906, at the height of that era's period of mass emigration for Jews, the total number of Russian Jewish emigrants to the United States was slightly over 125,000 – a number smaller than what is expected in Israel alone this year and in years to come.

And so, for us in Budapest, seeing these Jewish souls in transit, the pieces suddenly came together. It is a tragic truism that there is no undoing the Shoah. But what is being acted out now, in numbers once again nearly unimaginable, is in eerie and ironic contrast to the awful events of fifty years ago.

At the airport that Saturday night, we saw and spoke with Jews from throughout the Soviet Union, from Moscow and Leningrad, from Riga and Siberia, young and old, healthy and disabled, eager and anxious, smiling and tense, all being transported in a complex project coordinated like a military operation, 24 hours a day, seven days a week. As opposed to what happened at the notorious Birkenau selection site at the end of the railroad line, which we also had seen, every Jew coming though Budapest, by train, plane, car or whatever other means, is personally met and treated with human kindness by representatives of the Jewish Agency. In contrast to those who were packed in trains relentlessly rolling to Auschwitz, with its perverse sign cruelly pretending that their work would make them free, these people board El Al airplanes on the last leg of their flights to true freedom and to dignity as Jews in Israel. Theirs is a journey not to death but to life, not to a brutal end but to a new beginning.

We left with images before our eyes not of the Eastern Europe photographed in an earlier era which has now vanished but of the new realities and with a renewed dedication to do what we can to spread the word and play a part in facilitating these historic developments.

Letter from Prague: Time of Renewal

The Forward, June 14, 1993

• • •

From the most improbable sides Jews are threatened with danger,
or let us, to be more exact, leave the dangers aside and say
they are threatened with threats.

Franz Kafka, in a letter to Milena Jesenska

"**P**rague spring." The phrase resonates. To come to Prague in springtime these days is inevitably to think of 1968 and the attempt to humanize a communist country which, though cruelly quashed by Soviet tanks, remained a harbinger of the dramatic changes that came to Central and Eastern Europe some 21 years later. But for one tuned in to the Jewish experience in this part of the world, there are other associations with springtime as well.

In the spring of 1389, when Passover and Easter coincided, as they did this year, a massive pogrom took place in Prague, in which some 3,000 members of the Jewish community were murdered, many of them in the Altneuschul, the oldest synagogue still in use in Europe. An elegy on the pogrom, written by Rabbi Avigdor Kara, continues to be read locally on Yom Kippur. As late as 1899, Easter in Prague was marked by an anti-Semitic outburst revolving around ritual murder charges in the infamous Hilsner affair. It was in that season too, March 15, 1939, that the Nazis marched into Prague.

Still, there is more to the Jewish experience in Prague than a chronicle of persecution might suggest. And in a tentative manner there may, at this season of rebirth, be hope for at least a modest renewal of Jewish life in this former center of Jewish culture, where a first-time visitor is moved by the city's beauty and touched by its history.

Looming above Prague is Hradcany Castle, which was the seat of power for rulers who alternately served or oppressed the Czech people, not to mention the Jewish community. The Czechs attempted to take their destiny in their own hands through a 19th-century national revival that proceeded with fascinating parallels and interlockings with modern

23

Zionism. A plaque expressing gratitude for the help that Czechoslovakia provided Israel in the war of 1948 now hangs outside the Jewish Town Hall in Prague. And the similarities between the two states were alluded to when, in speaking to the Fourth Congress of Czech Writers in 1967, the playwright Pavel Kohout described a small country besieged by its larger, hostile neighbors, and then told his listeners that though they may have thought he was referring to Czechoslovakia, in fact his subject was Israel.

Only in 1989 did Czechoslovakia finally liberate itself from Soviet control. Since then, with Vaclav Havel demonstrating friendship to Israel, relations between the two countries have been reestablished. Today, Czechs appear to hold warm feelings for Israel, despite or perhaps because of the Soviets' hostility to the Zionist state.

This spring works by Israeli artist Yosl Bregner were on exhibit in Prague. The show was organized by the Franz Kafka Society, whose vice president, Vladimir Zelezny, a writer blacklisted by the Communists, is committed to addressing the prevailing ignorance about both Kafka and Jews at this crucial moment in the reestablishment of Czech democracy. The archetypal modern author and dominant figure among the German-speaking Jewish Czech literati of the early 20th century, Kafka, who seems to have lived practically everywhere in old Prague and died in 1924 with most of his writings as yet unpublished, became a virtual non-entity in his home city between 1939 and 1989. Both Nazis and Soviets banned his works, with their eerie anticipation of totalitarianism, and as fashionable as images of Kafka are in the current tourist milieu, most contemporary Czechs have little direct knowledge either of Kafka or of Jews in general.

Mr. Zelezny speaks of wishing to build on and strengthen the Czech tradition of tolerance and pluralism by promoting Kafka and other writers in his circle, such as Max Brod and Franz Werfel. Wishing to demonstrate that the explosion of German-language Jewish creativity of the early 20th century was integral to Czech culture and is of great value, he hopes the Kafka Society will make it possible for him to teach contemporary Czechs about Jews in a positive manner, before those who are less sympathetic fill the vacuum.

Overall, the Czech republic seems relatively free of the resurgent anti-Semitism that has surfaced in other countries of the region, including the Slovak republic that was born amid the dissolution of Czechoslovakia this past January. Czechs say that it is only because of German influence that there is a small skinhead movement here, and contemporary Czech nationalism has not generated anti-Semitic activity of note. Indeed, when an unfriendly journalist several months ago published a list of 160 leading figures in Czech culture who were supposedly Jewish, rather than stimulating fear of Jewish control he was sharply criticized from both leadership and people on the street.

Still, given their history of suffering, many remaining Jews in the Czech republic, particularly the older ones, are not without concerns and are reluctant to identify themselves publicly as Jews. Some survivors of the Holocaust are even unwilling to participate in the community's Yom Hashoah observance, held in the renovated 16th-century Pinkas Synagogue, where the walls are being covered with a list of the names of the members of the Czechoslovak Jewish community murdered by the Nazis. An earlier version of that listing was erased during the communist era.

Today, there are approximately 1,000 registered members of the Jewish community, or kehillah, in Prague, and purportedly at least that many who are hesitant to identify themselves. But while some Jews or people of Jewish background continue to hold back, others are increasingly impelled to assert and rediscover their heritage. Tomas Kraus, executive director of the Federation of Jewish Communities in the Czech Republic, lists the Prague community's priorities as building an infrastructure, supporting the elderly, who make up some 75 percent of the community, and reaching the young.

Of immediate concern is advancing restitution and property claims. Legislation currently on the books provides for the return of property that was nationalized from 1948 onward, a date chosen to block claims by ethnic Germans accused of collaborating with the Nazis whose property was taken over by Czechs after the war. Additional legislation has been introduced that provides an exception under which the Jewish community can reclaim property taken prior to 1948. Its prospects for passage are reportedly good, and Mr. Kraus, who has prepared an inventory of the property that the community hopes to reclaim – including some 200 synagogues and 400 cemeteries – is hopeful.

A vast number of Jewish artifacts are found in Prague as a result of Nazi confiscations. The Nazis planned a "museum to an extinct race" here, and so the precious legacy of the lost Jewish culture is preserved, on display in several remaining synagogue buildings in Prague's former ghetto.

But Jewish Prague today provides more than a poignant reminder of a destroyed past. A rabbi, native to the Czech lands and educated in Israel, returned last fall to preside over the community's spiritual life. Holidays are again celebrated. The Jewish Agency and the American

Jewish Joint Distribution Committee are providing Hebrew instruction, youth programs, and other links with Israel and world Jewry. Other organizations are to be found on the scene as well. The emergence of new leadership and the interest in Judaism among the young people is impressive.

The clocks above the old Jewish Town Hall – including one that designates the hours with Hebrew letters and whose hands move right to left – mark the forward passage of time, and the Town Hall itself is in active use as the remnant of a once-thriving Jewish community attempts to rebuild itself in the post-communist era.

Then and Now:
A Visit to Today's Germany
JUF News, August 1993

• • •

I had never visited Germany. At first, that was deliberate. Some three decades ago, on a post-college graduation "grand tour," I made stops in neighboring Austria, Switzerland, and France. None of them had a pristine record during the Nazi era, to say the least, nor had they faced their own history with total honesty. Still, I, like others, chose not to visit Germany as a pleasure-seeking tourist.

Through the years, my habit of avoiding Deutschland continued, even though West Germany made clear efforts to strengthen its character as a liberal democracy. Then, last March, things changed briefly when, taking a vacation trip to visit our son who was spending the year in the Czech Republic, my wife and I flew into Frankfurt, where we boarded a train for Prague.

The idea of entering a German railroad car to head east was unsettling. We first went through passport control in the airport. My reaction on seeing a uniformed German official was an urge to ask him what he, or his father, did during the war. I didn't. The train ride itself was routine except for occasional associations with the past brought on by such factors as a brief stop to change trains in Nuremburg.

Despite my earlier recalcitrance and discomfort, when the opportunity for a full-scale visit of a non-touristic kind recently presented itself, I was ready to accept it. Over the past year, with anti-foreigner violence and anti-Semitic activity on the rise in Germany, the Jewish Community Relations Council has repeatedly sounded an alarm. Much of our contact on the matter has been with officials of the local German consulate, who have been forthcoming in listening to our concerns and open in their own responses. Thanks to a recommendation made by the consulate, I was invited to participate in a two-week program called Germany Today sponsored by the German Academic Exchange Service. I agreed to go. And so, in mid-June, I boarded a plane and took off for Berlin, the capital of the Third Reich.

I arrived on a Friday afternoon and first took a walk through the no-longer-divided city, from west to east. The sites resonated with memories of what was. That evening I attended an Oneg Shabbat in the former East Berlin. I said kiddush and, after we ate, my son, who had come up from Prague, led the Birkat Hamazon for the group, members of the local Jewish community who gather weekly to reclaim their heritage and who, as they put it, are happy when they can learn from visitors.

The experience was a touching one, parallel to others I've been privileged to have in Russia, the Czech Republic, and elsewhere where Jewish life and culture were once richly alive, then virtually wiped out, and now are being revived by a remnant of our people. But it was also hauntingly different to have such an experience in this setting, so close to the very places where the Holocaust was forged.

The Germany Today program itself began in Bonn, the current capital, on Sunday evening. During the 10 days I was with the group I joined 16 other participants in the program – academics, politicians, journalists, and individuals involved in international trade – in a series of lectures from a range of experts, in meetings with political and academic leadership, and on several tours.

Bonn is a sleepy university town on the banks of the Rhine River. It is a musical city where Beethoven was born and where Robert Schumann died. It is a city of culture where a memorial to the Jewish-born poet Heinrich Heine, built to replace one destroyed by the Nazis elsewhere, is exhibited. It is a town with block after block of charming 19th century homes where, due to a strange quirk, a brand new super-modern building has thus far proved unusable for Germany's parliament, the Bundestag.

Shortly after its dedication some months ago, the building's acoustics and sound system were found to be inadequate. With serious corrections deemed necessary, the delegates had to troop back to the refurbished 19th century waterworks building which had been used by West Germany's parliament for the previous six years. It is almost as though the soul of the city was asserting itself in an attempt to continue to tie those charting the course of post-war Germany to the country's better days and better nature.

No matter which Bundestag building in Bonn is used during the next few years, Berlin will once again become the capital of reunified Germany. The main reason for the decision to move was to be able to "give" something to the former East Germans, who in many other ways are finding themselves very junior partners in the reunification of their once-divided country. It was a controversial decision because of the expense involved, but moving the seat of government into Hitler's former capital raises questions of another kind as well.

I had the opportunity to ask about that when our group had a session on the planning of the new capital city with the director of the City Forum. She pointed out that the role of Berlin as capital preceded the rise of the Third Reich. She added that planners are proceeding with sensitivity to the history and geography of the city. Pressure to build on the site of Nazi headquarters, left desolate after those buildings were destroyed and now home to a small museum called "Topography of Terror," is being resisted. The neighborhood that was predominantly inhabited by Berlin's pre-war Jewish community will be restored and there are plans to erect a Holocaust memorial. The Ministry of Defense will be located on a street named after the German general who led the plot to assassinate Hitler in 1944, where a memorial and a museum on the German resistance are now found.

Issues surrounding reunification were in the forefront of consideration for our program, as they seem to be in the country in general. What one hears most is that the Germans were unprepared for reunification, with the West Germans ignorant of the decayed condition of the East German physical infrastructure and the low productivity of the East German industries.

When the Berlin Wall came down on November 9, 1989 (by chance, the 41st anniversary of Kristallnacht), there was widespread rejoicing. The East had been released from the hold of Communism, and by the following year, the country had formally been made whole again. Unification of the two economies, however, has turned out to be a daunting task, and social unification has proven to be equally difficult. The impact of living in two cultures in separate parts of the divided Cold War world, with little contact or knowledge of one another, created a divide of a more than physical kind between the inhabitants of the split land.

An especially troubling development in the post-unification era has been the rise of a violent skinhead youth culture, susceptible to neo-Nazism. The surfacing of behavior of that sort has been more common in the East, and the after-effects of the break from Communism have been seen as a reason. A meeting which our group had in Dresden with a panel of officials of the state of Saxony proved illuminating.

The Minster of Science and Arts described the Marxist indoctrination before reunification when the Holocaust was seen merely as an expression of class warfare. He said that efforts are now being made to help students understand the Nazi era as it truly was. Other speakers indicated how, following the changes of 1989, young people were unexpectedly confronted with freedom, with few tools to understand what that means beyond what they could see on Western television programs.

Much of the neo-Nazi activity, the speakers asserted, is a form of reaction, a version of free expression of a kind previously forbidden. "If you hold a pendulum firmly in place on the left," said one panelist, "then when released it swings to the right."

While such an explanation helps account for the neo-Nazi skinhead phenomenon in the East, the fact is that in the former West Germany, too, there has been a rise in such activity, with some of the worst violence having taken place there. However, though there has been some vandalism of Jewish cemeteries and Holocaust memorials in Germany over the past year, the primary targets of those who evoke the Nazi past have been foreigners. At a time of economic slowdown complicated by the difficulty of making reunification work, Germany has suddenly been witness to a large upsurge in asylum seekers, who, along with foreign workers, have suffered scapegoating and violent attacks.

It has been claimed that the energy which German law enforcement has used to combat terrorism on the left has not been replicated in responding to that now coming from the right. There is need, it is said, for greater effectiveness in preventing violence, greater success in the apprehension of perpetrators, and more effective use of sentencing as a deterrent.

Also needed is stronger leadership to counter the current trend. Speculation about the reasons for Chancellor Kohl's failure to speak out more quickly and firmly against the violence leads in many directions, with nobody having a certain answer. Most common is the view that he has been motivated by political calculations, catering to voters on the right. Whatever the motivation, to the extent that their Chancellor seems to equivocate in taking on the perpetrators of right-wing violence and in sympathizing with its victims, Germany's image in the world will continue to suffer.

This highly significant issue has meaning far beyond German's borders, with Germany, in effect, at the cutting edge in defining what Europe will be like in the post-Cold War era. Somehow, it seems to a visitor, there needs to be a solution to handle the political and economic refugees on the move on the Continent. By making entrance to the country so much more difficult, as it did on July 1, Germany is putting the problem in the laps of other countries – notably the Czech Republic and Poland – but not solving it.

Somehow, too, it seems that there needs to be a solution to accommodate the growth of foreign populations such as that experienced by Germany and other countries relatively unaccustomed to such heterogeneity. The question here is whether they will adjust to these plu-ralistic, multicultural trends in a manner which respects individual and group differences while maintaining a legitimate sense of national iden-tity and purpose, or whether ugly xenophobia will rule the day. There is also the question of what happens when, as in the former Yugoslavia, ethnic strife emerges and the threat of genocide arises. Do other states have the obligation of stepping in or do they simply stand by and, at best, provide refuge for the victims, ironically facilitating the goal of "ethnic cleansing"?

There are many ironies to all of this in reference to the Nazi past. It is ironic to be calling for strong leadership in Germany. But it is indeed strong leadership, of a democratic kind, that is needed to counter those who model themselves on the Nazis. It is ironic to talk about Germany's obligation in the international arena, which at times might even mean foreign military involvement. But in today's Europe, with Germany the strongest power, that might indeed make sense, to help prevent a conflict like that in Bosnia from spreading further, just as Hitler, if confronted and not appeased at the beginning, might have been stopped. In applying lessons from the past, reunified Germany can become less paralyzed by its history and better able to help forge a future free of the horrors of that time.

. . .

Reminders of the Jewish past in Germany and of the cataclysm which almost wiped it out dot the national landscape. Hitler may have thought of Jews as outsiders, but it is believed that they came with the Romans, possibly as early as the First Century. A mikva in front of Cologne's old city hall, excavated after World War II and renovated in 1979, bears wit-ness to the existence of a Jewish community there from at least the 12th century. A square near the site of that city's former synagogue, destroyed on Kristallnacht, is now named after the composer Jacques Offenbach, a native son whose father was a local cantor.

Intimations of what used to be are sometimes found in unexpected places. A painting in Dresden's museum of Old Masters by the 18th cen-tury artist known as Caneletto is labeled a view of the city's market square from the direction of the Jewish Quarter. Another painting shows Jews leaving the city's large synagogue on what must have been the Sabbath or a holiday. Today, a Jewish cemetery with a small synagogue continues to exist. In front of the synagogue is a memorial listing the names of Jewish citizens of the community who died between 1914 and 1918, presumably in World War I while serving what they regarded as their homeland.

A handful of synagogues in Berlin outlasted Kristallnacht. According to a guidebook, the New Synagogue (which opened in 1866, with Kaiser Wilhelm I present, and was protected in 1938 as a historic building) stood virtually abandoned in East Berlin, with trees growing inside. It now is being restored to its former grandeur, with a community building housing a kosher restaurant down the street. In the former West Berlin, a Jewish community building was erected on the site of the destroyed Liberal Synagogue, making use of that building's front arch. Plans now exist to build a wing of the Berlin Museum devoted to Jewish subjects.

And there are additional reminders of Germany's once-thriving Jewish community. A much smaller community exists now, augmented by the addition of newcomers from the former Soviet Union.

Relations between Germany and Israel are close. Recently the Israeli novelist Amos Oz was awarded a prize at the Frankfurt Book Fair, with his acceptance speech attracting considerable attention. The German Parliament has passed legislation outlawing compliance with the Arab boycott of Israel at least as strong as that which is on the books in the United States. And twice during my stay I was caught off balance, once by seeing a dubbed television program made in Israel portraying the establishment of the Jewish state; another time by hearing Hebrew spoken by other visitors touring the Bundestag and discovering that they were members of a delegation from Tel Aviv.

Experiences like these were reassuring. Not that relations between Germany and the Jews are entirely "normal." They aren't and never can be. And at the same time, if economic recovery fails to precede the elections in 1994, a swing to the right is generally predicted, with the right-wing Republikaner Party possibly obtaining enough votes to enter the Bundestag. The problem is not that it is or will be 1933 all over again. Even observers with very sharp antennae for this sort of thing insist that Germany today is solidly rooted in democratic traditions. Still, I left as I had come, believing that concerns about conditions in Germany today are not without foundation.

And I returned home with a new perspective on America. In Cologne, after the guided tour, our group was given 45 minutes to see sites on our own. There was the city's towering Gothic Cathedral. There were some inviting museums. But I chose to take a look at the inside of the building which had been used as Gestapo headquarters, where, as we were told, several cells had recently been found in the basement, with handwritten messages on the walls from their doomed occupants.

Accompanying me were the two other Chicagoans on the trip – an African-American who was reminded of cells for slaves that he had seen in South Carolina, and an Asian-American who had himself been born in a Japanese-American internment camp on the West Coast in the early 1940s. America has blots of its own on its history and we have troubles of our own dealing with the issue of diversity. But thinking of the efforts being made to promote intergroup harmony and the distance we have come in building appreciation for pluralism, I couldn't help feeling grateful for the principles of freedom and equality that guide our country.

In the end, I was glad I had accepted the invitation to visit Germany. I was also very glad to come home.

. . .

Postscript

In the summer of 2012, my wife and I, traveling back to the States from a visit to Israel, made a brief stop in Berlin. The city had changed considerably since my earlier visit 19 years before. The hotel we stayed in was in a now-upscale area of the former East Berlin, near Museum Island. Transformed into a stylish hub beckoning artists and young people, Berlin also had by then created a number of memorials – such as the striking one at the Topography of Terror site I had seen during my first visit to the city – which showed a readiness to honestly face Germany's Nazi past in impressive fashion.

Walking back to our hotel at one point, we discovered that a free outdoor concert was scheduled to take place nearby, with Daniel Barenboim conducting the Staatskapelle Berlin (the orchestra of the Berlin State Opera) and Yefim Bronfman playing Tchaikovsky's First Piano Concerto. And thus, the following day, we went to join the thousands of Berliners sitting in their folding chairs and enjoying what was a delightful performance on a lovely summer afternoon. But I couldn't help feeling a multi-layered chill when realizing that these two Jewish musicians who had each spent formative years in Israel were performing at the very spot where, just 79 years before, a 40,000 person mob made up of other Berliners had been stoked to a frenzy by Joseph Goebbels as he and his fellow Nazis embarked on a massive book-burning, with much worse to follow. While the Israeli/Jewish identity of the lead performers whom I and the others in the audience listened to added a sharply ironic dimension to the moment, illustrating how much things had changed, the situation encapsulated how, for my wife and me, whatever was going on during our visit to Berlin, we were constantly conscious of the cloud cast over it all for us by the awful history of the Holocaust in that city.

Confronting the Holocaust Fifty Years Later: Reflections on a Visit to Lithuania and Poland

This piece was the basis of an address delivered at the University of Chicago Divinity School Wednesday Luncheon on March 5, 1997. *It was subsequently included in the Spring/Summer 1997 issue of "Criterion," a publication of the Divinity School.*

• • •

The Books Of The People

I had been to Poland before, though never to Lithuania. Still, this was a very different kind of trip from any I had previously been on.

It began with a call from the office of Richard Durbin, recently-installed U.S. Senator from the state of Illinois, to say that during the upcoming mid-February congressional recess he would be traveling to Lithuania and Poland, and I had the opportunity of joining him. Others on the delegation were the Senator's foreign policy staffer and brother Bill Durbin, along with two leaders of Chicago's Lithuanian-American community.

One of the purposes of the trip was to deal with a large collection of Hebrew and Yiddish books in Vilnius, Lithuania (known as Vilna in Yiddish and Russian), which had been the object of considerable attention since the appearance of a front-page story in the New York Times a couple of months before.

Durbin's office had been in touch then too, to indicate his interest in the subject and readiness to be of assistance, and we had continued to stay in contact and to work together on the matter. A letter to the Lithuanian prime minister, which the Senator had initiated along with Congressman Ben Cardin of Maryland, had been signed by 56 fellow senators and congressmen. Among other things, Durbin wanted to deliver it by hand during the forthcoming visit.

The books had special meaning to me, as they do to many others in the Jewish community, and the New York Times article had struck a chord even before I had heard from Durbin the first time. Ancestors of mine had lived in the Kovno (now Kaunus) region until the second half of the 19th Century, when they had moved to Poland, and my grandfather had brought to North America a collection of Hebrew texts, many of them published in Lithuania, which have been passed down in the family.

Vilna (where, according to a German-language memoir published in 1910, the British philanthropist Sir Moses Montefiore had stayed with a certain "Reb Michel Kotzen" while on his way to meet with the Russian Czar on behalf of the Jews of the region in 1846), was once a major center of Jewish learning and culture. Known as the "Jerusalem of Lithuania," it had housed the great Strashun Library and, in the early decades of this century, was the founding home of the YIVO Institute for Jewish Research. There were many famous yeshivas throughout the country, with a particularly notable one being in the town of Telz.

When the Nazis occupied Lithuania in 1941, the Jewish population was rounded up into ghettos. As the Jews were slaughtered their centers of prayer and study were destroyed, but not before large numbers of books were hidden, while others were confiscated. During the period of Soviet occupation, many of these volumes ended up in a former church building which became an annex of the Lithuanian National Library.

The Times article, with a Vilnius dateline, had opened by announcing that "tens of thousands of rare Hebrew and Yiddish texts lie in dusty heaps in a Roman Catholic church here, desiccated and forgotten." I represented the Jewish Federation of Metropolitan Chicago and Senator Durbin at a heavily-attended meeting in New York which was convened by the National Foundation for Jewish Culture shortly after that article appeared. Its purpose was to set the American Jewish community's priorities for dealing with the subject in a coordinated fashion.

I had continued to work with the steering committee established at that meeting, consisting of officials of the Foundation, YIVO (now based in New York), and the National Conference on Soviet Jewry. The trip with Senator Durbin offered a chance to see firsthand what the situation regarding the books actually was, and what could be done to deal with them in a proper and constructive manner.

Like a delegation that had proceeded us under the aegis of the American Jewish Committee and included representatives of YIVO and B'nai B'rith, we found most of the items that are kept in the church and in the adjacent building, once a monastery, to be in better condition and better cared for than the New York Times article had suggested was the case.

During a visit conducted by Dr. Regina Varniene, Deputy Director of the National Library and Director of the Centre of Bibliography and Book Science, we learned that there are, in all, close to 125,000 volumes in the Judaica collection of the Bibliography and Book Science Center. Of these, there are a total of 38,476 books which have been catalogued and are currently on shelves, 10,800 of them "first copies" of Hebrew or Yiddish books published in Lithuania which are kept in acid-proof boxes in an "Archive" section in the former monastery. Approximately 13,000 more books, most of which are on shelves in the former church, are still awaiting cataloging. Additionally, there are some 73,409 periodical volumes, all of which have been catalogued and are being microfilmed, and it is suspected that a number of additional periodicals may be mixed with other collections at this time.

The magnitude of what is there is one thing, and it should be added that, in the cavernous old church building, the Jewish texts are joined by hundreds of thousands of volumes on other subjects which together fill the room wall-to-wall, from the floor to shelves accessible only by high ladders. Even more impressive than the number of volumes, however, is their nature.

There we stood, in the former monastery in the heart of Vilna, holding a book written by one of the foremost scholars of 18th Century European Jewry, known as the Vilna Gaon. It was a volume stamped with the imprimatur of the Strashun Library, the site of which, now an empty space in the center of Vilna's Old Town area, I had sought out just that morning.

There we stood in the chilly former church, some of its decorations still visible, in our overcoats, holding a prayer book stamped with the markings of the Great Synagogue of Vilna; holding another book in which a child had doodled on the inside cover, afraid that we knew but still wondering what had become of that child. There we stood, looking at the pages of periodicals which, week after week, month after month, had told the tales and reflected the lives of a people with a vibrant, centuries-old culture in that country.

There had been Jews in Lithuania even before the country became Christian at the end of the 14th Century. Jews had constituted some 40% of the population of pre-war Vilna, maintaining their own community while playing active roles in the overall life of the city. There had been around a quarter of a million Jews in pre-war Lithuania. And then, in a flash, almost all of them were gone. These books, with their worn covers, some of them falling apart, these books, we recognized, standing there in awe, were survivors in their own way.

Beyond the books and periodicals, there is something else in the National Library's Judaica collection that we asked to see, though this material is even less well-known and less frequently seen than the books and periodicals and was not even referred to in the New York Times story. It consists of some 371 scrolls --mostly Torah scrolls or fragments thereof but some of them megillot, scrolls of the Books of Esther or Ruth or of other books of the prophets or writings of the Bible.

Most of these are badly damaged or otherwise defective, but a number may be usable or repairable. All are stored in the manuscript collection in the main building of the National Library, to which they were moved from the church in the past few years.

We were able to take two of the scrolls off of the shelves and out of their canvas coverings and to unroll them on a table, which we understood was rarely allowed. Again we were moved, this time to speculate on the exact circumstances which had caused the damage (apparently from a fire) that one of the scrolls we looked at had suffered. We marveled at the fact that the second scroll we looked at, which seemed to be in decent condition, had remained that way throughout the Holocaust and after.

In a subsequent meeting with Prime Minister Gediminas Vagnorius, where we were joined by the American ambassador, James Swihart, and where I was honored by Senator Durbin's request that I describe the Jewish people's concerns, we asserted that whatever questions might be raised about the ultimate disposition of the books, the scrolls should be thought of in an entirely different fashion. They are not objects for inclusion in a library of any sort, we said, but religious articles that should be returned to the Jewish community as soon as possible, either to receive a proper burial or to be put in use if still judged acceptable for that purpose by religious authorities.

While the prime minister seemed sympathetic to our arguments, he was not prepared to make an immediate decision in that regard. He did, however, speak positively about his desire for moving forward in resolving the overall situation of the books in a manner which would ensure their preservation and accessibility.

The letter presented by Senator Durbin spoke of exploring issues involved in the ultimate disposition of the volumes. We learned of three alternative venues in Lithuania alone where the collection might end up: the National Library, to which an additional wing is being added; the (government-owned) Jewish State Museum; and a site to be controlled by the Jewish community. Beyond that, some people have spoken about possible locales in America and Israel, while YIVO and perhaps others feel they have ownership claims on some of the books. During the meeting with the prime minister, the idea was floated that an international committee of experts could be established through which all of the interested parties, from Lithuania and abroad, could work together to forge a set of recommendations. It is an idea which we strongly supported and which has been reiterated in subsequent correspondence between the Prime Minister and Senator Durbin.

The books were discussed in various conversations and meetings with government officials and others during our four-day stay in Lithuania. All in all, while much remains to be done, there was, we felt, significant movement on this subject during our visit.

Lithuania Today

Our group arrived in time to join in the celebration of Lithuania's independence day. Having emerged from over four decades of Soviet domination, Lithuania today is a country proud of its national identity, exuberant in its sense of freedom, committed to democracy, and worried about Russia, which even long before the Soviet era was wont to exert its rule westward. The dominating political topic during the four days we were there was the possibility of Lithuanian membership in NATO. Whenever Senator Durbin faced questioning, which was often, that topic came first.

But there were also personal dimensions of the visit for all of us. Long a champion of independence for Lithuania, Durbin had been there three times previously. His brother Bill, however, had not been there before, and each of them paid their first visit to Jubarkas, the town west of Vilnius where their mother was born. They were extremely touched by the stop there as they discovered not only information about their mother's birth and baptism but the existence of relatives they never knew they had.

And as crowded as the Senator's schedule was with political and personal matters, there still was time for relating to subjects with Jewish interest, even beyond the books. Thus, entering Kaunus, we stopped at the Holocaust museum at the Ninth Fort, an outpost built by the Russians in the 19th Century which was used by the Nazis as a prison and a place to murder the Jews from that city and elsewhere.

During our stop in Kaunus we visited with the local Jewish community leadership. Before that, in Vilnius, we had been joined at lunch by the chairmen of the Lithuanian Jewish community and of the Vilnius Jewish community. In both places, I was able to find additional time of my own to spend with these and other members of the Jewish community, most of them survivors, former partisans, people who had spent the war years in the USSR, or children of individuals within those categories.

It is eerily haunting, in Lithuania today, to remember how great and how rich Jewish life was in that center of Talmudic and Haskalah (Enlightenment) teaching, of Hebrew writing and printing, and of Yiddish culture, that place where Zionist and Bundist ideology flowered. It is painful beyond measure to think of how it was that such Jewish life ended. And yet, if you do not remember what was and do not know how it came to an end, there is very little to let you know.

In the Old Town area of Vilnius, where the Jewish community thrived, one street is named after the Gaon, another is still called "Jew Street," and that is about it. There are no explanations of why those streets have those names or why the Jews themselves are no longer there. There are no plaques or markers where the destroyed synagogues or other institutions formerly stood. There may indeed be some Holocaust museums in the country, such as at the Ninth Fort, where the Soviets erected a striking monument on the site of the killing fields and burial pits. But visits to such a place are not, I was told, part of the required curriculum in the school system.

At the same time, as if to rub salt into a still-open wound, there are reminders that anti-Semitism persists. The leaders of the Kaunus Jewish community were dismayed that, just a few days earlier, when scenes of Mardis Gras were on Lithuanian state television, the only masks which revelers were shown wearing were of Jews, Gypsies, and devils. In Vilnius, Jewish leaders described an article written just last summer in which Jews were accused of inviting the genocide perpetrated against them in Lithuania by supposedly having welcomed and aided the Soviets who briefly ruled Lithuania before the Nazi invasion.

Meanwhile, Aleksandras Lileikis, who directed the Lithuanian security police in the Vilnius district during the war and who last June returned to Lithuania after being stripped of his U.S. citizenship by a federal court in Boston for having lied about his role during that period when he entered this country, has yet to go on trial for participating in the Nazi acts of genocide. It is suspected by some that prosecutors are hoping that time will take care of the 89-year-old man before they have to deal with him. At the same time, serious questions go unanswered about the "rehabilitation" of a number of individuals who had been incarcerated during the Soviet era for acting in complicity with the Nazis, even though the government of independent Lithuania has admitted that errors were made in their haste to rectify Soviet injustices.

Still, this is a government which has in a number of ways shown its sympathy and understanding for the Jewish community. The well-known chairman of the Parliament, Vytantas Landsbergis, is himself the son of a mother honored by Yad Vashem as a Righteous Gentile. This past September, as the genocide against Lithuanian Jewry was being commemorated, President Algirdas Brazauskas declared that "there can be no lenience or prescriptive principles granted...those Lithuanian residents who participated in the killing of the Jews." He called for visits to the "memorial sites of the victims," saying: "After all, it is a loss, a pain and an unhealing wound for all of Lithuania's people."

For all of the distress voiced by the leaders of the Jewish community in Kaunus regarding on-going manifestations of anti-Semitism, they are quick to add that, since independence, Jewish cemeteries and the sites of mass shootings have been properly cared for, and to show their appreciation for the freedom which now exists in Lithuania. And they are exceptionally proud of the active organizational life they now direct.

With some 700 members, Kaunus's Jewish community offers an educational program for their youth, a Maccabbee sports club, associations of veterans and of survivors, cultural programs, and religious activity headed up by the Chabad. They do this with the help of the American Jewish Joint Distribution Committee, funded in Chicago by the Jewish United Fund, out of a newly-rehabilitated set of offices in a former synagogue.

In Vilnius, the director of the Jewish State Museum of Lithuania, Emmanuel Zingeris, who dreams of once again making that city a center of Jewish study, is a member of Parliament and a significant figure in the current government. At the same time, members of the 4,000-person Jewish community are particularly proud of their accomplishments in reviving Jewish life there and are looking forward to next September, when the 200th anniversary of the death of the Gaon will be observed.

Simonas Alperavicius is chairman of the Jewish community of Lithuania and Boris Borisov is chairman of the Vilnius Jewish community. With them and Al Domanskis, a fellow traveler from Chicago who joined me and served as translator, I sat in the home of the Grodnik family one late afternoon. With their 25-year-old daughter Liora I did not need a translator, for she spoke a fluent Hebrew learned during a year's stay in Israel.

On the television screen we watched videotapes of Liora performing songs in Hebrew and in Yiddish on the stage in Vilnius. In the room was a cupboard full of menorahs and Jewish art objects. On the table were drinks and sweets with smells and tastes I had not encountered since my childhood, in my grandmother's dining room in Chicago. "We are re-building Jewish culture here," said the mother, chairman of the committee established by the local community for that purpose. "We have been here for 600 years," she proclaimed in the apartment where she herself had been born 50 years before.

On my last night in Lithuania Emmanuel Zingeris and I talked for a while in my hotel, then made some stops. First we went to his office in the Parliament, where he gave me several books and articles he has worked on regarding Jewish culture in Lithuania. While we were there he put me on the phone with his brother Mark in Kaunus, a Jewish playwright eager to discuss literature and amazed to learn that I had once had Saul Bellow as a teacher. Our next stop was outside of the massive former Yiddish theatre, now scaffolded, with reconstruction stalled.

Finally, we drove to the small wooden building where that museum's current exhibit on the Holocaust is on display. Near that former house stands a monument to Chiune Sugihara, the Japanese diplomat based in Kaunus who had saved thousands of Jews from the Holocaust by making travel visas available before he was forced to close the consulate there in August of 1940. Placed in a small lot, the monument, in the Buddhist style, is entitled "Moonlight." Standing together on a snow-covered lot at midnight that chilly evening, we and the statue were ourselves magically bathed in the light of a nearly-full moon which suddenly broke through the clouds above. Nine hours later I was on a Lithuanian plane, headed for Warsaw.

Poland

Before leaving Chicago, I had obtained from a cousin the names of the towns in the Kovno area where, according to family records and lore, ancestors and other relatives had lived in the 19th Century. On the way from Jubarkas to Kaunus, we drove through two of those towns, Raseiniai, where my grandfather's father had lived and my grandfather himself had been born, and Ariogala, where my grandmother's grandfather had been an innkeeper. In speaking with the leadership of the Kaunus community I was able to learn that, as late as 1980, a Kotzin had lived in that city.

Flying from Lithuania to Poland, I more or less retraced the route followed by my grandmother and grandfather. In Poland, as in Lithuania before, the senator's itinerary, while greatly focused on international politics and economics, continued to have a significant Jewish component.

For me, there were intense personal dimensions to the visit as well.

As in Lithuania, in Poland too there were, repeatedly, signs of the two sides of the coin regarding attitudes towards Jews in that part of the world today. Just three days before we arrived, a Catholic priest named Henryk Jankowski had complained to a reporter that Poland is being ruled by a Jewish minority which has decided to persecute him. He made that statement following a court appearance brought about by the fact that local government prosecutors had charged him with group defamation for equating the Jewish star to Nazi and Communist symbols while delivering a sermon in church. A couple of weeks after we left, Polish prosecutors dropped legal action against Jankowski.

At a meeting with our delegation the first day we were in town, a leader of a recently-formed rightist party called the Movement for the Reconstruction of Poland (ROP) opined that the Jewish perspective on matters has been effected by the experiences Jews suffered, while, according to him, Polish suffering during the war has generally not been acknowledged. Asserting that bystanders should not be blamed for what happened to Poland's Jews in the Holocaust, he offered no admission of participation in the Nazi atrocities by any Poles nor even that there was a history of anti-Semitism in Poland.

Walking the streets of Warsaw not long after that meeting, I saw one slogan painted on a building wall calling for the expulsion of the country's "Jewish occupiers" and another calling for that of the "Jewish president." Under the latter was an apparent reaction to it from a critic of the political party we had just heard from, who equated the ROP with the Nazis. Most disturbing of the anti-Semitic graffiti I saw that afternoon were drawings showing a Jewish star at the end of a hangman's noose on a gallows.

I saw a variation of such a drawing, with the star inaccurately drawn, the next day as well, in the company of the non-Jewish guide who had just taken our group through the former Warsaw Ghetto. While the rest of the group went to meetings elsewhere, he and I walked alone toward the back of the Umschlagplatz, the site where the trains had departed packed with Jews being sent to the camps. There on the wall was that image.

"I am sorry you have to see this," the guide said with profound empathy. It was shortly after I had mentioned to him that Warsaw relatives of mine had perished in the Holocaust. A native of that very part of town who has become an academic expert on the Ghetto and who had just completed a study of victims' memoirs found there, this young man conveyed a sensitivity and appreciation for the dignity of the Jews who had lived and died in Warsaw which sent a powerful message about the manner in which some members of his generation are dealing with the past.

Likewise, the schoolteacher who guided us through Auschwitz-Birkenau the next day seemed overtaken by a solemnity and agony of his own. Looking at one of the displays there, he said that for him, of particular poignancy were the shower heads. He noted that whenever he sees them he imagines the feelings of those doomed human beings who had looked up from below wondering and fearing what would be coming from the last object their eyes focused on.

The current Polish government, we were told, has been responsive to concerns related to the history of the Jews of Poland. Though the site of the Auschwitz-Birkenau death complex has itself been a subject of controversy in recent years, while we were there the government was working on a proposal for ensuring its proper preservation in consultation with the United States Holocaust Memorial Council and Jewish groups. Since we left a draft of that proposal has been agreed to in principle. During the time we were in Warsaw, one of the chambers of the Polish Parliament approved legislation providing for the return of Jewish communal property. The vote in the lower house was 339 to 34 with 30 abstentions.

Just a few days after we left, as Polish media devoted airtime to reporting on the vote, an arson attack was directed against the lone synagogue still in use in Warsaw, which I had visited during our three days in the country. The Polish president quickly condemned the attack, as well as violence against the Jewish community in general. Two sides of the coin.

In Kracow the night before we went to Auschwitz, we sat in a Jewish-style restaurant called "Ariel," with Klezmer music in the background, joined by Stanislaw (Yitzhak) Zohar, the JDC's local representative in Poland, and his wife. Zohar told us how he had fled Kracow and survived the Holocaust, then had gone to Israel to have an impressive military and diplomatic career before joining the staff of the Joint Distribution Committee. A few years ago he returned to Kracow with his wife to assume his current responsibilities, which include bringing comfort, companionship, and support to the lonely survivors living out their final years and days in Poland.

Three million Polish Jews were wiped out in the Holocaust, out of the 3.5 million who lived there before the war. The experiences of Kracow's Jewry have received widespread visibility through the film "Schindler's

List" which, as it happens, received its first American network television screening some three days after we were in that city. The street where we had dinner, in the heart of the old Jewish area, was used in the filming. Steven Spielberg himself, we were told, nightly ate in the same restaurant we did while he was working on the movie.

Still, Poland today is a site not only for remembering what was, mourning the lives that were taken, and aiding the survivors. For in Poland too, particularly since the fall of Communism, a modicum of Jewish life is being reborn among a population whose number is uncertain but small by anyone's count.

As described in an article in the Jewish Telegraphic Agency Daily News Bulletin which was published only a few days after our return, a conference held in January under the sponsorship of the JDC brought more than 150 Polish Jews together in Warsaw to discuss the future of the community. Young Poles, some of them formerly "hidden children" saved and adopted by Catholics, others children of survivors who covered up their own Jewishness, are only now learning of their Jewish origins. As the Washington Post reported in a recent article, they are coming out of the woodwork as they discover their Jewish identity. Others who have known they are Jewish are becoming more involved in Jewish activities.

The last night in Warsaw, while Senator Durbin attended a private dinner at the American Ambassador's home, Bill Durbin, the other Chicagoan, and I, joined by our driver, went to a new Jewish-owned restaurant for dinner. After eating in the upstairs dining area, we were shown the rest of the establishment, including a section which is designed to reproduce the cellars used formerly in the city for eating, drinking, and listening to Jewish music. On one of the walls leading into this "Karczma," along with messages written by other visiting dignitaries, we unexpectedly saw the bold Hebrew script of the Israeli novelist Amos Oz. It provided a refreshing and uplifting counterpoint to the hostile graffiti I had come upon previously.

Though on an entirely different scale, the small revived Jewish communities in Poland and Lithuania, like the state of Israel which was born out of the ashes of the Holocaust, constitute a rebuttal to Hitler. They are evidence that, successful as it was in many ways, in the long run the Nazi's evil program failed. They are, in their fashion, affirmation of the fact that Jewish life goes on, that the Jewish people live.

A Final Word: The Dead Hand

The week we were traveling, the international editions of Time and Newsweek ran cover stories entitled, respectively, "Echoes of the Holocaust" and "War Without End: Why World War II Still Haunts Us All," while an article in the New York Times elaborated on what its headline called "World War II's Unfinished Business."

As these reports indicated, while Switzerland and France have been drawing the greatest attention, nearly a dozen European countries, confronted by facts which they had ignored, denied, or distorted, have been taking new looks at their pasts. What we were witness to and involved in on our trip was, in its way, an aspect of a development which is increasingly and dramatically being brought to the fore.

As today's world is propelled forward to the new millennium there is, it seems, a countervailing pull back to the past. It is a pull which brings to mind what the 19th Century British writer George Eliot evoked with the phrase "The Dead Hand" in "Middlemarch," her novel about change.

The Holocaust was a defining event in our century and for our civilization. It is an event with which most of the countries involved had failed to come to grips factually and morally before moving on. The rapid arrival of Communist control for some, and of Cold War involvements for others, facilitated their failures to face up to that earlier period. With the passage of 50 years and the fall of Communism, archives are being opened, old information is coming to the fore, and many countries are finding themselves unable to avoid realities long kept under the carpet.

Though some commentators may have seen the fall of Communism as an end to history, it has instead revealed itself to mark a return to history. Released from the yoke of Soviet oppression, nations in Eastern and Central Europe are reaffirming their national identities. As they and Western countries attempt to forge new relationships and to move forward, they all seem fated, whether they wish it or not, to have to face that cataclysmic dark age which marked the fourth and fifth decades of this century.

Some nations acted cravenly and viciously then; some acted nobly and heroically; most had mixed records. Now there are myths to defuse, historic facts to acknowledge, and moral conclusions to be drawn. And it seems as though this simply must happen before the world can move forward.

Europe is haunted by the ghosts of its Jews, a people who were practically wiped out during the Holocaust, a people who, even when living out their separate minority existence were also part of a more diversified mix than what now prevails in many of those countries. (Ironically, in an age when heterogeneity seems to be a fact of social life, some countries in Eastern Europe today are, internally, even more homogeneous than they once were.) And thus, there are many countries which need to look at what they were, at who used to be part of their national demographic makeup but is no more, and at why that is the case. And they need to recognize and to embrace the reemerging communities made up of remnants of that people of the past who are now part of their present too.

Hitler's goal was to annihilate the Jewish people and to eradicate Jewish culture. A fitting way to remember the millions who perished and to ensure the ultimate defeat of Nazism would be not just to establish museums with relics of the past and to erect memorials at the places where Jews were slaughtered, but to support the modest revival of Jewish life now taking place in those cities and countries with respect and with understanding for Jews and Judaism, along with recognition that the center of global Jewish life has shifted.

As this happens, the countries involved must deal honestly with their own behavior at that earlier time. They need to do that not only to guarantee the civilized world's victory over the evil of Nazism but for the redemption of their own national souls. The Nazis brought death as they transformed themselves and those who aided them in the pursuit of their goals into monsters. The forces of life and humanity must confront the past lest they continue to be pulled back by its dead hand.

In this context, the books currently housed in that former church in Vilnius and the adjacent building take on added significance. There is something both tangible and symbolic about those volumes, those repositories of Jewish wisdom and emblems of the personal and communal existence of the People of the Book. For the Jewish people they are links with a time which is no more, even as they have continuing meaning and value. For the Lithuanians they are reminders of what their country once was like, and of who once lived with them.

The manner in which the situation involving these books is resolved will do and show much. Hopefully, the visit paid to Lithuania this February by a new American senator from Illinois and the delegation which traveled with him was helpful in moving matters toward a positive solution.

Visiting Andalucía

JUF News, February 2011

• • •

"Jews don't travel to Spain," I remember my mother telling me back in the early '60s. European born, she was expressing a longstanding tradition that reflected the impact of the events of 1492 and after, when Jews, after centuries of living in what they called Sepharad, were expelled unless they converted to Catholicism. Those who remained without choosing to comply, or were suspected of not doing so sufficiently, became victims of the brutal Spanish Inquisition that remained in place until the nineteenth century.

It was not as though no Jews ever set foot there again, of course, and Jewish idealists formed a sizable percentage of the American volunteers who went off to fight in the Spanish Civil War in the late 1930s. Indeed, on our bookshelves at home, now in my own library, there was a copy of *The Old Bunch,* the 1937 novel about the Jews of Chicago by Meyer Levin that the author had given to my father with the signed inscription: "For Dr. J. A. Tropp [a person I have never been able to identify, even with the use of Google] and the Loyalist cause in Spain."

As the years went by after my mother and I had our conversation, the world changed in a number of ways. The reign of Franco, the dictator who came to power as a result of the civil war, ended. The new Spanish government made moves to come to terms with its country's history and reached out to the Jewish people. Today there are few people, I suspect, who even know about that earlier prohibition on travel, and for Jewish tourists Spain has become a destination like many others. These days the Jewish people's image of Spain is marred again, now by reports of the embrace of anti-Semitic stereotypes and by the expression of anti-Israel attitudes. But Spain is not the only European country so characterized.

My wife and I first visited Spain nearly 10 years ago, when we made stops in Madrid, Barcelona, and the northeastern part of the country portrayed by George Orwell in his classic account of the civil war, *Homage to Catalonia.* Reading Hillel Halkin's stunning new book about Yehuda Halevi, the great Sephardic writer who lived in Spain in the eleventh and twelfth centuries, much of that time in the southern cities of Andalucía, I was inspired to pay another visit, this time to that region. And so, late in

2010, my wife and I linked up with Israeli friends of ours and set out on a vacation which included two days each in the three most notable cities of Andalucía, Seville, Granada, and Cordoba, which had once been centers of Jewish life for nearly a millennium and a half.

It is understood that Jews first came to Spain during the Roman era, numbers of them after the destruction of the Second Temple in Jerusalem in 70 CE and the expulsion that followed. The subsequent Barbarian invasion from the north, which led to the establishment of the Visigoth kingdom and the rise of Christianity in Spain, brought forced conversions and persecution. When Muslim invaders coming from North Africa conquered much of Spain in 711, they were welcomed by the Jews, whose status improved decidedly.

During most of the next three centuries the Jews of Andalucía lived a rich communal life, especially in Cordoba, the seat of the Muslim caliphate, but also in other cities, with individuals from the Jewish community rising to key positions in Muslim society. Meanwhile, the Muslims themselves were often divided, with continuing waves of invaders from North Africa bringing increasing conflict, especially from the eleventh century onward. In Granada, where the Jewish statesman and poet Shmuel Hanagid had risen to great prominence earlier in the eleventh century, thousands of Jews were massacred in the year 1066. And during the centuries that followed until the Christian reconquista moving down from the north had completed its task, persecution was not uncommon, even while there was a flowering of Jewish culture and thought. Indeed, that was so much the case that for parts of this period the Jews actually fared better in areas of the north already ruled by the Catholics.

Many of the unpleasant realities that prevailed during the long centuries of Muslim rule are today often obscured by portrayals of a permanent, happy multi-cultural existence. But though more than half a millennium has now gone by without a viable Jewish presence in this region, even a short visit reveals signs of conditions that prevailed in a part of the world where, however much they achieved, the Jews often had fraught relations with their neighbors. Andalucía, as elsewhere on this globe of ours, is haunted by echoes of a previous Jewish presence.

In Cordoba and Seville there still are neighborhoods called the Judería. One can only wonder what the residents of these cities thought of, through the centuries, when they continued to use that label to identify those areas, utterly depleted of the living Jews who had once filled them. In Seville, according to Halkin, a portion of an earlier synagogue has been incorporated into one of the churches. As I walked through that city's striking Alcázar palace, built by the Muslims, then altered by their Christian conquerors, and the site where Ferdinand and Isabella greeted Christopher Columbus upon his return from the New World, I found myself in something call the Courtyard of the Levies, so named, the tourism sign said, for its incorporation of a "Wall of the Levies," with its graceful Moorish-style arches, taken from a building once in that city's Jewish Quarter.

In Granada, too, the guidebooks talk about a Quarter once inhabited by that city's Jews. And in Cordoba, where the Judería forms the heart of today's primary tourism district, not only are there squares named after Yehuda Halevi and Maimonides (and a statue of the latter figure), but there is also a gem-like medieval synagogue whose interior walls are covered with striking stucco designs that had been found beneath the plaster in the late nineteenth century. Close by that synagogue is a building called Casa de Sefarad, Casa de Memoria, a small but movingly- and professionally-designed museum, opened about four years ago, that charts the history of Spanish Jewry through the Inquisition.

Cordoba today is proud to honor Maimonides as a native son. In the museum of the city, his is one of a handful of waxwork figures on display. What is not generally pointed out, however, is that, although he indeed was born in the city and surely benefitted from its intellectual and cultural climate, because of the prejudices and uncertainty that permeated the atmosphere there, he and his family left at about the time of his bar mitzvah, never to return. The bulk of his highly significant career was spent elsewhere, much of it in Cairo. As for Yehuda Halevi, after having moved from place to place and then spending a decade in Granada in the late eleventh century, he moved about still more. According to Halkin, in around 1108 he left Muslim Andalucía for Christian Toledo, and moved back to Cordoba around 1130. And then, in 1140, Halevi set sail via Egypt for the land of Israel, arriving and almost immediately dying there in 1141.

Though Halevi's motivation for that final journey and his fate have been interpreted in various ways, for Halkin and many others he was, in effect, a proto-Zionist who acted in line with the message of his best-known poem. It declares: "My heart is in the East/But the rest of me far in the West," and ends by saying "Yet gladly I'd leave/All the best of grand Spain/For one glimpse of Jerusalem's dust." (Halkin's translation.) As accomplished and comfortable as the Jews of Andalucía at times were in that land when it was controlled by the Muslims, and at times in Christian-controlled parts of Spain as well, they were always, Halevi and history tell us, in exile. The Muslims, in contrast, whose numbers and power were much greater, came to see Spain as "their" territory.

Seeing what is left from the time of Muslim control, its beauty and grace, its hints at the nature of the civilization that once was, one can sense the glory of that age. For all of the Christian triumphalism evidenced in efforts to symbolically "convert" Muslim architectural masterpieces as they did the people, notably in the Giralda Tower and the Alcázar in Seville, the Alhambra in Granada, and the Grand Mosque in Cordoba (which has a church imposed upon it to create a hybrid as architecturally awkward as the modernized Soldier Field), the artfulness and sublimity of the original Muslim structures still come through.

It is not difficult to understand the connections that Muslims of today must feel with Andalucía, which their ancestors ruled, in part or in whole, for nearly eight centuries, presiding over one of the most advanced civilizations of their day. But separated from nostalgic romanticism and instead attached to resentment, hatred, and violent irredentism, the energy connected with this longing has merged into one of the most destructive forces in our world today.

It is the force which last fall drove the Yemen-based Al-Qaeda group to direct two package bombs to the addresses of buildings in Chicago that until a short time before housed local synagogues—and to put on those packages the names of, in one case, a leader of the Crusaders who occupied Jerusalem, and in the other case the head of the Spanish Inquisition who succeeded Torquemada. The message surely intended by that choice of names and addresses was not only that Jews around the world are today a primary target of Al-Qaeda but also that the pain inflicted by the Muslim world's occupying enemies centuries ago will be avenged. Just as the Muslims of that earlier day defeated the Crusaders and reversed their control of the Holy Land, so Islamist terrorists of today who have shown their readiness to bomb the Madrid train station have their eyes on lost Andalucía and the rest of Spain. And Jews are in the crosshairs as well.

So what, then, is the closing impression of a Jewish visitor to Andalucía? It is of a region rich in historical resonance, connected, but yet not altogether connected, to its past. The region is pointed to by some these days as modeling for us the ability of the three Abrahamic faiths to live together in harmony. That may indeed have happened at times, in some of the places in that region. At the same time, though, the region's record of interfaith—and intrafaith—conflict, of invasion and conquest, which is not so often called to attention, stands as a warning of the bad times that might come again, and in certain ways are already upon us.

For Jews, whose presence in that earlier world is often evoked without full acknowledgment of why that presence ended, it is a region of both rich memories to embrace and painful ones not to be ignored.

So let this be an homage to Andalucía, a region with its ubiquitous orange trees and peaceful gardens, with the intricate tile and stucco designs of its castles' interiors and the calming bubbling of its serene fountains, a region that was once the home of a thriving Jewish community that produced poetry and philosophy and scholarship of the first order, accomplishments which benefit the Jewish people and the world to this day. But a region, too, with a history that was still felt at least through my mother's generation, in which the fate of the Jews would stand as a paradigm and warning of how tenuous a home built in exile can be, no matter how deep the foundation or how long it has lasted; a region from whence the anticipatory Zionist intuition of Yehuda Halevi would emerge to be validated by the cataclysms of the twentieth century. And a place where, today, our people's and our world's current challenges are evoked.

A Family Visit to Odessa

The Times of Israel, July 25, 2013

• • •

It started as a whimsical notion a few years ago, when a couple of cousins and I began to speculate on what it would be like to visit Odessa to see what we could find of our family history there. But then, as time went by, it became a serious idea. Though the complexity of scheduling prevented us from finding a time that was good for everybody, at the very end of this past May, after closing out a week-long visit to Israel, my wife and I boarded a plane for Kiev along with my sister who lives in Jerusalem and, after joining up with another cousin and his wife at the Kiev airport, continued to Odessa. It was, I had realized when thinking about the calendar as the trip approached, exactly 100 years since our family had left there for Canada.

Walking around Odessa the morning after we arrived, we immediately fell in love with the city. That was especially so for its central, seaside part, where we were staying, with its beautifully-rehabbed early-nineteenth-century buildings; with the "Potemkin" steps (the steps!); with the overlook of the Black Sea and the port (though the unexpected, view-corrupting eyesore that a post-Soviet developer built out into the sea at the bottom of the steps was shocking); with its aura of a pleasure-providing resort; and with its incredible cultural traditions and wealth of astonishingly important historical Jewish connections. But the family reasons which drew us there in the first place were a significant priority for the visit. And we weren't disappointed in that either.

Though we knew that our ancestors had left the region for good in 1913, toward the end of the vast wave of Jewish emigration from the Russian Empire's Pale of Settlement, we did not have very much information about the family history there. Furthermore, a number of the details that we had been made aware of by our mothers and an aunt didn't necessarily connect. Trying to reconcile the parts of the story that we brought with us, we came up with what has now established itself as the prevailing family narrative.

One of the things we had known was that the 1913 departure was not our forbearers' first exodus from that region. In 1906, following the pogroms of 1905, the family – consisting of our grandparents and four children of theirs, though not my mother, who had not yet been born – like many other Jews at that time, left for North America. Their original point of departure was a town in the Odessa region called Berezovka. They got as far as Nova Scotia and then, however, had to turn around because one of my uncles was diagnosed with an eye disease – a situation, I understand, not all that uncommon among the immigrant populations of the time.

Return they did, and our belief is that at that point they settled in Odessa proper, which is where my mother always said she had been born, an event which took place at the end of 1907. My cousin's mother and another aunt had talked about the time that they and our grandmother had been treated for typhus in the Odessa Jewish Hospital, and for that reason too it made sense that they would have been living there at the time. The hospital is referred to in a number of texts by Isaac Babel, born in Odessa in 1894 and the author of several powerful stories about Jewish life there, many of them set in the Moldavanka neighborhood. Aged and decrepit like so many of the Odessa buildings outside of the central city, the hospital is still extant, and we were able to see it and stand outside of it.

Our grandfather died in 1908, when my mother was just a few months old. Family lore has it that he was a peddler during those brief Odessa years, and the conclusion we came up with during our visit was that, following his death, our grandmother, lacking a "bread winner" and with five children to care for, one of them an infant and the oldest only eight years older, took her brood back to the town where she had lived previously with her husband. His family came from there, and it was where she very likely had a support structure to turn to. Furthermore, my cousin's mother and another aunt – the oldest of the siblings – had talked about living in Berezovka as children, which would make sense in this scenario. And the pieces continued to fit when, on our second day in Odessa, with those relatives' sparse recollections to guide us and curious about what else we would find, we set off for the town along with our guide.

To say that the road to Berezovka that our van drove on once we got out of Odessa proper was worse than any I have ever been on is to engage in drastic understatement. Back in Chicago we joke about the potholes that develop on the Outer Drive and the expressways each winter. But what we confronted here were far more than mere potholes. They were deep ruts and incipient sinkholes just a couple of yards apart, all along what once, apparently, had been a paved two-lane highway. Navigating this treacherous obstacle course involved veering from one side of the road to the other while hoping the gravel or dirt shoulders would hold when needed. After slowing down to a crawl for much of the 90 kilometers from Odessa, we finally made it to our destination.

The Berezovka we saw was a town consisting mostly of old homes and small buildings, a great many of them clearly from the era when our family had lived there. Replicating something we noticed during our drive, many of the homes had goats tethered or wandering nearby — goats like the one in a lithograph I now have that my mother loved. The artist was Todros Geller, who had been born in another town in the Ukraine and as a teenager had studied art in Odessa before leaving for Canada and then moving to Chicago.

What made the visit "work," to our good fortune, was that our guide had established contact with a resident of the town born in 1937 named Isaac Greenberg, who was able to take us to several sites and answer a number of our questions. The first place he directed our driver to was the Holocaust memorial on the edge of town, haunting in its simplicity. Having seen the few references to Berezovka in Charles King's 2011 book *Odessa: Genius and Death in a City of Dreams,* all of them Holocaust-connected, and having learned more from our guide, I already knew a bit about what had occurred in and around the town during the War. But Mr. Greenberg and a woman we would spend some time with later that afternoon filled out the painful picture in a very personal way.

The German invasion of this part of the Soviet Union had brought with it Romanian troops and civilians, who became the occupiers. Recognizing that Sevastopol, home of the Soviet naval base on the Black Sea in nearby Crimea, had far more military value than did Odessa, the Soviets had pulled out of the Odessa region. In the case of Mr. Greenberg and his family in Berezovka, and a number of other Jewish families there and elsewhere in the region as well, the adult males were conscripted into the Red Army, while women and children were evacuated, in his case to Kazakhstan. The remaining Jews – and there were plenty of them, since before the war Odessa was nearly 40 percent Jewish, as were a number of these towns – were at the mercy of the Romanians, whose cruelty often rivaled that of the Nazis.

The horrors the region's Jews faced are rendered in a memorial we saw the next day at a large square in Odessa's Moldavanka neighborhood. Though, as Charles King observes, the memorial makes Odessa's non-Jews seem more helpful than most of them in fact were and gives the Romanians a free pass altogether, it still is moving in its way. And standing as we were while looking at it on the site of what we were told was a wide-scale roundup of the city's Jews where a "Death March" commenced, we read the memorial's inscribed listing of the towns toward which that march proceeded, the second of which was Berezovka.

Many Jews died before leaving Odessa and others died while traveling by foot or train en route to those destinations. Most of the rest were murdered after they got there. King cites supposed "rumors" circulating in Odessa in 1942 by escapees "about people being machine-gunned in a ravine at a place called Berezovka," and then adds: "We now know those rumors to have been true. The escapees were reporting on one of the worst massacres to have taken place under Romania's watch, the killing of about twenty-eight thousand Odessa Jews by SS units recruited from among the *Volksdeutsche*." As for the Jews of Berezovka itself, the Jewish Encyclopedia asserts that they "all perished during the German occupation in World War II."

As much as the Jewish history of Berezovka, like that of other towns and cities in the region whose populations were heavily Jewish, is tied up with the pogroms of 1881 and 1905 and with ensuing Holocaust events, before the Shoah there was also a thriving Jewish communal life there. And our family, like others, was part of it. Mr. Greenberg showed us a building that once housed a Jewish school, and he took us to a place where there once stood two synagogues. One of them, after having become a movie theater in the post-war period, was now razed to the ground, and the other – though the building still stands – is now a well-appointed Baptist church.

It was in noticing the latter building that we had one of our most meaningful revelations. My cousin's mother, in recollecting her childhood, used to talk to my cousin about the family's living in a house next to a courtyard and about looking up a nearby hill to see a red brick building. And indeed, in Berezovka today, small old homes from that era, with courtyards (though the very term makes them sound more elegant than they now are, and probably were then as well) still exist on a street that goes up a hill, at the top of which stands that former synagogue, now with a red tile roof. Why my aunt did not identify it as a synagogue who knows, and we had no way of knowing whether the building itself was once made of red brick or whether it always had a red tile roof. But we felt it was no stretch to conclude that we had visited the place where the family had lived and that we had seen the building on a hill that my aunt long remembered.

Mr. Greenberg also took us to a very large, hilly area on the edge of town which had once been the site of the Jewish cemetery. We found hardly any gravestones there – just a handful of them, on most of which the writing had worn down long ago, with almost all of them now knocked over. (Our guide from Odessa said that it was her understanding that the worst desecration had occurred after the Soviet era.) Within this weed-overgrown, devastated area, though, we did find, next to one another, gravestones with engraved dates clear enough to read, of three individuals, born in 1903, 1904, and 1907 respectively. Given those dates, we imagined these were people with whom our aunts and uncles had very possibly played during their childhood years.

Before coming to Odessa, we had figured that the height of success would have been to find our grandfather's grave and to say Kaddish for him there. Once we arrived, put the dates together, and saw the conditions of the cemeteries we visited, we realized there was no way that could happen. Assuming as we now did that he must have died in Odessa proper and been buried there, we did not believe that the burial site could be here in Berezovka. Nor could it be in the existing Odessa Jewish cemetery, which we saw on our way to Berezovka, with its impressive memorial to the victims of the 1905 pogrom, since that was not established until about a decade after our grandfather had died.

The place most likely for him to have been was buried, we concluded, was in the old Jewish cemetery written about by Babel in his *Odessa Tales.* Though we made a stop at that site during our time in Odessa, there was nothing to be seen but a huge forested area planted by the Soviets after they razed the cemetery itself. The only thing connected with that cemetery still left is a large cement structure that we were told was part of its entrance gate, kept intact by the Soviets as the site of the assassination of Communist heroes. Still, it was there that my cousin and I decided to lay a couple of stones in our grandfather's memory, assuming as we did that he had been buried somewhere in that former cemetery, and that this was the closest we were ever going to get to his grave.

As for the Berezovka stop, it provided one more highlight, which came after we saw all of the relevant sites that we could with Mr. Greenberg. To close out the visit we were taken to the home of a woman named Lydia who, we learned, had been a small child at the time of the Death March from Odessa. As she and her family had walked past the people of Berezovka, the story goes, one of them snatched her from her mother's arms and thus saved her from the ravages of the Nazis and their accomplices. After the war, she was given to an orphanage, and though she never learned her family name, she regained and maintained her Jewish identify, such as she could through the Soviet era. And now, she was enormously proud to tell us, she feels deeply tied to the Jewish people, keeping up with the news from Israel, where two of her four grandchildren live.

Drinking tea and eating cake in her small home's all-purpose living room/dining room/kitchen, we felt like we were connecting ourselves with this town's past. And everything was capped off when, in answering a question as to whether she had ever heard Brickman, the family name, referred to in the town, she said she recalled a conversation back in the mid-'50s, when people were reminiscing about families that had emigrated from Berezovka in earlier years, and the Brickmans were indeed named as one of them.

The ride back from Berezovka was no easier than the one going there, but in this case we traveled with a sense of deep satisfaction that we had made the trip. And as we had done in going the other direction, we admired the beauty of many of the fields we were driving through, fields of grain that once had made Odessa a major provider of wheat to all of Europe. It was a view that, it occurred to us, was replicated in a way by the fields that the family must have seen when they at last arrived at their Canadian destination in Winnipeg, Manitoba, where my grandmother joined her older brother. Along with another brother who immigrated there as well, those families started new lives that surely were not only better in many ways than what they had been experiencing in the Russian Empire, but that saved them from the fate which Jews in that region, and beyond it, were to suffer less than three decades later.

With a sense of "mission accomplished," we had two-and-a-half more days to enjoy Odessa's attractions. That included going to the glorious opera house, where we saw ballet performances of Stravinsky's "Firebird" and "Rite of Spring"—a work which by chance had its famous premiere in Paris in 1913, the year our family departed for North America, on almost the exact same date when we viewed it one hundred years later. Our time in Odessa also gave us the opportunity to savor cuisine we remembered from our youth. Eating what the menu translated as "stuffed fish," I thought of the line in a Babel story when, describing a Sabbath meal his grandmother had prepared, he talks of *"gelfilte* fish with horseradish sauce (for which it is worth becoming a Jew)."

We also learned more about Odessa as it was a century ago, when it was one of the great Jewish cities of the world and where much of great importance to the Jewish people was percolating. Taken on a tour of Jewish sites in Odessa, we saw homes where once lived writers

– acknowledged by plaques – ranging from Babel to Chaim Nachman Bialik to Ahad Ha'am to Sholom Aleichem to Mendel Macher Sforim. This also is where the early Zionist thinker Leo Pinsker lived and worked, and for a shorter time the Jewish historian Simon Dubnov. Another native son, born there in 1880, was Vladimir (Ze'ev) Jabotinsky, who was a journalist and activist in Odessa before going on to become a major Zionist leader. Jabotinsky's *The Five: A Novel of Jewish Life in Turn-of-the-Century Odessa,* published in 1936 and translated from Russian into English just in 2005, with its intimations of some of the wellsprings of his Zionism, evocatively captures the "feel" of the city and its Jewish community as they were in those earlier years. Reading it while I was in Odessa gave the book particular resonance.

Contemplating the strong Zionist component of Odessa's Jewish community early in the twentieth century (the first mayor of Tel Aviv, Meir Dizengoff, also hailed from there), while standing alone one morning on the Black Sea shore where a key scene in *The Five* is set, I imagined the romantic pull there must have been for many of Odessa's Jews back then. They themselves could have stood on that shore, I thought, looked out on that body of water, and imagined themselves getting on a ship, sailing through the Dardanelles, making their way to the Mediterranean, and ultimately arriving at the port of Jaffa.

And what a world we live in today, it also struck me at that moment. Just a handful of days before, I had been standing in Jaffa myself, looking at the Mediterranean and at Tel Aviv, now a vibrant metropolis in its own right. There were a few Israelis who had departed Tel Aviv on the plane with us and who had also made the connecting flight to Odessa in Kiev, and we had gotten to know some of them while filling out forms and commiserating together late at night in the Odessa airport after discovering that our luggage and theirs had been left in Kiev. (We finally got it nearly 24 hours later.) We also saw them the following morning, standing with other Israelis at the top of the Potemkin steps and listening to a Hebrew-speaking tour guide describe the dramatic events that had taken place there in 1905. And then, as if to provide a symbolic frame for the visit, as my wife and I were sitting in a restaurant called Kompot and having a late breakfast on our final morning in Odessa, before we returned to Chicago and my sister returned to Jerusalem, we found ourselves next to two Israelis who had just arrived the night before, and we immediately struck up a conversation with them.

The Jewish people have been fundamentally affected by key developments of these past 100 years. The Soviet Union denied Jews the opportunity to live full-fledged Jewish lives; the Nazis and their allies destroyed Jewish life altogether; and the part of the world we had come to visit is no longer a center of gravity for the Jewish people. Meanwhile, though, those Jews whose families survived the Shoah and who are now living in Odessa are rebuilding their Jewish identities, helped by the American Jewish Joint Distribution Committee, whose "Chesed" program services Jews throughout the area – including, as we saw on a map in their headquarters, 17 of them in Berezovka. At the same time, the State of Israel has come into being and, despite ongoing challenges, Jewish life is thriving in the two major locations where Jews live today – Israel and North America – thanks in great part to the Jews who came from this area both earlier and again more recently. And while no family's story is altogether "typical," the family whose experiences of a century ago my relatives and I traced during our visit to Odessa, and whose experiences of today we live daily, exemplifies much of what was, and what is.

The Terrorist Threat
at Home and Abroad

For years before the timeframe of the pieces in this book, Israelis had been targets of terrorist attacks at home, in the air, and in places abroad like Munich, scene of the Olympics of September 1972. In Buenos Aires, Argentina, terrorists bombed the Israel Embassy in 1992 and then the Jewish Community headquarters in 1994. America, too, had been victimized by earlier terror, but it was the World Trade Center attacks of September 11, 2001 that brought the scourge of international terror to America's shores big time and made Americans acutely aware of the phenomenon.

Already attuned to the terrorist threat, in part because of familiarity with what was happening in Israel and in the global Jewish world, the Federation's Jewish Community Relations Council (JCRC) was in a position to understand and flag these matters at an early point. The JCRC called attention to the fact that a group called the Islamic Association for Palestine – identified by media sources and later by law enforcement as being involved in providing financial support for Hamas – had a base of operations in Chicago. And a conference convened in 1996 by the JCRC's Terrorism Awareness Project which examined the global and local situations also noted a law passed by the Illinois legislature with JCRC support that outlawed the raising of funds for terrorist purposes, the first of its kind in any state in the country.

The items in this section include a paper prepared for the JCRC publication linked to that conference, preceded by a piece about Hamas that appeared in the Chicago Tribune. They are followed by a number of pieces which reflect on implications of the 9/11 attack and related terrorist activity in America. The section concludes with remarks prepared following the January 20 terrorist attack in Mumbai, India.

Halting the Madness of Hamas

Chicago Tribune, March 21, 1996

• • •

As Joseph Conrad's 1907 novel *The Secret Agent* draws to a close, an explosives-making terrorist known as "Professor" passes through the streets of London. "His thoughts caressed the images of ruin and destruction. He walked, . . . terrible in the simplicity of his idea calling madness and despair to the regeneration of the world."

Unlike the anarchists in Conrad's book, which was based on an 1894 attempt to blow up the Greenwich Observatory, the Hamas terrorists who have recently brought so much attention on themselves have a religion-based motivation and a localized political agenda. Unlike the hapless bomber in Conrad's novel, who accidentally blows himself up while leaving his target undamaged, they have deliberately taken their own lives while bringing death and destruction to Israel's cities. But they can indeed be said to be driven by the madness and despair which Conrad's "Professor" invoked.

"The Last Hour would not come until the Muslims fight against the Jews and the Muslims . . . kill them," reads a text cited in the 1988 Hamas Charter. The despair of the Hamas operatives derives from the fact that developments seemed to be moving away from their goal of destroying the state of Israel and replacing it with an Islamic entity.

Recent months have seen greater and greater reconciliation of Israel and its neighbors, with Israel an increasingly accepted component in the Middle East. The assassination of Prime Minister Yitzhak Rabin in November, perpetrated by an Israeli Jew opposed to the direction in which the peace process was moving, made the Israeli public even more supportive of that process.

Despite Hamas calls for a boycott of the subsequent Palestinian elections, the turnout was heavy and Yasser Arafat obtained legitimacy as the head of the Palestinian Authority.

With revision of the PLO covenant on the horizon and final status talks between Israel and the Palestinians scheduled to begin shortly, the endgame in the Israel-Palestinian negotiations seemed to be drawing near. And meanwhile, with talks between Israel and Syria moving forward, there was the threat that President Hafez Assad's hospitality toward terrorists groups would become a thing of the past and that freedom of action within Lebanon would be curtailed for Hezbollah, another Islamic terrorist organization.

Made desperate by these developments, Hamas felt a clear need to strike out. And strike out they did, in a series of acts in Jerusalem, Ashkelon and Tel Aviv that emphatically showed all the world the madness of their methods.

The anarchists described by Conrad picked their target, where time is measured, for symbolic reasons. For Hamas, the consideration in choosing where to blow themselves up has been simply to take as much innocent human life as possible. So they have picked out crowded buses on the rush hour streets of Jerusalem and the busiest shopping center in Tel Aviv on the afternoon of a holiday when children in costume were gathering.

In the words of its own motto, "Death for the sake of Allah is [Hamas'] most coveted desire." The barbaric, death-embracing cruelty of the Hamas killer staggers the mind and chills the heart.

Although the ultimate end that the latest acts aim at bringing about is clear, the means intended to achieve that end are complicated. Trying to enhance their organization's power within the Palestinian world, Hamas strategists apparently believe that Arafat will pretty much leave them alone, letting them grow as a force; or, if he takes them on, he will enhance their prestige in another way.

At the same time, they aim to reverse advances in Palestinian self-determination and are ready to bring frustration to their people in order to mobilize Palestinian support for their nefarious purpose. Thus they are trying to cause Israel to pull back from the peace process and, first of all, have provoked Israel to close off the Palestinian-controlled areas and to take other security measures that affect the Palestinian people.

It is essential to see the Hamas attacks for what they are: not isolated acts by reckless individuals but planned maneuvers by an organization (however fragmented it may be) with a complex infrastructure and with recruiters and teachers able to persuade young men to carry out such outrages.

Though Israelis are the immediate targets of these bloody attacks, Yasser Arafat and the Palestinian Authority are threatened by them as well. And, at the same time, the United States and other Western countries, along with many Middle East nations, are threatened by the broader forces of Islamic extremism backed by Iran and other "rogue states."

Recognizing the immediate and longer-term implications of the recent Hamas attacks, world leaders have formed an alliance against international terrorism, which is significant both practically and symbolically. As the U.S., Russia, Israel and Saudi Arabia met in Egypt to consider measures to be implemented in the effort against terrorism, they demonstrated a passing of the old divisions between East and West, Arab and Jew.

But for the current challenge to be successfully faced, it is absolutely necessary for Yasser Arafat to take effective steps against Hamas in those areas that he controls. And it is to be hoped that there will be understanding for the measures Israelis must take to protect their people. In addition to weakening the Hamas infrastructure and the ability of Hamas operatives to kill Israelis while they blow themselves up, opponents of the current regime of terror also need to counter the readiness by Hamas followers to engage in such behavior.

The spiritual head of the Islamic Movement in Israel has described the scenes of death and destruction in Israel as not consistent with Islamic beliefs. His call on international Muslim leaders to place a religious ban on suicide attacks merits support. And those preachers and others within the Palestinian world advocating and celebrating terrorist violence in the name of Islam must be placed beyond the pale.

And finally, there are steps that can and should be taken to make it more difficult for Americans to provide support for such activity. The time has long passed for passage of a strong effective law to combat terrorism in the United States. Here in Illinois, which has been described as a major support base for Hamas, pending legislation that would criminalize fundraising for terrorist activities is important as well.

Conrad treated his ineffectual terrorists with irony and scorn. In the last words of his novel the Professor is shown walking in London "unsuspected and deadly, like a pest in a street full of men." A century later, the madness and despair of which the Professor spoke, combined with powerful explosives and a malignant ideology supported by a handful of pariah states, has let loose a destructive force that has appalled the civilized world and provoked an international crisis. It must be addressed.

Terrorism Today and the Chicago Connection

from *Confronting International Terrorism*
at the Local Level: The Illinois Model
October 1996

• • •

Terrorism is hardly a new phenomenon. A number of nationalisti-cally-based terrorist movements have been active on the world scene for years, and in the post-Cold War environment their numbers have increased. At the same time, however, the overall face of both international and domestic terrorism has been strikingly altered in the wake of the collapse of the Communist system.

In the international domain, the disintegration of the Soviet Union removed a major source of aid and inspiration for terrorist states and organizations. But state-sponsored and group terrorism of another kind has emerged as a significant force, driven not by Marxist ideology or the geo-political interests of a Russian-dominated bloc of nations but by religion-based passions and the desire to spread extremist Islamic beliefs in opposition to the secularism, modernism, and Western democratic values represented by the United States. (Ironically, some of the militants who now direct their wrath at the West received Western backing while fighting the Soviets in Afghanistan.)

On the domestic level, with the Soviet Union no longer a threat to American freedoms, the United States government itself is seen by some of its own citizens as surrendering their independence and engaging in an oppressive global conspiracy. The government is thus regarded as the enemy by violence-inclined right-wing groups, some of which embrace a "Christian identity" ideology that sees white Aryans as the true chosen people, demonizes Jews, and regards blacks as inferior.

While there are important differences between these two contemporary sources of terrorist activity, each embraces an image of an idealized past in which their predecessors had more power than they themselves do today, and they share an apocalyptic vision of their future. Desperate to alter the course of events before it is too late and ready to take up arms against innocent civilians and to bomb symbolic targets, each of them wishes to bring about cataclysmic change as the end of the millennium approaches.

Both of these sources of terrorism thus target the United States and oppose the "New World Order" which, in their different ways, they see America promoting. Another characteristic they share is that both maintain support bases on American soil. That the domestic groups would do so is one thing. Less expected has been the way some international terrorist organizations have taken advantage of constitutional protections, of limited recognition of their nature and goals, and of the presence of potential supporters to obtain financial backing and to establish structures for recruiting, training, and directing operatives. This is of particular significance to the citizens of Illinois, for as the facts have become known, the Chicago area has frequently been seen at or near the center of attention in connection with one particular organization responsible for some of the deadliest acts of terror on the globe, namely the Palestinian group called Hamas.

In January 1993, Israeli security forces detained two Chicagoans suspected of bringing large sums of money to aid terrorist activities conducted in Gaza and the West Bank by members of Hamas, an organization dedicated to advancing the radical Islamic cause by eradicating the State of Israel and establishing Muslim rule over all of Palestine. One month later, in a February 17 *New York Times* article, Judith Miller, a *Times* correspondent with years of experience throughout the Middle East, reported on implications of the interrogations of one Chicagoan, Mohammed Abdel-Hamid Salah of Bridgeview. Miller observed that "Hamas, the Palestinian group that has attacked Israelis and Palestinians, has drawn critical financial support and political and military guidance from agents in the United States." (In *God Has Ninety-Nine Names,* a recently-published book that elaborates on the activities of Salah and others in the framework of Islamic militancy throughout the Middle East, Miller reveals that she had personally watched an interrogation of the Hamas suspect.)

In a Hebrew-language book on Hamas published in Jerusalem in 1994, the Israeli journalist Ronni Shaked, along with Aviva Shabi, provided more details on the activities of Salah and Muhammad Jarad, the other Chicagoan who had been picked up and who was later released. And they elaborated further on Chicago-area connections with Hamas, describing both fundraising activity and the manner in which a Palestinian visitor to the United States named Nasser Issa Jalal Hidmi participated in a 1990 training session near Chicago. At that session, for which Salah provided the invitation and made the travel arrangements, Hidmi and others reportedly learned how to make explosive devices.

On the *MacNeil/Lehrer News Hour* of October 20, 1994, the investigative journalist Steven Emerson described other Hamas activities in Illinois. On November 13, 1994, on CBS's *60 Minutes,* Oliver "Buck" Revell, former head of counterterrorism for the FBI, asserted that "Hamas, in the United States, collects money, produces propaganda, films, video . . . recruits and even engages in paramilitary training." He responded to a direct question by affirming that the area "outside Chicago" was a place where such training had taken place.

The July 1995 arrest at Kennedy Airport of Mousa Mohammed Abu Marzook, a top Hamas leader, followed by an extradition request from Israel, led to a May 8, 1996, federal court ruling which brought more Chicago connections to public knowledge. Reporting on the determination that Abu Marzook can be extradited to Israel to stand trial for murder and terrorism in connection with violent acts carried out by Hamas from 1990 to 1994, The New York Times quoted Salah's saying that "an enormous amount of money" was collected in Chicago on behalf of Hamas. Another statement cited by the judge provided evidence of Salah's supplying $96,000 for weapons procurement to a Hamas operative in the West Bank city of El Bire.

The hearings documented the fact that Abu Marzook had transferred hundreds of thousands of dollars to Salah's accounts in Chicago banks, from whence they were presumably meant to be distributed to Hamas operatives in Gaza and the West Bank. In January 1995, in the wake of a number of dramatic bombings around the world, President Clinton issued an executive order to freeze the assets of a dozen terrorist groups, and in March of 1996 the *Chicago Tribune* reported that assets worth about $800,000 were seized after the issuing of that order. More recently, in a *Wall Street Journal* article on August 5, 1996, Steven Emerson identified Marzook and Salah as two of the three holders of accounts whose funds had been seized. (Emerson also bemoaned the fact that the Treasury Department has not gone after more of the "tens of millions of dollars" worth of assets which investigators reportedly linked to terrorist groups operating in over 12 states.)

Testifying before the U.S. Senate's Subcommittee on the Near East and South Asia on March 19, 1996, Emerson spoke about Chicago connections a number of times, even including a section on "Hamas in Chicago" in his written presentation on "Terrorism and the Middle East Peace Process: The Origins and Activities of Hamas in the United States." Highlighted in that section was reference to a program held at Bogan High School on October 3, 1994, called the Jerusalem Festival

1994. According to Emerson, the event included the sale of "radical pro-Hamas publications," and the program "featured songs of revolution and speeches by Hamas leadership both in the United States and abroad."

Quoting some of the speakers, Emerson emphasized their praise of those who have maintained the conflict against Israel. At one point in the program, according to Emerson, "following a song by the band, a section of the audience broke into a popular Hamas chant that glorified the Iz ad-Din al-Qassam military squads – the very same death squads that carried out the series of four suicide bombings in Israel during the past four weeks." At another point in the rally, the director of the Texas-based Holyland Foundation for Relief and Development, which Emerson calls "Hamas' open charitable arm," reportedly solicited funds. According to Emerson, "tens of thousands of dollars were raised that night."

The rally, Emerson reported, was sponsored by the Islamic Association for Palestine (IAP), an organization frequently linked to Hamas. In his August 5, 1996, *Wall Street Journal* article, Emerson cites Oliver Revell, the former FBI official, as straight-out calling the IAP a Hamas front, while in *God Has Ninety-Nine Names,* Judith Miller says that the IAP "has close ties to Hamas and Islamic Jihad." On April 8, 1996, the *Dallas Morning News* reported that "public records, materials from the [IAP and the Holyland Foundation for Relief and Development] and interviews over seven months show a pattern of personal, financial and philosophical ties between Hamas and the two non-profit groups." And the paper also pointed to Chicago connections with the IAP, then based in Richardson, Texas.

The Dallas paper noted that two Chicagoans, Rafiq Jaber and Sabri Ibrahim, were "current president and vice-president, respectively, of the Islamic Association for Palestine." The *Morning News* went on to declare that "the association is planning to move its headquarters" to Chicago. Since the spring of 1996, Action Alerts to members, press releases, and membership forms have been circulated with Chicago area addresses and telephone information, supporting the inference that the IAP headquarters has indeed been relocated to Illinois.

The Islamic Association for Palestine for North America was created in 1981, and, according to Emerson, Abu Marzook was one of its founders. In an article in the *Jerusalem Post's* International Edition for the week ending August 26, 1995, Emerson was quoted saying that the IAP was actually started in Illinois, then moved to Texas, with branch offices established in Illinois and other states. Hamas itself was established in Gaza in 1988, but according to Emerson its uncompromising charter may actually have been written in the United States.

The charter, known in English primarily through a translation prepared by the Islamic Association for Palestine in 1990, proclaims that Hamas, whose name means the Islamic Resistance Movement, "works toward raising the banner of Allah on every inch of Palestine." The document goes on to say that "the Islamic Resistance Movement is a link in [a long] chain of the Jihad against the Zionist occupation," and that "it looks forward to fulfill the promise of Allah no matter how long it takes because the Prophet of Allah (saas) says: The Last Hour would not come until the Muslims fight against the Jews and the Muslims would kill them." The self-definition of Hamas is encapsulated in its motto which proclaims: "Allah is its Goal. The Messenger its Leader. The Quran is its Constitution. Jihad is its methodology, and Death for the sake of Allah is the most coveted desire." Rather than regarding the Israeli-Palestinian conflict as a resolvable clash between two nationalist movements, Hamas, expressing vitriolic anti-Semitic notions, sees Jews *per se* as the enemy and utterly rejects the legitimacy of the Jewish State of Israel.

With the Israeli government and the Palestinian Liberation Organization joining together in a peace process, Hamas' attempts to torpedo Israeli-Palestinian reconciliation became increasingly destructive. In early 1996, those efforts culminated in a series of suicide bombings which put at risk a centerpiece of U.S. foreign policy in the Middle East and threatened to bring intensified instability to the region. Meanwhile, American troops were themselves directly targeted by Middle East terror in the June 1996 bombing in Saudi Arabia.

With international terrorism thus showing itself as an increasingly ominous threat to America's friends, American interests, and American lives, the need for our nation to take appropriate legislative, security, law enforcement, and even military steps to counter such a threat has become more and more apparent. That is so, whether it means coming to grips with the sponsorship of terrorism by states like Iran, Libya, and the Sudan, or whether it means confronting the way terrorist organizations like Hamas and Islamic Jihad have established support and operations centers in states like Illinois, Texas, Florida, and Virginia in our own country.

As we oppose the terrorist menace, we must be careful to avoid stereotyping and scapegoating a group of people – a consequence that has unfortunately, at times, followed revelations about the religious and cultural links of some who engage in such activities. There are obviously many terrorists on the world scene who are not Muslims and who have nothing whatsoever to do with Islam. Likewise, however much practitioners of the sort of international terrorism I have focused on may link themselves with the Islamic religion and may invoke its beliefs and terminology, they should not be regarded as representative of all Muslims. Knowledgeable scholars have pointed out that the principles and practices of these terrorists are actually at odds with the essence of the Islamic faith; thus, the behavior of that limited number of Muslims who participate in terrorism and deliberately lend support to it should not be seen as characteristic of all followers of Islam.

At the same time, while it is incumbent upon all people of goodwill to speak out against stereotyping, against false generalizations, and against bigotry directed against the Muslim community, sensitivities regarding such matters should not prevent us from dealing with a very real and very important situation. Without implicating all Muslims or their religion, institutions of our society need to join one another in confronting that wave of international terrorism emanating from people and organizations which deliberately associate themselves with Islam, while we stand resolutely together against the overall threat of terrorism our nation faces as new dangers replace old ones on the world scene.

Israel Not the Main Issue in Terrorists' Hatred of America

Chicago Tribune, October 7, 2001

• • •

Experts on terrorism and the Middle East have identified a visceral hatred of America and what it stands for as the primary force motivating the terrorist movement that struck so devastatingly on September 11. As President Bush said about that group when speaking to Congress and the American people nine days later, "Its goal is remaking the world--and imposing its radical beliefs on people everywhere."

"These terrorists kill not merely to end lives," he went on to say, "but to disrupt and end a way of life."

There is an alternative view being circulated by some, a view positing that American support for Israel brought about the current crisis. To properly understand and face our adversary, we need to recognize the wrong-headedness of this claim.

Hatred for America within the Arab world is not entirely unrelated to hostility toward Israel. That link was graphically demonstrated when, upon hearing of the horror unleashed in New York and the Washington area, Palestinians danced in the streets.

The essential point, however, is that, at its core, the terrorists' animosity toward America and the rejection of Israel by certain Arabs and Muslims have a common denominator. Both reactions reflect a culture-based objection to what is seen as the intrusion of non-Islamic, Western, democratic people, practices and values into the Muslim world. As the Iranians put it, America, especially in an era of globalization, is the "great Satan" and Israel is the "little Satan."

The notion that September 11 happened because of America's alliance with Israel – or, a variant of that, because the Bush administration had not played a more active role in helping resolve the Israeli-Palestinian conflict – is out of sync with the facts.

For one thing, the Osama bin Laden network that apparently produced the culprits has not made the Palestinian anti-Israel cause a major part of its agenda. Yes, bin Laden has occasionally talked the talk in bad-mouthing Israel. But he has far more often declared that it is America that must be punished for contaminating holy Muslim places by stationing its forces in his native Saudi Arabia and for generally being like the medieval Christian Crusaders whose invasion was overcome by Muslim resistance.

While there is at least one reported instance of an attempt by bin Laden to place operatives in Gaza, through the years the terrorism attributed to his group has featured primarily American targets.

Glib assertions that these terrorists hate us because America has been too inclined to take Israel's side in its conflict with the Palestinians ignore the readiness that our nation has demonstrated to be involved in resolving the conflict in a fair manner. Also ignored are the friendships we have shown toward the Arab world; Egypt is the second-largest recipient of our foreign aid. In light of the fact that the September 11 attack was planned over several years, the claim that it was provoked by the relative non-engagement of the Bush administration is utterly incongruous, because that administration has been in office a mere eight months.

In a way, any argument about America's evenhandedness is beside the point. For many of the Palestinians and their supporters, the problem is not that America is not sufficiently committed to working to help bring about a just peace between the Israelis and Palestinians. For them, the problem is that we are committed to doing that, because for them the real goal is not a just peace but the destruction of Israel.

Hamas and Islamic Jihad certainly aspire to that goal. Members of these Islamic terrorist organizations have virtually patented the practice of killing themselves to murder as many civilians as possible (what they call "martyrdom" and others call suicide attacks). And they share more than that tactic with the bin Laden group. Perverse as their beliefs may be, like the followers of bin Laden, they, too, see themselves as the true protectors of Islam from the democratic, modern world of the West.

A particularly chilling attempt to absolve the bin Laden terrorists and scapegoat Israel and its friends for the September 11 attack on America is brought to light in reports that many Pakistanis and Egyptians believe the outrageous claim that Jews rather than Muslims were the perpetrators. Incendiary rumors that 4,000 Jews stayed away from the World Trade Center that day because they had warning are being circulated even in this country.

In sum, despite the spin that some – maliciously or not – may put on the answer to why the World Trade Center and Pentagon were attacked on Sept. 11, and despite all of the coverage the Palestinian-Israeli conflict ordinarily receives in our media, the Israel factor is not the dominant issue for the world's Muslims, is not at the core of U.S.-Muslim relations, and is not at the heart of the reason why we have been targeted by our terrorist enemies.

It is more accurate to say that militant radical Muslims are anti-Israel because they see Israel as imbued with American values than it is to say that they are anti-American because of our ties to Israel.

Plainly put, those individuals who inspired, conceived of, plotted and carried out the horrifying acts of September 11 were driven by hatred of all that America stands for: of our commitment to personal freedom; of our proclaiming the right to liberty and justice for all; of our egalitarian, democratic principles; and of our affirmation of diversity. We are hated by these enemies not for anything we have done to them or to anybody else, nor because of any of our alliances. They hate us, quite simply, for what we are.

War Memories Among School Children

JUF News, February 2002

• • •

My father remembered World War I.

He was a child then, growing up in a Polish town, and in later years he liked to talk about how it was, first when the Russian soldiers went by on their way to the front, then when the Germans defeated them and occupied the city until their own fortunes changed and they abandoned it.

After emigrating to Canada, he and his family arrived in Chicago in 1923. When World War II came my father was told he was too old to serve. I myself was a small child at the time, and I remember little connected with that war except that we had a "Victory Garden" in our back yard where we grew some of our own vegetables.

I also remember how, in subsequent years, I played with the white helmet my father had been given when he had served in the Auxiliary Police – an arm of that war's version of what is now called Homeland Security – which trained at Soldier Field.

Those memories began to come back to me a few weeks after the attacks of September 11, when I drove past our former home in West Rogers Park and was startled to see statues of Uncle Sam festooned in red, white, and blue planted in front of it. I was in the old neighborhood on my way to Rogers School, the elementary school I had attended, where I was about to serve as "Principal for a Day" in a wonderful program introduced by Mayor Daley a few years ago.

Walking down the school's old hallways, I remembered the air raid drills that were held during the Cold War, when there were fears that America might be targeted. I thought I recognized the very locker that I used to stand in front of, my arms raised behind me and folded to protect my head, with a classmate at my back doing the same, in preparation for an attack which, thankfully, never came.

My generation's war was the one in Vietnam. I was in graduate school in Minnesota then, and rather than participating in that conflict I was a protester against it. I continue to believe that what I and others did was right, but I also now regret that the movement we were a part of helped spawn generic anti-war and anti-government attitudes that, to an extent, continue to afflict America.

When I said that to a friend recently, he observed that the fault lay in the injustice of that war, not in our actions, and that the problem is that today's protesters do not make such a distinction. All the same, even though opposition to today's war and a readiness to blame America itself for what has been done to it largely remain limited to parts of academia and some other precincts where attitudes of my generation hold sway, the country continues to pay a price for some of what happened in the '60s.

Having obtained an academic appointment at Tel Aviv University, with my wife I left Chicago and the domestic agitation surrounding the Vietnam War just days after the infamous 1968 Democratic convention hosted here. Five years later, our war came.

In the summer of 1973, I had been drafted by the Israel Defense Forces, but given my age and family status I had had only a cursory basic training and was put in a reserve unit that did little beyond light guard duty. Then, on Yom Kippur, when an unprepared Israel was attacked, my unit was called up.

While we were spared direct engagement, after the first days of the conflict a number of us were upgraded, retrained, and put in a combat unit on the tense border with Jordan. Viewing Amos Gitai's film *Kippur* a short time ago, my wife and I both found ourselves viscerally moved, with powerful memories brought to life. It was as though we were back at that time of trauma and tension.

Living through an experience like the Yom Kippur War offers preparation of a sort for the shock and uncertainty which struck America when this country too suffered a devastating surprise attack. The question arises, however, whether America has yet found an Israel-like balance between sharp, unrelenting awareness of its new reality and the ability to maintain a form of day-to-day normalcy.

There indeed may be new airline security measures, but recurring breaches of security make it clear that full-scale arrangements are not yet in place. Travel and tourism may indeed be down, but it is not apparent what other changes there have been in people's lives or in their attitudes.

The country knows we have been attacked by commandeered jets, and the anthrax mystery remains unsolved, but it sometimes seems that the memory of September 11 needs to be reinforced and that Americans have yet to fully recognize who and what was behind that attack. Though President Bush properly insists that this is not a war against Islam, the people who struck that day were not generic "terrorists" but, as various commentators have noted, Islamists who use terrorism as their primary instrument.

On the day of my visit, the principal of Rogers School, Constance Roberts, told me of the way the school had treated the events of Sept. 11 and then took me to several classes. In the hallway where my classmates and I used to cover our heads in preparation for an attack that never came, I saw drawings of American flags taped up shortly after September 11, when the attack for which the nation was not prepared did come. On a stage where, during our graduation, my classmates and I had presented the patriotic "Ballad for Americans," I heard today's students energetically chant the Pledge of Allegiance.

Observing an English instruction class, I saw new Americans from places we had only learned about – places as diverse as Bulgaria, Mexico, Korea, Haiti, and Pakistan – join together to learn a common language in a school where they will also learn the common values of a modern pluralistic democracy, values for which America's enemies wish to destroy it.

How, I wondered in my old elementary school, will the children of today remember the new kind of war in which we are currently engaged? What, I have continued to wonder, will their memories of this war be like?

Tolerance and Reality in Collision

Chicago Tribune, November 17, 2002

• • •

We do not yet know everything about John Allen Muhammad and perhaps never will.

But more and more information about him has been emerging since he and his 17-year-old companion, John Lee Malvo, were apprehended in connection with the shootings in the Washington, D.C., area. One thing that has become clear is that the common profiling of a serial-killing sniper was widely off the mark in this case.

Muhammad's ties to the Nation of Islam surfaced soon after his arrest, along with reports that he had sympathized with the 9/11 hijackers. Now, along with allegations that he and Malvo may have been linked to a robbery and shooting in Alabama and another in Louisiana, come reports of possible links to a murder in Tacoma, Washington, and the firing of shots into a synagogue there last May. And it is reported that Muhammad spoke disparagingly about Christians and Jews, according to a friend in Bellingham, Washington, where he occasionally visited.

Tentative as one must be in drawing conclusions from all of this, two other murderous sequences, one of which claimed victims in Chicago a little more than three years ago, suggest parallels, different as the situations might at first appear to be.

On the Friday evening of July 2, 1999, Benjamin Smith, the disciple of a white supremacist hate group, began a holiday weekend shooting spree by wounding several Jews coming home from synagogue in Chicago's West Rogers Park. After that, he drove to Evanston, where he gunned down former Northwestern University basketball coach Ricky Birdsong, an African-American who was jogging in his neighborhood. He fired at other members of minority groups in Indiana and Illinois, killing one more person. Pursued by law enforcement, he ended the rampage by taking his own life.

Theories about Smith's motivation, choice of targets and timing remain speculation. Still, what we seemed to be seeing then was not an individual carrying out the operational plan of a specific white supremacist organization but a lone true believer under the influence of that movement.

A person with hatred in his heart, Smith directed his hostility toward specific categories of people. When something or other put him over the edge, individuals became the targets of his violence based solely on their religion, race or ethnicity. On that weekend, he went on a crusade aimed at shaping his kind of America, free of Jews, blacks and other minorities.

Three years later, on another July 4th, another murderous outburst took place in America, this one at Los Angeles International Airport. In this case the perpetrator was an Egyptian resident of the U.S. said to be associated with radical Islamist beliefs. He, too, apparently acted on his own, selecting those targets that his ideology had taught him to abhor. He went to the Israeli airline El Al's counter and opened fire, killing two before being killed by security guards.

There surely continue to be potential lone wolves in America like Benjamin Smith, likely to act out the messages of violence preached by the home-grown white supremacist movement. That movement, with its link to a perverted version of Christianity known as "Christian Identity," reminds us that no religious source has a monopoly on producing polluted streams that adherents might choose to follow.

We now also know that there are those whose version of Islam – considered a perversion of that faith by outside scholars and most believers – teaches that it is Jews, Christians and other Americans who are the evil enemy.

With feelings strong and the danger of stereotyping always present, we need to be careful to avoid impugning all Muslims for the acts committed by some. But we would be dangerously shortsighted to ignore the lessons of September 11, when individuals operating in the name of Islam perpetrated the greatest act of terror committed on American soil. In addition to taking thousands of lives, they provided inspiration for those vulnerable to the messages of hate delivered in certain mosques and schools in the Islamic world and in parts of the West as well.

The variation on Islam that John Allen Muhammad would have been taught as a follower of Louis Farrakhan's Nation of Islam is distant from the mainstream of that religion in several ways. But Farrakhan himself, at a news conference held five days after September 11, 2001, at which he expressed his condemnation and horror at what had occurred, went on to say, "When a nation becomes the only remaining superpower ... and that nation then has a spiritual lapse and begins to sink into moral decline ... the Koran teaches that Allah then seizes that nation with stress and affliction, that it might humble itself."

We do not know precisely what conclusions John Allen Muhammad may have derived from the acts of September 11 in the framework of the religious convictions that he embraced. But in the post-9/11 world, it is reasonable to suggest that his beliefs had something to do with his and Malvo's alleged campaign of terror in the environs of our nation's capital.

At a time when we are concerned about homeland security, it would be foolhardy to ignore these apparent implications of the shootings. The new reality we face certainly presents challenges of one kind to law enforcement, whose job it is to keep us safe, and of another kind to all Americans, as we strive to maintain our traditions of tolerance and fairness. It is a reality we would fail to face at our peril.

Reflections on the Mumbai massacre
from Chicago's North Side

Remarks prepared for neighborhood memorial, January 2009

Following the January 2009 terror attack in Mumbai, India, Chicago's Indo-American Center, based on California Avenue near Devon, planned a Solidarity Memorial and invited me to speak there. Though the Center needed to cancel the observance shortly before it was scheduled to take place, these remarks were shared with the Center and were printed in the JUF News.

．　．　．

I would like to begin these remarks in an autobiographical, personal way. As it happens, I grew up in this neighborhood. The synagogue where I received my early religious school education and observed my bar mitzvah was across the street. The apartment where my family lived until I was one year old, when we moved a mile or so north, is one block from here. The apartments and homes where my grandmothers, aunts, uncles, and cousins lived are a stone's throw away. And the library where I spent innumerable hours is not much farther.

While the Jewish population's percentage of the neighborhood was more considerable in those years, there remains a significant Jewish presence. Meanwhile, the population has been heavily augmented by individuals who hail from the Indian subcontinent or whose ancestors did, and who still have strong ties to their cultural and religious roots.

I reflect on all of that now because the people who live in this Chicago neighborhood today, and who have come together this morning in common purpose, with shared emotions and shared convictions, make up a microcosm of the demographic that came under attack during those horrifying days in Mumbai. And the democratic values that we all hold dear – our commitments to religious and cultural pluralism, to tolerance, to equality, and to freedom of thought and expression – are precisely those values that enrage the terrorists who attacked that day and that propel them to plan and carry out acts of barbaric violence against those whom they hate.

The targets that day, along with Americans, Britons, and other Westerners, were the Hindus, Muslims, and other Indians who subscribe to Western values and practices in a way that has come to define Mumbai as a leading global metropolis. And among the targets, very specifically, were Jews – a group with whom today's Islamist terrorists seem to have a pathological obsession.

Back, briefly, to autobiography. After growing up in Chicago and going elsewhere for my advanced education, in 1969 I headed to Israel to teach English literature at Tel Aviv University. Soon after arriving there I made the acquaintance of the departmental librarian, a woman who had immigrated to Israel from India where, I learned, her family had lived for generations. It was the first time I had become aware of the fact that Jews lived in India, and through her I learned details about the history of the community there, a community that has been the subject of a number of media reports since the Mumbai massacre took place.

Jews began to live in India over 2,000 years ago. What are known as "Baghdadi" Jews – the group of which my colleague was a part – came from the Middle East in significant numbers in the 19th century. While the quantity of descendants of all of those "local" Jews has declined from what it once was, a core group remains, and today there is also an ongoing flow of Jewish visitors, particularly Israeli travelers, many of them young people who feel an affinity for India and its people and who have brought aspects of the Indian lifestyle back to Israel.

It was primarily to serve the visiting Jewish businessmen, tourists, and travelers that the Chabad movement opened its center in Mumbai, as it has done to provide hospitality and connections with their Jewishness for visitors in far-flung locales around the globe. And it was that center in Mumbai that the terrorists made a prime target on their hit list, there that they murdered six Jews, whose bodies were subsequently brought to Israel for burial – six victims among the nearly 200 people whose lives were so cruelly taken during those awful days in Mumbai.

Never before in the history of India, it has been said, were Jews victimized by anti-Semitism and targeted for being Jews. But we all now live in a new world, a world with global terrorists who think it is so important to kill Jews that, in the vast city of Mumbai, they were prepared to devote 20 percent of their attack force – two of the reported 10 gunmen – just to take over the Chabad House and murder whatever Jews they found there.

And so today, in this Chicago neighborhood where Indians and Jews live together, we have come together to mourn the victims of the Mumbai terror – the Indians, the Jews, the others, all of them. As we grieve, we affirm that we will continue to stand together – literally and symbolically – in opposition to the barbarism of the terrorists.

The story of the orphaned two-year-old child of the slain directors of the Chabad center, who was rescued by his Indian nanny and has been brought with her to Israel, breaks our hearts. But like the Chabad leaders, who have made clear that they will rebuild their center and use it once more, we must dedicate ourselves to counter evil with goodness. And in defiance of the murderers of Mumbai and those who would follow after them, we must reaffirm those democratic values by which their victims lived in faraway India, values which we uphold by coming together and living together in Chicago today.

Anti-Semitism Old and New: From Farrakhan to Delegitimization

Understandably, I expect, this is the longest section in the book. I say understandably because, despite the comfort level that most Jews enjoy in today's tolerant America, anti-Semitism remains one of the most significant issues that a Jewish communal organization faces. Dealing with this matter has for many years been a key part of my portfolio, and from an up-close position, I have confronted and thought about the nature of anti-Semitism as it has presented itself and as it has evolved over the last quarter-century.

After a couple of items from early in the '90s which offer views of the state of anti-Semitism in America at that time, this section moves on to a number of pieces about Louis Farrakhan. The Nation of Islam leader, based in Chicago, for many years has garnered both local and national attention for his provocative enunciations of anti-Semitic concepts, most of them variants of traditional themes. The first of those pieces, printed in *The Christian Century* magazine in 1994, analyzes what I consider to be the anti-Semitic core of Farrakhan's world view and rhetoric, and the others demonstrate the longevity of his presence.

Following the pieces on Farrakhan, which have been deliberately grouped together, is an article from the late '90s about Arthur Butz, a professor of electrical engineering at Northwestern University whose espousal of Holocaust denial beliefs exemplifies another way in which anti-Semitism has manifested itself in recent decades. That piece calls attention to the use of the Internet to spread anti-Semitic views, a development that has become increasingly relevant in considering the reach of extremist groups and individuals and their views.

While practitioners of traditional forms of anti-Semitism remain "out there" to this day, their numbers and power have diminished, and what has been seen more frequently as we have moved into and through the early years of the current century is a new form of anti-Semitism. This contemporary version of that ancient hatred shifts the target of attack from individual Jews and Diaspora Jewish communities to the State of Israel – the Jewish collective – and its supporters. Not all criticism of Israel partakes of anti-Semitism – and supporters of Israel need to be careful to avoid charging anti-Semitism when such an accusation is not justified. But as several pieces in this section demonstrate, when verbal attacks use familiar anti-Semitic tropes and when criticism crosses into hate-filled rejection of the legitimacy of Israel as the nation-state of the Jewish people, anti-Semitism indeed comes into play. As common as this new form of anti-Semitism has become, however, the need to advance recognition of what it is and to demonstrate the danger it poses presents an ongoing challenge.

Duke of Hazard:
He represents dangerous trend
JUF News, December 1991

• • •

The good news is that David Duke was decisively defeated in his run for the governorship of Louisiana, receiving only 39 percent of the vote. In an ordinary election, that would be regarded as a wipeout. But his was no ordinary election.

So much for the good news. Nearly 700,000 Louisianans, representing 55 percent of the white vote, were ready to make Duke Governor despite his neo-Nazi and Ku Klux Klan past, his indirect appeals to bigotry, and his lack of qualifications for the job. Beyond that, Duke was able to attract substantial funds not only from Louisianans but from people throughout the country, including Chicago. And through the media attention which his campaign attracted, Duke was able to project himself on the national scene. Duke and what he stands for are likely to be with us for a while.

I first learned about Duke back in 1979, when I joined the staff of the Anti-Defamation League in Atlanta. Duke, who was a notable figure in the extremist movement in the South, had already discarded his Nazi uniform for the sheets of the Ku Klux Klan. More than that, wearing three-piece suits, he had begun to use his smooth speaking style on radio and television talk shows, presenting himself as a new kind of Klan leader.

The evolution of Duke's public persona continued once he left the Klan in controversial circumstances. He set up his own organization, called the National Association for the Advancement of White People, and he gradually moved into politics as a way to expand his influence. He ran for president as a candidate of the Populist Party, won a race for state representative in Louisiana, then failed in bids for the U.S. Senate and, now, the governorship.

Duke's surface evolution has thus been a steady march from the extremist fringes into the apparent mainstream. Just as he has changed his uniforms and his organizational affiliations, so has he changed his physical appearance, thanks to plastic surgery and a new hair style. His public rhetoric has also been moderated. Duke now claims that certain comments and actions, like the wearing of the swastika, were youthful indiscretions which he has left behind. Many of those who voted for him indicated they believed those claims.

In this effort, Duke has played the media like a violin. Appearing on *Nightline* the night before the election, Duke maligned the so-called liberal media, which, in fact, had ensured that he was politely given a fair hearing. Duke's standing as a candidate provided the legitimacy that made him a worthy subject to be interviewed about his ideas and proposed programs. Duke milked that legitimacy for all it was worth, at the same time as he castigated his media hosts for their supposed unfairness, thereby both projecting himself as a worthy political alternative and enhancing his image as an outsider ready to stand up to the establishment.

Duke explained his purported change by asserting a conversion to Christian belief and a religious rejection of his past. But a notable event in the closing days of the campaign involved the defection from the Duke forces of an organizer who concluded that the professions of faith were a sham. And indeed, one "religious" group which has helped Duke and with whose members he has been associated is a movement called the Identity Church, which preaches that Jews are the agents of Satan and white Christians the true chosen people.

Anti-Semitic concepts, it is safe to say, remain central to Duke's true belief system, with hate more than love providing the emotional underpinning of his appeal. Even if his organizational affiliations changed, through the '80s he continued to celebrate Adolf Hitler's birthday. In a 1986 speech he said that "I think they [the Jews] are trying to exterminate our race." Anti-black attitudes are even more a part of his political pitch than anti-Semitic ones. But it is cold comfort to the Jewish community that, though his hardcore followers and some others may share and be attracted by his anti-Semitism, it is doubtless his racism which got him more votes.

Jews and blacks thus stand together as the targets of this classic bigot at a time when anti-Semitism and an inverted version of racism are being expressed by another person getting national attention, Leonard Jeffries, the City College of New York professor. Ironically, Jeffries and the demagogues who exploited and exacerbated the tensions in the New York neighborhood of Crown Heights are busy making Jews scapegoats for the black community's problems while real enemies like David Duke stalk the American scene.

For the Jewish community, David Duke's emergence comes after the news about Jeffries, Crown Heights, Cardinal Josef Glemp's visit to the United States, and President George Bush's September press conference with its troubling language about the powerful group lobbying in Washington. What all this suggests is that the potency of the lessons of the Holocaust is diminishing and the dangers of anti-Semitism are becoming less widely recognized. Somehow, it seems to be more acceptable to echo traditional anti-Semitic notions about Jewish power and malicious Jewish control.

The persistent presence of the Holocaust denial movement, another development with which Duke has associated himself, is a symptom, I believe, more than a cause of the fading familiarity with the reality of the Holocaust. The readiness of some Louisianans to vote for a candidate known to have championed not just the perpetrators of Jewish genocide but America's World War II enemy shows how much history has been forgotten. Decreased knowledge and understanding of both the Holocaust and the civil rights era's fight against discrimination have helped make people less inclined to be repelled by Duke's message.

Thus, even if David Duke's anti-Semitic and racist beliefs are not all that has gotten him as far as he has gotten in his political career, they doubtless have been part of the attraction for some, and they haven't hurt him with others as much as they should have. Duke is a glib speaker able to tap into several emotional issues — fear and uncertainty about the future; resentment of others who have or who are thought to have advantages; hostility to traditional governmental figures. With that happening, and in a climate in which all kinds of verbal expression once taboo are no longer off limits, David Duke and those like him are more likely to gain increasing exposure and to be listened to as though what they have to say has a degree of legitimacy. This is not to say that stark anti-Semitism and racism have yet become entirely okay, nor that they are likely to. Duke is unlikely to gain much real power through his political endeavors. But the danger is that he will gain an increasingly large audience for the expression of his ideas, coded though they may now be. And the more he is around, the less unacceptable it will be for a public figure to have an extremist record like his and to project the kinds of messages which he does.

The antidotes to Duke and those like him are exposure and condemnation. More and more as the campaign developed, Duke was shown for what he is, and in this the media played a useful role. The fact that Duke ended up receiving a smaller percentage of the vote than many expected suggests that this exposure had an impact.

Jewish organizations, because of their non-profit status, were constrained from public condemnation during the time when Duke was a formal candidate. There was also local concern that visible opposition, especially from those out of state, would have strengthened Duke's claim that he was fighting outsiders. With his status as a candidate now a thing of the past, there is the opportunity to speak out and work in opposition to him and what he represents. It is to be hoped that more and more people of goodwill, aware of the danger which bigotry poses both to its targeted groups and to society, will take the Duke candidacy as a warning and work to counter him and the threat which his candidacy revealed.

Numbers Game: Statistics and Anti-Semitism

JUF News, April 1993

• • •

With the horrors of the Holocaust providing a graphic lesson, one might have hoped that anti-Semitism would have been a thing of the past at this point, 50 years after the Warsaw Ghetto uprising. Unfortunately, that is not the case, as developments of the past year or so have continued to show. But our ways of evaluating and understanding this troubling phenomenon may not be as helpful as they could be.

In Europe and parts of the former Soviet Union, the collapse of communism has been followed in many places by the resurgence of nationalism, often with an anti-Semitic component. In our own country, we've seen the candidacies of David Duke and Pat Buchanan and the events in the Crown Heights area of Brooklyn, likened by some to a pogrom. The media, meanwhile, often seem to go easy on anti-Semitism. In January, for example, the *Chicago Reporter,* a publication on race relations, took notice of an anti-Semitic book as though it merited credible attention. Though its author, Michael Bradley, is white, the book, called *Chosen People from the Caucasus,* enlarges on racially-based anti-Semitic notions of the sort enunciated by Leonard Jeffries, professor of Afro-American studies at the City College of New York.

Bradley regards Jews as the most Neanderthal of all white people and thus as particularly aggressive. After attempting to deny Jews a history of suffering of their own, even as slaves in Egypt, he sees them as active in the slave trade which victimized blacks. The book's subtitle, "Jewish Origins, Delusions, Deceptions and Historical Role in the Slave Trade, Genocide and Cultural Colonization," makes clear its perspective.

Recognition of Jewish vulnerability seems increasingly hard to come by these days. The State of Israel is seen as far less endangered than it once was, with anti-Israel propaganda and public opinion portraying Israelis themselves more as victimizers than victims.

At the same time, though, recent studies and reports confirm that anti-Semitism remains a fact of life. These include a study focusing on New York conducted for the American Jewish Committee; another conducted for the Anti-Defamation League by the polling firm of Marttila and Kiley; statistics on hate crimes released by the FBI; and the

Anti-Defamation League's annual audit of anti-Semitic incidents. The Marttila survey, released in November 1992, concluded that "roughly one in five Americans, or between 35 and 40 million adults, hold a collection of views about Jews which are unquestionably anti-Semitic." And the ADL audit talked about a significant increase in anti-Semitic incidents on college campuses over the past five years.

Ironically, these studies and their troubling conclusions, along with the recent surfacings of anti-Semitic behavior, come at a time when Jews increasingly seem to have made it in America. In his book, *A Certain People,* Charles Silberman charted the manner in which American Jews since World War II "have moved from the periphery of American society into its mainstream."

As an example of how far we continue to go, it can be pointed out that there now are 10 Jewish United States senators. Indeed, the conclusions drawn by the 1990 National Jewish Population Survey conducted by the Council of Jewish Federations suggest that a greater threat to the survival of the American Jewish community comes not from anti-Semitism but from the assimilation made easier by our being more widely accepted.

Still, the alarm level about anti-Semitism remains up in much of the Jewish community, encouraged by the facts and the polls. Without derogating these concerns, I think it can be said that perhaps the polls, and especially the manner in which their results are presented, may be creating a misleading impression of prevailing conditions.

The Marttila and Kiley survey, for example, used 11 descriptive phrases about Jews to measure the prevalence of anti-Semitic attitudes in America today. The conclusion was that the 39 percent of Americans who agreed with none or one of 11 tested attitudes can be regarded as being free of anti-Semitism; the 40 percent who agreed with two to five of the views can be regarded as holding a middle ground; and the 20 percent who agreed with six to 11 of the attitudes can be regarded as most anti-Semitic. But questions can be raised about seeing those results in a totally negative manner.

First, a number of the notions in the tested list might be regarded as reflecting positive and not negative attitudes toward Jews. Some of them might even be held by Jews. One, for example, says that "Jews stick together more than other Americans," and another says that "Jews always like to be at the head of things." There is also the opinion that "Jews have a lot of irritating faults," which gets chuckles when repeated in Jewish audiences.

More to the point, I believe that serious questions can be raised about the interpretation of the one determinant with which a great percentage of Americans now agree, namely the one which says that "Jews have too much power in the United States today." It is indeed distressing that the percentage of people who support this belief went from 11 percent in 1964 to 31 percent in 1992. But with 50 percent of respondents thinking that whites in general have too much power and 20 percent thinking that blacks do, it seems that more may be going on than a simple enlargement of support for that anti-Semitic stereotype.

As the recent political campaign suggested, we live in an era when many people are full of resentment toward others and when there is a feeling of personal disempowerment coupled with a sense that members of other groups are privileged with unfair advantages. One wonders if those feelings may not have affected the responses to the question on the survey which asked about Jewish power.

The impression of most people who heard about this surrey is, I suspect, that the news it brought was mostly bad. The emphasis has been on the fact that 20 percent of Americans hold several negative stereotypes, not that that statistic is down 9 percent from 1964. Furthermore, John Marttila has asserted that the real purpose of the survey was not to measure the extent of anti-Semitism in America but to help us understand who holds anti-Semitic views. That is hardly, I believe, the way most people in the Jewish community saw it reported.

Another way to attempt to measure anti-Semitism is by tracing the incidents which take place, as is done by the Anti-Defamation League. The ADL's audit of anti-Semitic incidents for 1992 was released in early February, with most of the press reports leaving the impression that the results showed that things have been getting worse.

While that may be so on college campuses, which were emphasized in those reports, in most other ways the report actually charted improvements over the previous year. Violent criminal acts are down. Skinhead activity is down. Acts of vandalism are down. (In Illinois they have gone from 33 recorded incidents in 1990 to 27 in 1991 to 23 in 1992.) Acts of harassment are down (though they went up in Illinois over the past year). And overall figures are down.

Part of the problem with this kind of study is that it puts the emphasis on national results, and they can be skewed by significant local shifts. Volatility in New York over the last couple of years has been especially notable. Thus, while the national statistics in 1991 were up from 1,685 incidents to 1,897, which might have seemed to mark a major national trend, of the 194 additional incidents, 158 of them took place in New York. By the same token, this year the national numbers are down by 149 incidents, but with New York down 129 incidents most of the improvement was in that one location.

A second problem with this kind of survey is that while the report itself breaks down the numbers into two categories, one for acts of vandalism, the other for acts of harassment, threats, and assaults, those numbers in recent years have generally been issued together. As a result very different kinds of acts, of different degrees of seriousness, get lumped together. Additionally, the category of harassments, threats, and assaults in itself is a hodgepodge, merging not only physical attacks on individuals but the far more inconsequential instances of name-calling or expressions of invective through correspondence or written statements (some of them from isolated crackpots who make it a habit of circulating such material), anonymous phone calls, or personal verbal exchanges.

The ADL itself acknowledges some of these factors and emphasizes that the results of the annual audit provide only one kind of measure of anti-Semitic activity. Nevertheless, the kinds of reservations I have raised are seldom widely noted when the audit is reported on or commented upon, and the audit is often used as a barometer of the status of anti-Semitism in America generally.

In trying to get a handle on the nature of contemporary anti-Semitism, one of the key questions which I believe we should ask is whether it is a distinct phenomenon or just one of several forms of prejudice which are or seem to be on the upswing in America today. The latter view, supported by the Marttila and Kiley survey, which links anti-Semitism to racism and intolerance, has considerable merit to it. Historically America has been more free of ideological anti-Semitism than Europe, and that seems to be true today as well, with the religious basis for prejudice fading away as well. At the same time, expressions of bigotry are said to be up overall in recent years, at least in part because of an increasing freedom for expressing such attitudes.

But at the same time as it is important and useful to look at current manifestations of anti-Semitism in the context of other modes of bigotry and of a breakdown of restraint in America today, that is an incomplete approach. When all is said and done, anti-Semitism remains not just one type of prejudice but unique and special as well. The historian Gavin Langmuir has charted the emergence of anti-Semitism not just as a mode of intergroup conflict but as an irrational hatred. Given its historic sources and manifestations, anti-Semitism brings much baggage to the modern moment, with Jews being Western civilization's classic scapegoats and with a core of stereotypes and images available to trigger hostility and to be called upon and used as a mode of attack.

Jews are not just any "other." They are Western culture's archetypal outsider. In the most enduring of the malevolent anti-Jewish concepts, they are the controlling enemies of order and of goodness itself. These notions are capable of being held even in places where there no longer are Jews, as in parts of Europe, or hardly ever were, as in Japan, a condition which does not apply as much for the other common varieties of intolerance. As different as America may be from Europe, it would be risky to try to insist that Americans are totally immune to these impulses.

Support for the view of anti-Semitism as special can be seen in a study of hate crimes that took place in Chicago from 1986 through 1991 which was prepared for the Chicago Commission on Human Relations. Titled *When Worlds Collide: Culture Conflict and Reported Hate Crimes in Chicago,* the study draws upon statistics which show that the largest target group for hate crimes was non-whites, the second largest whites, and the third largest Jewish individuals and institutions. According to Garth Taylor, author of the report, incidents involving people in the first two categories resulted from the fact that "there are certain high-tension areas of the city where racial groups are in conflict with each other and commit hate crimes against each other." For Jews, in contrast, it is as though they or their institutions, by the very fact of their existence, evoke hostility.

Anti-Semitism thus can both be tied to a general trend in our society and regarded as a problem in its own right. Realizing that certain statistics on anti-Semitism may go up at the same time as comparable statistics regarding other forms of prejudice in America increase provides us an important context for understanding and responding to anti-Semitism on the one hand. But on the other hand, given the specialness of anti-Semitism, including its potential to take on a life of its own, we have the right, indeed an obligation, to have special concerns about it.

And so data telling us that Americans think that Jews have "too much power in America," without being exaggerated, indeed deserve a careful look. Without concluding that it is the 1930s all over again, Jews are right to take note of nationalism-linked anti-Semitism wherever it may appear. We are right to be bothered by anti-Semitism among blacks, themselves also primary victims of bigotry and one-time partners in the civil rights movement. And developments on campuses, where the America's leaders are being educated and the nation's future may be taking shape, merit special concern.

But information needs to be as correct as possible; details need to be explored; conclusions need to be kept in perspective; and we should be prepared to acknowledge the good news as well as the bad. We need, in sum, to maintain a levelheaded approach to the continuing existence of anti-Semitism, respecting the anxiety felt by many in our community while seeing the problem accurately and in appropriate context, the better to understand and effectively confront it.

Louis Farrakhan's Anti-Semitism:
A Look at the Record
The Christian Century, March 2, 1994

• • •

A venomous anti-Jewish speech given by Kahlid Abdul Muhammad, a spokesman for the Nation of Islam, has caused a national furor. The remarks — which included the claim that "the so-called Jew... is sucking our blood in the black community" — were made in late November at Kean College in New Jersey, but it was not until January that the controversy developed. In a column on the op-ed page of the *New York Times* on January 8, Roger Wilkins, a black professor of history at George Mason University, took to task those blacks who had failed to condemn the speech. "Sometimes," he said, "it takes strength for teachers to say such things to students when a truly wicked and destructive message has just pandered to their deepest injuries and insecurities." A. M. Rosenthal wrote about the subject in a hard-hitting column on the same page three days later. But it was only after January 16, when the Anti-Defamation League of B'nai B'rith placed a full page ad in the Times with excerpts from Muhammad's remarks, that the issue exploded.

In an interview published in the *Times* on January 23, Jesse Jackson condemned the remarks as "racist, anti-Semitic, divisive, untrue and chilling." Labeling Muhammad a "surrogate" of the leader of the Nation of Islam, Minister Louis Farrakhan, Jackson called on the latter to respond, noting that in the previous few months Farrakhan had supposedly been reaching out to the Jewish community. African-American leaders such as Benjamin Chavis, executive director of the National Association for the Advancement of Colored People; William Gray, president of the United Negro College Fund; and Kweisi Mfume, congressman from Maryland and chair of the Congressional Black Caucus, condemned the speech. But Farrakhan's only public reaction was to accuse Jews of "plotting" against him and trying to divide his organization.

The issue would not go away. On February 1 Vice-President Al Gore condemned the speech and called on Farrakhan to denounce it as well. On February 2 Mfume announced that the Congressional Black Caucus was pulling back from the "covenant" which he had earlier said was being formed with the Nation of Islam.

Finally, on February 3, Farrakhan spoke out. Removing Muhammad from his post for the time being, Farrakhan said: "While I stand by the truths that he spoke, I must condemn in the strongest terms the manner in which those truths were represented." And he went on to accuse the Anti-Defamation League of trying to destroy him and his organization. Farrakhan was willing to be publicly critical of Muhammad's exceptionally provocative style, but in lashing out at a Jewish organization and endorsing the substance of the Kean College speech Farrakhan revealed his essential stance – one at odds with the way he has been portrayed in recent months.

When Farrakhan appeared before nearly 25,000 people at the Javits Convention Center in New York in December, the *Times* described him as a person who, "while admired by many young black people for his message of economic power and discipline, has been bitterly criticized by many people for his comments nine years ago calling Judaism a 'gutter religion.'" Though commentators often have acknowledged Farrakhan's notoriety, they have generally limited themselves to citing that remark, sometimes along with another 1984 comment in which he described Hitler as a "great man." Meanwhile, attempting to polish his public image through a performance of Mendelssohn's violin concerto and other means, Farrakhan obtained a series of platforms which helped enhance his stature and acceptability. These included an appearance before an interfaith assembly while Nelson Mandela was in the Midwest, another before the Parliament of the World's Religions in Chicago in the summer, and another before the Congressional Black Caucus in September, along with Jackson and Chavis.

Non-Jewish religious and community leaders generally remained silent at this development, and some African-American leaders stressed the need for black unity, portraying Farrakhan as an ally in the fight against drugs and violence in the inner city. But the Kean College episode and Farrakhan's reaction to it demonstrate that the man continues to subscribe to a belief system which is at its core bigoted and anti-Semitic.

Indeed, careful observers have noted for some time the nature of Farrakhan's views. In July 1992 Henry Louis Gates, chair of the African-American Studies Department at Harvard, wrote "Black Demagogues and Pseudo-Scholars" for the Times. The prime offender was Farrakhan, and the primary text cited was a 1991 volume prepared and issued by the Nation of Islam called *The Secret Relationship between Blacks and Jews.* Labeled by Gates "the bible of the new anti-Semitism," it is a work which continues to be promoted by the Nation of Islam, has turned up on a college reading list, and provided the topic of the Kean College speech by Khalid Muhammad. At his February 3 news conference, Farrakhan held up a copy of the book and championed its contents.

The book's thesis is that "the most prominent of the Jewish pilgrim fathers used kidnapped Black Africans disproportionately more than any other ethnic or religious group in New World history and participated in every aspect of the international slave trade." Gates pointed out the speciousness of that assertion and contended that Farrakhan's purpose in rewriting the history of the relationship between Jews and blacks is to attempt to restructure the present nature of the relationship. Farrakhan, says Gates, not only wishes to sever what remains of the civil rights era coalition of Jews and blacks but aims at undermining the notion of bridge-building between African-Americans and other groups in order to promote his own separatist ideology.

Farrakhan's treatment of Jews as the primary scapegoats for black suffering goes beyond tactics, however, and reveals some essential attitudes. Farrakhan and his followers not only distort the role of Jews in the development of slavery but also deny Jews their history and their role in the cosmic scheme itself. That role and, in a way, even that history are appropriated for African-Americans.

A 1992 book published by the Third World Press in Chicago titled *Chosen People from the Caucasus: Jewish Origins, Delusions, Deceptions and Historical Role in the Slave Trade, Genocide and Cultural Colonization* asserts that the biblical Israelites did not really suffer so badly under slavery in Egypt. The book's foreword is by John Henrik Clarke, professor emeritus at Hunter College, whom Farrakhan describes as influenced by Elijah Muhammad and whom Khalid Muhammad calls a "grand master historian." Clarke attempts to undermine what he calls "Black America's sentimental attachment to the Jewish people," which is "in actuality an indulgence in fantasy and biblical folklore."

The Secret Relationship proclaims that "Jews have been conclusively linked to the greatest criminal endeavor ever undertaken against an entire race of people – a crime against humanity – The Black African Holocaust." In drawing upon language ordinarily used to describe the catastrophe suffered by European Jewry in the 20th century, this passage simultaneously transfers the quality of suffering from Jews to African-Americans and makes Jews the inflictors of it. Theologically, the denial of historical status to the Jewish people and the attachment of it to American blacks involves the notion of "chosen-ness." The thesis of an ironically titled work like *Chosen People from the Caucasus* is that most if not

all of today's Jews are not truly (i.e., racially) Jews at all, having supposedly descended from Khazar converts. It is that premise which lay behind
one of the many deliberately insulting passages in Khalid Muhammad's
speech; directly addressing the "so-called Jew," he said: "You're not the
true Jew .... You are a European strain of people who crawled around on
your all fours in the caves and hills of Europe, eating juniper roots and
eating each other." Muhammad was also drawing upon these concepts
when he asserted: "No white Jews [were] ever in bondage in Egypt for
400 years. You're not the chosen people of God. Stop telling that lie."

For Farrakhan, if there were any Jews who once functioned as the
chosen people, they forfeited their right to that status, and it is he and
his followers who deserve the title today. Speaking to the Gang Peace
Summit held in Chicago in late October, he called for a truce among
the participants because, in part through their actions, "we have offended
God, who has chosen us after 400 years of suffering to be his chosen
people." As Khalid Muhammad puts it: "We can find no other people
fitting the description of the bible prophecies... except we, the 50 million
or more mentally and spiritually dead black men and women here in the
hells of North America." And as he told the blacks in his Kean College
audience: "You are the true Jew. You are the true Hebrew. You are the
true ones who are in line with bible prophecy and scripture, so teaches the
most Honorable Elijah Muhammad and the Honorable Minister Louis
Farrakhan." Farrakhan's view of Jews thus combines admiration for the
power which he attributes to them and apparently wishes to obtain for
himself with resentment of the fact that they have maintained the unde-
served trappings of chosen-ness, along with animosity toward them for
denying him his rightful status. An interview with Farrakhan published in
the *Chicago Sun-Times* last July brought to the surface significant aspects
of the pattern of thought which he has been publicly developing in recent
months. "When I talk to the Jews, I am talking to a segment of that quo-
rum that holds my people in their grip," Farrakhan said. And he added:
"I want you to know, as God is my witness, in my heart I don't have that
much desire to harm one Jew. I want to see black people free."

Mary Johnson, the *Sun-Times* reporter who conducted that interview, has since provided this account in a piece in the *Chicago Reporter.* "I
asked him, 'if Jews were so wrong, and you never said anything so bad,
then why would you extend the olive branch?' He said he was doing it
to free people like me who are working for the white man." In terms of
the biblical analogy, in portraying Jews not as victims but as victimizers
Farrakhan sees them as the contemporary Pharaoh, continuing to enslave

his people. Khalid Muhammad picks up on this comparison when he says to the Jewish community: "Like ancient Pharaoh... your heart is hardened."

Making the biblical analogy explicit, a massive headline filling the front cover of the September 22 issue of *Final Call,* official publication of the Nation of Islam (repeated in an equally massive two-page center spread in that issue), reads: "Minister Farrakhan to Jewish Leaders: Let My People Go!" Writes Farrakhan: "This is the way it was in Egypt under Pharaoh. The Elders of Israel were controlled and dominated by Pharaoh... So it is today,... We must be free from this inordinate influence and control by members of the Jewish community. So, I say to those powerful Jews who wield this kind of influence and power: 'LET MY PEOPLE GO!'" Farrakhan thus not only sees today's Jews as the new Pharaoh and African-Americans as the new Jews, but suggests that he is the new Moses.

Another revealing scriptural role has been attributed to Farrakhan in a series of articles which have appeared in *Final Call* over the past several months in a column titled "Farrakhan: the Traveler," by Jabril Muhammad. In a piece in the November 24 issue headed "Farrakhan Heralds Presence of Messiah," Jabril Muhammad elaborates on an anecdote referred to in the October 27 column, which had the headline "Wise Opponents Know Farrakhan's Identity." "The Honorable Elijah Muhammad," Jabril Muhammad writes, "told me of certain wise Jews with whom he met in the 1930s – long before he was publicly known – who recognized him. He went on to tell me this is mentioned in the Holy Qur'an, wherein it is written that they would recognize him as they recognize one of their sons. Likewise, these wise Jews recognize the honorable Louis Farrakhan as the herald of the Messiah as they recognize one of their sons .... The Almighty promised through all of His servants, the prophets, that what we are seeing and experiencing would take place at this time. These promises include the coming and work of the Honorable Louis Farrakhan."

By saying that Jews know that Farrakhan is the messenger of the Messiah but are trying to hide that truth from others and are setting themselves up in direct opposition to the Messiah's agent, Jabril Muhammad is portraying the Jewish people in a classical anti-Semitic manner. And these notions are emphasized by Khalid Muhammad as well. Besides telling his listeners that "it was the Jews who crucified Jesus, the so-called Jews of his day," Muhammad climaxes his prepared speech by announcing: "You are the chosen of God. And God has chosen you to be his people and he, to be your God. And he is raised up in your midst a divine messenger, a divine Messiah, and a divine warner, and the extension of that divine work is operating in your midst today in the person of the Honorable Minister Louis Farrakhan."

Many of these ideas come together in the December 8 issue of *Final Call* in which Jabril Muhammad asks: Have the Jews "figured out how they are going to deal with the manifestation of that which they know is written in the Torah? They know that they have no ancestors who served in Egypt for 400 years in fulfillment of the divine promises God made to Abraham. Even if that was the case, they cannot truthfully deny that they have forfeited any claims to the benefits of the promises God made through the prophets; especially those to be fulfilled in these days – unless, of course, they accept the Messiah, who is now present in the world. And you can't do that without accepting Minister Farrakhan, who represents the Messiah!"

It is no wonder that Farrakhan endorsed the "truths" of the speech delivered by his disciple – a speech also laden with racist, anti-Catholic and homophobic attitudes, and containing personal attacks on other blacks. Farrakhan and his followers are giving new life to traditional anti-Semitic notions of Jewish conspiracies, of Jewish control, and of Jewish villainy. This form of anti-Semitism comes not from experience or fact but from certain earlier images about Jews which have taken on mythic potency and which fit Farrakhan's worldview. In this respect, ironically, Farrakhan is a soulmate of right-wing white supremacists who see Jews much as he does, but regard themselves as the chosen people.

As evidenced by his own words, by those of his followers, and by publications put out by the Nation of Islam, the profound bigotry which has been at the heart of Louis Farrakhan's belief system for years continues to inform his teachings and sometimes to drive his preachings. To see him as a person meriting mainstream stature who simply made one or two disturbing statements a number of years ago and has now gotten attention because of the unfortunate rantings of an aide whom he has disciplined is to ignore an abiding and chilling reality about him and the organization which he leads.

Confronting the 'Farrakhan Problem'

Chicago Tribune, October 23, 1995

• • •

Media commentators on Monday's Million Man March in Washington quickly called special attention to the passage in Louis Farrakhan's 2 ½-hour speech in which he offered to sit and dialogue with the Jewish community. It would be nice to think that this was a sincere offer and that whatever issues may exist between the Nation of Islam leader and the Jewish community will soon be overcome. Unfortunately, it is impossible to see how the leadership of the Jewish community might take this gesture seriously.

It should be emphasized that the problem with Farrakhan is not that he and his followers occasionally come out with a comment here or there which, as some reporters are occasionally prone to say, are "alleged" to be anti-Semitic. Those comments are merely the tip of the iceberg, revealing not just an intense hostility toward the Jewish people but an ideology which is anti-Semitic at its core. Farrakhan is driven by a belief system which sees Jewish villainy, Jewish conspiracies, and Jewish control everywhere.

Farrakhan teaches a complex theology which sees him and his followers as the true Jews, as chosen people who have suffered 400 years of slavery in America, a destiny prefigured by a biblical narrative. It is he who has been chosen by God to take them out of that oppression.

After successfully pursuing a meeting with some local rabbis a couple of years ago, Farrakhan asserted his confrontational purpose with the front page of the Nation of Islam's Final Call publication reading: "Minister Farrakhan to Jewish leaders: Let my people go!" (That episode offers one more reason for skepticism regarding the Farrakhan's latest overture: as they say on the street, "Been there, done that.")

When Khalid Abdul Muhammad's foul-mouthed bigotry was brought to public attention in early 1994, Farrakhan, condemning "the manner in which those truths were represented," said: "I stand by the truths that he spoke." In an interview with Larry King only a couple of hours after delivering his Million Man March speech, Farrakhan proclaimed, as he has many times, that everything he has said about Jews is "the truth."

Farrakhan had the opportunity to be a true symbol of the march's themes of repentance, atonement and responsibility that day. In his speech he outlined steps to be taken toward reconciliation. However, he failed to take even the first of them, which would have meant accepting the judgment of others that he has been wrong in his expressed attitudes toward the Jewish community.

People can change and the day may indeed come when a sincere demonstration of change by Farrakhan will open the door for true reconciliation. Sadly, though, signs of that remain absent. What we have in their stead is what can only be seen as a posturing show of outreach, not the real thing.

As we in Chicago have good reason to know, attempts by Farrakhan to refurbish his image are nothing new. The aforementioned meeting with local Jewish leaders came shortly after he had performed Mendelssohn's violin concerto. ("Farrakhan makes new music" read one headline, as though the metaphor made it so.) Meanwhile, his public appearances in mainstream settings multiplied at that time from a speaking opportunity at an interfaith luncheon held for Nelson Mandela and an appearance before the Parliament of the World's Religions in Chicago to a session with the Congressional Black Caucus in Washington, D.C. The Khalid Abdul Muhammad embarrassment set things back a bit, but now, through the Million Man March, which he created, Farrakhan has gone mainstream big time.

Unfortunately for him, with the media citing not only the record but also a number of black spokespersons who have been ready to tell it like it is, he has not been able to shake off his reputation for racism, bigotry, homophobia and above all, anti-Semitism. In response, Farrakhan has claimed that his remarks were taken "out of context" (as if there is any acceptable context for calling Jews "bloodsuckers") and charged that the media is out to get him.

Seeking to improve his image and to enlarge his following with people who, ignoring the bigotry and other Nation of Islam principles, have championed aspects of his message. Farrakhan seems to have concluded that if only the Jewish community would give him a clean bill of health by meeting with him, that might do the trick.

The problem is that Farrakhan, in attacking the Jews as he repeatedly does in preachings to his followers, in portraying the Jews as he does in his teachings, is a messenger of hate and a force for divisiveness. It is easy to say how wrongheaded it would be for the Jewish community to give him the legitimacy he seeks.

Outraged by the anti-Semitism of Farrakhan and those who echo him, some Jewish people may be inclined to turn away from the black community. Most, however, while firm in abhorrence of what Farrakhan represents and disturbed by his ascension, remain committed to the vision of a diversified, but unified, America.

These are difficult times in our nation as we struggle to learn how to live with one another. At the same time, there is encouragement to be found in the positive energy set loose in Washington.

I am told that even while Farrakhan was enhancing his status, large numbers of those on the Capitol Mall were inspired with a greater commitment not only to do something for their community, but to work in concert with others, including Jews who had stood and worked with them in the past.

Farrakhan Once More

JUF News, January 1998

•   •   •

It can be regarded as a fact of contemporary life that Louis Farrakhan will periodically surface as a source of controversy causing headaches for the Jewish community. Such issues will most likely play out in the media, which the Chicago-based leader of the Nation of Islam is a master at exploiting. The latest local episode of this sort has grown out of a meeting Farrakhan had with Mayor Daley in City Hall on November 21.

Learning of that meeting, reportedly arranged by the alderman of the ward where the Nation of Islam is based and owns considerable property, Jewish community leaders were concerned that this could become one more in a series of meetings with public officials through which Farrakhan has tried to achieve mainstream status. Concern was compounded when news stories reported that the mayor encouraged dialogue between the Jewish community and Farrakhan, and even "hinted" that the city might refrain from providing approval for Nation of Islam development plans on the South Side unless such dialogue took place—a situation that could lead to the Jewish community's being portrayed as blocking economic improvement in the inner city.

Even before those reports of the mayor's meeting with Farrakhan surfaced, the Jewish Community Relations Council (JCRC) had asked for a Jewish organizational meeting with the mayor to discuss this situation. That session, which in addition to the JCRC involved the American Jewish Committee, the American Jewish Congress, the Anti-Defamation League, and the Chicago Board of Rabbis, took place on December 5. There matters were put in quite a different light than initial media reports had described them.

Mayor Daley told us he had opened the meeting with his previous visitor by making clear that there is no place in the city for the kind of bigotry Louis Farrakhan espouses. Understanding the Jewish community's refusal to enter into so-called "dialogue" with Farrakhan as long as he promotes anti-Semitism, the mayor went on to tell us that he had not called for such an exchange. He indicated he had told the leader of the Nation of Islam that he needs to stop excluding other groups from his projects, and that Farrakhan had a problem which he himself would need to find a way to correct.

Most of our meeting with Mayor Daley, where he was joined by Clarence Wood, commissioner and chair of the Chicago Commission on Human Relations, revolved around the question of how the anti-Semitic bigotry of a Louis Farrakhan might be countered in the city of Chicago. On these matters the mayor demonstrated penetrating insight and sensitivity. He made clear that Farrakhan's scapegoating of Jews for problems faced by members of the African-American community is unacceptable. And he conveyed his recognition of the fact that, while Louis Farrakhan may wish to create the image of an ongoing conflict between himself and the Jewish community, his inflammatory expressions of bigotry are detrimental to all citizens of Chicago and must be condemned first and foremost by leaders of the community at large.

Leaving the meeting, I and others indicated that we had been reassured by the mayor's comments and by his forthright stand against anti-Semitism. Asked by members of the City Hall press corps whether I didn't think that the mayor had nevertheless contributed to the "mainstreaming" of Louis Farrakhan by meeting with him earlier, I responded that that depended on the manner in which the earlier meeting was portrayed.

Since our conversation with the mayor took place, attention to the subject has continued to focus on the question of whether Jewish community leadership is prepared to enter into dialogue with Louis Farrakhan. Organizational spokesmen have continued to emphasize that a readiness to enter into such contacts before Farrakhan rejects the many anti-Semitic positions he and his followers continue to promulgate would only provide him with unmerited legitimacy and a platform for continuing to attack the Jewish community.

We say this in part on the basis of a number of experiences, the most recent of which occurred several months ago after newsman Mike Wallace brought Farrakhan and World Jewish Congress President Edgar Bronfman together over dinner in New York. Farrakhan's continued verbal assaults on Jews immediately after that led Wallace to conclude that "the man is a mystery to me." In an interview on NBC television's *Meet the Press* two months ago, Farrakhan, even when talking about his purported desire for dialogue with members of the Jewish community, stirred things up by referring to Jewish "arrogance." He also reaffirmed his commitment to the baseless and bigoted slurs he regularly circulates about the Jewish people, by saying he needs to be "shown that there is something that I said that is untrue."

In response to those who might still urge the Jewish community to seek reconciliation with Farrakhan through dialogue, it must be made clear that the onus for the absence of such contact rests not on the Jewish community but on the minister. Meanwhile, shortly after the recent incident, Farrakhan embarked on an extended world tour that is likely to bring him into the company of leaders around the globe, among them dictators in several terrorism-supporting countries. He is even talking about making a stop in Israel, where government officials have already rejected his request for official meetings. Media attention and controversy are thus likely to continue to follow this divisive figure before he returns home and starts to stir things up here once again.

Farrakhan's 'False Jews' Rhetoric Is Age-Old Bigotry

Chicago Sun-Times, March 13, 2006

• • •

Louis Farrakhan is back. For decades he has gained notoriety for making provocative statements about Jews and others, statements that he and his followers have routinely then attempted to explain away.

What is at stake is far more than a loosely uttered phrase or two. In his rhetoric, Farrakhan has given new life to traditional anti-Semitic themes of Jewish conspiracy, Jewish control and Jewish villainy. He has used age-old images that demonize the Jewish people.

So it was on Feb. 26, when Farrakhan trotted out a concept that derives not from contemporary reality but from age-old bigotry, proclaiming to a packed United Center that "neo-cons and Zionists have manipulated Bush and the American government, and our boys and girls are dying in Iraq and Afghanistan for the cause of Israel, not for the cause of America." His audience surely knew what was implied when he referred to those "neo-cons" as constituting "the synagogue of Satan" and when he spoke of the "wicked state of Israel."

When Sister Claudette Marie Muhammad, a Nation of Islam official named last August to the reconstituted Governor's Commission on Discrimination and Hate Crimes, invited her fellow commissioners to Farrakhan's speech, this was what she was bringing them to hear. Her subsequent failure to condemn Farrakhan's language or even disassociate herself from it then brought its own fallout.

Sister Muhammad not only did not repudiate what Farrakhan said. She actually echoed some of Farrakhan's most inflammatory language. Farrakhan asserted that "false Jews promote the filth of Hollywood that is seeding the American people and the people of the world and bringing you down in moral strength." Explicitly linking his anti-Semitism to homophobia, he went on to say: "It's the wicked Jews, the false Jews that are promoting lesbianism, homosexuality."

Farrakhan's contemptuous talk of "false Jews" as opposed to "true Jews" could have reminded his listeners of an infamous speech given in 1993 by another Nation of Islam follower named Kahlid Abdul Muhammad, who had proclaimed that "the so-called Jew ... is sucking our blood in the black community." Muhammad had gone on to tell his audience of kindred spirits that "you are the true Jew."

When Sister Muhammad defended her suitability for remaining on the commission by saying, "I respect those who practice the true tenets of their faith, be it Islam, Christianity, Catholicism, Judaism or any other religion," she was picking up on vocabulary and concepts long espoused by both Farrakhan and other Nation of Islam spokesmen.

There are contemporary echoes of this kind of language that help explain why members of the Jewish community are taking all of this so seriously. For example, a leader of Hamas, the Islamist Palestinian terrorist organization dedicated to eliminating Israel that has patented the use of suicide bombing, was quoted in the Feb. 27 issue of *The New Yorker* saying: "Now the fashion world, the media -- it's controlled by Jews.... Freud, a Jew, was the one who destroyed morals, and Marx destroyed divine ideologies. ... And now it is the Jewish lobby in the United States that is setting policy in the world and causing the United States to wage war all over the world." You might almost think that he and Farrakhan have the same speechwriter.

As the local crisis has evolved, the Governor's Commission on Discrimination and Hate Crimes has ironically become a platform for circulating the kind of hate speech that it was created to combat. Anti-Semitism has been turned loose.

But while many political figures and editorial writers around the state have condemned Farrakhan's bigotry, in many quarters this controversy, like many previous controversies involving him, has somehow been falsely cast as a battle between the Jewish and African-American communities. Its true meaning and impact have thus not been adequately addressed.

This crisis that never needed to happen is a human relations disaster playing out in the political arena. The longer it lasts, the more the societal atmosphere in Illinois will be poisoned by the rhetoric of Louis Farrakhan and his followers, and by the silence of those who let it stand as mere words.

Louis Farrakhan at It Again

JUF News, July 2010

• • •

For well over two decades Minister Louis Farrakhan, head of the Chicago-based Nation of Islam, has been involved in a double-edged exercise. For one thing, he has repeatedly maligned and attacked the Jewish people, seeing them as conspiring enemies of his own people in general and of himself personally. But at the same time as he has maintained that extremist profile, he has attempted to garner mainstream acceptability and credibility, even reaching out – or at least assuming the posture of one who is reaching out – to Jewish communal leadership.

True to the pattern, last week he sent a letter to Abe Foxman, National Director of the Anti-Defamation League, with open copies to well over a dozen other national Jewish leaders. One of them was Jerry Silverman, President and CEO of the Jewish Federations of North America, the umbrella body that includes this Federation. The letter, while ostensibly calling for dialogue, closes by threatening dire consequences emanating from divine sources should the community choose not to engage with him. Accompanying the letter were two volumes produced by the Historical Research Department of the Nation of Islam aimed at documenting a history of Jewish anti-black villainy over the centuries – one of them focusing on *Jews Selling Blacks* and the other on *How Jews Gained Control of the Black American Economy.*

The latter book is identified as Volume Two in a series charting *The Secret Relationship Between Blacks and Jews.* Volume One, which focused on the slave trade, was issued in 1991. Discredited in its primary thesis and many of its details by various scholars who analyzed it shortly after it was issued, that volume was described by Henry Louis Gates, Jr., the eminent African-American scholar, as "the bible of the new anti-Semitism" in a *New York Times* column headed "Black Demagogues and Pseudo-Scholars." Gates' theory was that by producing such a work, Farrakhan aimed at severing what remained of the old civil rights coalition of Jews and blacks and at advancing his own separatist agenda.

Whatever purposes he may have had in mind in that book and related publications, in continually scapegoating the Jewish people for the difficulties African-Americans have suffered in America and for his own inability to achieve the leadership status he craves – a failure brought about in part because of the very bigoted excesses he demonstrates in his rhetorical treatment of Jews – Farrakhan is revealing a deep-seated animus. And his provocative portrayal of the relationship goes on in other ways too – as in a June 26 speech to a 5,000-person audience in Atlanta in which, the Nation of Islam's *Final Call* publication reported, he proclaimed that "Blacks in America are God's people, not those who inhabit land in Palestine."

And so Farrakhan's obsession with the Jews continues. One can expect reputable scholars to once again reveal the objective shortcomings of the research carried out by the Nation of Islam for these new volumes, despite the plethora of footnotes and the extensive bibliography that the second of them contains. Meanwhile, astute analysts will perhaps have more to say about the kind of factors that would drive Farrakhan and his followers to spend years compiling reports like these and then sending them out with inflammatory commentary from Farrakhan himself, such as that contained in the latest cover letter.

The truth is that there was no historic "secret" relationship between Jews and blacks, and however much the painful legacy of slavery and segregation may have affected American society, Jews are surely no more – and probably less – responsible for that legacy than other Americans. At the same time, though, even as Farrakhan continues to sing his same old song, significant strides have been made in addressing racism in our country.

As the years go by, Farrakhan and his abiding message of hate and separation become more and more marginalized. What he needs to do if he really wants to meet with responsible Jewish communal leadership is to unequivocally make clear that he now recognizes the mendacity and maliciousness of the anti-Semitic rhetoric he has been enunciating for decades, and that he realizes and regrets the harm he has done in generating hostility toward the Jewish people. Put simply, he needs to repudiate what he himself has said before he merits mainstream acceptance and before there can be any meaningful dialogue.

His latest maneuver, rather than being a step forward in that direction, is instead but one more example of how locked in he remains to the old way of doing things that has kept him on the fringes. Based on the record of his behavior and prevailing signs, there appears to be little likelihood that there will be a meaningful change on his part. He certainly has not yet demonstrated that he is ready to give up his longstanding prejudices and give up his long-held positions – and accordingly, local and national Jewish community leaders can be expected to continue to reject his entreaties.

The media, it seems, remain fascinated by the man and his behavior and ever-ready to give him the air time he craves, no matter how much he repeats himself. Still, after garnering a flurry of media attention, this endeavor, like the ones that preceded it, will probably then be forgotten, if it hasn't already been ignored by most of the general public. Meanwhile, the venom contained in these new books and in Farrakhan's words continues to be out there, potentially poisoning followers of his who, sadly, might take them seriously.

Letter from Chicago: Ifs Ands – and Butz

The Forward, February 7, 1997

• • •

Northwestern University, in suburban Evanston, immediately north of Chicago, once had a quota to keep Jews out. Now it is known for being very hospitable to Jewish students, faculty, and administrators. Its Jewish Studies program includes an annual joint lectureship with Chicago's Jewish Federation; the university offers a number of Holocaust-related courses. But these days Northwestern is also gaining attention as the institution that for more than two decades has included on its faculty one of the nation's most prominent Holocaust deniers, an associate professor of electrical engineering named Arthur Butz.

Mr. Butz came to the fore in 1976 with the publication of his book, *The Hoax of the 20th Century.* He already had tenure. The community came to accept his presence given certain ground rules; namely, he would not be allowed to advocate his outrageous positions in class. While he has been an embarrassment to the university, attracting occasional notice as successive generations of students have become aware of his presence, he has kept to the arrangement.

Now, however, Mr. Butz's activities have become an issue once again with the discovery that he is disseminating his pseudo-scholarly poison through a home page maintained on Northwestern's Internet server. A story in the *Chicago Tribune* recently publicized the existence of the site while reporting that the contract of an unpaid volunteer instructor in the same department who had refuted Mr. Butz's views in class had not been renewed.

For the past several weeks the president of the university, Henry Bienen, who himself has labeled Mr. Butz's ideas "monstrous" and "idiotic," has been besieged by calls, letters and (appropriately) e-mail messages from alumni, members of the community and others. The International Socialist Organization has picketed Mr. Butz's classes demanding that he be fired. *The Daily Northwestern* commemorated 20 years of Butz-linked controversy by reprinting letters to the editor published over the years supporting or opposing his retention.

The university's position is now, as it has always been, that Mr. Butz has the right to say whatever he wants out of the classroom, even though his ideas have "no factual basis whatsoever and are a contempt-ible insult to all who have experienced [the Holocaust] and their fami-lies." University spokesmen say that allowing material on its Internet server is no different from including it on library shelves. What principle, they ask, might be enunciated to determine what is allowed there and what isn't?

While endorsing the principles of free speech, others, such as a del-egation from the Jewish Community Relations Council and Hillel that held a two-hour meeting with Mr. Bienen, the university provost, and its primary Holocaust specialist, have argued that this case is different. They insist that by allowing Mr. Butz to use his home page to circulate Holocaust denial materials, the university, despite a generic disclaimer, is providing an implied endorsement of the potential legitimacy of these nefarious views. Some go so far as to suggest that by providing Mr. Butz with a home page the university is in effect subsidizing the circulation of his opinions.

Taking their lead from the *Tribune* article, the JCRC/Hillel delega-tion pointed out that not all universities seem to have as free-wheeling a policy regarding use of their Internet servers as does Northwestern. The University of Iowa, for example, cites an expectation of "ethical and responsible behavior by its faculty, students, and staff" and calls on us-ers to "take all reasonable steps to ensure the accuracy...of the informa-tion that he or she compiles or provides." Iowa's policy also authorizes "individual units within the university [to] define conditions of use for facilities under their control."

"The Internet," wrote Claude-Anne Lopez in a recent issue of *The New Republic,* "is becoming the newest purveyor of prejudice in America. Its misuse has opened a free and universal platform for ignorance and hatred."

Noting the above, many of those troubled by Northwestern's position argue that the current situation is different in both degree and kind from what was the case before.

When Mr. Butz – never a distinguished academic – came on the scene with the publication of his book, he could be regarded as an isolated crackpot. Now, it is clear that he is part of a widespread denial movement whose pernicious premises and malicious goals are well-known. Indeed, he is looked upon as a pathfinder within that movement; what he has to say is not merely "personal opinion," as it is sometimes referred to in university materials on the subject.

The Holocaust itself is now 20 years further in the past; today's students and others of their generation are even more innocent of its facts than their predecessors were two decades ago. In that context, the Internet has become a prime means of presenting loony and prejudice-filled conspiracy theories. Mr. Butz is taking advantage of it, and of his status on Northwestern's faculty, in order to enhance his visibility and his credibility.

What the current controversy boils down to is a conflict between one position that asserts a university's need to be as protective of freedom of expression as possible, no matter what is being said and another that holds that distinctions about what is said can and should be made in the name of institutional responsibility.

Members of Chicago's Jewish community who hold the latter position are driven in part by consciousness of the evil done in our century and provocatively denied by Mr. Butz and his ilk, an evil committed by people driven by bigotry and encouraged by the written and spoken word. It is, ultimately, the power of language that is at the core of the current local debate, as a major American university struggles with a question brought to the fore by a new technology and an old hatred.

Anti-Semitism Reborn
JUF News, April 2003

• • •

As war against Iraq appeared increasingly imminent, a charge previously heard in this country only sporadically, and mostly from the
radical fringes, began to have more widespread circulation. In brief, the
charge was that certain Jewish officials in Washington whose primary
loyalty is to Israel were driving America to war with Iraq in order to free
Israel from the threat of Saddam Hussein and to enable Israel to expel the
local Palestinian population under the cover of war. This specious theory,
labeled "toxic" by Lawrence Kaplan in a *Washington Post* article that did
much to bring the problem to public attention, is a dramatic instance of
the way that traditional anti-Semitic concepts—in this case, notions of
dual loyalty, inordinate Jewish power, and Jewish conspiracies—have
been reborn in the context of Israel's conflict with its Arab neighbors.

As violence between Palestinians and Israelis has intensified over
the past two years and their conflict has taken on more and more of a
religious dimension, many supporters of the Palestinians have been directing their hostility not just against the State of Israel or its government
but against Jews *qua* Jews and against Judaism itself, and the anti-Israel
campaign has increasingly taken on an anti-Semitic character.

This is not to say that the policies or actions of any given Israeli government or institution cannot be questioned or criticized and that every
critic deserves to be labeled an anti-Semite. Israel's leaders, like those of
any country, certainly can be challenged, and not all expressions of criticism merit being regarded as anti-Semitic. Still, a cogent argument has
been made that when Israel, a boisterous democracy with an independent
judiciary and a free press, is cited in the most deprecating of ways—with
calls for punishment in the form of economic and other sanctions for
alleged human rights offenses far less damning than those committed by
a host of other countries—that singling-out offers evidence that the critics
may be motivated less by objective concern than by subjective bias. As
Harvard President Lawrence H. Summers said in a breakthrough speech
on the divestment campaign and related campus-based activities that
recklessly invoke the stigma of apartheid in attempting to treat Israel like
a new South Africa, even if the intent of such actions is not anti-Semitic,

the effect can be.

Some of the Israel-linked rhetoric has been unequivocal in its anti-Jewish thrust. When Israel's Mossad was inexplicably blamed for what happened in America on Sept. 11, 2001, with the fantastic, conspiracy-haunted lie that 4,000 Jews stayed home from work in the World Trade Center that day spreading like wildfire throughout the Arab and Islamic worlds and taking on a life of its own, a frightening manifestation of anti-Semitism was surely at work. And classic anti-Semitism was surely at play as well when Egyptian television ran a 42-part series, a special for Ramadan, set during the late 19th- and early 20th-century period when British colonialists assumed control of Egypt, that drew on the discredited forgery from Czarist Russia known as *The Protocols of the Elders of Zion.* Implying that a Jewish conspiracy laid the groundwork for the establishment of the State of Israel as part of an attempted takeover of the entire world, the plot of the series echoed ideas with a pedigree going back to medieval Europe.

What is classic about such anti-Semitic material is not only its provenance but its purpose. Just as Jews were singled out as scapegoats for the hurts and frustrations of the past—such as the plague in the Middle Ages and the economic and social failings of Weimar Germany—so the Jews and Israel are being blamed for the humiliations, failings, and misery of life in much of today's Arab world. Just as Jews were earlier portrayed as conspiratorial and demonic, so they are being seen and portrayed today. A pernicious mode of regarding the "other" cultivated in Christian Europe is finding fertile soil elsewhere. One thing new about the current anti-Semitism is the extent to which it is being generated out of the Arab and Islamic worlds.

In a striking instance of the way this old wine is being poured out of new bottles, the typological image of the crucified Christ is being transferred to the suffering Palestinians, with the Jews once more being shown as tormentors. Thus, an "Easter Message" from the Sabeel Center in Jerusalem last spring declared: "In this season of Lent it seems to many of us that Jesus is on the cross again with thousands of crucified Palestinians around him. Palestine has become one huge Golgotha. The Israeli government crucifixion system is operating daily."

This certainly does not mean that today's anti-Semitism comes only from Muslims (nor, it should be said, that all Muslims partake of it). In another troubling dimension of what is going on, some of the classic renderings of Christian anti-Semitism, which had been dumped into the dustbins of history by the Vatican and other official Christian bodies, are coming to the surface in the West once more as well. In Europe, fascistic politicians and gangs have produced echoes of last century's horrors, but now they have been joined by radical leftists with their own anti-Semitic biases.

If, for the former, the sin of the Jews is, as it was, that they are rootless, cosmopolitan outsiders who undermine national cultures, for the universalistic latter it is that they insist on their own state, which is seen as a *prima facie* racist act and an affront to human rights principles. As the Canadian Professor of Law and Member of Parliament Irwin Cotler, one of the most perceptive and eloquent commentators on this subject, says, for such ideologues human rights has become the new religion and the Jews the new anti-Christ.

Some analysts see European anti-Israel attitudes as in part an extension of anti-globalism-linked anti-American feelings, and they also connect the mode of Israel-bashing there to an urge for cathartic release from Holocaust-related guilt. On a stop in Zurich while flying back to Chicago from Israel last summer, I saw graffiti calling Ariel Sharon Hitler's pupil, a cruel and increasingly common sort of analogy that was particularly galling coming from the Swiss. With the mantle of victimhood passed to the Palestinians and with the Israelis regarded as the new Nazis, the slate can be wiped clean. The anti-Semitism of the past is expunged as, ironically, a new form of it is adopted.

Even here in the U.S., where FBI figures showed an increase in anti-Muslim hate crimes in 2001 in light of the impact of 9/11, the number of anti-Semitic acts for the year was still double that total. The Iraq-linked canard cited earlier is an especially troubling reminder that anti-Semitism cannot be ignored in America, that attitudes which had gone underground can come back to the surface, especially in a heated ideological climate. Still, the overriding fountainhead of the new anti-Semitism is the Middle East, and so, for example, most of the upsurge in anti-Jewish violence in France has been attributed to that country's Muslim population, to people incited by their imams and by what they see on Middle East-based television networks to seethe with anger at Israel's alleged treatment of the Palestinians.

Another defining characteristic of the new anti-Semitism, and a reason it is proper to talk about certain kinds of treatment of Israel today as having an anti-Semitic quality, is that it is directed not just against Jews as individuals but against the Jewish people collectively, and most particularly against the Jewish State of Israel. Whereas in the Middle Ages individual Jews were blamed for poisoning the wells, today the State of

Israel is seen as responsible for bringing misery to the rest of the Middle East and beyond.

Where previously it was Jews as individuals who were singled out for discrimination, who were said to have merited the curse of exile and eternal wandering separate and apart from their non-Jewish neighbors, today it is Israel which finds the members of the United Nations applying disparate treatment in ganging up on it. Israel is singled out for condemnation where others equally or more "guilty" are not. Israel alone is earmarked for pariah status amongst the nations of the world.

Finally, and this is at the heart of the matter, where all else is leading, among the nations of the world it is Israel alone whose very right to exist is challenged, as the Jewish people's right to maintain sovereignty in their ancient homeland is called into question and as Zionism, the national movement of the Jewish people on whose philosophical principles that sovereignty is based, is impugned as evil. That is the crux of the situation as the anti-Semitism of the past, which put in jeopardy the lives and survival of Jewish individuals and communities, has been reborn in a manner that threatens the existence of the Jewish collective, the Jewish State of Israel.

At the same time, the physical threat to the Jewish people has gone beyond Israel. The Tunisian synagogue targeted by al-Qaida was as symbolic in its way as the American sites of 9/11 were in theirs, and the attacks on Israelis vacationing in Kenya and on an Israeli aircraft there highlight this addition to the list of al-Qaida's intended victims of religiously motivated mass murder. The merger of radical Islamist fervor and anti-Israel, anti-Jewish hostility threatens to become radioactive—literally so, especially to the extent that Iraq and Iran become involved in developing and enabling the proliferation of weapons of mass destruction.

This, then, is what is at stake for Israel and the Jewish people. As far as the West is concerned, it is curious to note that these trends are greatly a development of the last several years, and most especially of the last two years. Yes, some of this has been around for some time. Still, there is no question but that the situation has changed and grown worse during the post-Cold War period, especially in a Europe marked not by the "end of history," as some said it would be, but by a return to history—to local ethnic conflicts and to a waning of some of the taboos surrounding anti-Semitism.

Observers close to the scene have reported that the Palestinian populace was never informed that at Camp David the Barak government offered the possibility of a Palestinian state with a compromise regarding

Jerusalem, and that Yasser Arafat walked away without even offering a counterproposal. Certainly the Palestinian Authority's failure to prepare its followers for concessions on the right of return and other issues, along with use of the media and other means to incite the local population, has affected Palestinian behavior. And Muslims around the world too have been relentlessly incited against Israel by the inflammatory international Arab television developed over the past decade.

Anti-Israel cadres in the West, who could have known better, have followed suit in their way as well, as they have shut their eyes to the responsibility of the corrupt, mendacious, autocratic Yasser Arafat and his circle, along with death-embracing terror groups, for the suffering of the Palestinian people. These cadres' readiness to ignore or distort that reality while jumping on Israel and making the anti-Israel cause fashionable in certain circles adds credence to the sense that what is in play now is not a legitimate reaction to what is really going on. An inescapable explanation for what we are seeing at least in part involves the rising to the surface of dark feelings and impulses regarding the Jewish people and the Jewish state.

Supporters of Israel have an obligation to be careful in our use of the term "anti-Semitism" and to recognize that it is legitimate to raise questions about the actions and policies of any country, including Israel. And it is important for members of the Jewish community to acknowledge that, troubling as things may be, neither the medieval era nor Hitler's Germany have re-emerged full-blown. Today's Jews, with a strong State of Israel, with a self-assured American Jewish community, and with friendship from the American government and people, are not helpless or abandoned.

Still, the way things are going, there is a real danger that the anti-Semitic passions which have increasingly colored anti-Israel agitation in the Arab and Islamic worlds will continue to intensify and spill over into the Western world. Enlightened forces thus have an obligation to resist the blandishments of those who deny the anti-Semitic component of much anti-Israel rhetoric by making overstated claims about censorship and McCarthyite tactics. The new manifestations of this oldest of prejudices must be recognized, condemned, and opposed before they truly do get out of hand.

The New Anti-Semitism:
Sources, Symbols, and Significance

Lecture presented at the Catholic Theological Union, Chicago
February 24, 2004

Printed in JUF's "Emerging Issues" series, March 2004

. . .

In Phillip Roth's 1993 novel *Operation Shylock,* an antiquarian dealer in rare books based in Tel Aviv, referring to the well-known character from Shakespeare's Merchant of Venice, says: "For four hundred years now, Jewish people have lived in the shadow of this Shylock. In the modern world, the Jew has been perpetually on trial; still today the Jew is on trial, in the person of the Israeli."[1] With that as text, the remainder of my talk will be commentary.

Just two days after I was invited to give this lecture, Mahathir Mohamad, then Prime Minister of Malaysia, spoke at an Islamic summit conference at which 57 nations were represented. With the audience applauding, he declared that "1.3 billion Muslims cannot be defeated by a few million Jews." Mahathir went on to say, "Today the Jews rule this world by proxy," and he talked further of "the enemy, . . . a people . . . [who] have now gained control of the most powerful countries."[2] On a Sabbath morning one month later, two synagogues in Istanbul were bombed, with many lives taken, and a Jewish school in France was burned to the ground. That same day, the well-known Greek composer Mikis Theodorakis was cited saying of "the Jews," "This small people is at the root of evil, not good."[3]

As these episodes demonstrate, we are talking about a toxic use of language and imagery coming not just from fringe figures, and about dangerous, sometimes-lethal, actions. Though these examples may represent the extremes of the phenomenon called "the new anti-Semitism," they are hardly isolated cases, and they make clear just how serious this subject is.

While something novel has indeed been happening over the past several years, it's not as if the old anti-Semitism has gone away altogether. After months of escalating hype, tomorrow will bring to commercial screens around the country a movie produced and directed by one of

Hollywood's most popular celebrities which potentially threatens to bring before millions here, and millions more around the world, a dramatic evocation of the deicide charge that generated hate and violence over two millennia. Meanwhile, modern versions of familiar anti-Semitism continue to be practiced by right-wing extremist groups at home and abroad, as we were chillingly reminded last October when a member of the German Bundestag called Jews a "people of perpetrators" for their involvement in the Bolshevik revolution.[4] The "old" populist, nationalism-based anti-Semitism can today be seen staging a revival in the republics of the former Soviet Union, while admirers of the Nazis can be found even in this country. Still, the fact is that something new is now happening as well, and that it presents the greater threat in today's world.

As far as I have been able to discover, the phrase "the new anti-Semitism" was first used as the title of the closing chapter of Bernard Lewis' 1986 book *Semites and Anti-Semites*. Though Lewis at that time was able to express the hope that the trend he was describing might dissipate, when the book was republished in 1999 he found himself saying that "anti-Semitism has conquered new territory and risen to a new intensity."[5] Since then, there has been still greater intensification, and the term "the new anti-Semitism" has become widely used to describe what is going on. Attention has been drawn to the subject by Irwin Cotler, recently named Attorney General in Canada, and Natan Sharansky, Israel's Minister of Diaspora Affairs, both of them major figures in the global human rights arena, while scholars in this country and elsewhere have by now come together in numerous conferences and written scores of articles on the topic. In the last several months, three books have been published with the phrase "the new anti-Semitism" in their titles: one in England edited by Paul Iganski and Barry Kosmin, the others in the U.S. by Phyllis Chesler and by Abe Foxman, while Gabriel Schoenfeld has written still another on the subject, along with a fourth called *The Return of Anti-Semitism.*[6]

The basic components of what is meant by the term "the new anti-Semitism" already appeared in Lewis' discussion. First, as the quotation from Roth's novel asserts and as Mahathir's comments make clear, whereas in traditional anti-Semitism it was individual Jews, Jewish communities, and the Jewish people who were maligned, discriminated against, and in the most extreme instances, fingered for extinction, the central target of the current animosity is the Jewish collective as constituted in the State of Israel; individual Jews are increasingly targeted for their identification with that nation. Secondly, as Lewis had already observed when he said that "classical anti-Semitism is an essential part of Arab intellectual life at the present time,"[7] while the key themes and images which help to define today's anti-Semitism have sources in the Christian West, their current fountainhead of dispersion is in the Arab and Islamic worlds. Finally, when this new anti-Semitism locates itself in Europe, it is generally a phenomenon not of the right but of the left -- something not altogether new, but also not commonly recognized.

As suggested above, however recent uses of the label "the new anti-Semitism" may be, many of its components are not all that new. While the Islamic world was historically far more benign in its treatment of Jews than Christendom, and while that history continues to be pointed to with pride by many Muslims, the motifs of Christian European anti-Semitism were imported into the Middle East as far back as the turn of the last century, while certain Arab leaders subsequently demonstrated a clear affinity for the beliefs and programs of Nazi Germany. By the 1950's, an Islamic validation for hating Jews appeared in the teachings of Sayyid Qutb, the ideologue of the Egyptian Muslim Brotherhood and perhaps the most important intellectual influence on today's radical Islamist movement. He portrayed Jews as conspiring to subvert and destroy Islam. In his pamphlet *Our Battle Against the Jews,* Qutb wrote: "With their spite and deceit, the Jews are still misleading this nation, and distracting her away from her *Qur'an* in order that she may not draw her sharp weapons and her abundant ammunitions from it."[8] And for some time, official Arab media outlets have drawn upon Nazi-style imagery as governments have exploited popular anti-Semitism to redirect social unrest.

The attempt to paint Zionism as equivalent to the Nazi ideology and Israelis as heirs to the Nazi regime began in the Soviet Union after the Six-Day War. These charges gravitated to the Soviet clients in the Arab world, and they became even more widespread following Israel's military venture into Lebanon in 1982. But as significant as all of these developments were, it was the events and zeitgeist of the late 1980s and '90s that were especially important in creating an environment in which the new anti-Semitism could take shape.

Fresh from routing Soviet troops from Afghanistan, one of the triggering events in the fall of the U.S.S.R., the radical Islamist movement evolved into a global terrorist enterprise. With the Soviet Union out of the way, America was next, with the World Trade Center itself first attacked in 1993. And Israel and the Jewish people were on the hit list as well.

The Lebanon-based Hezbollah group, it is widely believed, was linked to two bombings in Buenos Aires -- one of the Israel Embassy, which took 29 lives in 1992; the other of the Jewish community headquarters, which killed 86 people in 1994. Accompanying such terrorist activity is a bigotry-laden ideology. As Jeffrey Goldberg has written in *The New Yorker,* Hezbollah is "not merely anti-Israel but deeply, *theologically* anti-Jewish."[9]

The charter produced by the Gaza-based Hamas organization in 1988 is itself unequivocal about that group's ideological views and goals. The historian Omer Bartov wrote in a recent article in *The New Republic* that the charter "contains among its fundamentalist Islamic preachings, the most blatant anti-Semitic statements made in a publicly available document since Hitler's own pronouncements."[10] In the words of the charter, "The Zionist plan has no bounds, and after Palestine they wish to expand from the Nile River to the Euphrates. When they totally occupy it they will look towards another, and such is their plan in 'the Protocols of the Learned Elders of Zion.'" In the document, Hamas says of itself that is has "raised the banner of Jihad in the face of the transgressors to free country and folk from [the transgressors'] filth, impurity and evil."[11]

Hamas grew in size and impact in the '90s against a backdrop of the unfolding Oslo Process. The potential success of that endeavor in establishing peace between the Jewish state of Israel and a presumably secular state of Palestine made Hamas and other Islamists all the more desperate, and they carried out a string of suicide bombing attacks on Israeli civilian targets. During those years, the more secular Palestinian Authority itself inculcated a culture of hatred for the Israelis through classroom curriculum and mass media even as it was supposed to be preparing its people for reconciliation.

As elements in the Islamic and Arabs worlds were increasingly becoming promulgators of the new anti-Semitism in the '90s, developments in Europe were making that territory a more fertile field for the metastasized form of a prejudice to which it itself had originally given birth. The face of Europe was changing thanks to the accelerated immigration of large numbers of Muslims, especially from North Africa, many of them with few resources and limited employment opportunities. Feeling displaced and unwelcome, incited by extremist Islamist preachers in their mosques, they have at the same time been seen as forming a block to be reckoned with politically. According to reports, the Muslim population of France has just about doubled over the past decade, to now be approaching ten percent of the total population of that country.

With the end of the Cold War, Europe changed in other ways as well. University of Chicago professor Mark Lilla posits that what he calls "the end of politics" in Europe has created a circumstance whereby all nationalism is suspect — and Jewish nationalism, expressed through the Zionist philosophy on which the State of Israel is based, is considered particularly objectionable.[12] This approach of course ties in with the fashionable anti-colonialism which disparagingly portrays Israel as a colonial power.

Complicating things further are ways the Holocaust began to be approached in the '90s. While the Shoah had destroyed European Jewry and opened deep wounds in the nations from which the perpetrators and their sympathizers and collaborators had come, many of those wounds were either deliberately unacknowledged or just left untended in the rush to forge Cold War alliances. Then, with the end of the Cold War, the wounds were suddenly reopened. For many in today's Europe, a theory goes, though there is recognition that there can be no moving forward until the Holocaust issues are resolved, and though many meaningful steps have been taken, the way these issues are being dealt with in some quarters is not through acceptance of responsibility but through attempts to evade and dispense with the whole package. In this framework, the equation of Israel and the Jews with the Nazis serves the purpose of expunging guilt, since the Jews can now be regarded as at least as bad as the Europeans themselves were.

A significant number of Jewish communities are being rebuilt in Europe today, though they are smaller than they once were. At the same time, though, with regionally based ethnic groups playing a growing part in the new Europe, Jews, having no land base on the continent, may be as much the misplaced outsider and "other" as they were in the era of the European nation states. Finally, as strategic ally and ideological soul mate of the U.S., Israel, along with its supporters, has also been affected by post-Cold War Europe's resentment of unipower America, with its globalist reach. Anti-Semitism and anti-Americanism have thus been linked in a number of ways.[13]

These, then, are the sources and the precursors of the new anti-Semitism and the conditions in which it has taken shape. Its full-fledged maturation coincided with the upsurge in violence directed against Israel that began in September of 2000, the outbreak of the terror war that Palestinians named the Al-Aksa Intifada, which was accompanied by a rash of assaults, acts of vandalism, and other incidents throughout Europe. Expressions of that new anti-Semitism have proceeded over these past three-and-a-half years, with certain key triggering "markers" along the way: the ironically named World Conference Against Racism, Racial Discrimination, Xenophobia and Related Intolerance, which took place in Durban, South Africa, in September 2001, consolidating the ideological strands of the new anti-Semitism and energizing its proponents; the impact of the September 11, 2001, terror attacks on America; and the spring 2002 reaction to the Israel Defense Forces' actions in Jenin, provocatively mislabeled a "massacre," as Israel responded to the slaughter of its civilians at a Passover Seder in Netanya. Along the way, Arab television stations like Al-Jazeera have circulated inciting images and messages to viewers around the world, while the European media, much more than our own, have portrayed the Israelis as brutal oppressors and the Palestinians as mere victims, as today's "wretched of the earth," to use a phrase from the revolutionary rhetoric of the '60s, when elements of today's left-wing ideology were shaped.

Having named this stage of their "uprising" after the mosque on the Temple Mount, for the Palestinians the conflict with Israel is increasingly taking the shape not of a political difference which can be resolved by compromise but as a religious war, a fight to the finish. It is not just the Islamists but Yasser Arafat and his followers as well who call for jihad and describe the suicide bombers as martyrs. Arafat's Camp David insistence on a "right of return" for Palestinian refugees and their descendants and the continuing echoing of that demand by many Palestinians is endorsement of a formula for the dissolution of Israel as a Jewish state. During these past three-and-a-half years challenges to Israel's very legitimacy and right to exist have been bluntly enunciated by Israel's adversaries. At the core of the new anti-Semitism is this denial to the Jewish people of a basic national right, an act equivalent to the denial of basic rights to Jewish individuals and communities in earlier times.

In the current framing of the Israel-Palestinian conflict, the language of genocide has been used more and more by the declared enemies of Israel and the Jewish people, accompanied by murderous attacks. Citing a Hadith, the Hamas charter apocalyptically declares: "The Last Hour would not come until the Muslims fight against the Jews and the Muslims would kill them."[14] "The Jews," the former Rector of the Islamic University in Gaza preached in an October 14, 2000, sermon broadcast on Palestinian Authority television, "are the ones who must be butchered and killed, as Allah the Almighty said."[15] In a Gaza sermon in April 2002, a Palestinian Authority Imam proclaimed: "Oh, Allah, annihilate the Jews and their supporters."[16]

Acting out this injunction, Hamas, Islamic Jihad, and the al-Aksa Martyrs Brigade (an arm of the "secular" Fatah movement whose very name demonstrates the radical Islamicization increasingly permeating the Palestinian cause) have carried out horrendous attacks on Israeli civilians. Meanwhile, anti-Jewish violence perpetrated by al-Qaida and groups associated with it since 9/11 have included the bombing of a Tunisian synagogue; the cruel murder of Daniel Pearl, made to affirm his Jewishness before being beheaded; the bombing of Jewish sites in Morocco; the attack on an Israeli tourist hotel and attempt to bring down an Israeli civilian airliner in Kenya; and the bombings of the Istanbul synagogues.

Accompanying the violence of the Palestinian and Islamist assault against Israel on the ground has been a campaign of internal incitement and external propaganda. Basic to the rhetoric are those themes and symbols which have come to be characteristic of the new anti-Semitism as rendered both in the Arab world and in the West.

Most traditional are the themes and iconography of Christian anti-Semitism. In May of 2001, Syrian President Bashir Assad scandalously welcomed the Pope to Syria by invoking the notorious deicide charge repudiated by the Church forty years ago. "Our brethren in Palestine are being murdered and tortured," he said, "by those who even killed the principle of equality when they claimed that God created a people distinguished above all other peoples. . . . They try to kill all the principles of divine faiths with the same mentality of betraying Jesus Christ and torturing Him."[17] A less well known but equally insidious variation on the deicide theme was expressed in the 2002 Easter message from the Sabeel Center for Liberation Theology in Jerusalem, which said: "In this season of Lent, it seems to many of us that Jesus is on the cross again with thousands of crucified Palestinians around him . . . . The Israeli government crucifixion system is operating daily."[18] This notion was echoed in a cartoon that appeared in the Italian newspaper *La Stampa* in the spring of 2002, while Israeli troops surrounded the Church of the Nativity in Bethlehem; it portrayed the baby Jesus lying in a crèche in front of an Israeli tank saying: "Don't tell me they want to kill me again."[19]

Related to this theme is the blood libel charge that had so much currency and did so much harm during the Christian Middle Ages. The atavistic accusation that Jews drink non-Jewish children's blood and bake matzoh with it has had a modern history and contemporary life in the Arab world. It was asserted in a 1983 book by Syria's current Minister of Defense, and it has recently been repeated in one way or another in various Arab countries, including Egypt and Saudi Arabia (where Purim became the holiday of choice).

An especially gruesome evocation of the theme appeared in England in a cartoon printed in the January 27, 2003, issue of *The Independent.* The cartoon, which was actually awarded a prize this past December, shows a grotesque, naked Ariel Sharon eating the bloody body of a Palestinian youth. "What's wrong," says Sharon, "you never seen a politician kissing babies before?" In the background a tank and helicopters wreak devastation while calling out: "Vote Sharon."[20] Defenders of the cartoon say the image innocently simply replicates Goya's famous "black" painting called "Saturn Devouring His Children." But in a 2001 study, Fred Licht argues that Goya himself may have been well aware of blood libel charges against Jews and was possibly deliberately alluding to that canard when painting the original. Consciously or not on their part, the cartoonist and his acolytes stepped into traditional anti-Semitic territory.[21]

The central symbol of the new anti-Semitism also has its origins in the old, though in this case it takes on its meaning precisely because of the inverted way in which it is used. I refer to the swastika, the symbol of identity and pride for the Nazis which is now used to brand Israel and its supporters as the "new Nazis." Linked to that image are various statements which explicitly or implicitly elaborate on that concept.

Though, as I noted earlier, this application of the swastika has origins in Soviet anti-Semitism, it today has taken on a life of its own, a development not without irony. The Soviets, after all, were trying to identify Israel and Zionism with their people's World War II enemy, whereas the Arabs are using this Nazi sign even though their own leaders had demonstrated sympathy with Hitler and his followers during World War II. Furthermore, many of the same forces that are promoting the analogy today are also engaged in stepped-up Holocaust denial -- so much so that the French Minister of Education has recently expressed the need to address teachers' reports that Muslim students rejecting the validity of the Holocaust have disrupted classes in which the subject has been taught.[22] Still, this emotionally charged symbol has become today's leading visual device for maligning Israel and, by extension, the Jews.

At the NGO Forum of the Durban World Conference, the Arab Lawyers Union distributed a book on the cover of which was a Jewish Star superimposed over a swastika along with the words: "That is the fact -- Racism of Zionism & 'Israel,'" while the analogy was repeated in various cartoons and other materials circulated there.[23] On the streets of Europe today, demonstrations are replete with banners showing the swastika equated with the Star of David. A "greater than" symbol has also appeared between the two, meaning that the Jews are even worse than the Nazis.[24] Such signs express the feelings of those who hold them and are meant to appeal to an European sensibility which regards Nazism and all that it stands for -- fascism, nationalism, racism, violations of human rights -- as the prime evils of our time.

However cynically some of the enemies of Israel may be using this symbol, it has taken on its own power in transferring a *frisson* of abhorrence from the Nazis to Israel and, by extension, to the Jewish people, symbolized by the star. The image and ideas echoing it are ubiquitous. On a visit to Barcelona a year ago last summer, my wife and I discovered that a swastika had been painted over Hebrew writing memorializing a rabbi's residence there in the 7th century, with the phrase "Palestina Libre" printed underneath. Even at that site in Spain, a graffiti artist had used the Nazi symbol to vandalize the record of an historic Jewish presence and to promote the supersessionist impulse of the new anti-Semitism. The swastika is an insulting tool for directly assaulting Jewish sensibilities and thus a vehicle of anti-Semitic attack, and it has become the primary contemporary device for symbolically maligning Israel and the Jewish people.

Another recurring characteristic of the new anti-Semitism is its obsessive attachment to the charge that Jewish conspiracies seek control of the world. Besides going back to at least the Christian Middle Ages, this theme is the message of a basic modern text, *The Protocols of the Elders of Zion,* a czarist era forgery described by Norman Cohn in his study of its influence on the Nazis, as a "warrant for genocide."[25] Although the *Protocols* has long been circulated in the Arab and Muslim worlds (and was translated into Arabic as early as 1927) the work and references to it have become especially prevalent. During the month of Ramadan in November of 2002, a 42-part television series based on the Protocols called "Horseman Without a Horse" was broadcast nightly in Egypt. In 2003, the *Protocols* was drawn upon for a series produced by Syrian Television and aired by the Hezbollah Al-Manar satellite television station in Lebanon, a frequent source of anti-Semitic material. A long catalog could be prepared referencing the places where the *Protocols* continues to turn up and to be cited. Significant in itself for creating a hate-filled image of Jews as villains to be destroyed, its driving notions permeate the rhetoric and haunt the imaginations of the exponents of the new anti-Semitism.

Most striking in this regard was the absurd charge that the 9/11 attacks were carried out not by al-Qaida terrorists trying to inflict harm on the U.S. but by Israel and the Jews, whose conspiratorial goal was to turn the U.S. against the Islamic world. Premised on the baseless assertion that Jewish workers in the World Trade Center had known what was coming and had thus stayed home, the charge circulated throughout the Arab and Islamic worlds like wildfire, and reportedly continues to hold sway in the minds of millions of individuals. This kind of evasion of the truth and attribution of malicious power to Jews, paralleled by Holocaust denial claims that the Shoah never took place and that the Jews have manipulated the world to believe that it did, is an extreme symptom of the new anti-Semitism.

Related to the belief that the Jews wish to control the world is the notion that they already control America. Such a notion is heard, directly and in innuendo, even from voices more sophisticated than one might have expected to be enunciating it. It comes into play in comments about supposed Jewish control of the Bush Administration and its formulation of Middle East policy. A visual rendering of this concept as applied to the UK appeared on the cover of the January 14, 2002, issue of the British publication *The New Statesman,* which showed a Jewish star stabbing the Union Jack with the caption: "A kosher conspiracy?"[26]

Bringing together some of these observations, it strikes me that it might be useful to begin to talk about the new anti-Semitism as a postmodern expression of the world's oldest hatred. In the post-modern mode, it is post-colonialism (though one can argue that in accepting the prejudices of Western anti-Semitism many Arabs have allowed their minds to be colonized by some of the worst that Europe has had to offer); it is post-nationalism (at least in its rejection of Jewish nationalism, though its supporters seem to have no problem with Palestinian nationalism); it is global (and this is a major aspect of the new anti-Semitism, with modern media, particularly television and the Internet, providing global communication links); it is rooted in a series of "texts" with tenuous ties to objective reality which elicit reaction in their own right (the fraudulent *Protocols;* the fantastic attribution of blame for 9/11; the manufactured charges of a massacre at Jenin); and its signature image is an abstract symbol taken not from external reality but from the history of anti-Semitism itself (and that symbol now has an applied meaning that turns that history inside out).

Interesting as it might be to pursue this line of thought, in the limited time I have for today, I'd like now to turn to the third element in the title of my talk, namely the significance of the new anti-Semitism. I will do that by first considering some of the areas of contention that have emerged in other discussions of this topic.

One of the issues now in dispute circles around the question of just how severe the current problems are. On one side are those observers who say that the world has returned to a condition much like the 1930's, when the engine which drove the Holocaust was moving into high gear and little was being done to slow it down; on the other are those who say that conditions now are significantly different from what they were in the '30s, and that as troubling as current developments may be, Jews are more secure in today's world than they were then. I myself incline to the latter position for a number of reasons, but with sympathetic understanding of where those who take the former position are coming from, especially given the history of the world's treatment of the Jewish people.

The question I would raise, particularly to a non-Jewish audience, is not about how similar to the '30s things now are, but why, given the nature and extent of current anti-Semitic discourse and behavior, it has taken so long for the problem to gain appropriate attention. In an interview in *La Stampa* on December 21, Roger Cardinal Etchegaray said: "The path that leads to Auschwitz is always in front of us," and he went on to declare: "There is a return of anti-Semitism in our Europe. . . . . Not to recognize it, not to call it by its name, is an unwitting way of accepting it."[27] In the last few months, more and more religious and political leaders are also speaking out, and the EU held a major session on anti-Semitism just last Thursday. But how could it be that a mere 60 years since the Holocaust, taboos which built a bulwark against anti-Semitism could be allowed to be weakened, and that today's version of anti-Semitism could be pretty much dismissed if not ignored as it began to cover the globe, riding mainstream currents and returning to the very soil of Europe?

Suspicions as to why this development has been discounted in Europe were kindled two months ago, after it was made public that a report on Manifestations of Anti-Semitism in the European Union requested by the European Monitoring Center on Racism and Xenophobia, though completed in October 2002, was denied exposure by the EUMC until protests brought it to public attention. The authors of the report at the Center for Research on Anti-Semitism in Berlin speculate that the reason the study had not been released was that it showed that "Among the perpetrators of anti-Semitic attacks especially in France, Belgium, the Netherlands and Great Britain are young Muslims of Arab or North African background." They went on to say: "There also appears to be discomfort in the EUMC with the naming of anti-Semitic tendencies in certain left-wing groups . . .

which cross the line between legitimate critique of Israeli politics to instrumentalization of anti-Semitic stereotypes." And they added: "These prejudices also have spread to the middle of society."[28]

The researchers at the Berlin Center insist that the young Muslim offenders described in the study "themselves are suffering from massive discrimination, living on the fringes of society and seeking a scapegoat for their poor living situations." Indeed, many observers of the current scene point to the imperative need for European countries to address that festering problem. But that does not change the facts. As the German newspaper *Die Zeit* wrote: "The study makes it clear that this Islamistic hatred of Jews is not merely a reaction to the Israeli occupation politics in Palestine, but is based on a firmly established anti-Semitic ideology."[29]

All of us who deal with these issues surely have an obligation to make clear that though we are talking about a trend which has come to the fore in certain Muslim circles, we are not saying that such views are universally held in the Muslim world. But by the same token, those who approach current developments primarily as defenders of the good name of Islam have an intellectual and moral obligation to admit and address prevailing realities. When Osama El-Baz, a leading Egyptian intellectual, spoke out against "Horseman Without a Horse," he was taking an important step in this regard. But he has had far too few counterparts.

As the discourse on this subject has played out, one of the most specious approaches to it has been taken by those who not only play down the prevalence of anti-Semitism but malign those who call attention to it by charging that Israel's supporters call all criticism of Israel anti-Semitic in order to block any criticism of Israeli behavior. Like any other country, Israel is properly susceptible to criticism of the decisions and actions of its leaders, and in fact such criticism is rampant, both in boisterously democratic Israel itself and abroad. Rather than its being Israel's supporters who are trying to block criticism of that country by talking about anti-Semitism, it is, I would suggest, Israel's antagonists who are trying to prevent discussion of today's anti-Semitism by going on the offensive against those who speak about today's anti-Semitic trends.

Then there are those who, while not denying the existence of the new anti-Semitism, blame it on Israel itself and on the policies of its current Prime Minister. Such a blame-the-victim approach is of course all too prevalent in many circumstances, and here, as in most of them, is suspect. The current upsurge in global anti-Semitism preceded Ariel Sharon's election to Prime Minister. It had its origins in an earlier era altogether and was solidified in its current form during the Prime Ministership of Ehud

Barak, at the very time when he and other government officials were offering unprecedented negotiating terms. It was Palestinian violence and accompanying rhetoric which brought Sharon into office, not vice versa, and it was not until he had been in office during several more months of terror that Israel reoccupied Palestinian cities and took other strong defensive measures. Furthermore, as many commentators have shown, if one is only interested in challenging Sharon's policies, that can certainly be done without crossing the line into anti-Semitism. Indeed, Phyllis Chesler and Omer Bartov themselves -- along with others -- demonstrate that such criticism can be offered at the very same time as the upsurge in anti-Semitism is described and those who promulgate it are condemned.[30]

While the focus of this talk has been on the way the new anti-Semitism is playing out in the Arab and Islamic worlds and in Western Europe, and while the problems without question are far more severe there than elsewhere, I'd like to close with some reflections on the state of affairs nearer to home. First, I would say that the closest thing we have to replicating the situation in Europe can be found on the nation's campuses, where the anti-colonialism argument is frequently attached to Israel and that nation's right to exist is sometimes denied; where the swastika-Jewish star analogy is promulgated by demonstrators; and where anti-Jewish hostility at times surfaces directly. A striking instance of the latter phenomenon occurred a year ago, when the campus newspaper at the University of Illinois in Urbana-Champaign ran a letter to the editor with a headline -- chosen by the editors -- proclaiming that "Jews Manipulate America."[31]

A few months later, the *Chicago Tribune* carried a cartoon featuring an image of a hook-nosed, mercenary, America-controlling, Jewish Star-labeled Ariel Sharon. The cartoon, using the iconography of traditional anti-Jewish stereotyping to make a baseless comment about Israel, offered a textbook example of the way elements of the new anti-Semitism have entered mainstream discourse even in this country.[32] Just one month ago the *Christian Century,* a national mainline Protestant magazine published here in Chicago, printed a cartoon which showed the Three Wise Men stopped by a barrier labeled "Sharon's Wall," with the caption reading: "Bethlehem: You can't get there from here" -- implying that the current Prime Minister of Israel would have ruined the first Christmas had he been around then.[33] Elsewhere too, Christian circles within our own country have treated Israel in a way that resurrects some of the kinds of ideas and attitudes which many of us thought had been irrevocably deposited in the dustbins of a dark history.

At the same time, the kind of inflammatory rhetoric emanating from radical Islamic circles elsewhere in the world has also been heard in this country, especially this city. A February 8 *Chicago Tribune* article about the mosque in suburban Bridgeview reported that its religious leader, Sheik Jamal Said, while speaking at a prayer service last May (where he was raising funds for a University of South Florida professor charged with being the U.S. leader of the Palestinian Islamic Jihad terror group), called Israel "a foreign, malignant and strange element on the blessed land."[34] Previous reports indicate that, during Thanksgiving weekend of 2000, just two months after the upsurge in violence against Israel began, Said spoke at a convention in Chicago to raise funds in order, in his words, "to pay for the family of a martyr." A Kuwaiti speaker at that conference who insisted that "Palestine will not be liberated but through jihad" went on to say: "The Jews will meet their end at our hands."[35]

The conference at which those last two remarks were made was organized by the Islamic Association for Palestine, a Chicago-based group that has been described as the major propaganda support arm for Hamas in this country. In 1990 the IAP translated the Hamas charter into English, and the organization has posted that document on its website. Other Chicago-based events recently noted in the news include a 1991 fundraiser for Islamic Jihad at which a Palestinian imam arrested by the FBI in Cleveland last month was videotaped referring to Jews as "the sons of monkeys and pigs" and calling for rifles to be directed at them.[36] An article in the *Wall Street Journal* two months ago profiled an Indian college student recruited into the Muslim Brotherhood who attended a 1994 meeting in Chicago at which "six or seven masked young men dressed as Hamas militants ran down the aisles, waving the organization's green flags and shouting 'Idhbaahal Yahood!' ('Slaughter the Jews!')"[37]

Conditions in America, I hasten to reiterate, have not come close to replicating those elsewhere. But here as elsewhere, I believe, it is the obligation of anyone speaking on this topic at this time to not only analyze it but to sound an alarm about it as a global problem which cannot be ignored. Yes, the topic has been gaining increasing notice. But the time is long past for the forces of decency to more effectively come together to firmly repudiate the tenacious evils of the new anti-Semitism.

And that is where I intended to end this talk. But then, a few days ago, I read something which has led me to add this coda. It was a remarkable interview with the Israeli novelist Aharon Applefeld, conducted by Ari Shavit in the newspaper *Ha'aretz* and entitled "A Jewish Soul." And so, just as I began with an 11-year-old quotation from Roth, I'd like to close with an 11-day-old quotation from Applefeld. It comes when

Appelfeld, a Holocaust survivor from Central Europe, responds to the question: "Did anything in these years of terrorism bring back something of the old Jewish fear?" After making some personal remarks, he says: "When I look at the whole picture, I see the Jewish fate here. The issue of deicide pursued us for a thousand years in Europe, maybe longer. So we thought, fine, we'll start again, we'll start somewhere else. Maybe here all that will calm down. So we came here and we started again. But it's starting here, too. In other words, we tried to escape from the fate of a persecuted minority, but the fate of a persecuted minority pursued us here, too. Despite all our efforts, we didn't succeed in escaping it."[38]

That, in a nutshell, is how a Jewish soul sees things in the winter of the year 2004.

NOTES

[1] Phillip Roth, *Operation Shylock: A Confession* (New York: Simon & Schuster, 1993), p. 274.

[2] Text of Mahatir Speech of October 16, 2003, from www.ezboard.com. See also Manfred Gerstenfeld, "The Mahathir Affair: A Case Study in Mainstream Islamic Anti-Semitism," Jerusalem Center for Public Affairs, November 2, 2003.

[3] Cited in Chris McGreal, "The 'New' Anti-Semitism: Is Europe in Grip of Worst Bout of Hatred Since the Holocaust?" *The Guardian,* November 25, 2003, online edition.

[4] Cited in Omer Bartov, "He Meant What He Said: Did Hitlerism Die with Hitler?" *The New Republic,* February 2, 2004, p. 30.

[5] Bernard Lewis, *Semites and Anti-Semites: An Inquiry into Conflict and Prejudice* (New York: W.W. Norton & Company, 1999), p. 262.

[6] Irwin Cotler, "Human Rights and the New Anti-Jewishness: Sounding the Alarm," The Jewish People Policy Planning Institute, November 2002; Natan Sharansky, "On Hating the Jews," *Commentary,* November 2003, pp. 26-34; Paul Iganski and Barry Kosmin, *The New Antisemitism? Debating Judeophobia in 21st-Century Britain* (London: Profile Books, 2003); Phyllis Chesler, *The New Anti-Semitism: The Current Crisis and What We Must Do About It* (San Francisco: Jossey-Bass, 2003); Abraham H. Foxman, *Never Again? The Threat of the New Anti-Semitism* (New York: HarperCollins, 2003); Gabriel Schoenfeld, *The Return of Anti-Semitism* (San Francisco: Encounter Books, 2004). For early treatment of this matter as it surfaced post-September 2000 see Jonathan Rosen, "The Uncomfortable Question of Anti-Semitism," *New York Times Magazine,* November 4, 2001, online edition; Hillel Halkin, "The Return of Anti-Semitism," *Commentary,* February 2002, pp. 30-36; Marvin Perry and Frederick M. Schweitzer, *Antisemitism: Myth and Hate from Antiquity to the Present* (New York: Palgrave Macmillan, 2002), see Introduction, pp. 9-16, Conclusion, pp. 263-264.

[7] Lewis, *Op cit.*, p. 256.

[8] Cited in Yigal Carmon, "Contemporary Islamist Ideology Permitting Genocidal Murder," The Middle East Media Research Institute (MEMRI), Special Report No. 25, January 27, 2004, p 18. See also Robert S. Wistrich, *Muslim Anti-Semitism: A Clear and Present Danger* (New York: The American Jewish Committee, 2002); Menahem Milson, *Countering Arab Antisemitism,* Institute of the World Jewish Congress, Jerusalem, 2003; Jonathan D. Halevi, "Al-Qaeda's Intellectual Legacy: New Radical Islamic Thinking Justifying the Genocide of Infidels," Jerusalem Center for Public Affairs, December 1, 2003.

[9] Jeffrey Goldberg, "In the Party of God: Are Terrorists in Lebanon Preparing for a Larger War?" *The New Yorker,* October 14 & 21, 2002, p. 192.

[10] Bartov, *Op. cit.,* p. 32.

[11] "Charter of the Islamic Resistance Movement (Hamas) of Palestine," *Journal of Palestine Studies,* XXII, No. 4 (Summer 1993), p. 132; p. 123.

[12] Mark Lilla, "The End of Politics in Europe, the Nation-State, and the Jews," *The New Republic,* June 23, 2003.

[13] On these and related developments in Europe, see Alvin H. Rosenfeld, *Anti-Americanism and Anti-Semitism: A New Frontier of Bigotry* (New York: The American Jewish Committee, August 2003); John Rosenthal, "Anti-Semitism and Ethnicity in Europe," *Policy Review,* October 2003, online edition; Shalom Lappin, "Israel and the New Anti-Semitism," *Dissent,* Spring 2003, online edition; and Josef Joffe, "The Demons of Europe," *Commentary,* January 2004, pp. 29-34. Joffe is editor of the German weekly *Die Zeit.*

[14] Hamas Charter, *Op cit.* p. 124.

[15] "PA TV Broadcast Call for Killing Jews and Americans," Middle East Media Research Institute (MEMRI), October 14, 2000.

[16] Cited in Goldberg, *Op. cit.,* p. 191.

[17] Speech of President Bashar Al-Assad, Syrian Arab News Agency, May 5, 2001, available at www.adl.org.

[18] Naim Ateek, "An Easter Message from Sabeel," 2002.

[19] Cited in Cathy Young, "The New Anti-Semitism," *Boston Globe,* December 22, 2003, online edition.

[20] *The Independent,* January 27, 2003.

[21] Fred Licht, *Goya* (New York: Abbeville Press, 2001), pp. 220-221.

[22] Elaine Sciolino, "French Assembly Votes to Ban Religious Symbols in Schools," *The New York Times,* February 11, 2004, Section A, p. 3. Also see, on this and other matters, Haim Musicant, "Anti-Semitism in France, an Assessment," December 30, 2003. This report, which originally appeared in the CRIF English-language newsletter, is available at www.adl.org.

[23] See in Wistrich, *Op. cit.,* p. 23.

24 Photo of Palestine rally, London, 2002, on back cover of Paul Iganski and Barry Kosmin, *Op. cit.* On use of the "Zionism equals Nazism" charge and other phrases currently in play, see Manfred Gerstenfeld, "Language As a Tool Against Jews and Israel: An Interview with Georges-Elia Sarfati," Jerusalem Center for Public Affairs, February 1, 2004.

25 Norman Cohn, *Warrant for Genocide: The Myth of the Jewish World-Conspiracy and the Protocols of the Elders of Zion* (London: Eyre & Spottiswoode, 1967).

26 *New Statesman,* January 14, 2002.

27 "Cardinal Sees Anti-Semitism Rise in Europe," *International Herald Tribune,* December 22, 2003, online edition.

28 "Anti-Semitism Study in the Spotlight," Centre of Research on Anti-Semitism Newsletter, No. 26 (December 2003), p. 2.

29 *Ibid.,* p. 2; p. 4.

30 Chesler, *Op. cit.;* Bartov, Op. cit.

31 *Daily Ilini,* January 22, 2003, online edition.

32 *Chicago Tribune,* May 30, 2003, Section 1, p. 26.

33 *Christian Century,* January 13, 2004, p. 6.

34 Cited in Noreen S. Ahmed-Ullah, Kim Barker, Laurie Cohen, Stephen Franklin, Sam Roe, "Hard-Liners Won Battle for Bridgeview Mosque," *Chicago Tribune,* February 8, 2004, Section 1, p.15.

35 Steven Emerson, *American Jihad: The Terrorists Living Among Us* (New York: Free Press, 2003), pp. 100-101.

36 Michael Fechter, "Imam Who Touted Al-Arian Charity Arrested," *The Tampa Tribune,* January 14, 2004, online edition.

37 Paul M. Barrett, "Student Journeys into Secret Circle of Extremism," *Wall Street Journal,* December 25, 2003, online edition.

38 Ari Shavit, "A Jewish Soul," *Ha'aretz,* February 13, 2004, online edition.

The Continuing Challenge of Anti-Semitism

Lecture presented to International Council of Christians and Jews
Chicago, IL, July 26, 2005

Printed in JUF News, July 2005

• • •

A little more than six years ago, a homegrown white supremacist with hatred in his heart and the words "Sabbath breaker" tattooed on his body drove to the most Jewishly-identified neighborhood in Chicago and opened fire on a number of observers of the Jewish Sabbath on their way home from Friday evening worship. The evening marked the beginning of the July 4th holiday weekend. After wounding several Jewish Chicagoans, this opponent of the principles of religious, racial, and ethnic diversity celebrated on that distinctively American holiday continued his shooting spree, murdering an African-American basketball coach in nearby Evanston and an Asian student in Bloomington, Indiana, before taking his own life during a police chase.

As it happens, Matt Hale, the notorious mentor of the individual who carried out those acts, was just recently sent to prison for planning the murder of a federal judge in Chicago whose husband Hale mistakenly accused of being Jewish. Clearly, old-time anti-Semitism, coming from the far right, remains alive in America, and given the violent inclinations of many of its advocates, it certainly cannot be ignored. But neither should it be exaggerated. Its practitioners are few, and they are for the most part marginalized by the American mainstream. As we take stock of the current state of anti-Semitism, we cannot ignore this strain of it, but we also should not fail to recognize the development of a new, post-modern form of anti-Semitism. That is a phenomenon far more common in Europe than in America, but one which certainly can be seen here as well, and it will be the focus of my remarks today.

Many of the themes, concepts, language, and imagery of the new anti-Semitism are familiar, but they are incorporated into a unique syndrome that has three defining features.

First, whereas traditional anti-Semitism emanated from Christian Europe, this latest incarnation of the world's oldest hatred is most significantly generated in the Muslim and Arab worlds. While the Islamic world was historically more accepting of Jews than was Christendom — albeit assigning them a second-class status — over the past century or so, patterns of prejudice that originated in Christian Europe have found a home in Arab and Muslim lands.

One way in which this has worked is illustrated in an article in the June issue of *Commentary* magazine by the historian Paul Johnson. Johnson talks about the impact of the czarist-era Russian forgery *The Protocols of the Elders of Zion* on the Palestinian grand mufti, Muhammed Amin al-Husseini, saying, "Al-Husseini was already tinged with hatred of Jews, but the *Protocols* gave him a purpose in life: to expel all Jews from Palestine forever." After citing the mufti's ties with Hitler and other Nazis, Johnson goes on to say: "Over the last half-century, anti-Semitism has been the essential ideology of the Arab world." As if to confirm this claim, a Pew Global Attitudes Survey released less than two weeks ago shows that 99 percent of the public in Lebanon, 100 percent of it in Jordan, and 88 percent of it in Morocco view Jews in an unfavorable fashion.

While the Holocaust that was wrought on European soil left a residue of shame which rendered anti-Semitism a blight to be shunned there, at least in official circles, the *Protocols,* labeled Hitler's "warrant for genocide" and long discredited in the West, has been kept alive in the Arab world, where the book's contents reinforce conspiracy-haunted, hate-filled stereotypes of Jews. Over the past several years, as the Muslim population in Europe has skyrocketed and as local guilt feelings over the Holocaust have receded, some of the old attitudes which were born in Europe have been brought back.

Another defining attribute of the new anti-Semitism is that, as it grows in the Western world, its primary locus is not on the right, as was that of the old anti-Semitism, but on the left side of the political spectrum. This is not an altogether new phenomenon in itself, with the Soviet Union having been a center of anti-Semitism in the post-war period. What is new is the phenomenon's growth in the post-Cold War environment, especially over the past five years, during which much of the radical left seems to have found a new "cause" in the Palestinian struggle.

Radical Muslims and post-Enlightenment leftists have thus formed an unholy alliance on European soil. Together they march and together they embrace a particularly perverse trope with precedent in the Soviet Union that has become a recurrent theme of the new anti-Semitism, namely the equation of the Jews and the Nazis. As Jews are seen as the new Nazis, as practitioners and not victims of racism, the paradigmatic evil of our time, they become fair game for the left. There are of course several layers of irony in all of this given the afore-noted support for Hitler's Nazis from certain Arab leaders and given the strength of the Holocaust denial movement in the Arab world today. But irony aside, the insulting equation is repeatedly rendered in placards, cartoons, and anti-Israel propaganda.

The third element that characterizes the new anti-Semitism has to do with the nature of its target. No longer does the hatred primarily focus on individual Jews or Jewish communities. Instead it is aimed at the Jewish state of Israel and, by association, at Jews who are identified with that nation.

For those in the Arab and Muslim worlds with unremitting hostility to Israel's very existence, there is no place in what they regard as their part of the world for a Jewish nation. Israel's very presence is an affront to their sense of themselves and their view of their proper relationship with the Jews. For the European leftists who have taken up this cause, the presence of a particularist Jewish state and the insistence on its legitimacy are an affront to their concept of a post-national globe where universal values reign. Israel, from that ideological perspective, is not the product of the Jewish people's return to self-determination and sovereignty in their native land, a land to which they had remained attached through all the centuries of exile. It rather is a colonialist enclave, the fruit of imperialism sustained through its friendship with the leading force for contemporary imperialism, the United States. From this perspective, Israel is sometimes seen, in the mode of historic anti-Semitism as promoted in the *Protocols,* as controlling the United States, and it is at other times seen as merely a tool being used by America to extend its own global reach.

In earlier eras, Jews like Shakespeare's Shylock were regarded as threatening the happiness and even the existence of the Christians in whose world they lived while following their own materialist, money-grubbing code. But they at least could convert. In the 19th century — as captured in the portrayal of Fagin by Dickens and his illustrator Cruikshank — the demonic Jew had become racially determined and, as Hitler insisted, could only be annihilated. Today, it is Israel and its Jewish supporters who, at the worst, are seen and portrayed as global outsiders with demonic powers, operating through conspiratorial means to take over the world. More commonly it is Israel that becomes the scapegoat for the Arab world's own frustrations, Israel that is blamed as the cause of regional instability and even worldwide terrorism, Israel alone that is seen as preventing a gentle peace from coming to its region. And it is Israel, alone among the nations of the world, whose academics are shunned, whose universities are boycotted, and whose very right to exist is challenged over and over, directly and indirectly.

This new anti-Semitism is no fringe phenomenon overwhelmingly condemned and rejected by the mainstream. Its themes and images have been enunciated and circulated without rebuke by politicians, journalists, academics, and clergy. Indeed, especially through much of Europe, it has become a trend. And with this anti-Semitism "in the air," Jewish individuals and Jewish institutions have found themselves targeted not only by expressions of hate but by violent actions, as synagogues have been firebombed and individuals have been attacked.

The situation in America is different from that in Europe for several reasons. Through the years, while there have been instances of anti-Semitism in American life, America has generally been far more tolerant and far freer of virulent anti-Semitism than Europe. At this time it also is experiencing less of a radical Muslim influx, and those Muslims who do come are, by and large, less inflamed by the preaching in their mosques and the messages on their computers and satellite TVs. They are more accepted into and accepting of the values of this pluralistic nation of immigrants. At the same time, the Jewish community, while a small minority, has numbers, status, and an organizational ability to protect its rights far more than do its counterparts in Europe. America's political leadership has been more sensitive about anti-Semitism and friendlier to Israel than much of that in Europe. And finally, the treatment of Jews and of Israel in the America media, while sometimes troubling in its own ways, is generally less provocative and unbalanced than much of what has appeared in Europe.

Still, this is not to say that some radical Muslims have not been actively promulgating anti-Semitic themes in the U.S. A court case recently pursued in Ohio revolving around the imam of Cleveland's largest mosque disclosed that at a 1991 rally held in support of the Palestinian Islamic Jihad terror organization right here in Chicago, he had called for "directing all the rifles at the first and last enemy of the Islamic nation and that is the sons of monkeys and pigs, the Jews." The new anti-Semitism has also surfaced close to the mainstream in this country. And much of that has happened at two primary venues: on some university campuses and within some Christian groups.

University campuses, it can be suggested, are the closest thing we have to Europe in many ways. Thanks to the behavior of numbers of faculty members and some students, an intellectual climate somewhat similar to that on the Continent has been created in conjunction with a post-modern, anti-colonialist ideology. At the same time, on some campuses there are politicized Muslim and Palestinian students who, frequently with the backing of off-campus supporters, aggressively assert a problematic anti-Israel agenda.

In the Chicago area this past year the Muslim Cultural Students' Association at Northwestern University brought former Congressman Paul Finley to campus. While his talk was ostensibly scheduled to be about cultural matters, the focus of his attention was predictably on a charge that, through conspiratorial power, the Jews manipulated America to serve Israel's interests and not its own by attacking Iraq. Another local Muslim student group, this one at Northeastern University in Chicago, was planning to have a memorial service for Sheik Ahmed Yassin, the leader of Hamas, a terrorist organization dedicated to Israel's destruction which is guided by a venomously anti-Semitic charter. Meanwhile, at Chicago's DePaul University, a group called Students for Justice in Palestine sponsored an art exhibit labeled "The Subject of Palestine" that mostly consisted of a series of portrayals of martyred Palestinians victimized by the brutal Israelis. The opening sentence in the exhibit catalog, repeated on a placard at the entrance to the exhibit, drastically distorted history and denied Israel's legitimacy by proclaiming that "Resistance is the Palestinian response to the tragedy known as the *Nakba,* when in 1948 statehood was lost to Israeli occupation." The exhibit was shown at the DePaul Art Museum and officially co-sponsored by a dozen DePaul departments and programs.

DePaul's administration says that before allowing the exhibit to open, they sought and received assurance from faculty members that the exhibit was not anti-Semitic. That these professors failed to identify the display and accompanying commentary as anti-Semitic is not altogether surprising in light of traditional ways to think of the term. Furthermore, those of us who are positing that there is a new anti-Semitism with hostility toward Israel at its core need to be careful not to assert that any and all criticism of Israel is labeled "anti-Semitism" and not to charge all critics of Israel with being motivated by an anti-Semitic animus. But when that criticism merges with an agenda aimed at dismantling the State of Israel; when it comes with disregard for or rationalization of the brutal murders of Jewish men, women, and children; and when it is couched in language and concepts saturated with the substance of traditional anti-Semitism — then, I would assert, the charge of anti-Semitism is appropriate.

To be sure, there still is educating to do, both within the Jewish community and without, to help people understand what the nature and the boundaries of this new anti-Semitism are. But when the committee investigating charges that some Columbia University faculty members exhibited an anti-Israel bias inside and outside of the classroom and intimidated student supporters of Israel concluded that no anti-Semitism could be found, and when the *New York Times* highlighted that finding in the headline of its first report on that study, in effect dismissing other aspects of the report, an oversimplification was clearly in the works on the part of people locked into the old definition of the term. And when Norman Finkelstein, a DePaul faculty member listed as an advisor to the Palestinian students who put together the exhibit on their campus and whose new book is due out next week, provocatively proclaims that it is Israel and the "American Jewish elites" who are "the main fomenters of anti-Semitism in the world today," even while conducting his own attacks on what he calls "Israeli crimes" and making his own assertions about Jews' "abuse of formidable power," as he did in *Tikkun* magazine, he is obfuscating what is going on and is contributing to the problem at hand rather than helping to illuminate or address it.

This brings me to the final locus of the new anti-Semitism in America that I would like to talk about, one which has particular relevance in this setting. I refer to certain Christian churches and individuals.

This manifestation too has sources and analogues in earlier developments. What we are seeing taught and implied in certain Christian quarters today is a new form of replacement theology, one that sees the Palestinians as the new Israel, entitled to the land of Israel, and as the new Jesus, tormented and crucified by the Jews. The Jews thereby are at best undeserving of sovereignty in the land of Israel, and at worst merit the contempt and punishment dealt them through the ages.

A direct evocation of the deicide charge — repudiated by the Catholic Church forty years ago, and by many other Christian denominations as well — was rendered by Syrian president Bashar al-Assad when he welcomed Pope John Paul II to Syria in 2001. But it also is a recurring theme promulgated by Palestinian Christian leaders with a following in the United States, notably by Naim Ateek, former Anglican Canon of St. George's Cathedral and founder and current director of the Sabeel Ecumenical Liberation Theology Center in Jerusalem.

In a sermon entitled "The Zionist Ideology of Domination Versus the Reign of God," delivered in the Notre Dame chapel in Jerusalem on February 22, 2001 as part of a Sabeel conference, Ateek talked about "the evil structures that have dominated the Palestinians for the last hundred years." Mixing the language of religion and theology with that of politics and ideology, Ateek continued by saying: "I believe that the original sin and crime was Zionism in the way it turned into a colonial force. Israel still lives and acts in the same basic ideology." He closed this sermon by saying: "Jesus Christ, living in our country as a Palestinian under occupation, offers us a different model of power." In a sermon delivered in the same setting two days later, Ateek proclaimed that "Israel has placed a large boulder, a big stone that has metaphorically shut off the Palestinians in a tomb. It is similar to the stone placed on the entrance of Jesus' tomb. . . . We have a name for this boulder. It is the OCCUPATION."

These themes recur for Ateek. In an Easter message from Sabeel in 2001 to which the ICCJ took strong exception at the time, he specifically declared that "In this season of Lent, it seems to many of us that Jesus is on the cross again with thousands of crucified Palestinians around Him . . . . The Israeli government crucifixion system is operating daily." At the opening worship service of the Sabeel International Solidarity Visit in Jerusalem on April 17, 2002, he asserted that "Palestinians have been condemned as a nation by Israel, and sentenced to destruction. The accusations of people in power are strikingly similar throughout history to the charges leveled against Jesus in this city -- terrorist, evildoer, or rebel and a subversive person. Palestinians are being crucified today for refusing to succumb to Israel's demand for greater concession on land."

Ateek's thesis and language have been picked up on by followers of his such as Hilary Rantisi, a former staff member of Sabeel who in an Easter reflection of her own printed in the Winter 2002 issue of *Cornerstone,* a Sabeel publication, spoke of the way that "many Palestinian Christians refer to their experience living under occupation and the suffering they endure as 'walking the Via Dolorosa.'" She described the way that the Sabeel Center "leads what they call the 'Contemporary Way of the Cross,'" offering Western Christian pilgrims "the opportunity . . . to join Palestinians for an afternoon of making the modern stations of the cross, the ongoing suffering that Palestinians endure under occupation." Echoing her mentor, Rantisi went on to say: "Today, Palestinians are still walking the Way of the Cross, and anxiously awaiting the day of resurrection, the day the stone that blocks the tomb of occupation is rolled away."

Ateek's contemporary rendering of traditional Christian anti-Semitic motifs is widely circulated within Mainline Protestant churches in the U.S. I first came upon these notions in a Religious News Service report carried in the March 14, 2001 issue of *The Christian Century,* the mainline Protestant magazine published in Chicago, that described a Sabeel conference that "brought together several hundred Christians from 17 countries." According to the article, while observing Palestinians "huddled" outside the office of Israel's Interior Ministry, the participants heard a spokesman read from the Gospel of Matthew how "when Pilate saw a riot was gathering, he took some water and washed his hands in front of the crowd saying, 'I am innocent of this man's blood. It is your responsibility.'" We all know what comes next in the Gospel and can understand what is implied here.

Ateek himself has often come to the States to speak in church-sponsored programs, while Sabeel has established a network of supporters in North America which has become a vehicle for advancing his teachings. A conference initiated and coordinated by the Sabeel Ecumenical Liberation Theology Center in Jerusalem and the friends of Sabeel in North America will be held here in Chicago on October 7-8. The venue is the Lutheran School of Theology, which is a primary sponsor of the conference along with a number of other groups, including the Working Group on the Middle East of the Metropolitan Chicago Synod of the ELCA and the Middle East Task Force of the Chicago Presbytery. Ateek himself will be a primary speaker.

Not all of the thinking, writing, and speaking of this sort is originating in the Middle East. To give one example of others within Mainline Protestantism who have been advancing such attitudes, I would cite the Presbyterian minister and director of the Center for Middle Eastern Studies at North Park University in Chicago, Donald Wagner. His 2003 book, *Dying in the Land of Promise,* is subtitled *Palestine and Palestinian Christianity from Pentecost to 2000.* Summarizing the book, my colleague Rabbi Yehiel Poupko has pointed out that for Wagner, "the Jewish people ceased to have any attachment to the Land so very long ago, and were replaced by the real Israel, the Palestinian Christians." The theme of the book is encapsulated by its cover, a photograph of a mural at the Christian Lutheran Church and International Centre in Bethlehem, whose pastor and director, Mitri Raheb, is another promulgator of the kind of replacement theology I am talking about. This mural portrays thirteen Palestinian men in a local setting engaged in an apparent reenactment of The Last Supper — or perhaps it is meant to be understood as a picture of the original Last Supper itself. In the theology of the new anti-Semitism the two are one, as the Palestinians become both the new Jews and the new Jesus.

Recent developments make clear that the impact of these ideas is not merely academic. A news article by James Besser and an accompanying editorial in the latest issue of the Jewish Week, published in New York, report that representatives of Sabeel had significant impact at the recent meeting of the United Church of Christ, influencing that body as they have other American mainline denominations as decisions have been made about divestment from Israel. After citing Sabeel's benign description of itself, Besser says, "A number of analysts say the center is playing a much more malevolent role, pressing for punitive actions against Israel, ignoring Palestinian violence and ultimately arguing against the legitimacy of a Jewish state." And he quotes several experts, some of them here today, who make the kind of argument I have been developing today regarding the theological underpinnings of this kind of behavior.

In a talk presented at a community forum organized by the Jewish Community Relations Council of the Jewish Federation of Metropolitan Chicago this past April, the British journalist Melanie Phillips, who has done major work on this subject, talked about developments in England. Speaking of the way that "some of the most virulent and disproportionate attacks upon Israel are made by Christian aid agencies, clerics, and church newspapers," she said that "church newspaper editors and others say the churches' hostility to Israel is rooted in a theological dislike of the Jews," and concluded that "this is because Palestinian politics and Christian theological prejudice have become inextricably intertwined."

As Phillips' talk demonstrated and as I have observed, the situation in England and on the Continent certainly is more severe than that in America. But these trends cannot be ignored or minimized in either place. In Europe, through the OSCE and moves by various governments, measures have begun to be introduced to counter the new anti-Semitism. More remains to be done there, and we need to sound a proper alarm and address these trends before they grow and do greater damage in our country as well.

The radicalism of some within America's Muslim population absolutely must not be seen as characterizing that entire community. But neither should that radicalism be excused through post-modern verbal jujitsu or justified as the understandable reaction of people concerned about the suffering of their overseas brethren, as it has been. This applies to campus radicalism as well. The encroachment there of the new anti-Semitism must be recognized for what it is and treated with the opprobrium that such bigotry surely merits. Finally, it must be made absolutely clear that there is no room in theological discourse or in political discourse about the Israel-Palestinian conflict for language which resurrects the theological anti-Semitism which was widespread in Christendom for so many centuries. The circulation of such concepts, impeding rather than advancing the true peace with justice that their advocates claim to wish to see in the Middle East, poisons the relations between Jews and Christians in this country and introduces a dangerous venom into the bloodstream of the body politic.

Charges of anti-Semitism may occasionally be misplaced, and those of us who use such terminology need to be careful. By the same token, though, there indeed is a new anti-Semitism abroad in the land. Its promulgation is a serious matter that cannot be ignored.

A New World of Anti-Semitism

Chicago Sun-Times, August 23, 2006

• • •

Two seemingly disparate events took place on America's West Coast within 24 hours in late July. In Los Angeles, the well-known movie actor and director Mel Gibson, stopped for a driving infraction, expressed views that made the incident a cause celebre. In Seattle, an unemployed man named Naveed Afzal Haq entered that community's Jewish Federation headquarters and began shooting. Different as those two incidents were in many ways, what they had in common was a key anti-Semitic component.

Pulled over for speeding while under the influence of alcohol in the early hours of July 28, Gibson reportedly cursed the Jewish people and asserted that "the Jews are responsible for all the wars in the world." Implying that the Jewish people were somehow conspiring against him, he asked the arresting officer if he were Jewish. (As coincidence would have it, he is.)

That afternoon, Haq, with two automatic handguns, waited outside the entrance to Seattle's Jewish Federation until able to force himself past security. He then opened fire on staff members, killing one and wounding five before he turned himself in. Haq reportedly said that he picked the Federation after searching the word "Jewish" on the Internet, and that he made its occupants his targets because, as he told a 911 dispatcher, "these are Jews and I'm tired of getting pushed around and our people are getting pushed around by the situation in the Middle East."

The anti-Semitic aspect of Gibson's early Friday morning arrest did not come to light until the weekend, so it cannot be said to have influenced Haq. Furthermore, while Haq's premeditated attack quite clearly seems to have been motivated by anti-Semitic impulses, for Gibson, the act for which he was arrested merely provided the occasion for a spontaneous anti-Semitic outburst. Still, the language that came out of each of their mouths reveals a strikingly similar animus.

In speculating on the sources of Gibson's anti-Semitism, one thinks of ideas and attitudes he may have picked up from his father, who has expressed Holocaust denial beliefs, as well as Christian teachings from an earlier era echoed in Gibson's *The Passion of the Christ,* which, though repudiated by the Catholic Church decades ago, remain alive in some quarters. Haq, who reportedly identified himself to his victims as a "Muslim-American" who was "angry at Israel," may have absorbed some of the classic anti-Semitic notions that tenaciously remain in Western culture. But he very likely also drew from newer sources with a non-Western connection. Therein lies the greatest difference between the two forms of anti-Semitism in these incidents.

The views Haq expressed and the emotions linked to them emanate in large measure from the Middle East, where a nationalism-driven conflict between Israel and its Arab neighbors has morphed into a religious war spearheaded by the radical Islamists of Hamas, Hezbollah and Iran. The ideological underpinnings of their proclaimed jihad partake of an incendiary anti-Semitism that is being promulgated in schools and mosques, circulated on TV stations and the Internet and vocalized in street demonstrations. Such messages very likely reached Haq, one way or another.

The new anti-Semitism acted upon by Haq is on the ascent globally and is a potential threat here too. Evidencing the extended presence of attitudes like Haq's, at a rally organized by local Muslims organizations in Chicago early in July, one placard could be seen equating Nazism and Zionism (a major theme of the new anti-Semitism), with another itself consisting of a Nazi-like caricature portraying Jewish control of America and through it the world. The flier announcing the rally included a photo that appears to be cropped and otherwise manipulated showing President Bush with his hand over his heart while standing next to an Israeli flag, insinuating that he feels greater loyalty to that country than his own.

It certainly is legitimate for any American to publicly convey his or her views on the conflict in the Middle East. But all steps possible should be taken to ensure that that conflict is not acted out similarly in America, as language and imagery that crosses the line threatens to make happen. Public officials and leaders of local and national Muslim-American organizations properly condemned the Seattle violence. But they often went on to talk about the need to provide security for local mosques in light of a supposed possible backlash. That kind of response is both gratuitous and insufficient.

Besides condemning such an act, it is also important for them to speak out specifically and firmly against the inflammatory anti-Semitic concepts that lay behind it, lest such views become more common and acceptable in this country and anti-Jewish violence becomes more than the isolated instance it was in Seattle.

Engaging the Battle against the New Anti-Semitism

JUF News, February 2009

• • •

On Feb. 15-17 the London Conference on Combating Anti-Semitism brought together members of more than 40 national parliaments along with experts on the subject and community representatives.

The conference, co-sponsored by the steering committee of the Inter-Parliamentary Coalition for Combating Anti-Semitism, grew out of work done by the Global Forum to Combat Anti-Semitism, which has convened annually in Israel for several years. After having participated in the last two meetings of the Forum, I was invited to this conference—and what an experience it turned out to be, given the surge in anti-Semitism particularly in the wake of Israel's military operation in Gaza, and given the venue.

Here in Chicago, the Jewish United Fund has worked to create awareness of what has come to be called "the new anti-Semitism" and to respond to local anti-Semitic incidents. The first thing that struck me in London, hearing from counterparts involved in similar work there and in Europe, is how similar are the issues we face here, but how much more severe the situation is over there.

In England, where the Jewish community is only slightly larger than that of the Chicago area, there were some 250 anti-Semitic incidents during the four weeks following the beginning of Israel's operation in Gaza. In Chicago, troubling as they may have been, there were fewer than a dozen such incidents. In the British media and on campuses, where boycotts of Israeli academics have been promoted and some faculty members and students are especially hostile, things are far more problematic than they are here.

Similarly, issues resonate more strongly in proximity to the countries where the Holocaust took place, where the presence of large Muslim populations with active radical elements adds significantly to the problem.

Finally, with economic difficulties being a historic trigger for anti-Semitic activity in that part of the world, today's downturn is an additional source of disquiet, especially where Jewish communities are smaller and less comfortable in speaking out to centers of power than is the case here.

During the first day of deliberations the experts and lawmakers met in separate working groups but joined together to hear remarks from conveners of the conference and from Franco Frattini, the foreign minister of Italy and formerly the European Union's Commissioner for Justice, Freedom and Security.

For me, one of the most striking and meaningful aspects of the conference was the appearance of non-Jews in positions of influence who grasp the nature and seriousness of what is happening these days. They well recognize that today's venomous hostility toward Israel is expressed in ways that echo traditional anti-Semitism and that anti-Zionism is the new anti-Semitism.

With representatives from communities as varied as Venezuela, Turkey, and France, and with Iran on our minds as a center of today's anti-Semitism, we were sharply aware of the imminence of the threats to individual Jews, Jewish communities, the Jewish state, and the Jewish people in today's world. As many of the speakers stressed, however much anti-Semitism may concern Jews, it is a danger and challenge for society at large. Moral moorings are at risk and the connection with reality itself is made tenuous when individuals, groups, nations, and cultures are overtaken by perverted images of Jews, which have always been at the core of anti-Semitism, and by Jewish conspiracy theories, which inevitably drive those who are obsessed by anti-Semitic beliefs.

During the second day of the conference the parliamentarians gathered to create The London Declaration on Combating Anti-Semitism, whose intention is to "draw the democratic world's attention to the resurgence of anti-Semitism as a potent force in politics, international affairs, and society." The Declaration goes on to proclaim: "We are alarmed at the resurrection of the old language of prejudice and its modern manifestations—in rhetoric and political action—against Jews, Jewish belief and practice and the State of Israel." Alluding to Iran (and perhaps others), it says: "We are alarmed by government-backed anti-Semitism in general and state-backed genocidal anti-Semitism in particular."

The Declaration lays out principles for action in challenging anti-Semitism, and lists a range of specific steps in identifying the threat and establishing effective countermeasures. The Declaration itself is an impressive and important step. But implementation of its action steps is critical, as is the need to spread understanding of the new anti-Semitism.

In the working group on "Fighting Anti-Semitism in the Political Sphere," I described the frustrations we sometimes feel here in Chicago when certain public officials and organizations, even those of goodwill, describe anti-Semitism merely as one of many forms of discrimination. It is particularly problematic to talk about anti-Semitic incidents merely as hate crimes without dealing with their specific attributes and characteristics—especially when Jews and Jewish institutions are attacked as a way to channel hatred of Israel (for example, when synagogue walls are vandalized by the spray painting of the words "Death to Israel"). To do so fails to come to grips with the nature and challenge of the new anti-Semitism. As the practices for fighting anti-Semitism called for in the London Declaration are implemented, it will be important for these kinds of distinctions to be made.

In a similar vein, the conference's recurring calls for Holocaust education—while surely well-intentioned and desirable in their own right—do not necessarily represent the most effective way to confront today's anti-Semitism, which mostly is advanced by ideological activists and Muslim extremists who in many ways are different from the people and movements that drove the Holocaust. Indeed, there may in general be a significant failure to fully differentiate the nature and the sources of today's anti-Semitism from what prevailed during the Holocaust era. We need world leaders to speak out against Holocaust denial and to remember what happened during the Shoah, when the full fury of anti-Semitism was unleashed. But the Jewish people today are not nearly as weak and helpless as were the victims of that era, thanks in great part to the existence of the State of Israel. To be truly effective, today's measures need to be framed in reference to today's realities.

The London conference may not have covered all the territory related to its topic in full detail and depth, but it was a remarkable first-time endeavor with major and important accomplishments. Much credit and appreciation is due to the organizers and participants in this event, which will hopefully prove to be a landmark moment in the battle against the new anti-Semitism.

The Language of the New Anti-Semitism

*Presented at the Conference "Global Antisemitism:
A Crisis of Modernity"
Sponsored by the Yale Initiative for
the Interdisciplinary Study of Antisemitism
August 24, 2010*

Printed in Volume V: Reflections, *in the five-volume series on
Global Antisemitism: A Crisis of Modernity.
New York: ISCAP Books, 2014*

. . .

For several years now scholars and commentators have been talking about the new anti-Semitism – a contemporary manifestation of the age-old hatred whose themes, as well as the vocabulary and imagery through which they are expressed, are mostly traditional. Though this manifestation sometimes takes new shape or is expressed in new venues, what is particularly distinctive about this trend is the fact that the targets of today's attacks are not so much individual Jews or Jewish communities per se, as was the case formerly, but the Jewish collective – that is, the State of Israel, along with individual Jews based on their association with that entity.

When Naim Ateek and his Jerusalem-based Sabeel Center for Liberation Theology sent out an Easter message in 2001 saying that "In this season of Lent, it seems to many of us that Jesus is on the cross again with thousands of crucified Palestinians around Him," and when they went on to say that "the Israeli crucifixion system is operating daily," they were providing an example of the rebirth of Christian anti-Semitism in this new form. Though the Catholic Church and a number of Protestant denominations have explicitly repudiated the deicide charge that was at the core of anti-Semitic activity for centuries, that charge is an anti-Semitic trope that is now being conveyed through allusion and analogy in the works of Ateek and his followers and by representatives of mainline Protestant denominations in the U.S. and elsewhere.

Similar discourse appeared in the draft of a report issued by the Middle East Study Committee of the Presbyterian Church USA this spring, preceding that church's General Assembly in Minneapolis. In a critique that appeared in the *Christian Century* magazine issue of June 29 entitled "Habits of Anti-Judaism," Ted A. Smith and Amy-Jill Levine, both of them from the Vanderbilt Divinity School, cited a number of examples of this sort of rhetoric in the document. They concluded that the Presbyterian report "evokes old echoes of theological supersessionism" and that it "describes Jacob in ways that resonate with anti-Jewish stereotypes," and they noted multiple other ways that the report used tropes with origins in Christian anti-Judaism.

Reacting to the Smith-Levine critique and to the comments of other critics of the Presbyterian report, James Wall, himself a former editor of Christian Century and an ordained United Methodist minister, similarly resurrected traditional anti-Semitism in new garb in a piece headed "Israeli 'Agents' Infiltrate Presbyterian General Assembly." Alluding to a familiar New Testament phrase that referred to the episode in which Herod murdered all boys under the age of two in the Bethlehem area in an attempt to kill Jesus, Wall spoke of the way that "the slaughter of the innocents began with the Nakba in 1947."

Applying the themes of a stolen birthright and of supersessionism in the framework of his own hybrid application of religious traditions, the Nation of Islam's inflammatory Minister Louis Farrakhan resurfaced this summer, baiting American Jewish communal leaders and proclaiming as he has in the past that "The Honorable Elijah Mohammad said that almighty God Allah revealed to him that the Black people of America are the real children of Israel and we are the choice of God." Insisting that "To all of those who feel that the children of Israel are all over in that place they call Israel, you are mistaken," he added: "The wickedly wise... are working night and day to trick you out of the promise of God and take you down to hell with them because the time of their end has come."

Echoes of traditional Christian anti-Semitism can be heard not only in the words of theologians and spokesmen of religious bodies, mainstream or fringe, but also in more popular discourse. For example, working in a medium that favors short-hand allusions that accompany or are conveyed by starkly rendered graphic images, cartoonists have recirculated the blood libel charge that had so much currency and did so much harm in the Christian Middle Ages.

This theme was gruesomely evoked in a cartoon that appeared in the January 27, 2003, issue of *The Independent* in England. It showed a grotesque, naked Ariel Sharon eating the bloody body of a Palestinian youth. Another visualization of the theme appeared this past March in the form of a wall poster cartoon that was exhibited in the town square of Cologne, Germany. This drawing portrayed a person seen from chest level down who was wearing a bib with a Jewish Star on it, with a plate in front of him on which he was using a knife marked "Gaza" and a red, white, and blue fork to carve up a miniature, bleeding human figure dressed like a Palestinian (with a kaffiyeh around his neck). Beside the plate was a glass filled with a red liquid. Explaining why the public prosecutor's office declined to charge the poster maker with inciting racial hatred, a spokesman explained: "It is not a tendency of hostility toward Jews, but an actual criticism of the situation in Gaza. The cartoon is a sarcastic expression of the Israeli army in Gaza." I will talk about denial of anti-Semitism later in this presentation, but it is worth keeping this comment on a contemporary rendering of the blood libel theme in mind.

It has been widely noted by scholars that themes familiar from historic Christian anti-Semitism have found fertile soil in which to grow within the Islamic world. And thus the blood libel, for one thing, has often been repeated in Arab countries. But no theme from Western-generated anti-Semitism has become as widespread – both in the Islamic world and beyond – as the concept of a global Jewish conspiracy dedicated to controlling the world. It is a theme that Anthony Julius, in his recent book on the history of anti-Semitism in England, says was "new… in the late nineteenth century." As Julius puts it, "Anti-Semitism… ceased to address a problem within medieval life; it instead addressed the pattern of modern life."

Introduced at the time of the rise of modern Zionism, the theme was rendered in archetypal form in the notorious forgery called *The Protocols of the Elders of Zion* – an inspirational text for the Nazis which is now an accepted, widely-circulated source of ideas about Jews in the Islamic world. Nowhere can that be seen more clearly than in the Hamas Charter, a strikingly direct and extensive rendering of the language of the new anti-Semitism that was issued in 1988 and continues to define the group's nature and goals.

Hamas' use of the *Protocols* and belief in their validity is explicit. "Today it is Palestine, tomorrow it will be one country or another," reads Article Thirty-Two of the Charter. "The Zionist plan is limitless. After Palestine, the Zionists aspire to expand from the Nile to the Euphrates. When they will have digested the region they overtook [an animal metaphor consistent with the derogatory and dehumanizing way in which Jews are spoken about throughout this document and in other Hamas-endorsed frameworks] they will aspire to further expansion, and so on.

Their plan is embodied in The Protocols of the Elders of Zion, and their present conduct is the best proof of what we are saying." Similarly, in Article Twenty-Eight, the Charter speaks of the "Zionist invasion" as "a vicious invasion" which "does not refrain from resorting to all methods, using all evil in contemptible ways to achieve its end. It relies greatly in its infiltration and espionage operations on the secret organizations it gave rise to...and other sabotage groups. All these organizations, whether secret or open, work in the interest of Zionism and according to its instructions. They aim at undermining societies, destroying values, corrupting consciences, deteriorating character and annihilating Islam."

In this rendering of classic anti-Semitism in new garb, the word "Zionist" often replaces the word "Jew," as it already did in the title of the Protocols though that book was written when the Zionist movement was in its infancy and well before the establishment of the state of Israel. When Article 30 of the Charter talks about "the ferocity of the Zionist offensive and the Zionist influence in many countries exercised through financial and media control," we are hearing the language of the new anti-Semitism full-blown.

It is not only Hamas writing for its own followers and would-be followers who speaks this way today. Addressing the United Nations General Assembly on September 23, 2009, Mahmoud Ahmadinejad, the President of the Islamic Republic of Iran, referred to "barbaric attacks by the Zionist regime" on the Palestinians and, saying in that august setting the sort of thing he has said elsewhere as well, went on to proclaim, "It is no longer acceptable that a small minority would dominate the politics, economy and culture of major parts of the world by its complicated networks, and establish a new form of slavery, and harm the reputation of other nations, even European nations and the U.S., to attain its racist ambitions."

Ahmadinejad is often regarded as a crackpot, as a figure from another century if not from another world. But the kinds of ideas that he and his Hamas counterparts convey is becoming more and more common in the mainstream. This is so not only in England and Europe, where we have come to expect it, but in the U.S. as well. For one thing, that is especially true for Internet postings, where writers can give rein to unfiltered vituperation. And so, for example, John Petras, a former professor of sociology at Binghamton University, can write in an Internet newsletter called Dissident Voice that "[Elena] Kagan's ties to the staunchly Zionist faculty at both Chicago and Harvard Law Schools...account for her meteoric promotions to tenure, deanship and now the U.S. Supreme Court."

And he can go on to link those advances to her "ethnic connections" and can conclude that "another active pro-Zionist advocate on the Court will provide a legal cover for the advance of Zionist-dictated authoritarianism over the American people."

Even respected academics working through mainstream publications are joining the chorus in their way these days. In what began as a long article published in the *London Review of Books* in 2006, then turned into a book titled *The Israel Lobby and U.S. Foreign Policy* that was published in 2007 in the U.S., University of Chicago professor John Mearsheimer and Harvard professor Stephen Walt talked about their subject in more veiled language that, though they repeatedly deny meaning it to be heard that way, still sounds an awful lot like the way Jews and Zionists are portrayed by Hamas, Ahmadinejad, and the legion of other echoers of the concepts crystallized by the Protocols. Reduced to its essence, in the Mearsheimer/Walt construction, the supporters of Israel come together to exert an influence powerful enough to lead the United States to ignore its own interests in the Middle East and the world, and instead to be driven by what the lobby sees as in Israel's interest.

Mearsheimer and Walt may assert that they do not believe there is a Jewish cabal or conspiracy, and that in their minds the Israel lobby is like any other interest group or ethnic lobby. Still, for them the members of the so-called Israel lobby "are in an unusually favorable position to influence foreign policy" while "what sets [that lobby] apart is its extraordinary effectiveness." And in fact, throughout their book Israel's supporters are portrayed as constituting a powerful force undermining America's well being, with the members of that lobby skillful enough to cover up their behind-the-scenes subterfuge from others. The Hamas Charter calls it "sabotage." Mearsheimer and Walt may not overtly use the term in their text, but through their subtext they certainly convey a similar idea.

Since gaining widespread notice thanks to the book, Mearsheimer has continued to advance its themes, sometimes more bluntly. "In short," he said in a speech at the Palestine Center in Washington this past April, "President Obama is no match for the lobby." In an even more recent post on his blog, he proclaimed that "the lobby believes it can finesse any issue….America's interests and Israel's interests are going to continue to diverge. An end result of that…is that the lobby is going to have to work overtime to cover that up."

In that same post, Mearsheimer proclaimed that "The Israelis can do almost anything and get away with it….If I went to the Middle East, visited Israel, and I was killed, somebody shot me, do you think there would be any accountability? Seriously." Surely the venom verging on paranoia with which this notable professor now talks about Israel and its supporters has entered some very off-the-wall but familiar terrain.

In his April speech at the Palestine Center, Mearsheimer talked about what he described as the inevitability of Israel's becoming an apartheid state, entering into territory widely occupied today by those who have discovered that the term is an especially useful slur. In so doing, he himself engaged in a couple of revealing maneuvers. First, he switched from talking about Israel and apartheid in the future subjunctive, as though that linkage is only a hypothetical possibility, to doing so in the present tense, using a grammatical double move to make it sound like Israel has already become an apartheid state while leaving himself room to deny having said that. Secondly, he demonstrated how scornfully he regards Israel's mainstream supporters by using name-calling derived from South African history. Thus, after listing what he calls "righteous Jews" (including people who are prepared to sharply attack Israel and, in some cases, question its right to exist), he said, "On the other side we have the new Afrikaners who will support Israel even if it is an apartheid state." The people on the latter list, it should be noted, are not only personalities who might fairly be placed toward the right-wing of the political spectrum, but also others who objectively would not be regarded as having that political profile – including what he calls "individuals who head the Israel lobby's major organizations." Here it is worth citing Anthony Julius' observation that "the master trope, that there are 'good Jews' and 'bad Jews,' has been continuous in the political culture for at least the last hundred years. It... is itself an anti-Semitic construction."

The evocation of apartheid of course conjures up the racist regime of South Africa, which ultimately was overthrown. Numerous scholars have pointed to the differences between contemporary Israel and that regime, but despite that, references to the practice of apartheid and use of the word itself have become increasingly common as a way to malign Israel and, ultimately, deny its legitimacy. Such usage is one of the central ways that Israel and its supporters are linguistically tarred and feathered today, in an age in which racism is the prototypical sin and apartheid-era South Africa the model of a regime that did not deserve to exist.

Expressions of Israel-connected anti-Semitism keep turning up these days, even – or perhaps one might say particularly – in the words of celebrities who get widespread attention in our culture. Thus when a rabbi cum camera-toting YouTube reporter asked the aging but still active Helen Thomas, a respected journalist despite her cantankerous style, for a comment on Israel, she replied by saying: "Tell them to get the hell out of Palestine" and "go home" to "Poland, Germany, America and everywhere else." As commentators such as Jeffrey Goldberg and Shelby Steele have observed, this comment reveals both a denial of Israel's right to exist as a Jewish state and insensitivity to, if not blatant ignorance of, the realities of the Holocaust and its effects. Coincidentally enough, within a week or so of the Thomas incident, a Jewish dance group ironically named "Chaverim" was stoned while attempting to perform in the German city of Hanover when attacking youths, reportedly young Muslims themselves obviously well in touch with the language of the historic anti-Semitism of that landscape, shouted "Juden raus."

Even more recently, in another verbal outpouring that the perpetrator later said he regretted, the American film writer and director Oliver Stone told *The Sunday Times* in the U.K. that though "Hitler did far more damage to the Russians than the Jewish people," there is a greater focus on the Holocaust than on Russian suffering because of "the Jewish domination of the media." "There's a major lobby in the United States," Stone added in the Mearsheimer and Walt vein: "They are hard workers. They stay on top of every comment, the most powerful lobby in Washington. Israel has f***** up U.S. foreign policy for years." Whatever pro forma retraction Stone may have offered – and in what he said afterwards he really did not totally exonerate himself from the implications of all that he had been quoted as saying in the interview – his readiness to come out with such comments suggests the extent to which these attitudes and the kind of language used to convey them seem to be "out there" these days, beneath the surface if not always explicitly rendered.

The fact that both the Thomas and the Stone comments were connected with the Holocaust is not an incidental matter. Increasingly, the Holocaust context has become a dominating component of the new anti-Semitism. That can be seen in a number of frameworks, but the linguistic trope I wish to focus on here has to do with the way in which the Nazi war against the Jews, surely one of the most devastating expressions of anti-Semitism in all of Jewish history, as well as one of the most cataclysmic events of the twentieth century, is today itself being used to harm the Jewish people and the nation state that they established in their ancient homeland following World War II.

As Robert Wistrich and others have shown, comparisons of the Israelis and the Nazis could be seen as a theme in the Soviet Union, particularly following the Six Day War in 1967, and then in the Arab world as well. In the Soviet Union there was a certain appropriateness to the propaganda technique, since the Russians had been besieged and in their ways indeed victimized by the Nazis. And if you wanted to demonize the Israelis, it made a certain sense to say that the Nazis had been reborn in the Israelis' skins. For the Arabs, however, the approach was ironic, since key leadership of theirs had sympathized with the Nazis during the war and since some of their countries had provided refuge for Nazi war criminals. All the same, the equation caught on, and cartoons and other forms of propaganda promoting it were then reiterated and expanded at the time of Israel's invasion of Lebanon in 1982 and subsequently.

Still, it has pretty much been since the 1990s, following the collapse of the Soviet Union, and especially during the past decade, that the Israel/Nazi analogy has become a major motif in the West as well as in the Islamic world. It is now a leading weapon in the propaganda assault against Israel directed by activist Palestinians and other Muslims who have made their way to the West and by radical left-wing individuals and groups. With Nazism widely recognized as the most profound manifestation of evil in modern times, the painting of Zionism as Nazism reborn and Israel as the new Nazi Germany is an attempt to transfer the substance of that evil.

And so it is that, were you to have witnessed anti-Israel rallies in the streets not just of European metropolises but North American cities as well subsequent to Israel's military advance into Gaza in late December and early January 2008-2009, or following the recent episode involving the Turkish flotilla, you would have seen demonstrators waving the flags of Hamas and Hezbollah while holding signs bearing images equating the swastika and the Star of David and calling Gaza the new Warsaw Ghetto, labeling Israeli soldiers the new storm troopers, and accusing Israel of Nazi-like genocide. Dominating the rhetoric of these rallies, such signage — along with other signs and the chanting and speeches of the rallies —conveyed not sympathy for the Palestinians as much as hatred for Israel and its supporters. And meanwhile, this trope too has made its way into the mainstream — again often in the hands of a cartoonist like Pat Oliphant, who at the time of Operation Cast Lead, drew an image of a headless, brutal storm trooper to characterize Israel's behavior in Gaza.

In using swastikas and images of storm troopers to portray Israel and its supporters, Israel's enemies have appropriated motifs with a power that Hitler exploited in his time. It is the power of a stark twisted cross; the power of cruel Hitler-saluting soldiers in black boots, with which the power of the magnetizing madman Hitler himself is associated. Through the years neo-Nazis and other adversaries of the Jewish people have used the swastika to hurt individual Jews, painting swastikas on Jewish institutions, for example, as a form of anti-Semitic expression. Now, however, the swastika is used not just *against* Jews but, when attached to the State of Israel, to *portray* Jews. It is not just a vehicle for inflicting pain on Jews by trying to create the impression that their worst tormentors have returned, but a way to insultingly accuse them of having become those tormentors themselves.

In the new equation, not only have the Jews become the Nazis, but they have been replaced by new Jews, by new victims, namely the Palestinians, who are regarded as the true heirs to the Promised Land. Seen this way, the Nazi-Israel analogy is a contemporary equivalent of the replacement theology which drove Christian anti-Semitism for centuries, and thus can be likened to other current expressions of supersessionism.

The equation also creates a particular form of literal Holocaust revisionism, it can be suggested – that is, a way to lead the world to revise its thoughts and feelings about the Holocaust. For as this realignment of roles goes on, the Holocaust ceases to be regarded as the historic event it was, with facts and details to be learned about. It rather becomes a repository of images, of symbols of innocence and evil to be evoked and applied in whatever way one chooses to suit one's ideological purposes, however twisted that may be. It becomes, in sum, a toolbox full of icons to be taken out and assigned while the reality of the Holocaust, if not actively denied, melts away into a post-modern penumbra.

Traditional anti-Semitism demonized and scapegoated individual Jews and the Jewish people, regarding them as the evil "other" responsible for the ills of society and the world. The new anti-Semitism uses language that treats Israel and its supporters in similar ways. Whereas in earlier eras anti-Semitism, with its personal approach, caused Jews to be discriminated against, expelled from one country after another, and ultimately annihilated throughout most of Europe, it is the Jewish national state that today's anti-Semitism, serving a geopolitical agenda, would have treated as a pariah and ultimately eliminated. This goal is bluntly declared not only by the likes of Ahmadinejad and Hamas but in our own cities, for example by graffiti artists who, in this case abjuring the ubiquitous swastika, paint "Death to Israel" on synagogues they have vandalized. And a similar message is less directly stated but still implied by individuals and groups closer to the mainstream.

"In our time, political speech and writing are largely the defense of the indefensible," wrote George Orwell in his classic essay "Politics and the English Language" in 1946. The eras and contexts may have their differences, but Orwell's insights apply as well to the use of language I have been talking about, especially his observation that "if thought corrupts language, language can also corrupt thought." Like that before it, the language of today's anti-Semitism depends upon distortions of the truth to fulfill its purpose, a "hijacking of meaning" as Bernard-Henry Lévy called it when commenting on the post-flotilla demonizations of Israel. Some of those who call Israel an apartheid state or who equate Israel with Nazi Germany must realize that there are differences, and they can be said to be cynically corrupting language to promote such likenesses and to get others to believe them. But there are also people who truly believe even the extremist, delusional concepts about Israel and its supporters that they proclaim. Haunted by their obsessions, hatreds and intentions, they have allowed themselves to be separated from reality.

While the discourse of anti-Semitism is always drenched in corruptions of the truth and those who use and believe those corruptions are always separated from reality to some extent, there is something particularly troubling about the ways that the kinds of views circulating today are not only held by people clearly beyond the fringe but are also finding some degree of acceptance in the academy and elsewhere in the mainstream. That process is facilitated when mainstream figures who explicitly or implicitly use the language of the new anti-Semitism deny such intent and even dismiss the very existence of this new anti-Semitism, insisting that they and others like them are only criticizing Israel the way one can legitimately criticize any country.

The pattern is common. We have already seen it in the words of the spokesman of the public prosecutor's office in Cologne. Another example is provided by Mearsheimer and Walt, who devote a whole section of their book to advancing the misleading charge that "pro-Israel groups now claim there is a 'new anti-Semitism,' which they equate with criticism of Israel." Mearsheimer and Walt's insistent, repetitive use of the word "criticism" in this section as a description of what is being objected to becomes a stylistic tic, but that still doesn't make it accurate.

The reason they say this happens is because, they charge, Israel's supporters want to "silence" the country's critics. And they further advance their argument by turning other people's charges about the use of *concepts* into name-calling about *personalities* who *use* those concepts, deliberately conflating the two by saying, for example, "Anyone who criticizes Israeli actions or says that pro-Israel groups have significant influence over U.S. Middle East policy stands a good chance of being labeled an anti-Semite." While this labeling admittedly happens sometimes, it is not nearly as common as is implied by these authors and by others who would prevent readers from taking unfair attacks on Israel or expressions of the new anti-Semitism seriously. (After the recent flotilla incident, to give but one more example of this pattern, the cartoonist Oliphant drew a pirate with a Star of David on his head-covering climbing on board ship with sword in hand saying, "If you don't like piracy on the high seas, you're anti-Semitic.")

On the one hand, rejection of the existence of anti-Semitic meaning in statements partaking of the new anti-Semitism can be seen as a pre-emptive tactic which reveals an acknowledgment that, however much the taboo against anti-Semitism may have eroded in recent years, the charge still carries weight. On the other hand, though, attempts to obfuscate the difference between fair criticism of Israel and hate-filled rhetoric (a distinction Israel's supporters need to keep in mind too) leads to further corruption of language. Moreover, this new approach can be seen as problematic and even hostile in its own fashion.

In a way, active denial of the existence of the new anti-Semitism can be related to Holocaust denial. In the minds of those who embrace these positions, the twentieth century's Nazi-driven scapegoating and victimization of Jews and the early twenty-first century's demonization of Israel and its supporters are both considered myths made up by the Jews. For the Holocaust deniers, the first myth was created to evoke sympathy for the Jews and to elicit support for the establishment of Israel. (This is a leitmotif for Ahmadinejad, and the notion was rendered in shorthand by graffiti spray-painted in Rome last January that said "The Holocaust equals Zionist propaganda.") In the eyes of those who object to the claims that there is a new anti-Semitism, it too is a fiction, in this case created to block criticism of Israel and thus to maintain support for that country. Furthermore, in both cases there is an underlying belief that the ability of the Jews to get the world — at least the West — to buy into these fictions is proof of their skill in controlling others and thus of their nefarious, conspiratorial powers.

In fact, the world today truly is witness to the emergence of a new form of anti-Semitism, one that is no less potent than that of earlier eras. It is conveyed through language and images that are at once traditional in their substance and contemporary in their modes of expression. But experience reveals that for the man on the street, for the media, for officials in national governments and local jurisdictions, and for university administrators, there has been a serious deficiency in identifying and addressing this new form of hate.

The shift in the specific nature of the target apparently makes it difficult for people of goodwill who hold preconceptions based on the situation in earlier times and are thus programmed to recognize only the classic forms of anti-Semitism to understand immediately what is happening today, especially when those who circulate the new anti-Semitism do not want it to be acknowledged. But it is incumbent upon those who do realize what is going on, what it means, and what is at stake to speak out and to properly identify the danger that is out there. It is not just Israel's security and the safety of the Jewish people, but reality, justice, and just plain common decency that demand no less.

The State of Anti-Semitism:
Yom Kippur Musings

The Times of Israel, October 3, 2012

• • •

While sitting in my synagogue in a Chicago suburb this Yom Kippur, my thoughts turned to another synagogue, in Malmo, Sweden, where I had been a bit over a year before.

My wife and I had stopped in Malmo for a day and a half while visiting Scandinavia during a trip that had started in Israel, well aware of the reputation the city had gained as a center of anti-Israel and anti-Semitic activity. Seeing the designation of a synagogue on a street map, we walked over there from our hotel first thing in the morning, and when we got there we were greatly impressed by the beauty of the structure. At the same time, we couldn't help noting the total absence of any external signs or symbols designating it as a Jewish house of worship, save for the Star of David noticeable at the top — if you craned your neck and looked there.

Knocking on all of the building's unmarked doors, we were unable to gain entrance until a member of the local community – who engaged with us only when it became clear that we could converse with him in Hebrew – came for morning prayers. (When my wife asked him if there was a minyan, he said "I am it.") When, alluding to the prevailing hostile conditions in Malmo, I suggested that it must be rough for the community there, his quick reply was to the effect that "It's unsafe to walk around wearing a kippah in Brooklyn too." This statement, which conveyed a fatalistic acceptance of what he regarded as the universality of anti-Semitism in today's world, was revealing in what it said both about his limited understanding of Jewish life in the United States and about the reality of Jewish life in Malmo.

I have recollected that encounter a number of times since then. But it was acutely on my mind this Yom Kippur, when I thought of reports of recent incidents in several cities in Europe where public kippah-wearing and Jewish life in general have proven dangerous, and I contrasted that with the far more secure circumstances in which, contrary to the impression held by our new friend in Malmo, I and my fellow American Jews find ourselves.

Admittedly, my own synagogue had taken security measures on Yom Kippur, made necessary by the recurring targeting of Jews in to-day's world. But the American Jewish community, far larger than that in Europe and living comfortably with its non-Jewish neighbors while protected from violence by local civic authorities, enjoys far less threatening circumstances than those faced by our Jewish brethren in Europe, particularly those in the orbit of hostile neighbors. Then again, though, my synagogue musings continued, there certainly is no room for complacency, even for Jews living in the U.S.

With the incendiary, false charge that an "Israeli Jew" with Jewish funders had been behind the anti-Muslim video recently circulated around the globe having been so easily accepted, it is clear that a readiness to buy into anti-Jewish stereotypes has not gone away even in America. Indeed, on a popular television talk show, Zbigniew Brzezinski, a person of stature, was still picking up on the charge as a fact without correction the morning after it had been debunked in the American press. And as Yom Kippur was being observed throughout America, at the United Nations in New York, the country's largest city, there stood the Iranian president, perhaps the world's best-known bigot, at the podium of the world's most significant stage.

Actually, this year Ahmadinejad was more subdued than he had been at that location on earlier occasions – not to mention while on his home turf. But this time around, while preaching about the decline of the West and prophesying the return of the Mahdi, he still found the opportunity to echo the anti-Semitic conspiracy premise of *The Protocols of the Elders of Zion,* condemning "the hegemonic policies and actions of world Zionism." And in talking about today's headline issue, he described what he called the "continued threat by the uncivilized Zionists to resort to military action against our great nation."

Given Ahmadinejad's well-known record for verbal threats against Israel's existence, blatant anti-Semitic invective, and gross Holocaust denial, he of course needn't say a word to be recognized as the virtual incarnation of today's anti-Semitism. And in other appearances during his visit to America, he made sure to enunciate the preposterous and inflammatory claim that the people of Israel "have no roots there in history."

Ahmadinejad is hardly the only Iranian leader who has brought traditional anti-Semitic tropes into widespread circulation these days. And more than that, the threat from his country is hardly only verbal, with the Iranian nuclear project and Iranian belligerence posing a very real physical danger to Israel, the Jewish people, the Middle East, and American interests. These are uncertain and difficult times for the Jewish state and the Jewish people wherever they may live. With the solemnity of Yom Kippur setting the tone, the prevailing realities for Jews were surely sobering on this year's Day of Judgment.

And yet, I thought the day after Yom Kippur, there is also basis for affirming a more hopeful perspective. As the JTA News Service reported the day before Yom Kippur, there were signs that a corner may have been turned in Sweden, at least partly, countering both the ongoing anti-Semitism and the fatalistic acceptance of it I had witnessed there. In early September, JTA reported, some 1,500 people rallied in support of Israel in Stockholm and Gothenburg. Still earlier, Jews in Malmo had begun ignoring security protocol as they asserted their dignity and pride as Jews by wearing kippot on the streets. And on the Sunday before Yom Kippur, about 70 Danish Jews crossed the Strait of Øresund in a bus that traveled from Copenhagen to Malmo to show their solidarity with the community there, with the men deliberately wearing kippot.

Then, a bit over 24 hours after the end of Yom Kippur, a device was exploded at a Malmo Jewish community center, making clear that the issues there have hardly been overcome. But at least they have been engaged.

And meanwhile, during the Ahmadinejad days in New York, an activist organization called United Against a Nuclear Iran took up residence in the hotel where he stayed and organized a rally across from the UN that took place as he spoke there, not letting his visit go unprotested. And maybe, just maybe, the message that Iran will not be allowed to go nuclear is at last gaining serious, broad traction and is even being heard in Tehran.

Defending Israel in the Community, in the Media, and on Campus

As a number of pieces in other sections of this volume demonstrate, my portfolio at the Federation has included advancing understanding and support for Israel from the beginning. In September 1993, at the time of the announcement of the Oslo Accords, meant to end the Israel-Palestinian conflict, I was interviewed by *The New York Times*. Speaking of the PLO's longtime dedication to the destruction of Israel, I said that "the deep hope is that that's changed. But the risk is that the change isn't all that deep or all that permanent." Following the collapse of Oslo in September 2000, the possibility of a two-state solution was adamantly rejected by many Palestinian advocates and their supporters and the verbal attacks on Israel became harsher and more common in the mainstream. At the same time, the challenge of defending Israel grew while my activities and those of others in the community in that arena were intensified.

Mobilized Palestinian and Muslim groups began taking to the streets at the time to demonstrate against Israel, in some cases with the support of individuals asserting a Jewish identity. Denials of Israel's right to exist became more blatant. The Palestinian narrative at times was buttressed by media coverage of the conflict. Church groups became increasingly sympathetic to the Palestinian cause. Activist student groups and faculty members began making many university campuses centers of anti-Israel delegitimization activity. And the possibility of an Iranian nuclear threat added another layer of danger and complexity.

With all of this happening, the need for a sophisticated, effective defense of Israel on the American scene became all the more important, and has remained so. That is especially the case because support for Israel in America – in Congress, among government leaders, and in the realm of public opinion – is so essential for Israel's well-being. The pieces in this section track the way this issue has evolved during the current century, often with a Chicago focus given the activity that has transpired locally and the presence of several national players who are based here.

NOTE: In a number of these pieces, including the final ones, which come from early 2014, I reference the boycott, divestment, and sanctions activities that have come to play a central role in the global anti-Israel campaign. Much of that activity has been directed by the Boycott, Divestment, and Sanctions Movement, which likes to use the acronym "BDS," a label others have picked up. It is a phrase that I try to avoid, and I often urge others to do so as well. Boycotts, divestment, and sanctions are not ends in themselves, but means to an end – that end being the delegitimization of Israel and ultimately its destruction. The letters BDS are an abstraction which masks that goal, and I strongly believe that it behooves all of us who oppose the tactics and purpose of this assault on Israel's legitimacy to use language that makes clear what this movement's end game really is all about: the elimination of Israel as the nation-state of the Jewish people.

Orwellian Reading of the Middle East Conflict

Chicago Tribune, November 3, 2000

• • •

As the Israel-Palestinian conflict has taken a new turn, Israel and its friends have found themselves in an Orwellian universe in which distortions of the facts are presented as the truth. This goes hand in hand with the Palestinians' attempt to gain through violence and appeals to public opinion what they could not achieve through other means.

The riots and attacks on Israeli positions carried out not only by throwers of stones and Molotov cocktails but also by the illegal Yasser Arafat-linked militia known as the Tanzim and armed Palestinian "police," are called mere "protests" or "demonstrations." The regrettable Palestinian casualties, often suffered by youths who are cynically sacrificed on the altar of the Palestinian cause, are used to gain sympathy from the West and to further incite Palestinians.

In a recent visit to Israel, I and other Jewish community representatives were briefed on the Israeli policy of responding only when civilians or soldiers have been attacked or put in danger. This is a tricky policy to follow in a part of the world where restraint can be misinterpreted as a sign of weakness. Witness Israel's withdrawal from Lebanon, which some analysts have seen as emboldening Palestinians. All the same, it is the way the Israelis have operated and it hasn't saved them from being criticized for "overreacting."

Our group visited the Jerusalem neighborhood of Gilo 24 hours after gunmen, firing from an adjacent village under the control of the Palestinian Authority, had critically wounded an Israeli border policeman and left bullet holes in apartments on a quiet civilian street. Though Israeli tanks were in place between the neighborhood and the village and could easily have been used to take out the building from which the shots were fired, that was not done — because, we were told, others beyond the perpetrators would have been endangered. The chances of building a future in which the residents of the village and their neighbors could live together in peace would be jeopardized.

Since we were there, heavier fire has repeatedly been directed against the residential areas in Gilo. Israel, only after seeing this escalation of the attack on its civilians and after issuing a warning so that civilians in the Palestinian village could avoid harm, has begun to use greater force. The behavior of the Israel Defense Forces throughout the current conflict in no way justifies Arafat's reference at the recent Arab League summit to Israel's so-called "mass killing and barbarian bombing." Nor does it justify the votes of a string of countries which, following the Palestinians' bidding, have lined up at the United Nations to pass one-sided inaccurate resolutions about Israel's so-called "excessive use of force."

One listens in vain for meaningful UN condemnation of the way that Hezbollah, the Iran-linked militant Islamic group in southern Lebanon, has threatened to spread the conflict there by crossing the UN-validated border and abducting three Israeli soldiers. In Israel, our group met with the father of one of those soldiers, who identified himself as a long-time activist in Israel's peace movement and who pleaded with us to do what we could to ensure the safe return of his son and his comrades. One also listens in vain for the UN's condemnation of the lynching of Israel reservists who mistakenly ended up at a Palestinian checkpoint outside of Ramallah and thought they were safely under the protection of Palestinian Authority police.

The current crisis intensified after claims were made that a Muslim holy place on Jerusalem's Temple Mount was "defiled" by a visit there by Ariel Sharon, leader of the opposition in Israel's Knesset. The fact is the Al Aqsa mosque was untouched whereas a Jewish site in Nablus was destroyed by Palestinians. A 5th-Century Jewish synagogue in Jericho also was destroyed.

Palestinian casualties sadly mount while Palestinian spokesmen claim that what they want is a state of their own. But that is something which the Israeli government has already offered them. They say they want a shared Jerusalem, but that is something which Israel's Prime Minister Ehud Barak has offered as well. The conclusion becomes inescapable that, paradoxically, it was precisely because Israel was so forthcoming in the July peace negotiations at Camp David that Yasser Arafat, who was unwilling to meet Barak's concessions with concessions of his own, turned to violence.

With the moderate Arab states leading the way at the recent summit, most of the Arab world was unwilling to join in an all-out war. Arafat and his followers are left following a more limited – but dangerous – strategy, doing anything they can to gain sympathy and support and to make Israel look like the aggressive opponent of a fair resolution of the conflict. They are striving to replace a negotiating process with a set-up through which other world bodies attempt to pressure Israel to surrender to Palestinian demands that would put Israel's security in jeopardy.

A lieutenant of Arafat's, who has spearheaded the disorders in the West Bank, is quoted as saying he is leading a "peaceful Intifada." In truth, he and his comrades are using the methods of war. And as they do so they threaten Israeli security, Middle Eastern stability and American interests in the region.

Arab Leaders Must Abandon Pipe Dreams
Chicago Sun-Times, January 9, 2001

• • •

As I follow the latest developments in the Middle East, my thoughts go back to a day in 1974 when the effects of the Yom Kippur war of the previous October were still being sorted out. I was living in Israel and teaching at Tel Aviv University, and on the day in question I happened to be in Gaza City. When a local resident asked me where I was from and I said America, his face lit up and he began gesticulating. "America!" he said. "Kissinger! He will fly in. We will return to Ashkelon."

Listening to him, I experienced an epiphany, one of those rare moments when a core truth flashes before you. The conflict between Israel and its neighbors, it occurred to me, would never be resolved so long as Israel's adversaries not only attacked Israel but continued to look to an outside force to intervene to Israel's detriment and continued to believe that the Palestinians who had become refugees in Israel's War of Independence in 1948 would return to their families' former homes.

Despite setbacks since the Oslo Accords were signed in 1993, the Camp David talks of last summer seemed to offer the prospect that a resolution of the Israeli-Palestinian conflict might at last be at hand. Instead, Yasser Arafat walked away from those talks and, violating the most basic of the Oslo agreements, the Palestinians turned to violence. And now the Palestinian leadership appears to be driven by the same vain and counterproductive expectations that were expressed to me by the man in Gaza, and peace seems as elusive as ever.

Though the refugee question has been on the agenda from the beginning of the Oslo process, the Palestinians' insistence on a "right of return" became a central issue after President Clinton raised his latest proposals.

Anyone acquainted with the impact of this on Israel would have to be aware of two basic realities. The first is that Israel, a small country, would be committing national suicide by allowing a large-scale return. The second is that virtually no Israelis — no matter how far to the left, no matter how sympathetic to the plight of the refugees — will go along with that. And yet look what has happened.

The generation of that man in Gaza has been followed by another, and still another. Unlike the many groups that became refugees through the upheavals of the 20th century, and unlike what happened with an equal number of Jews living in Arab lands who ended up in Israel after the events of 1948, the bulk of the Palestinian refugees were not resettled. Reportedly denied even the benefits of funds provided to the Palestinian Authority after Oslo, frustrated refugees in Gaza, like those elsewhere, have been kept in squalid camps and inculcated with an intense hatred of Israel while being led to continue to believe that they will eventually be able to return to their families' former homes.

Instead of bringing peace closer by enabling their followers to come to grips with reality, Palestinian leaders through the decades have imbued them with futile dreams. The sincerity of those leaders' announced readiness to accept a solution whereby Israelis and Palestinians will live side by side in separate states is called into question by their insistence that the refugees, rather than becoming citizens of the new Palestinian state, should be allowed to flood into Israel.

Suddenly the refugees and their ambitions are everywhere — even on the cover of the journal of the Chicago-based American Bar Association. In December, the journal erroneously proclaimed that "international law is on their side," then in January it said that that is only what the refugees say. Meeting in Cairo, Arab foreign ministers upped the ante by talking about a "sacred" right of return. It will be hard enough for both sides to resolve their differences over what really is sacred, namely Jerusalem, without having every dimension of the conflict being given that status.

It is as clear to me now as it was on that day in Gaza 27 years ago that so long as the Arabs look for an outside power to force Israel to concede to illegitimate, destructive demands, and so long as the Palestinian refugees are encouraged to believe that they will return to their former homes en masse, the Israel-Arab conflict will remain unresolved. Sadly, at the moment, those lessons still seem unlearned by Arafat and the Palestinian leadership.

Covering the Coverage: Israel, the Media, and the Jewish Community

Remarks presented to American Jewish Press Association meeting, Chicago,
July 2, 2002,
on panel with Kevin Klose, President and CEO of NPR

• • •

I.

The Jewish community's reaction to media coverage of the Israel-Palestinian conflict has itself become a hot topic. Articles on the subject have appeared in JTA's *Daily News Bulletin, The Forward, Ha'aretz,* and *The Jerusalem Post,* and in such big city dailies as the *San Francisco Chronicle,* the *Los Angeles Times, The Washington Post, The New York Times,* the *Chicago Tribune,* and *The Boston Globe.*

As all of those stories report, the Jewish community has demonstrated deep concern about media treatment of Israel. In a way, it should be no surprise that the community is reacting in such a way. Since late September 2000, and even more so since March 2002, Palestinian terrorism directed at Israeli civilians has escalated, joined by a propaganda offensive aimed at enlisting international support for the Palestinians. Much of Europe and the rest of the world have fallen into place, criticizing and isolating Israel. Meanwhile, post-9/11 realities have made clear that the hatred and hostility of militant Islam is directed against America and Jews alike, with a global "new anti-Semitism" linked to anti-Israel attitudes rejecting the legitimacy of the Jewish state and giving new life to traditional forms of anti-Semitic rhetoric and behavior.

American Jews sense how much is at stake for Israel and the Jewish people. They recognize the importance of the media in impacting on public opinion and through it on the formulation of public policy, and they know that Israel's enemies would like the world's media to advance the anti-Israel cause. Meanwhile, like anybody else who has looked closely at the media, they see certain flaws and limitations in the way that it does its job of covering the news, and they occasionally see an unwelcome thrust on certain opinion pages or from electronic media talk-show hosts.

Given the nature of the visual images from the scene; the nuances of the language used to report on developments; the complexities of the issues; the tendency to avoid delving into those complexities and to eschew providing contextual background; and the limited background and understanding of some of the reporters who cover the story, it is no wonder that there should be concerns. Furthermore, through e-mail, members of the Jewish community can be plugged in to media watchdog groups and get forwarded messages from friends who point their fingers at the worst of what is being written, said, and shown around the world. And some of it, especially in the sharply hostile British and European media, can be very bad indeed.

In this overall framework, the Jewish community has responded to coverage of the conflict in various ways. Mainstream organizations by and large have maintained measured outreach and temperate exchanges with the media. At the same time, some groups and numbers of individuals have adopted a more aggressive and confrontational approach, sometimes reaching to demonstrations and boycotts.

In responding to all of this, the media have at times openly examined themselves, occasionally admitting mistakes. Increasingly, though, they have reacted by portraying all of the critics as emotionally driven members of a special interest group who do not recognize the nature of the media and who uniformly and unfairly charge all media outlets with bias and even with anti-Semitism.

"From Jewish Outlook, Media Are Another Enemy," announces the *L.A. Times.* "Caught in the Crossfire" proclaims the headline of a recent story on the subject in *The Washington Post.* "Pro-Israel groups take aim at U.S. News media" says the *Chicago Tribune.* Encapsulating much of this in a column in *The New York Times,* Frank Rich talked about what he called a relatively "widespread...conviction that the American press is engaged in a conspiracy to spread Palestinian propaganda and insidiously counter Israel interests."

This media perspective is itself off the mark, I believe, and it reduces the likelihood that those problems that continue to fester will be properly addressed. To illustrate the way the situation plays out in one city, I would like to consider the way a community organization like the Federation relates to the local media in its coverage of Israel, with the *Chicago Tribune* taken as a case in point.

II.

One of the largest circulation papers in the country, the *Tribune* is an influential force on the Chicago scene, and it is the local media outlet most likely to be regarded as problematic by members of Chicago's Jewish community.

For some time before the breakdown of the peace process a year and a half ago, the *Tribune* maintained an editorial stance that was often more critical of Israel and supportive of the Palestinians than was the case in most other American papers. Continuing in that vein, in its first editorial after the Palestinians turned to violence in September 2000, the *Tribune* attached primary blame to Israel and portrayed the Palestinians as the main victims of aggression. That editorial and the one that followed it baselessly implied that Ariel Sharon, then leader of the opposition, had deliberately provoked the violence.

When Sharon was voted in as prime minister, the *Tribune,* rather than acknowledging that the Israelis were responding to half a year of escalating violence which threatened their safety, mocked the maturity and political motivations of the Israeli electorate by asserting that "most Israelis appear ready to throw a national tantrum and depose Israel Prime Minister Ehud Barak." Though the *Tribune* repeatedly complimented Barak for his stance at Camp David, it also echoed the Palestinian perspective on the talks there and after, minimizing Israel's readiness to make peace by saying that in negotiations Israel "has insisted on giving Palestinians only half a loaf." While commentators on American Jewry's reaction to media treatment of Israel generally focus on news coverage and give short shrift to the editorial side of things, the impact of opinions and language like this cannot be ignored if justice is to be done to the topic.

As for its coverage, the *Tribune's* frequent stories on the Middle East are usually given prominent placement. At times these stories have a topic or use language that raises concerns. More often it is headlines, photos, and captions which have been regarded as problematic. This is not incidental, since these aspects of coverage — though often the choice of editors unfamiliar with details or complexities of the issues — are likely to have the greatest impact on most readers.

As community concerns about *Tribune* coverage grew early last fall, a story which, especially given its headline and accompanying photo, seemed to romanticize a Palestinian terrorist, was the "last straw" for a group of readers who took to the streets outside of Tribune Tower in protest and called for the cancellation of subscriptions. The Federation itself had long maintained open channels of communication with the *Tribune,* and at that time the paper's foreign editor invited the Federation and its JCRC to bring together representatives of several local communal organizations to hash these issues out with top editorial staff. Then, in December, leadership of the Federation had a separate meeting with those editors to review an academic study commissioned by the Federation some months previous.

The study compared coverage in the *Tribune, The New York Times,* and *The Washington Post* over 30 particular days during the first six months of what it called the "second intifada." It was referred to by the *Tribune's* public editor in one of his weekly columns a couple of months later, after he and other *Tribune* editors had appeared at two synagogue-based community forums. The Federation itself regards the study as an internal document used as the basis for constructive engagement with the *Tribune.* With its objective documentation of specific issues and analysis of apparent trends, in the context of an overall attempt by all three papers to present the news in an unbiased fashion, it provided a useful tool for give and take.

Significantly, by the time Federation leaders and *Tribune* editors had met to discuss the study, the paper's editorials had become more balanced than they had been earlier, showing a greater understanding of Israel's situation and greater readiness to be critical of Palestinian leader Yasser Arafat. This can no doubt be attributed, at least in part, to the fact that terrorism against Israeli civilians had escalated and that the responsibility of Yasser Arafat and other Palestinian leadership for the ongoing violence had become increasingly obvious. This is not to say that the *Tribune's* editorial page has come to replicate that of a consistently strong supporter of Israel like the *Chicago Sun-Times.* But in its sympathetic recognition of "the vulnerability Israelis must feel" and its condemnation of Arafat for having "no answer except more violence," its editorial stance has shifted in a meaningful fashion.

Whatever the reasons, the trend is worthy of note, as is much of the *Tribune's* coverage from Israel itself. The paper was early in reporting that, contrary to Palestinian claims, there was no massacre in Jenin, and it offered a moving description of reactions, one year after the Dolphinarium attack, in the Tel Aviv high school that most of the victims had attended. If for many of its members the community's view of the *Tribune* has not yet caught up to the positive editorial changes and mostly solid reporting, that in part derives from occasional coverage issues revolving around headlines, photos, story choices, and some specific language (such as the story that talked about Gaza as "the heart of Palestinian resistance since 1948," without explaining what that really means). And it especially derives from the impact of several writers whose work regularly appears on the paper's opinion pages.

These writers include Georgie Anne Geyer and Salim Muwakkil. The former, a syndicated columnist who has been on Israel's case for decades, has proclaimed that "every day, Israeli Prime Minister Sharon commits some new horror." After she claimed that Sharon had once announced to his Cabinet, "I control America," *The Wall Street Journal's* web site media watcher James Taranto did a search and concluded that the line "does not appear to have been reported by any legitimate news organization." Two months after the column appeared, an "Editor's Note" in the Tribune attributed that line to the "Palestinian press" and said that Geyer and her syndicator "regret not having attributed the quote more specifically."

Tribune columnist Muwakkil, an editor of the ideologically leftist magazine *In These Times,* likens Israel to South Africa of the apartheid era, and recently wrote, "We're complicit in one of history's most glaring injustices, the denial of Palestinian self-determination." Columnists such as Geyer and Muwakkil can be said to be "balanced" by the likes of the strong-writing Charles Krauthammer. However, most significant in keeping the pot boiling between the community and the Tribune has been the way that the paper's own public editor (and former editorial page editor), Don Wycliff, rather than being a listening post, has made himself a lightning rod in all of this.

With his public editor title prominently attached to it, Wycliff writes a weekly column, usually on whatever topic of the day commands his attention. He often deals with the Israel-Palestinian conflict, using loaded language sharply critical of Israel and sometimes going well beyond the paper's own editorials. "The government of Israel is demanding that the Palestinians allow their homeland to be colonized," he has written, "and that they do it without complaint." In calling for an imposed solution of the conflict, he has asserted that "Jerusalem [all of it, it seems] should simply be placed under control of the commander of [an] international force." He has referred to Israel's prime minister as "the egregious Ariel Sharon, one of the authors of the massacres at Sabra and Shatilla" (language he would later retract). In the same column, he called Arafat merely "ineffectual or devious" while showing a degree of understanding of the Palestinians' attempt to smuggle in arms and of Arafat's lying to President Bush about that. (In contrast, the *Tribune's* earlier editorial on the incident had blasted "Arafat and his minions" for "sabotaging peace.")

In writing such opinionated columns while serving as public editor, Wycliff is inevitably seen by readers as the voice of the paper itself. Even more troubling, in a way, have been those columns in which, as public editor, he has written directly about the paper's treatment of the Middle East.

While acknowledging that members of the Jewish community have conveyed concerns about the *Tribune's* coverage, Wycliff has declared that in his view the paper "has nothing to apologize for" in its Middle East coverage, as though that is what is being asked for. Stepping into one of the central flash points in current discussion of Middle East coverage was his particularly inflammatory March 21 assertion that, in contrast to the usage in its reporting on the 9/11 perpetrators, the paper does not — and should not — regularly use the word "terrorist" when talking about Palestinians who blow themselves up in a deliberate attempt to slaughter as many Israeli civilians as possible. Despite the U.S. government's own specific use of that label, for him that is because the Tribune is an "American" paper written for an "American" audience, and "to faithfully report and interpret the events [in the Middle East] for our American audiences, we must refrain from consistently labeling either party as terrorists, because to do so is, in effect, to declare it illegitimate."

Echoing this sophistry in an interview in the *Forward*, Wycliff said: "We won't call someone a terrorist, simply because today's terrorist sometimes turns out to be tomorrow's statesman," and he called the very word "terrorist" "tendentious" and "propagandistic." In still another column in the *Tribune*, he accounted for what he called the "devastating effect in Jenin" of Israel's military reaction to the Palestinian terrorist brutality that took so many civilian lives in March, by describing Israel as an annoyed "Superman." "The Palestinians yanked his cape with all those suicide bombings," he said, reserving his passion for knocking Israel later in the column.

While experts say that the common role of an ombudsman is to represent a newspaper's readers to it, the way Wycliff fills the role is by provocatively defending the paper against its readers. He often uses his column space not to respectfully address the Jewish community about its concerns but to implicitly belittle them for having such concerns. Thus, as open and responsive as many members of the *Tribune's* staff of editors and correspondents have been to ongoing exchanges, the image offered by the columns of the designated representative for such engagement has been of a very different sort. And the May 26 article about the Jewish community and the press carried by the *Tribune,* echoing those which have appeared in other papers, encapsulated its view of the current situation by positing that "pro-Israel organizations are pressuring news outlets" who "respond that the critics are not seeking even-handed reporting but advocacy on behalf of Israel."

III.

This brings me back to the point I made earlier, observing that a number of media outlets that are themselves coming under scrutiny today are increasingly dismissive of their critics as emotional advocates for one side, who are out of touch with the way the journalistic profession operates, who are unrealistic in their expectations, and who use heavy-handed tactics to advance their goals.

Understandable as it may be, given how much is at stake, some individuals and groups within the Jewish community frankly can indeed be said to get carried away in reacting to media coverage. Infuriating as media coverage can sometimes be, I believe that, in general, the community should try to demonstrate the kind of fairness and understanding about the media that we are demanding of them. And troubled as we may be about positions taken in certain editorials and opinion columns, and important as it is to respond in letters to the editor and otherwise, we can acknowledge that it is legitimate for opinions to be expressed there, so long as the language stays within certain bounds.

There may indeed be a "media war" in progress now, paralleling the battle on the ground. But the media, certainly the media as a whole, and especially the media in our country as opposed to that in England and Europe, are the battleground and not the enemy. An indiscriminate adversary approach to the media is neither justified nor helpful. It is unlikely to be productive in the short or long term, closing channels of communication, leaving the media feeling there is nothing they can do to satisfy this segment of the readership anyhow, so why try, and even creating a hostility from the media side with potential spillover.

That much said, it is important to emphasize that that is not the way the community's major organizations regularly conduct themselves in relationship to the media. In this city, the Federation, for example, is both critical and, when it is merited, complimentary. We are firm in our criticisms but ready to engage in dialogue about our concerns, with the hope that, as we rationally make our points, they will be understood, acknowledged, and acted upon by professionals attempting to do their jobs. In relating to virtually all of Chicago's media outlets, including the *Tribune,* we have found such channels available with journalists on both the news and opinion sides who, though they may not buy in to everything we have to say, have earned our respect both for the way they do their jobs and the way in which they have related to us.

If the entire Jewish community in every major city in the country is now going to be lumped together and defensively dismissed as a hotheaded special interest group, unjustified in its criticism of coverage and not entitled to be unhappy with commentary on the opinion pages with which it has differences, that approach is likely only to escalate tensions and acrimony between the media and a segment of their audience, provoking the emotional responses they purport to disdain. Such behavior sheds little glory on the professionalism of the journalistic enterprise.

The Israel-Palestinian conflict is a complicated one, with profound implications not just for partisans on each side but for the interests of our entire nation and the values it espouses and exemplifies. As the history of this time takes shapes, it is entirely legitimate to wish to see the media portraying unfolding developments in a fashion which brings accurate information and comprehensive understanding to their audience.

There are nuances of language and details of fact that make a difference. There are decisions of what to portray and what not to portray, about what to highlight and what not to highlight, about what to show and what not to show, about whom to interview and whom not to interview. As for the principle of "balance," it is not always achieved just because the two sides in a conflict are automatically treated the same.

In the case of the Middle East conflict, that does not mean that Palestinians have not suffered or that none of their grievances are valid. But something is drastically askew when terrorists and their victims, the aggressor and the side ready to make peace, are treated with moral equivalency; when the repeatedly false and exaggerated charges of one side are given equal credence to the verifiable statements of the other; and when as much time or space is given to describing a handful of counterdemonstrators as a mass of demonstrators.

Mistakes can be made by the media and they can matter, especially if they form patterns. A community that cares deeply about the security of the State of Israel and the well-being of its citizens can be expected to be distressed when it sees what it perceives to be an inaccurate and unfairly critical treatment of Israel. Yes, it is important for members of the Jewish community, particularly for those organizations which speak in its name, to be careful about the language they use in talking about and pointing to what they see as problems in media treatment. But it is at least as important for media outlets to avoid distorting the approaches of their critics and hiding behind global charges of being unfairly maligned. Instead, they need to engage in constructive dialogue, and be prepared to take a serious look at themselves to consider just how they are treating this topic, so that they can be sure they are living up to those values which they themselves espouse, and that they are properly playing the important role they should play in a democratic society.

Israel's Enemies Waging a Verbal Assault

Chicago Sun-Times, October 7, 2002

• • •

When the Iraqi foreign minister took the floor at the United Nations on Sept. 19 to read a statement from Saddam Hussein, it was like a scene from an earlier era, when denial of Israel's very existence was common for Arab countries and their friends at General Assembly sessions. Not once, as was reported the next day, did Saddam's statement use the word "Israel" when referring to that nation. Instead, it insistently spoke only of "the Zionist entity."

Iraq has its own reasons for touting anti-Israel credentials before the Arab and Muslim world these days. But it is not just from Iraq and not just at the UN that the rhetoric of rejectionism has returned.

Even as Israel has for two years been assaulted on the ground by a relentless Palestinian campaign of terror, so, even right here in America, supporters of the Palestinians have been challenging Israel's very right to exist. The language they use in doing so, however, is not always likely to be comprehended that way by the untrained listener.

When a group like the locally based Islamic Association for Palestine bluntly uses the word "Palestine" when referring to the territory that the UN and most of the world have identified as constituting the independent State of Israel since 1948 and labels all Israelis "settlers" regardless of where they live, it is pretty clear where they are coming from. Less brazen has been the rhetoric of Ali Abunimah, founder of a web site called *The Electronic Intifada,* who has emerged as perhaps the most visible local proponent of the Palestinian cause.

The son of a Jordanian diplomat with a British accent and a Princeton degree, Abunimah projects an image of moderation. He answers questions about his readiness to accept the existence of the State of Israel by saying he believes that "Israelis and Palestinians should live alongside each other in full peace, complete equality and profound democracy." But the Palestinian Liberation Organization, too, once endorsed such a one-state solution, a solution that in fact means that there would no longer be an Israel.

Then there are assertions of the "right of return" for Palestinian refugees and their descendants, a term also able to come in under the radar screen of an audience not tuned in to the lingo. In an article on his Web site headed "Palestinian Rights and the Document Shredder," Abunimah attacks the readiness of Palestinian intellectual Sari Nusseibeh to compromise on that "right" and to say that it would be sufficient for the refugees to relocate in a newly founded Palestinian state and to receive compensation. Similarly, on Sept. 29, some 500 Palestinians and supporters of their cause held a national "Right of Return" rally in downtown Chicago demanding that Palestinian refugees and their descendants be allowed to move to those places where they or their families once lived inside what is now Israel.

The refugees number some 3.5 million people, and for more than 50 years many of them have been kept in miserable camps by Arab regimes and fed a steady diet of Israel-hating invective. Advocates of their "return" well know that these efforts, if successful, would deconstruct Israel. "Palestine will be free from the river to the sea," proclaimed Intifada-praising T-shirts at the Sept. 29 rally. Though many who heard the chants and read the slogans may not have realized the implications of such words, the goal of those who marched certainly is to saturate Israel with a hostile population, which would eliminate that state.

The Oslo process, introduced in 1993, was aimed at moving Israel and the Palestinians toward a peaceful end to their conflict, with matters like the fate of the refugees to be resolved in a final status agreement arrived at through negotiations and a settlement of differences. With all the ensuing difficulties the process faced, in the summer of 2000 peace still appeared to have a chance. But then, after Yasser Arafat scorned unprecedented Israeli offers and American attempts to broker a fair solution of the conflict, the process collapsed.

At Camp David, Arafat himself resurrected the "right of return" as a central principle and balked at closing out all claims against Israel. Shortly afterward, the Palestinians began the violence that has now continued for two years.

The unraveling of Oslo on the ground has been paralleled by an upsurge in the use of bottom-line anti-Israel rhetoric by Palestinians and their supporters. Words like "apartheid" and "colonialism" — emotionally charged terms that distort the Israel-Palestinian reality and subvert Israel's legitimacy by drawing analogies to earlier ideological struggles — increasingly permeate the verbal battleground. In a shocking public return to the bad old days of widespread Arab maximalism and rejection of Israel, that country's very right to exist is now under broad linguistic attack.

In this country, the audacious pronouncement of such a radical notion would once have been as unimaginable as similar attacks on the national existence of any country, even America itself. Though the messages may sometimes need decoding, the legitimacy of the existence of Israel in the Jewish people's ancient homeland is today under verbal assault, including in our own backyard. Let there be no misunderstanding what is being said.

Terrorist's Bomb Shatters Israel's Glimpse of Tranquility

Chicago Sun-Times, August 25, 2003

• • •

Last Saturday evening, along with U.S. Rep. Jan Schakowsky and a Chicago family, I sat at dinner with Dr. David Zangen and his wife in a busy Jerusalem restaurant. A pediatrician affiliated with the Hadassah Hospital there, Zangen took several calls from the parents of patients with childhood diabetes, counseling them on how to handle ongoing difficulties.

Back in Chicago three days later, I thought of Zangen when news came of a devastating terrorist bombing on a Jerusalem bus in which 20 people had been killed and 100 wounded, many of them children. Zangen, I imagined, based on his descriptions of his life these past three years, was no doubt treating many of the wounded, victims of a mass murderer driven by ideology and hate.

The Israel we had visited for a week was different from what it had been at any other point over the past three years. The hotels were filled with tourists. The streets were filled with Israelis going about their ordinary business in the daytime, and in the evenings out to have a good time. They were all able to enjoy beautiful summer days and nights, ironically some 20 degrees cooler than the blistering conditions of the European cities from which many of the visitors had come.

The Israelis were thrilled by this taste of things as they once were and could again become. But they were also skeptical that the *hudna* that the Palestinian groups had declared could really last. The very term, after all, refers not to a cease-fire intended to precede a peaceful, permanent resolution of conflict, but rather to a pause in hostilities meant ultimately to be broken and historically used to enhance military capabilities.

Through the first half of the 90-day *hudna,* the midpoint of which came during our stay, the Palestinian Authority's prime minister, Mahmoud Abbas, and head of security, Mohammad Dahlan, had done nothing at all to weaken the powers of radical Palestinian groups like Hamas and Islamic Jihad, whose declared purpose is to destroy Israel and whose violent methods had been aimed at making life for Israeli civilians a living hell. Supported by funds from Saudi Arabia, Iran, and other global sources, those groups were rebuilding their infrastructure, damaged by Israeli defensive measures; enhancing their armaments; using tunnels between the southern Gaza Strip and Egypt to smuggle in arms, and developing and testing rockets in the northern Gaza Strip.

Not only do these groups have no interest in allowing President Bush's road map to run its course, with a Palestinian state headed by a responsible, peace-abiding government living side by side with the Jewish state of Israel, but that vision is their nightmare. It was only a matter of time until they would once again act to return the sirens and the suffering to the streets of Israel's cities in an attempt to keep the conflict going.

And so on Tuesday evening, a preacher from Hebron with a perverse dream of martyrdom, a man with children of his own and a pregnant wife, strapped explosives around his waist, disguised himself as an observant Jew, entered Jerusalem, boarded a bus packed with families riding home from Judaism's holiest site, and blew himself up to kill as many Israelis as possible.

The contrast between this lover of death, whose gun-toting image has now been broadcast around the globe, and the life-bringing physician with whom I had dined in that same city three days earlier, could not be more stark. A final irony is that the doctor's ordinary patient load is made up of at least as many Palestinian children as Jewish ones. Such coexistence is a reality that Tuesday's killer could not tolerate, one that he and his ilk would do anything they could to prevent from defining the future.

New Policies for New Problems on Campus

Remarks delivered at a Symposium for University Administrators,
University of Illinois at Chicago
October 23, 2003

• • •

On behalf of the Jewish Federation of Metropolitan Chicago, it is my pleasure to greet you and thank our partners in co-sponsorship of today's symposium, the Jewish Studies Program here at the University of Illinois at Chicago, for providing this wonderful facility.

I thank all of you for taking the time to be here. Fifteen campuses are represented, most from the Chicago area but others from beyond. The turnout, I believe, is testimony to a shared recognition of the seriousness of the subject matter we are here to discuss. It is subject matter that has been central to conversations and correspondence which I myself have had with several of you and your counterparts over the past three years, and it was to a great extent those conversations which led us to conclude that a day like this would be very much in order and could have important and productive results.

The campus-based concerns we are here to focus on affect students from diverse backgrounds. As we will hear, the language and actions of racist hate speech and hate crimes continue to surface on today's campuses, with African-American students feeling particularly threatened by that. Meanwhile, especially following 9/11, there have also been concerns regarding negative stereotyping and harassment of Arab and Muslim students. The Arab-American community and practitioners of Islam are still relatively unfamiliar minorities in this country, and with fear running deep and passions running high, special attention has been directed to the way they are talked about and treated. At the same time, though, it is clear that, as our keynote speaker, Stanley Fish, observed in an article in the *Chronicle of Higher Education* which focused on one aspect of these matters, most of the inflammatory issues of this sort which have surfaced on the nation's campuses over the past few years feature attacks on Jews – and usually, I would add, Israel is involved.

The Jewish Federation of Metropolitan Chicago supports the Hillel foundations which serve Jewish students at universities throughout Illinois, and we have direct contact with students and faculty. Beyond that, we represent the many members of our community who are alumni or parents of students at a host of universities. And we act on behalf of our broader community as well. Today's issues have been brought to our direct attention and otherwise noted by us, and what we have been hearing and seeing since the Israel-Palestinian conflict entered a new stage three years ago has been deeply troubling. This has been so in ways which, I would posit, are not only threatening to Jewish students and their beliefs, but at times seem to challenge the maintenance of traditional academic values.

Before I go any further let me make it absolutely clear that I do not believe that Israel should be immune from criticism directed at the policies of its government and leaders any more than any other nation should, nor that critics of Israel should be automatically silenced by charges of anti-Semitism. But when Jewish students and other supporters of Israel are physically threatened by uncontrolled pro-Palestinian crowds, as has been the case on campuses such as San Francisco State and Concordia University in Montreal, with scaled-down modes of this behavior seen on other campuses as well, then the boundaries of civility on which so many campuses pride themselves clearly have been transgressed. And when hecklers of pro-Israel speakers or when anti-Israel speakers have voiced gutter-level invective incorporating traditional anti-Semitic vocabulary and images, that has represented not the fulfillment but a travesty of the concept of the free exchange of ideas. When groups which condone terror exploit campus faculties to hold a conference aimed at undermining the right to exist of a country brought into being by the United Nations, then campus openness is, at least, being stretched to a questionable degree. When a letters to the editor section of a campus newspaper is exploited by a non-student, non-alumnus from out-of-state to convey grotesque yet familiar anti-Semitic concepts, then principles of free speech have been abused rather than respected in a manner that is frankly shocking to see on a supposedly enlightened and responsible university campus.

And, finally, when faculty members functioning outside and inside of the classroom associate themselves with some of the sort of behavior referred to above, or have "just" become aggressively partisan on the issues at hand, then they have at the very least provoked questions as to the misapplication of standards of academic freedom. I am thinking here of reports we have received from students telling us of situations in classrooms – in many of which the declared subject matter has nothing to do with the Middle East to start with – in which instructors have used that platform to malign Israel through highly questionable ideological language. Some of these faculty members, we have been told, refuse to either provide readings or allow students themselves to present the "other side."

The reaction of students who face this sort of behavior ranges from fear and intimidation which prevents them from speaking out, on the one hand, to outrage, anger and a readiness to stand up, on the other. In either case the reaction involves a sense of not feeling "at home" on a campus, and even of being demonized through association with the state of Israel and with fellow supporters of Israel.

These are obviously serious matters. I know they are taken seriously by yourselves and your counterparts and thank you for that. This subject was directly addressed by Harvard President Lawrence Summers a year ago September in a notable speech in which, reviewing certain developments on campuses in Europe and North America, he spoke about the way that "serious and thoughtful people" on those campuses "are advocating and taking actions that are anti-Semitic in their effect if not in their intent." My own belief that something new is going on worthy of consideration was strongly stimulated by a *New York Times* column by Edward Rothstein, published exactly eleven month ago. It was based on a Harvard episode having to do with an invitation given by the English Department, rescinded, and given again to a poet whose use of language had gone beyond mere hate speech into what could be regarded as incitement of murder – an episode which formed the basis of an extensive *New Yorker* article that suggested the widespread attention some of these matters are receiving.

The question Rothstein raised is whether the kinds of policies currently in place on university campuses to deal with such matters are adequate for the current times and the current challenges. It is that kind of question which will likely come to the fore today as, through discussion of the topics to be addressed, there will be an opportunity to review the policies and practices in place at various universities. Our intent is to let these discussions take their own shape, and we very much hope that you will find value in them in forging and implementing your own university's policies and practices on these matters.

I close in a personal fashion. Before I got into my current line of work, I myself was an academic, with a Ph.D. from the University of Minnesota, three years of teaching experience there, and a dozen years of teaching elsewhere. I come with what I hope is a continuing understanding of the nature and the values of university life, and with what I know to be an ongoing respect for the academic endeavor. Your readiness to tackle the issues on the table today demonstrates, I believe, that that respect is merited. On behalf of our community, I thank you, even before we get started, for the work you do, and for your readiness to enter into today's discussions.

Arafat Never Abandoned Goal
of Eliminating Israel

Chicago Sun-Times, November 8, 2004

• • •

Yasser Arafat's mother died when he was 4 years old. The loss was compounded when, sent to live with his mother's family, he was separated from his father.

There is irony here since, inverting the Palestinian narrative of dispossession that he would later embody, the young Arafat moved from Egypt, where he was born, to the Old City of Jerusalem. Still, one wonders to what extent he may have drawn upon the emotions wrought by the trauma of his personal loss and separation to imbue the national narrative with mythic qualities, and also to what extent that experience may have made him an uncompromising advocate for "return." In any event, Arafat became both the voice and symbol of his people's dreams and the major single reason why they and the Israelis have failed to resolve their conflict. And now, as I write this, his death appears imminent.

During his schooling as an engineer in Cairo, Arafat was exposed to the radical Muslim Brotherhood. He and several fellow students applied the then more fashionable leftist Arab nationalist ideology to the Fatah movement, which they founded, and to the Palestine Liberation Organization, made up of Fatah and other Palestinian groups. Taking over in the 1960s, he shaped these groups to advance the revanchist desires of the Palestinians.

Arafat and his followers became global masters of terrorism. In hijacking airplanes and raiding civilian targets, they defined the tactics of modern terrorist assault. In their gun-wielding, mask-wearing raid on Israel's athletes at the Munich Olympics in 1972, they established the popular image of the modern terrorist. And with his trademark kaffiyah, military garb, and pistol holster, Arafat put his stamp on the theatrical mode of modern terrorism, using the media to gain attention and project a romantic aura.

After being told that Arafat no longer sought Israel's elimination and that only he, the universally regarded representative of his people, could be an interlocutor, Israel was prepared to take a risk for peace, reversing its long-standing policy of refusing to talk to him and entering into the

Oslo Process.

But though he was now seen as a statesman and was even awarded the Nobel Peace Prize, Arafat's behavior belied that identity. Once he returned to Gaza and the West Bank to head the Palestinian Authority, he built up multiple police and military groups. Contrary to expectations, he never definitively challenged the growing Hamas and Islamic Jihad terror organizations. While others may have regarded those groups, with their Islamist ideologies, as threats to Arafat's power base, they kept alive the "armed struggle" he had championed, serving his longtime strategic approach even as he publicly committed himself to abandoning violence.

At Camp David in 2000, Arafat had the opportunity to obtain what he had proclaimed he wanted: an independent Palestinian state with its capital in east Jerusalem. But he walked away from that discussion, and the breakdown of those talks was followed by violence not only from the Islamist terror groups but also from offshoots of Arafat's PLO, with the latter soon adopting the suicide bombing tactics of the former. The terror war against Israel had resumed full scale. The Palestinians named it the Al-Aqsa Intifada -- a religion-based term for an increasingly religious conflict.

Arafat never espoused any vision of the kind of state he wanted for his people. He projected no sense of civil society, no social or economic philosophy, no consolidating statecraft. He enunciated no constructive hopes, but only repeated the mantra of leading a million Palestinian martyrs into Jerusalem. In continuing to encourage the Palestinian refugees and their descendants to believe they would ultimately return to their homes of a half a century before and making that a deal-killer at Camp David, he steadily championed a formula for the elimination of Israel, the only tangible goal that his voiced aspirations ever added up to.

The years of Arafat's stewardship over the Palestinian Authority were a disaster. Mafia-like fiefdoms were created by his henchmen, instituting a culture of corruption and neglect. Rather than teaching his people the ways of reconciliation and talking to them about the compromises needed to make peace, Arafat and company now had their own media and used it to inculcate hatred and resentment and to incite violence.

After giving up on Arafat following Camp David and then watching his continuing role in the terror war that followed, Israel declared him "irrelevant" and isolated him in Ramallah. And then the United States, witness to his part in the Karine A arms smuggling episode and his lies about it, concluded that for progress toward peace to be accomplished, the Palestinians would need to have another leader.

Arafat is credited with advancing the spirit of Palestinian nationalism while bringing his people's cause to the attention of the world. At the same time, his leadership repeatedly prevented the Palestinians and Israelis from resolving their differences in a peace that would address the legitimate needs of both peoples. He time and again brought suffering to both Israelis and Palestinians and foiled American plans for bringing stability to the Middle East.

With Arafat off the scene, there will be the opportunity for power to pass to a leadership that will take the Palestinian people on the path to a peaceful settlement good for Palestinians and Israelis alike.

The Withdrawal From Gaza:
Cautious Hopes for a Safer Future as Palestinians,
Abbas Now Face Test

Chicago Tribune, August 21, 2005

• • •

After a two-week visit, I departed Israel at 12:05 a.m. on Aug. 15, four minutes after Israel began its disengagement from the Gaza Strip. With its outcome uncertain, that voyage into uncharted waters is likely to have a significant impact on Israeli life while potentially restructuring the country's relationship with its neighbors.

In those ways, disengagement resembles such transformative events as Israel's War of Independence in 1948, the Six-Day War of 1967, the Yom Kippur War of 1973, Anwar Sadat's visit to Israel in 1977, the beginning of the Oslo process in 1993, and the collapse of that process in 2000.

For all of the divisions within Israeli society that I had witnessed during my visit there and that have been playing out on television screens worldwide last week, public opinion polls and conversations with intellectuals and ordinary people from across the political spectrum indicate that a broad consensus accepted the inevitability of disengagement from Gaza and parts of the West Bank. Yet most Israelis greeted disengagement not with joyous enthusiasm and great expectations but with, at best, a sober, muted hope for safer times.

Like the security barrier that Israel is constructing on the West Bank, disengagement was planned out of a sense that there was no partner with whom Israel could confidently attempt to make peace, no better way to protect its population from the vicious terror assaults that escalated beginning in fall 2000. Paradoxically, though, disengagement itself has created the framework in which such a partner might at last emerge, though such a result is far from certain.

In the days leading to disengagement, Hamas began boasting that Israel was retreating from the group's suicide and rocket attacks. A Hamas leader called disengagement "the beginning of the end of Israel." Palestinian Authority officials also began to talk about Israel's withdrawal as a retreat from violence, and Palestinian Authority President Mahmoud Abbas proclaimed, "Today we are celebrating the liberation of Gaza and the northern West Bank; tomorrow we will be celebrating the liberation of Jerusalem."

One can see why Hamas, whose leadership has been decimated by the Israeli military and whose terror tactics have been overcome by Israeli resilience, would make such claims to elevate its importance and to keep the conflict going. But it does not augur well that Abbas and other Palestinian officials are talking to their followers in a similar fashion. If their language reflects the way they understand Israel's reaction to the terror and the motivation for disengagement, and if it points to their future behavior, then they are misreading the Israelis and are miscalculating what they need to do to avoid taking their people down the path of continuing conflict and continuing misery.

What I frequently heard in Jerusalem on my visit, from Israelis and moderate Palestinians alike, is that this is a time of testing for Abbas and the Palestinian Authority. It is a time for them to act on their obligations in the "road map" to peace and to at last dismantle the terrorist infrastructure and establish a single, unified security force. It is a time for them to protect the rule of law, to end the corruption, and to construct an effective civil society for their people, rather than aiming at the destruction of the Jewish state of Israel. It is a time for them to teach their children the ways of reconciliation, respect and peace, rather than inculcating hatred, demonization and rejection of the Israeli "other."

That is the test Abbas and the Palestinians now face.

As the world has been watching the anguish of Israelis being removed from their homes and communities in Gaza and the drama revolving around Israeli disengagement, let it watch just as carefully to see whether disengagement proves to be a transformational event for the Palestinians as well. In passing this test, the Palestinians would be joining a process that could finally bring an end to the Israeli-Palestinian conflict.

It will take time to get there, and such a result surely will not be easy to accomplish. But if the Palestinians change their rhetoric and take the right steps, there is a chance that the painful, difficult measures initiated by Israel on Aug. 15, as the plane I was riding in cut through the midnight sky, might indeed help bring about a better day for Israelis and Palestinians alike.

Sights Set on "The Israel Lobby"

JUF News, October 2007

. . .

In late August, CNN-TV ran a three-part documentary called *God's Warriors,* with Christiane Amanpour, the network's lead foreign affairs correspondent, reporting. The series has been sharply criticized for its portrayal of its Jewish subjects and for implying a moral equivalence between the actions of the Jewish subjects of the first program and the Muslim extremists who are examined in the second program. Beyond that, though, I believe the series can be seen as feeding a troubling and increasingly mainstream undermining of American support for Israel.

Though few viewers not in the know were likely to have noticed it, in fact some professionals and lay volunteers involved in JUF activities made a very brief appearance in a section of the first program, labeled "The Lobby," where they are shown walking the halls of Congress. I am one of them, my back to the camera, greeted by Illinois U.S. Rep. Jan Schakowsky as we entered her office in Washington last February.

Before JUF personnel became subjects of filming CNN did in Israel as well as in Washington for this documentary, we were told by the network that it wished to use us in connection with what they described as a three-part series being put together to explore ways that religion-based communities in America are involved in public policy matters. A good deal of filming went on in both countries. In Israel, JUF representatives were shown helping to clean a bomb shelter up north, then calling Rep. Schakowsky to report on what they had seen there. In Washington, a reporter-producer and camera crew accompanied the group I was with as we visited congressional offices and expressed our concerns about a range of domestic and foreign policy issues.

At no time were we told that we were going to be shown in a series that would focus specifically on the ways that certain Jews, Muslims, and Christians around the globe are motivated by a sense that the modern world has gone off the tracks and that modern civilization needs to be brought back to acting in accordance with God's wishes, with some of the people reported on in the series and the groups they belong to prepared to act in extreme and even violent ways to advance that vision.

That was troubling enough. But more important than the way that

CNN misled us is the way that they misled their viewers. In the program in which my colleagues and I fleetingly appear, we are shown as members of a "loose coalition" that aims to advance American support for Israel and that functions as an enabler for God's Jewish Warriors, whose goal, the program posits, is to ensure Jewish control of all of the biblical Promised Land by building settlements in territory that came under Israel's control as a result of the Six-Day War.

In fact, the set of groups and individuals comprising the "lobby" which CNN was reporting on is no coalition at all, and it is not even much of a single lobby. We ourselves do not work in concert with everybody else who is considered part of this lobby, nor do we even share similar points of view with all of them on all issues, including some very key ones.

Given the purported subject matter of the broadcast, described as an investigation of the mentality and action of God's Warriors, one can only wonder why so much time and attention was given to this specific "lobby." That may in part have been because there was so little material directly related to the ostensible subject to focus on for the two hours about Jews. Thus, much of what got covered (especially regarding Jewish violence) is old news; thus viewers hear about Christians as well as Jews in this section, though the Christians got another two hours of their own in the third program; and thus there is a closing 10 minutes or so about a Palestinian man who was negatively affected by the building of Israel's security barrier, though it is quite a stretch to see that as connected with the proclaimed subject matter of the program in any way.

The "Israel lobby" is of course a hot topic these days, and maybe that's what qualified it for so much attention on this program. There it was, with people like former Sen. Charles Percy, former President Jimmy Carter, and Professor John Mearsheimer having the opportunity to tell the viewers what it is and how dangerous its actions are as, in their view, its members obstruct the coming of peace in the Middle East while advocating measures contrary to American interests.

In opposition to these three spokesmen the program presented the head of a pro-Israel PAC who is also the former head of a leading pro-Israel lobbying organization. While he is given opportunity to make decent counterarguments, one can't help suspecting that a neutral and naïve viewer would attach greater credibility to a former senator, a former president, and a professor at a major university, all of whom are on one side, than to a lone obvious partisan who is on the other. In fact, the former three individuals (or at least two of them) are just as partisan in advocating for one side in the Israel-Palestinian conflict as the latter individual is for the other side. By not including an authoritative figure with equally credible credentials to counter Percy, Carter, and Mearsheimer (and many could surely have been found), the program stacked the deck.

This omission is not of idle concern, because the program thus reinforced the pernicious notion that Jews and others who support Israel care more about Israeli interests than American ones and are leading America to take misguided steps. Unstated by authoritative voices in the program is the widely-held view that a close Israel-America relationship is very much in America's interest, and that whatever one might feel about the settlements, they are far from the major reason that peace has not been reached between Israel and the Palestinians.

Perhaps those putting this program together were driven more by the desire to make things fit the thematic approach of the series than by the need to answer the question of whether they really did fit. Whatever the reason, the result was more than unfortunate. Overall, the broad brush used to try to show the impact of those few individuals who might, based on the standards of the series itself, legitimately be called "God's Jewish Warriors," created significant distortions and took the program into problematic territory outside of its proclaimed subject matter, leaving viewers of the program more misled than enlightened.

Book continues trend

With its emphasis on "The Lobby," the CNN program fits a trend. Sept. 4 was the publication date for John Mearsheimer and Stephen Walt's *The Israel Lobby* and *U.S. Foreign Policy,* the expanded version of a monograph these two professors, the first from the University of Chicago, the second from Harvard, put on a Harvard website last year. Despite that rather obscure academic venue and parallel publication in the distant *London Review of Books,* their work attracted sufficient attention and stimulated sufficient controversy in America that a commercial publisher, Farrar, Straus and Giroux, apparently saw a potential goldmine in a book likely to bring the shaky and disturbing arguments of these writers much greater general attention.

With the imminent publication of this work troubling my mind, on the evening of Sept. 3, I set off with my wife and friends for a festive end-of-summer outdoor concert at Ravinia Park. Though it was Labor Day, the program actually was a lot more appropriate for July 4th (when the park had been closed) or any patriotic holiday. With the rest of the large crowd, I was energized and moved by music that included George Gershwin's "Of Thee I Sing," Irving Berlin's treatment of Emma Lazarus's words from the Statue of Liberty, the melody of Leonard Bernstein's "America," and in a rousing encore that had us all standing on our feet with tears in our eyes, Berlin's "God Bless America."

Listening to this inspiring music, I was struck by the thought that these Jewish composers and writers, conveying their own love of America, had helped generations of fellow citizens take pride in what America stands for and had given us the words and the melodies to express our own patriotism and love of this country. And now, I went on to think, come Professors Mearsheimer and Walt, implicitly impugning the loyalty of American Jews for the way we feel connected not only to America but also to the State of Israel, where Jewish sovereignty was reestablished in the wake of the slaughter of 6 million Jews who did not get out of Europe and were prevented from entering the ancient homeland of our people.

In our heart of hearts, I thought that evening and think now, we are certain that a strong Israel-America relationship is good for both countries, and that such ties are natural and correct, especially in today's dangerous world. Whatever pernicious message is stated or implied by academics or others with their own axe to grind, American Jews will continue to sing the songs that those who came before us gave to America, and we will continue to proudly advance the Israel-America relationship as we do.

New Era Is Born: Unlike Previous Critics, Mearsheimer & Walt Promote Anti-Israeli Views by Focusing on Jewish Lobby

YNET online, November 10, 2007

• • •

Last year it was a widely noticed, controversial book by former President Jimmy Carter. This year it is one by professors from two of America's leading universities. It seems that a trend is afoot that is changing the landscape regarding the way Israel is treated on America's campuses and beyond.

For background it is useful to recall a 2001 study called *Ivory Towers on Sand* in which Martin Kramer, then at Tel Aviv University's Dayan Center, traced the influence on Middle Eastern studies in the US of Edward Said, a professor of English and Comparative Literature at Columbia University.

Said's seminal book *Orientalism* was published in 1978. Along with the stocking of Middle East study centers and various departments at universities around the country with faculty hostile to Israel, his impact helped create a situation in which the Palestinian "narrative" held sway on many American campuses and Israel was regarded as a colonial intrusion into the Middle East.

Especially since the year 2000, when Israel began to be subjected to a terror war accompanied by an escalating propaganda campaign, various individuals and groups have reacted to the prevailing state of affairs. Students and others have called attention to the behavior of biased, one-sided professors. On the other hand, with a number of chairs established, with increasing numbers of visiting professors on the scene, and with new courses being developed, voices are now being heard that are more accurate and balanced in their treatment of the Israel-Palestinian conflict and that show an Israel not defined solely by the conflict.

More and more, Israel is being approached as a bona fide member of the world's family of nations meriting serious academic attention. Though Said still has a following and his impact lingers, beside the fact that he himself is now dead, the era that he personified and profoundly influenced is becoming increasingly passé. But now, with a rhetoric often characterized by belligerent shrillness, a troubling alternative approach is coming into the mainstream.

We have gone, it seems, from the age of Edward Said to the age of John Mearsheimer and Stephen Walt, with Jimmy Carter on one side and people like Norman Finkelstein on the other buttressing that trend. Center stage at the moment is the new book by Mearsheimer and Walt — an expansion of their earlier monograph — the bestselling *The Israel Lobby and US Foreign Policy*. (Interestingly enough, neither Said nor the current writers made a claim to academic expertise in Middle Eastern studies before publishing on the subject.)

At the time that Said was holding sway at Columbia, Rashid Khalidi, who has moved on to that institution to hold the Edward Said Chair, was ensconced at the University of Chicago, and Said's friend Ibrahim Abu-Lughod was at Northwestern University. With people like them leading the way, the pro-Palestinian cause was spearheaded by suave, articulate campus-based academics whose ideologically driven view of the past and present was offered with the patina of scholarship.

The key works of today, however, are less academic and much more clearly polemical. The hostility these books direct against Israel is blatant. And they are issued by commercial presses with full-blown publicity apparatuses that send the authors not just from campus to campus but from bookstore to bookstore and from media interview to media interview. Nothing is out of reach, it would seem, even a full-page ad in *The New York Times*.

Rather than coming across to the general public as partisan Palestinian Americans, today's promulgators of the anti-Israel agenda present themselves as authoritative figures whom the typical American can see as "one of us." Still, they are no less partisan than their predecessors.

Indeed, as much as these figures may declare that they affirm Israel's right to exist, in the ways in which they harshly criticize Israel while giving a pass to the Palestinians they undermine Israel's very legitimacy at a time when that legitimacy is increasingly under direct attack from other supporters of the Palestinian cause. And they bring a malignant tactic that was not previously provided such visibility and credibility, a frontal assault on the Jewish community and other supporters of Israel who are lumped together as members of an insidious and all-powerful "Israel lobby."

Here in Chicago, from whence I write, we have a front seat to this development. With Mearsheimer based on the campus that previously housed Khalidi (Walt is at Harvard,) and with the even more obviously polemical Finkelstein, just now denied tenure at nearby DePaul

University for his un-collegial excesses but still championed by other academics locally and nationally, the concepts I am positing are graphically demonstrated.

Like Jimmy Carter and others in this new school (might it be called the anti-Israel-lobby lobby?), Mearsheimer and Walt repeatedly insist that all they want is the right to criticize Israel, a right that, despite their own high profiles coast to coast, they say is denied them and others by an all-controlling Israel lobby. But they go beyond mere criticism by asserting that America's continuing support for Israel is justified neither on strategic nor moral grounds. And for them, the only explanation for that support is the power of the "Israel lobby" that in the eyes of these professors leads America by the nose, away from its own interests.

This is the new wisdom that is being promulgated not only from campus to campus but in public settings as well. Over the long term Mearsheimer and Walt's tome will most likely turn out to be less seminal and impactful in the classroom and research centers than was the work of Said. But it is symptomatic of a point of view which is now getting increasing attention in an America that is overwhelmed by the question of how the country got into Iraq and how it will get out, that is uncertain about what to do about Iran, and that is wondering if, when, and where there will be another terror attack on domestic soil.

The ideas promoted by Mearsheimer and Walt are reflected elsewhere too, as was demonstrated in a recent six-hour, three-part television documentary produced by CNN called *God's Warriors*. With the first installment focusing on Jews, Carter and Mearsheimer were themselves turned to as authorities as the program treated what it called "the lobby" in terms very similar to those used by Mearsheimer and Walt.

In looking for consolation, one can note that as this trend grows, a positive approach continues to gain momentum of its own as well, with the practitioners in the field of Israel Studies bringing a more accurate and comprehensive treatment of Israel to many universities. Meanwhile, supporters of Israel, not intimidated by the likes of Jimmy Carter, John Mearsheimer, and Stephen Walt, are challenging their theses, and the American Jewish community remains undeterred in advocating for a strong Israel/America relationship as something good for both countries.

All the same, however, although by now an impressive number of serious reviewers have been exposing the Mearsheimer and Walt book's shoddy scholarship, misleading claims, and tendentious arguments, their approach gains steam. At the moment, their book can be considered as much of a touchstone of the new age as *Orientalism* was for its.

Rallies Promote End of Israel, Not Conflict

Chicago Sun-Times, January 19, 2009

• • •

Reacting to Israel's action in Gaza, pro-Palestinian demonstrators have taken to the streets in Chicago and around the world. While in part conveying sympathy for the Gazan civilians sadly caught in the crossfire, demonstrators here as elsewhere have largely focused on denouncing Israel in a fashion that betrays an extremist perspective on the Israel-Palestinian conflict consistent with that of Hamas itself. These have not been protests against Israel's conduct as much as demonstrations of opposition to Israel's very existence, carried out in a way that is responsive to the Hamas call for "angry" demonstrations around the globe.

From London to Paris to Oslo to Algiers, rallies have turned violent. While the demonstrations in Chicago have been more tame, their messages are similar. On Dec. 28, a day after Israeli planes began to answer Hamas rocket attacks on Israeli civilian targets, demonstrators in Chicago chanted "Down, down, Israel. ... Free, free, Palestine." Hand-held signs included one, similar to those seen in Europe, with a map showing the entire area of Israel and the Palestinian territories labeled "Palestine." Alongside the map were the phrases "End the occupation of Palestine" and "Palestine forever, from the sea to the river."

Like Hamas, the Chicago demonstrators who envision a "Palestine forever from the sea to the river" are promoting the elimination of Israel. Signs calling for an end to 60 years of "occupation" decry the existence of Israel itself, from 1948 onward, not Israel's presence in territories it began to control in 1967, which in the case of Gaza ended in 2005. When demonstrators in Chicago and elsewhere hold signs insisting on a "right of return" for all Palestinian refugees and their descendants, they are likewise championing a step that would bring about the end of Israel.

Demonstrators in Germany and the Netherlands have chanted "Hamas, Hamas, Jews to the Gas." Associating themselves with the Palestinian terrorist group that provoked the current fight in Gaza, some demonstrators in Chicago waved the Hamas flag, and others, their faces hidden by Palestinian head scarves, carried a sign declaring "Hamas = Freedom Fighters."

Like Hamas in its charter, in its sermons, in its schoolbooks, and even in the children's television programs it produces, all of which viciously demonize the Israelis and the Jews, pro-Palestinian demonstrators around the globe are directing language and images full of venom against Israel and are evoking anti-Jewish animus.

The iconography of this form of attack is known to anyone familiar with today's standard anti-Israel propaganda and can be seen in signs held by men, women and children alike. Such signs portray the Israelis as Nazis, equate the star of David with the swastika, and accuse Israel of perpetrating a Holocaust and genocide. Using a contemporary term of abuse, they charge Israel with apartheid.

Anti-Semitic incidents have followed inflammatory rallies of this sort in cities throughout Europe. At a Jan. 9 afternoon demonstration in Chicago, both Hamas and Hezbollah flags were unfurled, and there was a large sign making the gross, incendiary charge that Israel and the Jews were responsible for the 9/11 attacks in New York. The night following that demonstration, four local synagogues were vandalized, some with the words "Death to Israel ... Free Palestine" painted on them.

An adversary portrayed the way Israel is at these rallies can hardly be considered a potential partner in peacemaking. Demonstrators who slander Israel in this fashion thus advance a formula for perpetuating the Israel-Palestinian conflict, rather than ending it in a manner that would allow Israelis and Palestinians to live in peace and security. The true freedom the Gazans need, which could help them achieve a far better life, is freedom from entrapment in Hamas' fanatical attempt to destroy Israel and to replace it with a fundamentalist Islamic regime.

As today's anti-Israel demonstrators take to the streets in implicit support of the Hamas vision, they fail to truly help the people of Gaza while inciting hatred of Israel and potentially provoking violence against the local Jewish community. It is a disturbing mix.

Pictures at an Exhibition: Art Galleries, the Academy, and Anti-Israel Polemics

Anti-Semitism International, Nos. 5-6, 2010

Also published in slightly different form in *The Fortitudes of Creativity: In Honor of Shlomo Giora Shoham (Israel 2010)*

• • •

Following the collapse of the Oslo Peace Process in the fall of 2000 and coinciding with the escalation of the Palestinian war of terror against Israel, a hardening in the tone and content of anti-Israel polemics became increasingly discernible. Going beyond mere criticism of Israeli government policies, more and more voices could be heard demonizing Israel in strident, extremist terms. Not only has Israel been accused of gross mistreatment of the Palestinians by those attackers, but the very legitimacy of the existence of the State of Israel has been implicitly called into question, and sometimes blatantly rejected by an approach that frequently crosses the boundaries of civil political debate and enters decidedly anti-Semitic territory. [1]

While such anti-Israel and anti-Zionist rhetoric has been less widely heard in America than in Europe, it has found a home in a number of American universities. This is especially so on campuses where faculty members, echoing the post-modernist intellectual tropes and postcolonial ideological themes espoused by their European counterparts, have become involved in Middle East-focused activities. The pattern has also been seen on campuses whose student bodies include active Muslim and Palestinian groups that embrace a radicalized, rejectionist Palestinian agenda — and in some cases are linked to off-campus organizations aiming to advance such agendas. [2]

Anti-Israel campus activity of this sort began to attract notice early this decade, when demonstrations, street theater, and other forms of on-campus public agitation surfaced. Some of it was quite confrontational, such as a series of annual conferences convened by the Palestinian Solidarity Movement promoting divestment from Israel. Over time, some of this kind of activity became less common, although annual events such as "Israel Apartheid Week" have become more widespread and Israel and its supporters have continued to face serious challenges both outside and inside the classroom.[3]

In this context, academy-linked advocates for the Palestinian cause have developed the use of art exhibitions – both the images on display and accompanying signage – as a distinctive device for advancing anti-Israel polemics. The tactic was notably used three times in the city of Chicago between 2003 and 2008, and the details of each instance, and their common denominators, are well worth considering.

The first example of this involved something called a "Video Petition Project." Created by the Artist Emergency Response (AER), a faculty-supported student group at the School of the Art Institute of Chicago, this installation was included in an exhibition called *War: What Is It Good For?* at Chicago's Museum of Contemporary Art (MCA) early in 2003. Lasting nearly an hour and a half, the video "petition" took the form of a series of head shots of individuals enunciating their perspectives on the Israel-Palestinian conflict. Virtually all these individuals were overwhelmingly supportive of the Palestinian cause or bitterly hostile toward Israel, or both.

While some interviews for this video were conducted at anti-Israel rallies and meetings in Chicago and other North Amer-ican cities, a student at the School of the Art Institute commented to me at the time that the students and faculty members comprising AER also did some of their filming on campus:

> They had the video petition playing at the entrance where everyone comes into the school buildings, and they passed out flyers with "sample things you could say" for the petition, and then they set up cameras on the lounge floors where people could go during their free time to make a statement for their video petition. The idea behind the petitions is you can either say one of the statements they had on the flyer…or something of your own. They asked me if I would make a statement, and when I said that I support Israel and her policies, they were no longer interested.

The student added, "There are flyers all over the school promoting the show, and I know of several teachers who have taken their classes there [to the MCA] specifically to see it."[4]

In fact, though its name *(Video Petition Project)* was intended to suggest that the installation was the video equivalent of a traditional written petition, this "project" differed from a standard petition in a number of key ways. For one, rather than signing their names on a piece of paper or on an e-mail document to endorse a particular position, the "petitioners" portrayed here appeared in front of a camera, identified themselves, and then made a statement that was either a verbatim recitation of a scripted text they had been given or an extemporaneous elaboration on the point of view suggested by that text. More significantly, whereas conventional petitions are directed to a specific audience, such as the President, Congress, and so forth, this "petition" was directed to no addressee in particular. It was designed to be exhibited to the public at large, with the purpose of influencing public opinion.

On its website, the Artist Emergency Response, which seems to have come into existence for the sole purpose of this project, defined the exhibit as "a visual testimony of North Americans voicing their opposition to the Israeli occupation and who seek a just solution to the Palestinian refugee crisis and an equitable and lasting peace."[5] Though the AER made many references to peace and justice in its materials, a close reading of the scripts provided shows that its approach to the Israel-Palestinian conflict was positioned in radical, rejectionist territory, placing the blame on Israel alone, and exclusively supporting Palestinian demands. While some interviewees were offered the possibility of endorsing a two-state solution to the conflict, others were urged to say, "I support one peaceful and democratic state for both Israelis and Palestinians." Jewish interviewees were encouraged not only to call for a "just solution in the Palestinian refugee crisis," but also to declare that "until Palestinian refugees are granted their right of return, I renounce mine." Incorporating language from the script of a flyer distributed by AER into their own independent wording, speakers referred to a "right of return" for Palestinian refugees, as well as to a "one-state solution" to the conflict, in a way that clearly implied that for many if not most of them, the "Palestine" they considered occupied by Israel was not the West Bank and Gaza alone, and the "just solution for the Palestinians refugee conflict" they endorsed was one leading to the end of the Jewish State of Israel.[6]

In specifically looking for individuals who would identify themselves as Jewish, AER may have thought that would make the video more acceptable to museum curators and viewers and, in particular, more persuasive to other Jews.[7] In practice, however, the attempt by such speakers to portray themselves as members of the Jewish community who are the most faithful to Jewish values was destined to outrage many Jewish viewers, and it accomplished just that.

When members of the local Jewish community and museum visitors began to hear of, and see, the exhibition, they were troubled. Reviewing the show in *The Chicago Tribune,* Julia Keller reported that the exhibition as a whole "ruffled some feathers," and she said this particular installation provoked "muttering from some museum-goers."[8] Reviewing the exhibition in the local Jewish community bi-weekly, *The Chicago Jewish Star,* and focusing on the "Video Petition," Gila Wertheimer concluded by declaring:

> A project that places people before a camera to record a single point of view over and over is unconvincing as a work of art. It is a record of denunciation, with an acknowledged political intent, but just because it utilizes an art medium – film – doesn't qualify it as art. Its inclusion discredits the theme of the entire exhibit.[9]

Museum officials were quick to respond to concerns. Writing to supporters, MCA director Robert Fitzpatrick said, "Our recent exhibition *War: What is it Good for?* has provoked many strong feelings from among members of our community. The intent of this current exhibition is to create a forum for discussion and debate – not to endorse any political position." He added that, "The MCA does not endorse individual viewpoints that may be expressed within the works in the exhibition and has not included any works to influence visitors to adopt any political belief."[10] Similar language was employed in new signage prepared to accompany the video petition, which also included language specifically identifying the installation "as part of a long history of artists' use of agitprop – something that serves the purposes of both agitation and propaganda." Simultaneously, the exhibition was expanded to include an Israeli video called *Keep on Dancing,* in which young Israelis portrayed their generation's commitment to leading normal lives despite the terrorism then being experienced in their country.

At the time this was happening, School of the Art Institute president Tony Jones sent a letter to supporters acknowledging that AER was "a recognized student group at the School," and that AER's website appeared on space provided by the School, but also declaring that "the video petition is not a School-based project." His letter added that "the views of the Artists Emergency Response (AER) and those of participants in the video petition project are those of the individuals themselves."[11]

In sum, despite the fact that key creators of this installation were associated with a school of art and were working in the *au courant* genre of video, aesthetics had little, if anything, to do with their motivation for putting it together. Rather, they clearly were driven predominantly by a desire to promote a political agenda. That reality was identified by early viewers of the exhibit, and then promptly acknowledged by officials of the museum itself, who proceeded to disassociate themselves from the exhibit's content and goals, while acknowledging that their own institutional purposes had been undermined.

Some of these factors also came into play in circumstances surrounding the exhibition *The Subject of Palestine,* that was displayed at the DePaul University Art Museum, on the university's Lincoln Park campus, from February 24 through May 6, 2005.

In her foreword to the exhibit catalogue, museum director Louise Lincoln declared that "Museums within university settings have an obligation not just to show art, but also to examine the relation between art and its social, political, and temporal context." She described the exhibition as a "grouping of works by artists of Palestinian identity, but differing in experience and perspective," and went on to say, "All the artists grapple with the way in which their identity is inextricably linked to one of the most charged political conflicts in the world. Taken together, the works give a profound sense of social complexity and painful emotion." Lincoln reported that "the initial proposal for the project came from a DePaul student group, Students for Justice in Palestine," a group that, as its name reveals, is driven by political and ideological, as opposed to aesthetic or even sociological, interests. Over a dozen departments and programs at the university served as co-sponsors. In addition, six faculty members were identified as having offered assistance. Among them was Norman Finkelstein, known for his provocative positions on the Holocaust and on the Israel-Palestinian conflict and for the inflammatory manner in which he expressed them, and who would be refused tenure by DePaul two years later. A local organization, the Arab American Action Network, on whose board sits Ali Abunimah, the most peripatetic, pro-Palestinian, anti-Israel advocate in the Chicago area, was said to have "generously contributed to the project." [12]

In all, the works of 16 artists were displayed in this exhibition, through drawings, prints, installations, and videos. As a unit, these works had the unifying theme of Palestinian suffering and exile, with titles ranging from "Sabra and Shatila Massacre," "Stateless Nation," "Martyr," and "Rabin Policy: Breaking Bones," to "Between the Bullets and the Stones," "The Baby Martyr Iman Hajjo," and "Home." While some works demonstrated artistic skill and complexity, and several did not seem to have an obvious "message," it was plain that the overriding purpose of the exhibition, as made explicit by the signage and catalogue, was blatantly propagandistic. The Palestinian "narrative" was advanced throughout, and the Palestinians were overwhelmingly presented as sympathetic victims, with virtually all the iconic episodes in the saga of Palestinian suffering portrayed in the exhibition. In contrast, the Israeli victimizers were mostly rendered as dehumanized, one-dimensional brutes.

Especially revealing was the opening statement in the exhibition catalogue's lead article, by guest curator Samia A. Halaby: "Resistance is the Palestinian response to the tragedy known as the *Nakba*, when in 1948 statehood was lost to Israeli occupation." And it was this sentence, extracted from the article, that was used to provide the introductory, defining, placard for the exhibition itself.

In a front page story in the *Chicago Jewish Star,* Douglas Wertheimer disputed the veracity of this and several other exhibit signs – including one describing how "At least 2000 Palestinians and some of their neighbors were murdered at Sabra and Shatilla because of Israel," another asserting that United Nations General Assembly Resolution 194 "affirms the right of Palestinians to return to their homes," and another claiming "that an Israeli tractor driver saw peace protestor Rachel Corrie 'and yet drove over her twice, killing her.'" Summing up his judgment on the bulk of the exhibit, Wertheimer concluded, "The feeling one gets from this presentation is that one is witnessing a propaganda display which promotes fantasies and illusions in order to perpetuate hate."[13]

"Tragedy and resistance permeate Palestinian national life and are the primary subject matter of Palestinian art," wrote Halaby in her article. After dividing the artists included in the exhibition into two categories, "heirs of the liberation movement" and "explicatory artists," she said that the former focused on "the struggle for freedom, support of political prisoners, and the right to return to their stolen homes and lands."

Describing the 2002 work, *Fire,* by Abd-al-Naser Amer, an artist in the first category, Halaby said it "tells of grief and anger in a turbulent, expressionist image of a man on a stretcher – an image of the victims of Israeli military attack which residents of Ghazza (Gaza) see far too often." Offering what seems to be her own judgment on the veracity of American and Israeli news media, Halaby also went on to say, "Amer renders his images on paper made of those Israeli and American newspapers that are full of lies, which he angrily tears, pulps, and reuses to tell the truth." Discussing another work, *The Baby Martyr Iman Hajjo,* Halaby described what she called "an image of respect, the respect of resistance to the daily humiliations imposed by Israelis on every detail of Palestinian life."

In contrast to the artists whom Halaby labeled "heirs of the liberation movement," are those she calls "explicatory artists." According to her, the latter "seek to explain Palestine, its history and its tragedy, to an audience perceived to have power over political reality – an audience whose good opinion Israel wants to maintain." The polemical goal of swaying such an audience to endorse the Palestinian perspective clearly seems to have been the very purpose of this exhibition.

It is a goal that is at odds with the museum director's proclaimed purpose of using university museums to "examine the relation between art and its social, political, and temporal context." In fact, DePaul took no steps to inform students and other visitors to the exhibition that the declaration in the introductory placard, like that in some other signage, was not a historically accurate description of events, but rather a distorted view of the past, conveyed in language that fed the group self-pity and animosity toward the Israeli "other" that permeated the exhibition. In showing the exhibition without such an accompanying clarification, but with signage advancing the political goals of Halaby and of the exhibition's student sponsors (and maybe some of its faculty sponsors), the DePaul University Museum participated in furthering those goals, however inadvertent this may have been.

The use of the opening passage from Halaby's catalogue article in signage providing the grounding for the exhibition as a whole exposed DePaul to criticism. As a representative of the local Jewish community's central organization, I wrote a letter to the university which said:

> The statement encapsulates a narrative in which Palestinians see themselves as martyrs victimized by the Israelis and in no way responsible for their own condition. Defying the historical facts, it asserts that "in 1948 statehood was lost to Israeli occupation," implying that Palestinians once had statehood, which they did not, and ignoring the fact that they could have had statehood at that point had they and the Arab world not rejected what the United Nations offered and Israel agreed to.

The letter continued by saying:

> Most revealing is the assertion that it was "Israeli occupation" that denied the Palestinians their state. By proclaiming that

even when Israel existed within the 1948 borders, that was "occupation," the statement implicitly rejects the legitimate re-establishment of Jewish sovereignty in the ancient homeland of the Jewish people – a legitimacy endorsed by the United Nations.[14]

The largest Catholic university in America, with over 23,000 students, DePaul is proud of its long history of inclusiveness. It welcomed Jewish students at a time when they could not attend other local universities, and today has a sizable Muslim student population. As had happened with the heads of the Museum of Contemporary Art, once DePaul officials realized they had been "used" by faculty-backed students with an anti-Israel political agenda who put together an exhibition open to criticism on intellectual grounds, they took steps to protect their academic standing. For one thing, they added signage distancing themselves from the exhibition and its message. For another, they used the university's official news source for faculty and staff, *Newsline,* to tackle the issue in a way designed to provide further official separation from the exhibition.

The lead story in DePaul's *Newsline,* entitled "Lincoln Park Art Exhibit Raises Historical Questions" (2005), quoted the passages from my letter cited above, and also quoted university president Father Dennis Holtschneider, who declared, "I believe that historical interpretation is critical, but first you must root yourself as deeply as you can in the facts." In compliance with Father Holtschneider's charge that it "set the historical record straight," the article then proceeded to review the facts of 1947-49. It continued by quoting Warren Schultz, an associate professor of history and one of the faculty supporters of the exhibition, who said he considered it important to discuss the language used to introduce the exhibit in context, saying that, for him, "It's presented as the point of view of the exhibit's guest curator. And in that sense, it needs to be understood as reflecting or giving insight to attitudes, approaches and past events that shaped the art in question." Daniel Goffman, chair of the History Department, added, "I think you can prove with evidence from 1948 that the statement, in and of itself without any context, is not accurate. But that's so deceptive in terms of what the statement says to that community." Putting all of this together, Schultz added:

Dan and I are in agreement that this is not a statement we would have made about the events in 1948, but I recognize that what this statement does reflect is a view of at least some Palestinians, and as such, it helps people to understand the art that is being produced.[15]

Though comments such as those by Professors Schultz and Goffman would have been illuminating had they been included in explanatory signage accompanying the exhibit and in the text of the exhibition catalogue, no such observations appeared in either of those places. On the other hand, the kind of comments made by them to *Newsline* suggests that exhibitions like this are able to find a home on university campuses not only because of agenda-driven students and lax exhibition standards (or inattentive officials), but also because of faculty members who are ready to offer a rationale for the distortion of historical facts, even if they themselves may not endorse the specific cause on behalf of which those facts are distorted.

In the third university exhibition referred to above, *Secrets,* a faculty member played a direct role. This exhibition was put together on the campus of Chicago's Columbia College. Now located in the city's South Loop area, Columbia College was founded in 1890 as the "Columbia School of Oratory." In 1961, it became a liberal arts college with, according to its website, "a 'hands-on minds-on' approach to arts and media education, and a progressive social agenda." Columbia College has grown greatly in recent years, and currently boasts a student population of nearly 12,000.[16]

Secrets opened in Columbia College's Glass Curtain Gallery in March 2008. The catalogue describes it as "A self-organized project initiated by the 6+ Women's Art Collective in collaboration with eight Palestinian women artists" that, before coming to Chicago, toured five other locations, which it presents as follows: International Center of Bethlehem, Palestine, September 2006; Khalil Sakakini Cultural Center, Ramallah, Palestine, December 2006; Al Hoash Gallery, Jerusalem, Israel, December 2006; The Paltel Virtual Gallery at Birzeit University, March 2007; The Dairy Center for the Arts, Boulder, CO, USA, April 2007.

By the time the catalogue was finalized for distribution at Columbia, a "correction" sheet (unsigned, but attributed to the 6+ collective) had been prepared, making it clear where the organizers of this exhibition came from politically and revealing their readiness to distort facts. The sheet, entitled "Notes on the Political Geography of Occupation," began by saying:

On page 3 of the *Secrets* catalogue, the location of Al Hoash

Gallery was incorrectly identified as "Jerusalem, Israel." In fact, Al Hoash Gallery is located in East Jerusalem, whose annexation by the State of Israel has never been recognized by the international community. Identifying and correcting this mistake has been, for us, an urgent call to reflect upon the ways in which the US-backed Israeli politics of aggression can become normalized and unwittingly reproduced.

While this "correction" sheet insisted that East Jerusalem was not to be considered part of Israel, it had no qualms about Bethlehem and Ramallah being called cities in "Palestine." It continued with a historical summary, declaring that Israel "forcibly placed East Jerusalem under its law, jurisdiction and administration," thus "denying the legitimacy of Palestinian sovereignty." Citing what it regarded as United States complicity with that deed, the sheet said that "The might of the United States continues to be openly leveraged against the international community." Describing Israel's Security Barrier erroneously in a number of ways, it continued:

> Israeli annexation of Palestinian lands continues today, under the guise of "security": the so-called Separation Barrier. This is a concrete wall 436 miles long . . . It surrounds Palestinian lands . . . devastating the Palestinian economy, while carving out more and more territories for protected Israeli settlements deep within the West Bank.[17]

A report on the exhibition broadcast on Chicago's public radio station, WBEZ, quoted Mary Rachel Fanning, an advisor and instructor in photography at Columbia College and a member of the 6+ Women's Art Collective, who was instrumental in getting the show placed at Columbia, saying, "The reason we chose the topic, 'Secrets,' was that the artists could respond to it intimately, in a personal way, but it also gave the artists an opportunity to respond to the topic in a political way."[18]

In an essay in the catalogue called "The Unearthing of Secrets," Maymanah Farhat admitted that "*Secrets* was organized without a particular curatorial premise that would serve as the basis of the selection of artists and artwork."[19] The lack of unity, indeed virtual incoherence, of this exhibit is thus apparently no accident. In its conclusion, the catalogue says: "By disregarding the purported need for curatorialship, 6+ allotted equal authorship to all fourteen of the exhibition's artist." After declaring that "The dominant American art sense is wrought with bias" in a "rigidly defined system [that] is directly tied to the American political sphere," the group goes on to assert that it "will now forge through the ideological barriers of the American consciousness and the mainstream art world."[20] These artists' anti-Israel animus is apparently tied to an overall revolutionary spirit, and they appear to view the assembly of the exhibition as itself an act of resistance.

In fact, Fanning's own mixed media installation had no apparent connection to the subject of the exhibition, while several other images and installations in the exhibition made no direct reference to the Palestinian experience either. At the same time, however, several works were connected to the pronounced pro-Palestinian, political orientation of the organizers through accompanying signage or by explication in the catalogue that often seemed a stretch of the imagination.

Some of these installations and images were quite touching. The video and sound installation, *Turning Our Tongues,* which has been displayed elsewhere, stood out in this respect. A collection of "Audio Journals from Dheisheh Refugee Camp," it consisted of recorded and photographed performances by young women ages 16 to 18 living in Dheisheh who related their life stories.[21]

What viewers were not told was that the reason why these well-spoken, apparently middle-class young women were languishing under severe conditions in a refugee camp, lacking greater personal opportunities, was chiefly because, for decades, their national leadership has chosen to keep them there and, at key moments, has refused to take the diplomatic steps enabling them to live in a state of their own, side by side with Israel. Instead, only Israel was blamed, and the only speaker who expressed impatience with her leaders mourned Yasser Arafat and wished Abu Mazen would be more radical and aggressive with Israel. The failure to contextualize the pathos attached to the situations faced by these young women, as well as the realities defining the conditions faced by the other subjects portrayed in the exhibition, is the real "secret" of this show, one that the museum organizers chose to withhold from viewers.

The lack of detail and context is particularly problematic in the cases of two other installations in the exhibition. One is a series of three photographs by Shuruq Harb, collected under the title, *Traces of Honor.* According to the catalogue, this series, portraying what is called "emblematic corpses," was "prompted by three 'honor' killings in 2005 in [Harb's] West Bank hometown of Ramallah and nearby Jerusalem city." Neither in the signage nor in the catalogue are visitors told that, as victims of honor killings, the women portrayed in these photos must have been murdered by fellow Palestinians. "Secrets," said the WBEZ radio report, "takes on the perspective of the Palestinian plight, with works that address Israeli occupation directly, and others that explore womanhood and war."[22] Given that kind of declaration, uninformed viewers had no way of knowing that the victims of honor killings portrayed were not murdered by the Israelis; on the contrary, they had every reason to believe they were.

Similarly, an audio video installation called *Transfiguration,* where visitors could look through a peephole at photographs from a boy's life, from baptism to funeral, sentimentally portrayed what the catalogue described as "the tragic story of a young man whose life was taken under the occupation." The catalogue went on to say: "It appears he became a resistance fighter shortly before he was killed, and is remembered as a martyr in his community." However, nowhere in the signage or in the catalogue were viewers informed precisely what kind of "resistance fighter" this young man was, or the exact circumstances of his death. Instead, referring to his "assassination," the catalogue told readers that:

> It is important to note that in Palestine, anyone killed as a result of the occupation is considered a martyr since it is understood that remaining in the territories, despite the danger it poses, is an act of political defiance and a sacrifice made on behalf of the entire community. [23]

In fact, according to *Israel Today,* the young man, Daniel Abu Hamameh, though a Christian, was killed while riding with wanted terrorists from the Al Aqsa Brigade in a car that "stormed through" a military roadblock. The human rights organization *B'Tselem* regards him as a "wanted person" who was driving "with two friends who were also wanted persons."[24]

As a whole, this exhibition contained images presenting Palestinians (mostly women) in a sympathetic manner. It was replete with signage that, ignoring Palestinian violence and terrorism, Israeli security concerns, and Palestinian rejectionism, had the potential to lead viewers to conclude that the suffering of the subjects was totally caused by the Israelis and by the conditions the latter unfeelingly and unjustifiably created and maintained.

Such a perception of the exhibition is supported by its catalogue, which was dominated by radical discourse replete with historical and descriptive errors. Most graphic in this respect was the opening chapter,

"Smoldering Secrets," by Lucy R. Lippard, a feminist art critic with no apparent background that would qualify her as a knowledgeable expert in Middle East issues. In her opening paragraph, she talked of "the way even indisputable facts engender accusations of anti-Semitism." Among the so-called "indisputable facts" listed in that same paragraph was a reference to "the divisive laws perpetrated by a theocratic society against second-class citizens of another religion that amounts to a new apartheid." Further on in this chapter, she stated that Palestinian art was "densely packed with history, both the recent 55 years of Israeli occupation and also the several thousand years of history that preceded it." With "Israeli occupation" beginning for her in 1948 (her piece, though published in the *Secrets* catalogue in 2007, was apparently originally written in 2003), and with Palestinian culture and society having existed for her from time immemorial, Lippard linked herself and, by extension, others involved in organizing and presenting this exhibit to those who deny the legitimacy of the founding of the State of Israel in 1948, and who reject the right of the Jewish people to self-determination anywhere in the Land of Israel. Though her provocative opening challenge regarding the validity of charges of anti-Semitism may have been an attempt to insulate herself against the same charges, her accusing Israel of "apartheid" can be seen as an exemplary representation of what has been called the new anti-Semitism. [25]

Lippard linked virtually every piece in the exhibition, however unrelated it might seem, to the theme she was promoting. Though she concluded by saying that the exhibition was the product of a "collective project, created by women artists defying national foreign policies and calling on the basic feminist values of 'generosity, empathy, and reciprocity,'" she herself demonstrated none of these values in the way she treated the Israelis. She even described them as possibly playing an obscure role in a British artist's portrayal of a preadolescent girl "lying on the ground with a bouquet of flowers on her chest." For Lippard, "This final image can be read as a death or a romantic swoon – tied into the Palestinian dilemma or simply a personal crisis of puberty."[26]

As in the previous two cases, the administrators at Chicago's Columbia College were unhappy when they learned that art exhibition space of theirs was being used by people with an agenda at odds with the university's academic principles. In this case, that realization came before the exhibit opened. They, too, then issued signage disassociating themselves from the political content of the exhibition. Furthermore, the egregiously ideological, and factually inaccurate, catalogue, on which

Columbia College's own imprimatur appeared, thus identifying the college as an institutional sponsor (along with three other universities), was not made freely available to visitors to the exhibition. Instead, a copy was displayed at the exhibition, with instructions how interested parties could order it directly.

What is it, one may wonder, that leads faculty members and students to wish to create exhibitions distinguished not so much by their aesthetic or academic features as by their advancement of a pro-Palestinian, anti-Israel agenda? The confluence of art and politics is, of course, not unique. The twentieth century alone witnessed, on the one hand, artists such as Pablo Picasso (in, for example, "Guernica") and Diego Rivera (in many of his murals) conveying political messages in their art and, on the other, Soviet and Nazi ideologues using traditional or popular art forms to advance their propaganda. Modern and contemporary artists have frequently been drawn to political and ideological engagement in their lives and in their art. And although the emphasis of this paper has been on the academic connections of the exhibitions under discussion, this is not meant to suggest that other venues are not being used in a similar way. As the list of locales for the *Secrets* exhibition shows, it was shown in several other galleries before arriving at Columbia College. Still, there is, I believe, something significant and instructive about the recurring overlapping of academia, art, and ideological anti-Zionism witnessed in Chicago in recent years, that may also be currently at play elsewhere on the American scene.

The current support for the Palestinian cause within academia and the art world expresses a fashionable endorsement of the Palestinian narrative, whereby Palestinians are viewed as today's "wretched of the earth," innocent victims of brutal Israeli colonizers. It is a narrative featuring claims of Palestinian dispossession that, focusing on American support for Israel, exploits the decline in America's stature abroad and the concomitant hostility against an America perceived in some quarters as an imperialistic power seeking global hegemony. It is a perspective that feeds on traditional anti-Semitic scapegoating, demonization, and conspiracy theories regarding Jewish power, while creating a new anti-Semitism that would deny the Jewish people a right to national self-determination, and that portrays Israel as a racist, oppressive, pariah-like, illegal entity – in short, as today's South Africa.

The globalized, intellectual readiness to accept the Palestinian narrative and embrace the anti-Israel agenda of radical Palestinian and Muslim groups has led academics and activists to join forces in a common front and to turn to art exhibitions as useful frameworks for advancing anti-Israel polemics in at least one major American city.

The advantage of utilizing art exhibitions to promote this cause is that, unlike the campus-based demonstrations and rallies, they are not so obviously partisan or such noisy turn-offs. Indeed, these exhibitions can be "sold" to university administrators and museum officials, who might be unaware of the extremist purposes they are endorsing, and the result is that these exhibits can then be brought before viewers without being immediately recognizable as propaganda vehicles. Once installed, the art works can evoke emotional responses, creating sympathy for the victimized Palestinians and hostility toward brutish Israel, while the signage and catalogues for these exhibits can be used to advance the Palestinian narrative and create support for the Palestinian rejectionist cause. And thus, as distortions of historical and contemporary realities are presented as facts to advance the cause for which these exhibitions are mounted, institutions of higher learning and art museums become accomplices, seemingly endorsing those claims.

As this review of three recent incidents in Chicago shows, officials at each host institution in question immediately took steps to distance themselves from each exhibition's message as soon as they realized how academic legitimacy and institutional credibility were being undermined. While it is likely that more institutions will be targeted for such exhibits in the future, perhaps some of them will be more wary than those were. Furthermore, with alert community organizations and informed Israel supporters on campus sounding the alarm, this component of the campus-based, anti-Israel propaganda offensive may have less free rein than it has had heretofore. And at the same time, with the field of Israel Studies growing in the United States and with increasing numbers of Israeli academics holding visiting positions at American universities, an alternative perspective is being offered to set the record straight.

Still, anti-Israel messages will undoubtedly continue to resonate in academia and to be advanced in various ways. With Hamas spokesmen in Gaza now calling for "cultural resistance" and the tactic having its appeal,[27] polemical anti-Israel art exhibits can be expected to continue to be seen in campus-based galleries throughout North America.

NOTES

[1.] Labeled "the new anti-Semitism," use of traditional anti-Semitic themes and imagery in an anti-Israel framework has been discussed in a number of books and articles, including the following: Paul Iganski and Barry Kosmin, *The New Antisemitism? Debating Judeo-*

phobia in 21st-Century Britain (London: Profile Books, 2003); Phyllis Chesler, *The New Anti-Semitism: The Current Crisis and What We Must Do About It* (San Francisco: Jossey-Bass, 2003); Abraham H. Foxman, *Never Again? The Threat of the New Anti-Semitism* (New York: HarperCollins, 2003); Gabriel Schoenfeld, *The Return of Anti-Semitism* (San Francisco; Encounter Books, 2004). A useful collection of essays and excerpts from other works is *Those Who Forget the Past: The Question of Anti-Semitism,* edited by Ron Rosenbaum (New York: Random House, 2004).

2. See *Academics Against Israel and the Jews,* edited by Manfred Gerstenfeld (Jerusalem: Jerusalem Center for Public Affairs, 2007), and Gary Tobin, Aryeh K. Weinberg, and Jenna Ferer, *The Uncivil University* (San Francisco: Institute for Jewish and Community Research, 2005).

3. For an eyewitness account of one of the most dramatic instances of campus-based anti-Israel agitation see Laurie Zoloth, "Fear and Loathing at San Francisco State," in Rosenbaum, pp. 258-262. On classroom-linked issues see Efraim Karsh, "Columbia and the Academic Intifada," *Commentary,* July-August 2005, pp. 27-32; Michael Kotzin, "New Era Is Born," http://www.ynetnews.com; November 11, 2007; and Mitchell Bard, "Classroom Battlegrounds: Pro-Israel Students Return to School Upbeat," *The Jerusalem Post,* http://www.JPost.com, September 4, 2008.

4. Personal communication from student at the School of the Art Institute. March 2003.

5. Website of Artist Emergency Response, http://www.artic.edu/webspaces/aer.

6. Flyer distributed by AER for taping of November 13, 2002.

7. On Jewish involvement in such efforts see Alvin H. Rosenfeld, *"Progressive" Jewish Thought and the New Anti-Semitism* (American Jewish Committee, 2006).

8. Julia Keller, "'War' Show Seeks to Incite Thought," *Chicago Tribune,* February 9, 2003, Section 7, p. 4.

9. Gila Wertheimer, "MCA's Politicized Anti-War Exhibit," *The Chicago Jewish Star,* March 14-27, 2003, pp. 1-2.

10. Letter from Robert Fitzpatrick (undated copy).

11. Letter from Tony Jones, March 7, 2003.

12. Louise Lincoln, Foreword to the Exhibit Catalogue, p. 1.

On Norman Finkelstein's tenure bid see Jennifer Howard, "DePaul U. Turns Norman Finkelstein Down for Tenure," *The Chronicle of Higher Education,* June 11, 2007. http://www.chronicle.com. For an update on Finkelstein, see Stewart Ain, "A Pariah in Exile," *The New York Jewish Week,* July 2, 2008. http://www.thejewishweek.com.

13. Douglas Wertheimer, "At DePaul, Anti-Israel Art," *The Chicago Jewish Star,* March 11-24, 2005, pp. 1-2.

A very different perspective was offered by the art critic of the *Chicago Tribune,* Alan G. Artner, who concluded that "these artists have voices that need to be heard, especially at an institution dedicated to the free play of thought." "Palestine Struggles are the Subject," *Chicago Tribune,* April 14, 2005, Section 5, p. 3.

All quotations from Samia H. Halaby are from "The Subject of Palestine," exhibit catalogue, pp. 1-3.

[14.] From letter dated March 24, 2005.

[15.] *DePaul University Newsline,* Volume 39, No. 14, April 15, 2005, pp. 1-2.

[16.] "A Brief History of Columbia College Chicago," http://www.colum.edu.

[17.] "Correction" sheet to exhibit catalogue.

[18.] "Art Exhibition Confronts Issues in the Middle East," WBEZ radio website transcript of broadcast of March 20, 2008. http://www.wbez.org/default.aspx.

[19.] Maymanah Farhat, "The Unearthing of Secrets," *Secrets* exhibit catalogue, 2007, p. 18.

[20.] *Secrets* exhibit catalogue, p. 50.

[21.] The installation is discussed on pp. 54-55 of the exhibit catalogue.

[22.] *Op. cit.,* WBEZ radio transcript.

[23.] Exhibit catalogue, p. 40.

[24.] *Israel Today,* June 28, 2006. http://www.israeltoday.co.il.

B'Tselem, Daniel Saba George Abu Hamamah, April 2006. http://www.btselem.org.

[25.] Lucy R. Lippard, "Smoldering Secrets," *Secrets* exhibit catalogue, pp. 7, 9.

[26.] *Ibid.,* pp. 12, 10.

[27.] See Ethan Bronner, "Hamas Shifts from Rockets to Culture War," *The New York Times,* July 24, 2009, Section A, p. 1.

The Shaping of the American Mind
The Times of Israel, March 11, 2012

• • •

This year's "Israel Apartheid Week" has come and gone.

While announced and promoted by a slick, highly professional video, and while anticipated in a batch of articles and opinion columns in the Israeli and American Jewish press, judging from reports from a number of cities, the whole thing was rather uneventful, at least in North America.

Here in Chicago, where the anti-Israel group known as Students for Justice in Palestine is particularly active on a number of campuses, and where last year's observance of the event brought "apartheid walls" plastered with inflammatory signage to three local campuses and other activities carried out elsewhere, things were quite quiet.

This isn't to say, however, that anti-Israel agitation on campus is an over-hyped thing of the past. For one thing, activities aimed at advancing a radical version of the Palestinian "cause" continue to be carried out on a year-round basis. And for another, the danger, while not to be exaggerated, should also not be lightly dismissed.

And so, for example, shortly before Israel Apartheid Week took place, an annual conference aimed at promoting boycott, divestment, and sanctions of Israel, which moves from campus to campus, was held at the University of Pennsylvania. Meanwhile, another conference, this one aimed at making the case for a "one-state solution" to the Israel-Palestinian conflict, has since been convened at Harvard University.

Gaining less attention, but nevertheless an example of the smaller-scale activity that goes on regularly around the country, an anti-Zionist Jewish psychologist named Mark Braverman, who has made it his mission to urge Christians to free themselves of guilt feelings about the Holocaust — which could interfere with a readiness to be harshly critical of Israel — came to visit the University of Illinois at Urbana-Champaign. Demonizing Israel and using anti-Semitic tropes while speaking at several programs on and off campus, he left Jewish students shocked and appalled.

Having grown accustomed to such activity over the past several years, community organizations like ours have developed a strategic approach that not only supports students in responding to the hostile attacks but pays a great deal of attention to advancing positive educational programming about Israel on campus. The goal is not just to oppose the tactics of those who would exploit the openness of campus culture to advance their destructive purposes but also to expose their true intent and counter their messages.

For what is currently happening on many North American campuses is a war of words and images generated by those who reject the right of Israel to exist as the nation-state of the Jewish people and whose aim is to erode the support Israel now has from its most important ally. It is a war that is conducted less through single battles of the sort that Israeli Apartheid Week epitomizes than by recurring offensives carried out in a cumulative war of attrition.

Consider the movement to advance boycott, divestment, and sanctions (BDS). The movement has few explicit successes to show for its efforts, certainly not on North American campuses. In fact it is unlikely that any serious direct harm could be done to Israel even if the steps were adopted in the places where they are promoted. The real purpose and impact of this agitation is to advance negative images of Israel, associating the country with the South African regime that actually did practice apartheid and that ultimately was brought down in great part by international sanctions.

Israel is likened to that regime to make it appear similarly illegitimate and evil, and the message is meant to seep in. And thus, for example, when DePaul University in Chicago last year was the site of a full-scale effort aimed at forcing a boycott on campus of something as seemingly trivial as Sabra hummus, the Student Union was plastered with posters calling for the boycott as a means of halting apartheid, posters that portrayed the Israelis as brutal baby-killers – and it was those terms and images that were really the crux of the effort.

Such incendiary, outrageous words and images are put out there, on campus after campus, over and over again: Comparisons of the Israelis to the Nazis; claims of Israeli genocide; assertions that Israel is a gross, deliberate violator of human rights; appeals to belief in democracy as a basis for supporting the eliminationist one-state solution. It is all part of an incessant campaign carried out through various means and in various settings. Even the naming of Students for Justice in Palestine – an organization that was invisible if not non-existent a decade or so ago but has emerged as the most dominant, ubiquitous anti-Israel group on one campus after another – reflects that gestalt.

With Senator Dick Durbin, his brother William, and guide at Auschwitz, February 1997.

With Senator Durbin and the Deputy Director of the Lithuanian National Library in Vilnius, February 1997.

Governor Jim Edgar signs JCRC-drafted counterterrorism legislation, with Federation leadership and statewide elected officials, July 1996.

With Mayor Harold Washington on Devon Avenue along with State Senator Howard Carroll, JCRC Director Peggy Norton, and other community leaders following a spate of anti-Semitic incidents, November 1987.

With Mayor Richard M. Daley and community leaders in West Rogers Park following anti-Semitic shootings in that neighborhood, July 1999.

With Joseph Cardinal Bernardin and the Reverend Michael Place during visit to Israel, March 1995. (Photo: Joel Fishman.)

With Joseph Cardinal Bernardin and Catholic Jewish delegation in Jerusalem, March 1995 (Photo: Joel Fishman.)

With Cardinal Bernardin and accompanying delegation meeting with President Ezer Weizman in Jerusalem, March 1995. (Photo: Joel Fishman.)

With Francis Cardinal George, Rev. Thomas Baima, and Steven B. Nasatir, Federation President, at Chicago Archdiocese announcing Federation/Archdiocese partnership for project at Israeli village of Fassouta, January 2008. (Photo: Linda Haase.)

With Cardinal George and Mayor George Ayoub at Fassouta, Israel, January 2008. (Photo: Debbi Cooper.)

With Congressman Bobby Rush and former Illinois Comptroller Dawn Clark Netsch at Yad Vashem, August 1995.

With Governor Pat Quinn at the Mt. of Beatitudes, July 2011.

Congresswoman Jan Schakowsky in Kiryat Gat Region, August 2003. (Photo: Linda Epstein.)

With Congresswoman Jan Schakowsky and Shimon Peres, Tel Aviv, August 2003.

With Senator Barack Obama and Chairman of the Executive of the Jewish Agency for Israel Ze'ev Bielski, along with Federation leaders Alan Solow and Midge Perlman Shafton in Jerusalem, January 2006.

Besides the fact that university campuses are the most likely places to find the right cohort to advance this campaign – a cadre made up of radical Palestinian and Muslim students and their ideology-driven student and faculty allies – they are also the prime battleground for another reason. For it is there that the leaders and voters of tomorrow – young idealists who are thought to be particularly vulnerable to the kinds of messages that are deceptively evoked – are coming of age. It is there that Israel's adversaries try to shape the American mind (to modify a phrase introduced by Allan Bloom 25 years ago) so Israel will no longer be thought of with sympathetic understanding.

For those of us who are concerned and involved in campus life, the challenge is to recognize this threat for what it is, to expose it, and to build countervailing attachments to the real Israel. To do that we need to be smart, fully attuned to the campus culture, and on the job 52 weeks a year — not just one.

Politics and the Modern Language Association

The Times of Israel, January 8, 2014

• • •

The recent passage by the American Studies Association (ASA) of a resolution declaring an academic boycott of Israeli universities alerted many members of the American Jewish community to the troubling views held by numerous activist faculty members on campuses throughout North America. Even though only some 800 ASA members voted for that resolution, in taking into account the motives of those behind the global Boycott, Divestment, and Sanctions (BDS) movement, which has called for such steps and which in truth constitutes an assault on Israel's legitimacy, concerns about this development are understandable. Equally understandable in their own way are the concerns of many communal organizations about what might happen when the Modern Language Association—a group some six times the size of the ASA—holds its annual convention in Chicago on January 9-12. But as important as the upcoming meeting and the resolution that will be introduced there are, it is equally important to keep in perspective what actually is on tap to happen at the MLA meeting, and to understand what it all means. For though what will be happening indeed matters to the Jewish community, what is going on most centrally is an internal battle regarding the meaning and purpose of the MLA itself, and it is that body which is about to face its moment of truth.

My own familiarity with this organization goes back over five decades, to a time when I was a graduate student in English at the University of Minnesota. The annual MLA convention is, among other things, a major job-hunting venue, and I lined up my first academic position at the 1967 meeting, also held in Chicago, where I was offered a position at Tel Aviv University. That led to my teaching there for eleven years, after which I returned to the States and began a very different kind of career in Jewish communal service. If no longer as central to my professional pursuits, my interest in literature continued. So it made sense when, two years ago, as I cut back my hours at the Jewish Federation of Metropolitan Chicago, I used some of the time made available to return to the classroom as a Visiting Professor at the University of Illinois for a semester and to begin to publish in scholarly journals once more. And when the program for this year's MLA convention was announced in early November, I renewed my membership and registered for the conference.

I continue to feel attachments to the historic purposes of the association. And I share the views of its members that the Humanities, which today suffer from decreasing support on the American educational scene, are of great value in general and in a democratic society in particular. Additionally, I have an ongoing interest in several of the fields the conference covers, and among this year's over 800 sessions, a number have topics that sound attractive to me. But at the same time, I have been troubled by the way that Israel has been treated at other academic conventions, and what I saw in this year's program led me and a number of longstanding members of the MLA with whom I have been in contact to have deep concerns about what was about to happen here.

While this year's MLA program does not include consideration of a resolution calling for an academic boycott of Israel like the one passed by the ASA, it does include a roundtable discussion session on the topic of academic boycotts whose panelists have all have gone on record in support of such boycotts or have otherwise demonstrated an animus for Israel. The line-up includes Omar Barghouti, identified in the conference program as an "independent scholar" but far better known for having founded the Palestinians' BDS movement. Another of the panelists is David Lloyd, a professor of English at the University of California's Riverside campus who wrote a column for the *Electronic Intifada* supporting the ASA vote and attacking what he called "the nightmare hidden within liberal Zionism." His primary target in that piece was the commentator Peter Beinart, whom he condemned for writing a column for The Daily Beast which, while criticizing Israel's settlements policy, also strongly affirmed the need for a two state solution to the Israel-Palestinian conflict. For Lloyd, who describes Israel as an "exclusively racist state," the "two state solution threatens Palestinians," and he decidedly rejects that solution himself.

In addition to that panel discussion, this year's MLA program also includes a resolution on Israel which, though not on the subject of academic boycotts, is troubling in its way. It calls for the association to urge the U.S. State Department "to contest Israel's arbitrary denials of entry to Gaza and the West Bank by U.S. academicians who have been invited to teach, confer, or do research at Palestinian universities." While on its face such language may sound reasonable to members of the MLA's Delegate Assembly who will vote at the end of this week, if examined carefully the resolution proves to be based on flimsy, limited evidence presented in a one-sided background report, and the resolution's charges are made without any suitable context. The resolution's insistence that measures taken by Israel in determining the implementation of its policies regarding foreign visitors are merely "arbitrary" is blind to the realities Israel faces. And the resolution's bias is evidenced in its unfairness in singling out Israel alone for engaging in a widespread global practice and in the assumptions it implies about Israel's motivation.

My early years as a member of the MLA took place in the '60s, a politically volatile time in America when I myself, outside of the classroom, was involved in the anti-Vietnam war movement. Despite whatever may have gone on in MLA conventions at that time, and although through the years various political causes may have been supported by the association, the MLA has continued to have the core identity of an academic and scholarly enterprise. What is happening now has the potential of changing that utterly. Accordingly, the central issue that is currently in play is not about a conflict of some sort between the Jewish community and the MLA, as some have suggested. Instead, the unfolding conflict is within the MLA itself.

Yes, the attempt to delegitimize Israel might get a bump if the supporters for implementing an academic boycott against Israel in the round-table discussion gain adherents. But that activity has never caught on in America as it has in England and Europe, and it remains unlikely to. Though Omar Barghouti may have called what happened at the ASA conference a "tipping point," the rejection of a boycott and strong criticism of the ASA for endorsing that position from one university president after another, and many faculty members as well, proves the contrary. Indeed, what the ASA did may have actually made the BDS movement weaker and less credible in America than it had been.

And yes, if the proposed MLA resolution passes despite its inherent flaws and despite the well-substantiated opposition of key MLA members, that probably would be portrayed by the resolution's supporters as a major victory, and some damage would indeed be done. In that regard, some members of the MLA opposed to this resolution suspect that it is a "stalking horse" which, if passed, could lay the groundwork for the introduction of a boycott resolution next year, and the anti-boycott momentum created recently by the sharp negative response to the ASA's action throughout the country could be blunted somewhat. But the resolution still is significantly weaker than what the ASA passed.

So as much as supporters of Israel are right to take seriously what is happening at the MLA convention, that concern should be kept in perspective. At this point it is not the MLA as an organization but some of its members who are creating a problem, and what is really at stake in these meetings is the future of the MLA itself. The key question at hand thus is whether the MLA will continue to be a body defined by its proclaimed mission of serving as an organization with the purpose of "promoting the teaching and study of language and literature" which embraces academic ideals and the advancement of scholarly pursuits. The stark alternative, which would follow if the MLA chooses to enter on the path which the ASA has taken, is that it can come to be regarded the way the ASA is today—as a fringe organization more concerned with the advancement of a one-sided, unfair, ideology-driven foreign policy agenda—rather than as a credible scholarly association. What is at stake in these meetings is the very soul of the MLA.

.

MLA Resolution: What's It All About?

JUF News, February 2014

• • •

On Jan. 11, the Delegate Assembly of the Modern Language Association (MLA) meeting in Chicago voted 60 to 53 to support a resolution which urged the U.S. State Department "to contest Israel's denial of entry to the West Bank by U.S. academics who have been invited to teach, confer, or do research at Palestinian universities." To become adopted by the organization as a whole, the resolution will next have to be approved by the MLA's Executive Council, scheduled to meet in late February, and if it passes it would face a vote of the total membership.

While the resolution passed by the MLA's Delegate Assembly thus has yet to be adopted, it still is a matter of concern and merits scrutiny. A useful way to approach it would be to apply a variation on the analytic terms first developed by medieval Kabbalists for reading the Torah, starkly different though the nature of these texts may be.

This approach proceeds by considering four levels of meaning, the first of which deals with the literal meaning of the text. Looked at on its face, the resolution thus is simply calling for certain State Department action. This reading is in tune with the claim made by one of the drafters of the resolution in opening the discussion at the MLA session where it was voted on, who asserted that the resolution should be taken only in the narrow sense of coming to the support of fellow academics.

But looked at only in this way, the resolution has hardly any value. It is hard to imagine the State Department truly "contesting" Israel's application of its security policies regarding academic visitors – especially because, as research done by a newly-formed group called MLA Members for Scholars' Rights showed, the proponents of the resolution could identify only one person who might have faced the problem, which is cited as the purported basis of the resolution.

Looking then for other meanings to this resolution, we can next see it as a symbolic statement of solidarity with the Palestinian people, whom the drafters and supporters of the resolution clearly regard as an oppressed people. If the resolution is seen this way, what matters is not what it calls for directly but how it could be taken by the Palestinians.

Their sense of grievance and victimhood was validated by the language of the resolution's backers, who repeatedly spoke about Israel's "racist" system and "apartheid" regime when they took the floor at the MLA meeting. Given that approach, this resolution and other statements like it can be seen as perpetuating the situation the Palestinians currently face, ultimately hardening both sides of the Israel-Palestinian conflict instead of advancing reconciliation and hastening the coming of the day when the Palestinians could have self-determination in a state of their own next to the state of Israel.

Moving on to the third level of meaning, the resolution can be seen as advancing a narrative which, as supporters of the resolution demonstrated, sees Israel as being a racist country practicing apartheid and using chemical weapons. As we dig deeper and get closer to the true meaning behind a resolution like this, we recognize that the rhetoric of its supporters is the rhetoric of the delegitimizers of Israel, of those who would marginalize the state for what they portray as its gross violations of human rights. This resolution may not go as far as the one passed by the members of the American Studies Association, whose right to call for an academic boycott was defended in an "emergency resolution" that failed to achieve consideration by the MLA. But the resolution's defenders talked about Israel with the same animosity as do the boycotters. The hostility of one speaker after another at the MLA session was tangible.

And this brings us to the resolution's deepest, fourth level of meaning, to what Cary Nelson, Professor of English at the University of Illinois at Urbana-Champaign, calls "the elephant in the room." That is anti-Semitism.

Those of us who talk about these matters need to use the anti-Semitism charge with care, both because its seriousness needs to be respected and also because, in attempting to pre-empt consideration of this issue, Israel's enemies are always quick to claim that Israel's friends use the term indiscriminately when talking about any critic of any of Israel's polices or actions. Though one of the supporters of the resolution at the MLA meeting attacked what he called the "rhetorical ploys" and "suppressive rhetoric" of Israel's supporters, it is in fact the enemies of Israel who try to suppress exposure of the anti-Semitism that often suffuses their own rhetoric and approach.

Thus, though we should be careful about using the term anti-Semitism, when anti-Semitic concepts can be identified within the verbal attacks on Israel, it is far from improper to point that out. So when one of the supporters of the resolution who took the floor during the Delegate

Assembly meeting talked about financial contributions to political can-didates in America by a "pro-Israel lobby," which, he implied, corrupt American foreign policy, the anti-Semitic reverberations were surely there.

That speaker, along with several others, was opposing the charge that there is something wrong with "singling out" Israel as does this resolu-tion. In fact, the pattern of singling out at the least raises the possibility that there is something off-kilter in such treatment of Israel, and those who do the singling-out don't like to be put on the spot about that. They talk about the amount of financial aid that Israel has received from the U.S. through the years and things like that as justifying particularist criti-cism of it. But with the proponents of a resolution that singles out Israel rejecting the replacing of it with a resolution that calls for freedom of movement for *all* academics, as was the case at the MLA meeting, it's hard not to suggest that the secret is out and that something is at play that is not just about the rights of traveling academics.

The introducer of this resolution, who spoke first at the meeting and who two days before had been a panelist on a discussion session that sup-ported academic boycotts of Israel, said he was insulted by the claim that this resolution was seen by some as laying the groundwork for a boycott resolution in the future. Whether or not that was the intent, there clearly is an affinity between the backers of this resolution and the supporters of such a boycott. Their shared methods, it has increasingly been recognized, marginalize Israel through a strategy of demonization and delegitimiza-tion which ultimately, it can be suggested, is intended to lead to Israel's elimination as a Jewish state, just as apartheid-ruled South Africa was brought down. And as much as the proponents of the boycott and other such measures may not like to have it said, the denial to the Jewish people of the right of national self-determination in their ancient homeland is an act of discrimination equivalent to the kinds of bigotry-driven acts carried out against Jewish individuals and Jewish communities in past eras.

So as much as it would be wrong in many ways to reduce everything to anti-Semitism, neither should we fail to identify what much of all of this is about. What we are witness to within the MLA and one academic association after another is the application of an anti-colonial ideology which, in the name of helping the Palestinians does quite the opposite, and which unfairly vilifies Israel as a racist violator of human rights that does not deserve to exist. Given the rhetoric with which these concepts are advanced, this ideology has become a key transmitter of the anti-Semitic virus in our time. That needs to be seen, and that needs to be called attention to.

Understanding Israel
As It Really Is:
Brand Israel and Israel Studies

During the period of time covered by this volume, members of the American Jewish community have recognized that the Diaspora's connections with Israel have evolved significantly. In earlier times those connections were largely created through the pride-filled emotional responses of people who personally witnessed the establishment of the state in the shadow of the Holocaust, who were aware of its early accomplishments and triumphs, and who experienced the initial fears and subsequent relief and joy connected with the Six Day War. Over the passage of time, the existence of emotional ties could no longer be taken for granted. And understanding of the totality of the real Israel has tended to be obscured as Israel has increasingly been seen primarily through the lens of its conflicts with its neighbors. To counter that trend, in recent years steps have been taken to reforge connections with Israel in a fashion appropriate for the current moment in time and to advance understanding of Israel in all of its complexities, both in and beyond the Jewish community.

I have had the opportunity to be directly involved in two of the main approaches that were initiated during the first decade of the current century to advance this greater understanding of Israel as it really is. The first revolved around the development of "Brand Israel" concepts that addressed discoveries made by a research group in America. At the breakthrough conference on the subject held in Israel at the end of October 2006, populated by experts from Israel and other nations, I delivered the paper included in this section of the volume that, talking about the American scene, applies the branding notions in territory beyond that for which they were first intended. Seen this way, Brand Israel concepts have the prospect of enhancing connections with Israel within the Jewish community and beyond. (This piece includes comments about then-Senator Barack Obama's first visit to Israel.) Applying these notions, colleagues in the Chicago Federation's Communications Department and I regarded the fundraising videos we produced annually as vehicles for presenting the Israeli people in a human fashion, as they coped with a difficult period of tension and violence with resiliency and strength of character.

During this same time period, I also became involved in advancing the field of Israel Studies in American universities and in establishing a Federation Israel Studies Project. That project supports programs on four major campuses in the state of Illinois in order to advance understanding of Israel in its complexity and to enable Israel to be better known in its proper place among the family of nations, at a time when international affairs have been receiving growing academic attention.

While the Brand Israel approach has not remained center stage quite the way it was intended to, its concepts have been integrated into the projection of Israel on the American scene in a number of ways. Meanwhile, the field of Israel Studies has grown enormously at multiple universities throughout the country, as is described in a piece published in 2013, part of which is included in this section. It was co-authored with Elie Rekhess, Visiting Crown Chair in Middle East Studies at Northwestern University.

The Role of the Organized Jewish Community in the Brand Israel Process

Presented at Brand Israel Conference, Tel Aviv

October 25, 2006

• • •

The structure I represent consists of 155 Federations and 400 independent communities throughout North America that are brought together in a continental framework by United Jewish Communities (UJC).* Jewish Community Relations Councils within those cities, along with several national organizations all of which are themselves brought together under the umbrella of the Jewish Council for Public Affairs (JCPA), form a component of that system. Given its wide communal base and national coordination, this organizational structure, with its access to both decision makers and the broad sweep of the American population, has the potential of being the most significant single delivery system for Brand Israel concepts in North America. Over the past year or two, this system has been increasingly mobilized to fulfill that potential.

At a breakthrough meeting convened in UJC's headquarters in New York last June that brought together officials from the Ministry of Foreign Affairs, the Brand Israel Group, and the UJC/JCPA system, these entities identified themselves as the three "pillars" which could most effectively advance the Brand Israel project in North America. At that meeting we brought one another up to date on our respective work in this area and discussed the parameters for framing a coordinated strategy for moving forward together. The conference opening here today marks a major next stage in that process.

Applying the insights that the Brand Israel process has thus far brought to bear, the UJC/JCPA system has been functioning in two fashions for two distinct yet overlapping audiences. First, in line with the original intent of the application of this branding is the area of advocacy, where the goal is to develop sympathetic understanding of the Israeli reality in a fashion that will maintain and advance American support for Israel. Secondly, we have seen great value in extending the concept of branding

---

*The organization's name was changed to the Jewish Federations of North America (JFNA) in 2009.

to advance the connection of members of the Jewish community with Israel. I will elaborate on this second approach shortly, but first I would like to speak a bit more about the advocacy dimension.

In carrying out its advocacy work in this area, the Federation system functions most especially through the Israel Advocacy Initiative that the United Jewish Communities and the Jewish Council for Public Affairs established during the recent terror war against Israel. This is a structure that provides assistance, coordination, and representation for the range of Federations and Community Relations Councils throughout North America. Its advocacy efforts take many forms, including contact with the media; outreach to elected officials and other "influentials"; work on campuses; and relationships with Christian, ethnic, and other segmented groups and their leaders. Most recently, the Israel Advocacy Initiative structure was able to fund the latest research carried out by the Brand Israel Group.

In its second, more innovative area of branding activity, the Federation system is particularly well positioned to reach out to the Jewish community through materials prepared by individual Federations in their various communities and by UJC nationally. In our own community, for example, we make use of a monthly publication that goes to over 40,000 households for ten months of the year and nearly 100,000 households in each of the two additional months; a website; a weekly "E-Alert" on Israel-related matters that goes to some 18,000 subscribers; and a wide range of campaign vehicles, including an annual video, printed materials, and other communications.

Here I would like to digress slightly to discuss why this second kind of branding outreach can be considered particularly important. Increasingly, the generations that remember the Holocaust and the founding of the State of Israel have been replaced by generations for whom not only those events are unknown in a first-hand fashion but also the Six Day War of 1967 and even the Yom Kippur War of 1973. Furthermore, as these newer generations are born and bred in a diversified America, they become more and more like other Americans. Brand Israel research that is focused specifically on the Jewish community has not yet been done, but it is reasonable to expect that when that happens it will show a declining differential between members of the Jewish community and other Americans. Outreach to the Jewish community that builds on the insights of Brand Israel research is thus extremely valuable, not only to maintain a level of support within the Jewish community that significantly serves Israel in the advocacy arena, but additionally to help maintain and strengthen connections between American Jewry and Israel — connection that are themselves of profound importance for both communities and for the future of the Jewish people. Such ties can no longer be taken for granted, and the branding of Israel that is now in the works can be an especially powerful and effective vehicle for addressing this essential need.

Let me add that while I have been making a distinction between advocacy for the general population to strengthen support for Israel's cause and marketing to the Jewish community as a means of sustaining and advancing ties between the North American Jewish community and the people of Israel, in many ways these two categories are overlapping. By that I mean that when Brand Israel concepts are used to promote advocacy efforts in the general community, they also resonate in a "marketing" fashion within the Jewish community; at the same time those approaches that are carried out with a marketing purpose within the Jewish community have advocacy impact as well. Thus, while I think it is useful to make the distinction between these modes of activity and to keep it in mind, each approach to branding provides strong reinforcement for the other.

In either case, the insights of Brand Israel research provide an extremely useful approach to draw upon in enabling audiences to perceive a new and additional reality of Israeli life beyond the conflict, one that resonates positively for those audiences and connects them with the country of Israel as an attractive yet still unique place whose people are vibrant and "like them." On the advocacy side, this branding approach can help make the American population sympathetic to Israel and more ready to support its cause. The ultimate impact of this approach is probably greatest only over a period of time, but the need to build up a readiness to be sympathetic to Israel is of great significance in the long term. Friends and supporters of Israel thus should realize that while all of this makes branding an important new component of the pro-Israel repertoire, that does not diminish the need to continue to directly and vigorously make the case for Israel in the realm of policymaking and public opinion. "Message" advocacy aimed at answering those who challenge Israel's rightness on particular issues and who reject Israel's very legitimacy therefore needs to be actively sustained as this approach is added.

And how does branding operate? In a conversation with a friend who is an expert in counter-terrorism work, I told him what I was doing in this realm and he reacted in a startled fashion. Saying that he had just completed the final draft of a book in which he describes ways in which America's counter-terror efforts are enhanced by contacts with Israel, he told me that the preface to his book begins by recounting an incident in which an African-American counter-terror official went to Israel and, on his first day in a high security installation, was pleasantly stunned to see his counterparts appearing not as the stiff, grim, militaristic individuals he expected to be working with, but people whose clothes and behavior were decidedly informal and whose interaction was warm and friendly. Such an experience is a prototype of the rebranding exercise, in which images framed by the notion of a harsh, cold, Spartan Israel possessed by its engagement in conflict are replaced by a very different Israel perceived through a "human lens."

As was the case for the individual in that anecdote, the goals of branding are most effectively achieved when foreigners visit this country and are given the opportunity to see Israel and the Israeli people as they really are. It is an experience that can shatter stereotypes and replace them with a new set of images more in touch with the total reality. Absent such a visit, branding in the realms of both advocacy and marketing is most effective when it offers a means to replicate that experience -- either by bringing aspects of Israel to the United States or via the media, though the latter approach is a particular challenge since coverage and images of the conflict so greatly dominate the media's treatment of Israel.

Let me give some examples of ways that the organized Jewish community can and does play a direct role in a branding approach defined in these ways. First, bringing people to Israel is one of the things we do. Last January, for example, two other representatives of Chicago's Jewish Federation and I accompanied Senator Barack Obama during his visit here. To provide him with a perspective on Israel and on our community's connections with it that he might not otherwise have, we arranged lunch with young Ethiopian Jews and others who could talk about the Ethiopian *aliyah* and the role that the American Jewish community has played in supporting it. We also took the Senator to the Christian-Arab village of Fassouta, where our Federation and the Chicago Archdiocese have a joint program and where, in meeting a number of residents and the head of the local Regional Council who spoke of the warm relations between Arabs and Jews in that area, he got a view of Israel strikingly contrary to that usually projected in the media.

A revealing exchange occurred the evening after the Senator had been helicoptered above the north of Israel and received a briefing from military authorities. Another Chicagoan asked him if he had seen or learned anything unexpected during that overflight. "I know what you expect me to tell you," the Senator answered. And then, validating insights of the Brand Israel Group's research, he went on to say: "But I was not surprised by Israel's overall smallness and the narrowness of its width. Those are details that I was already familiar with. What did surprise me was to see how green Israel is."

When the Chicago Federation brought Chicago's Mayor Daley to Israel last May, we deliberately spent time in Tel Aviv as well as Jerusalem. Sure enough, he loved the energy and spirit of the city's population. And having him here, along with the pack of Chicago television journalists who were on the trip, made it possible for coverage back home to include images of the city's beaches and cafes, the kinds of images that are needed to counter the prevailing perceptions revealed by the Brand Israel research. We also took Mayor Daley to Fassouta as well as to Kiryat Gat, where Chicago has its Partnership 2000 project and where he said to us, "This is what it's really all about: the people-to-people contacts." When speaking at the Federation's Annual Meeting four months after the trip, he declared, "After visiting Israel, I'm convinced that the news coverage focuses far too much on violence and far too little on understanding social and educational programs in the country."

I could elaborate on other visits we have arranged for non-Jewish public opinion makers from political life, academia, Christian denominations, and the media. Along with bringing those people to the country's national and religious sites and arranging meetings with elected officials, academics, and think tank analysts, we go out of our way to connect them with "ordinary" Israelis living vibrant and full lives.

Conversely, knowing that we cannot bring everyone to Israel, we do what we can to bring to the States representatives of the Israel that most Americans do not know and do not usually see. For example, a program that we have helped establish at the University of Illinois brings writers and other cultural figures who enable the students and faculty to learn about that facet of Israeli life. We have brought cultural figures to other campuses as well, and have also brought Israeli popular music groups who can connect with students in especially powerful ways. At the same time, for several years we have supported an Israel film festival in Chicago. Nationally, the UJC/JCPA Israel Advocacy Initiative convened a strategy session while the war with Hezbollah was raging and determined to bring a number of Israelis who demonstrate the diversity of Israel to cities throughout America, in a program called "Faces of Israel." It will take place beginning next month.

Our marketing outreach to the Jewish community is also greatly informed by the Brand Israel insights. On the national level this has especially been so since a group of UJC and Federation marketing executives held a seminar in Israel last December and began applying the concepts extensively in their ongoing work. We in Chicago and counterparts in some other communities had already intuitively begun doing this sort of thing even before knowing about the Brand Israel efforts, in some cases even before they began. The Chicago's Federation's campaign materials, for example, include an annual video that we use not only to stimulate donations but to enable members of our community to better understand Israel as it is and to connect with Israel and its people in a realistic fashion. Even as the recent terror war was unfolding, we strove to show Israelis not as pitiful victims but as resilient, proud, and vigorous men and women. With the results and insights of the Brand Israel Group's research in hand, we are able to move forward in these areas in a more deliberate, comprehensive, and strategic fashion.

The interest that the Federation system has in the Brand Israel process is demonstrated in part by the fact that a session was devoted to the subject at last year's UJC General Assembly, and another session will focus on it this year. During the next stage in the process initiated by the Brand Israel Conference that is opening today, our organizational advocacy and marketing structures will surely be able to carry out the kinds of steps I have been describing in an even more elaborate and effective manner than has been the case thus far. I personally am most pleased to be able to participate in this conference and in the ongoing work of the important endeavor of branding Israel.

Branding Israel: Effort to Brand Israel Aimed at Enabling Outsiders to Connect with Israeli Reality

Ynetnews.com, April 27, 2007

• • •

Research has shown that a very limited, in many ways distorted, image of Israel and its people has been allowed to shape the standard perceptions in the United States and other Western countries.

This is in part because of the relentless circulation of a false view by Israel's antagonists. It is also in part because of media outlets that find pictures of armed Israelis in uniform and of a concrete wall between Jerusalem and Bethlehem — and of black-clad bearded men in prayer next to the Western Wall — to represent the "typical" Israel. And it is in part because the friends of Israel and those making Israel's case have not been fully conscious of the problem or of ways to address it.

Drawing upon the research and counsel of professionals tuned in to the cutting-edge concepts of nation branding, Israel, led by the Ministry of Foreign Affairs, is currently engaged in a process aimed at addressing this problem. It is a process that many groups, including Jewish Federations in North America and their umbrella body the United Jewish Communities, see as having significant value in multiple arenas.

The process has not gotten underway without hearing from critics ranging from a skeptical former Foreign Ministry official (see Zvi Mazel in *Ynewnews*) to a scornful *al-Jazeera* commentator (see Sheikha Sajida in *al-Jazeera* column of March 26, 2007). Most of the criticism reveals misunderstandings or distortions of the purpose and methods of the branding practice — some of that stimulated by the nomenclature of "branding" and by the fact that the practice emerges from the world of advertising and public relations.

Israel's branding plan has been challenged for seeming to ignore the need for the country and its supporters to continue to engage the arguments of its adversaries and to directly take on a propaganda campaign aimed at vilifying Israel and undermining the very legitimacy of the Jewish State.

For those whose view of Israel is not hostile, the approach is seen as simplistically if not embarrassingly failing to confront serious issues. Unfriendly critics mock the Brand Israel process as a blatant attempt to manipulate the consumer public into "buying" an image of Israel aimed at deceitfully hiding the nation's destructive practices and evil nature.

In fact, the branding process is in no way meant to slight the ongoing need to directly challenge the arguments of Israel's adversaries while actively engaging in an issues-focused mode of advocacy. Branding is meant not to replace but to supplement that approach, and to do so in a fashion that, rather than distorting reality, is at its core utterly reality-based.

What might seem to be an unlikely source of elucidation of concepts on which the Brand Israel approach can be said to be based, knowingly or not, can be found in the views of Immanuel Kant. I refer in particular to his notions of *Verstand* (Understanding) and *Vernunft* (Reason,) especially as popularized in the English-speaking world by the Victorian writer Thomas Carlyle.

Consider, for example, the passage in Carlyle's epoch-defining essay "Characteristics" (1831), which proclaims, "The healthy Understanding, we should say, is not the Logical, argumentative, but the Intuitive; for the end of Understanding is not to prove and find reasons but to know and believe."

In his preceding sentence, Carlyle says, "As in the higher case of the Poet, so...in that of the Speaker and Inquirer, the true force is an unconscious one." Applying these concepts, it can be suggested that, while charges regarding Israeli "apartheid" can be rebutted by logical arguments disproving the accuracy of such terminology, the impression of Israel that branding is meant to reverse is of a harsh, brutal land whose residents are unwelcoming and utterly without feeling.

This perception would be best countered not through rational discourse but through an appeal to the unconscious that, poetry-like if you will, puts the perceiver in touch with the human element of Israel and thus discloses a deeper reality.

It might sound like quite a stretch to cite such concepts when talking about a project that is working through the contemporary media, a project whose implementers at the moment consider it an achievement to have lined up a photo shoot of Israeli women for the pages of an American magazine like *Maxim.* But when the experts working with the Foreign Ministry talk about trying to somehow capture the "essence" of Israel in language and image, this, I would suggest, is what their work is indeed about.

The impact of branding is conceived as long-term and is not supposed to fully register all at once. But as Israel continues to make its case in the arena of public opinion, it also makes great sense for it to project a truthful image of itself in the arena of public perception. The time is thus now ripe for replacing the prevalent limited images of Israel, not with alternatives that are false, but with something that is true, that effectively captures the transformative experience of a first-time visit to Israel and replicates the eye-opening and soul-touching impact of such a visit.

Other countries engage in nation branding to advance trade, tourism, and the like. For Israel, while those may be useful results as well, they do not frame the basic intent. To return to the framework of Carlyle and the German philosophers who inspired him, material ends like those are secondary for the Brand Israel effort.

At its core, it has the higher goal of enabling its audience to really "know" Israel and to connect with its ultimate reality. That is a goal worth aspiring to both for the general populations of those countries to which Israel is reaching out, whose sympathetic connection is so important, and also for the Jewish community, and especially its younger generations, whose connections with Israel are of such centrality for the future of the Jewish people and cannot be taken for granted.

These, then, are some of the characteristics of our time which the Brand Israel effort is tuned into and addressing. Neither petty nor perverse, as its critics and mockers would have it, it is a significant effort with the goal of advancing true understanding of the Israeli reality and meaningful connection with the country and its people.

The Jewish Community And the Ivory Tower: An Urgent Need for Israel Studies

The Forward, January 30, 2004

• • •

Across the country, college students are returning to campus from their winter breaks. Many, however, will be returning to classrooms where Israel is often a target of hostility and too seldom a subject of fair-minded academic consideration.

The manner in which Israel and the Middle East are taught about in the nation's university classrooms has increasingly come to the fore as one of the most difficult and far-reaching challenges facing the Jewish community. On many campuses there is instruction on various aspects of the Arab world, but there are no courses on modern Israel. Often the subject is treated only with reference to the Arab-Israeli conflict, frequently by instructors with pronounced pro-Palestinian leanings. Even in classes in other fields of study, faculty members with an anti-Israel animus regularly inject their political biases. Students sympathetic to Israel speak of the one-sidedness of reading lists and the hostile points of view espoused by faculty members, and of concerns about their grades should they object.

The extent to which faculty can or should be restrained when it comes to the expression of partisan points of view in the classroom is a sensitive issue. While some academics argue that political proselytizing has no place in the classroom, university officials are generally reluctant to take steps to prevent it.

One answer to this crisis is for members of the Jewish community to support the creation of academic courses on modern Israel, including its philosophical underpinnings in Zionist thought, its connections with a historic Jewish presence in the land, its culture and society, and its relationships and conflicts with its neighbors. Some donors have already begun to recognize the importance of expanding Israel-related offerings on campus, as evidenced by the recent establishment of an Israel Studies center at New York University and the endowment of a chair in the subject at Brandeis University. But much more needs to be done.

For its part, the organized Jewish community can do more to encourage such efforts. The Jewish Federation of Metropolitan Chicago is currently examining ways that it can work with local philanthropists to help ensure that academically credible offerings that are not unsympathetic to Israel will be made a more standard and universal part of regional university curricula. Hopefully other local Jewish communities will follow suit.

It is, of course, nothing new for members of the Jewish community to provide financial support to universities. The generosity of members of the community in this area is notable. Much of that giving, however, has had nothing to do with Jewish communal interests. When it does, it generally has benefited Jewish and Holocaust studies.

The proliferation of Jewish Studies programs has brought courses in Jewish history, thought and culture to numerous universities. Many donors who support this field take particular pride in noting the acceptance of Jews in America, which the tremendous growth of Jewish Studies both reflects and advances.

Holocaust studies, as Emory University historian Kenneth Stein has noted, began to be vigorously promoted within academia in the 1970s, when the Holocaust became an increasing focus of attention in the larger society. Jewish support for study and teaching in this area was motivated by a strong sense that it was necessary to prevent the Holocaust from being forgotten, as well as to ensure that it would never be repeated. Study of the Holocaust was perceived not only as a question of remembering the past but also as having bearing on the survival of the Jewish people in the future.

At the time, Israel Studies was not seen in the same urgent light, despite the widespread fears for Israel's survival, first on the brink of the Six-Day War, and then during the early stages of the Yom Kippur War. Jewish communal largesse in connection with Israel was conveyed via philanthropy aimed at helping the people of Israel. When such giving had an academic connection, it was to assist Israel's own universities.

Meanwhile, money from the Arab world and the federal government created university-based Middle East Studies centers that, as Martin Kramer showed in his 2001 book *Ivory Towers on Sand,* have come to be dominated by ideology-driven faculty members unfriendly to Israel.

Today, it is the future of Israel that is the most significant existential issue facing the Jewish people. As Israel comes under attack, as its right to exist is challenged, and as its history and actions are radically distorted in many quarters, it is increasingly clear that there is a profound need for American university students — the voters, opinion molders and leaders of tomorrow — to be taught about Israel in a comprehensive fashion and a non-hostile environment. And for that to continue to happen, a generation of teachers and scholars must be trained from a point of view that differs from that which currently prevails in much of academia.

The solution is not a simple one, as tensions surrounding some Jewish Studies programs in America suggest. On the one hand, there are those members of the community who see Jewish Studies programs as primarily serving communal needs by providing Jewish education to younger members of the community who may not have received it from other sources. On the other hand, there are those faculty members who see themselves as simply working in one academic field among many, and sometimes even feel that they must resist projecting the image of serving the community lest their academic credibility and status be jeopardized.

Such issues will likely come into play regarding Israel Studies programs as well. But these and other complexities aside, it is increasingly clear that serious steps must be taken to provide funding for courses in Israel Studies. University officials — who should care about their institutions' academic credibility as well as their image in the community — need to know that when they solicit Jewish donors for large gifts, this is an area that should be offered as waiting for support. Members of the Jewish community who are already prepared to make substantial gifts to colleges and universities need to be urged to support Israel Studies on campus.

And all community members with an abiding concern about the fate of the Jewish people need to be encouraged to add this area of giving to their philanthropic portfolios.

from

The State of Israel Studies:
An Emerging Academic Field

The article from which this material was taken was co-written
with Elie Rekhess, Visiting Crown Chair in Middle East Studies
at Northwestern University. Published in the Bloomsbury Companion
to Jewish Studies, edited by Dean Bell. London: Bloomsbury, 2013

• • •

Over the past decade-and-a-half, Israel Studies has grown rapidly in North America as a distinctive academic field. The purpose of this chapter is to provide updated data on this development, advance understanding of the field, discuss certain challenges faced by the field, and identify directions for future growth.

. . .

Israel Studies consists of multidisciplinary academic scholarship, research, and teaching on Israeli history, politics, society, and culture. It is focused on the modern State of Israel in the context of the historical developments that preceded its founding, its current characteristics, and its place in the Middle East. Israel Studies may be institutionalized in large university centers and institutes or smaller programs, or it may simply be taught by a chair or other faculty members. Research in this field aims to inform, raise awareness, and increase the knowledge and understanding of students, academics, decision makers, and other individuals with particular interest in the subject. The missions and priorities of Israel Studies programs may vary among scholarship and teaching, research, programming and events, the advancement of public understanding, and the preparation of policy studies.

Israel Studies as an academic discipline has developed significantly in the United States since the mid-1990s. Israel was previously taught about at times, but mostly in the context of the Israel-Arab conflict or in the framework of international relations. Israel was also often taught about in sociological and anthropological curricula, with a focus on modernization and immigration. However, as Ilan Troen, the Stoll Family Chair in Israel Studies and Director of the Schusterman Center for Israel Studies at Brandeis University, has observed, "Israeli history and society has only recently become a discrete topic or field of study within the humanities and social sciences, and included in university curricula."[1]

Troen believes that a foundational date in the establishment of Israel Studies was the appointment of Professor Ben Halpern to Brandeis University in 1960. A master historian of Zionism and the Yishuv, Halpern trained the first scholars who made Israel a major part of their oeuvre, among them Jehuda Reinharz and Ian Lustick.[2]

The founding of the Association for Israel Studies (AIS) in 1985 was another key development.[3] However AIS was not involved in institutionally promoting the teaching of Israel Studies, and the major initial growth of the field took place in the 1990s. First came the establishment of the Jacob and Libby Goodman Institute for the Study of Zionism and Israel at Brandeis in 1992.[4] Then came the establishment of the Institute for the Study of Israel in the Middle East at the University of Denver in 1996,[5] to be followed by the Institute for the Study of Modern Israel at Emory University[6] and the Center for Israel Studies at American University[7] in 1998. Six additional centers for Israel Studies were then established between 2003 and 2010.[8] In addition, during these early twenty-first century years, seven programs for Israel Studies were established and more than 25 chairs, professorships, and visiting professorships were formed.

Since early in this century, there has been a particularly notable surge of academic interest in Israel Studies. As Gal Beckerman has observed, "a study conducted by the Cohen Center for Modern Jewish Studies at Brandeis University found that among 246 American campuses surveyed, there was a 69 percent increase in the number of courses that mainly focused on Israel from the 2005–2006 academic year to the 2008–2009 year. Only 28 percent of these courses dealt with the Israeli/Arab conflict. Most of them examine Israel as a culture, society, political system, and historical entity instead of simply a point of international conflict."[9] Similarly, Ilan Troen has pointed out that in 2010 "there [were] some 1,300 courses on the State of Israel [taught] . . . in U.S. universities. That is three times as many as there were three years ago."[10] Likewise, Yoram Peri, the Abraham S. and Jack Kay Chair in Israel Studies and the Director of the University of Maryland Gildenhorn Institute for Israel Studies, indicated that the number of students enrolled in Israel Studies courses there rose from 200 in 2009–10 to 500 in 2011–12.[11]

The growing interest in Israel Studies has also been visible outside the classroom. Over the last two decades, three new journals have appeared in English: *Israel Studies,* published by Indiana University Press; *Israel Affairs,* published in London by Frank Cass Publishers; and *Israel Studies Review,* the official periodical of the Association for Israel Studies, published by the University of Maryland's Gildenhorn Institute for Israel Studies.[12] These periodicals operate with multidisciplinary editorial boards composed of scholars from the United States, Israel, and Britain. Moreover, academic publishers offer a greater number of monographs whether originally written in English or translated from Hebrew. The largest list is the State University of New York's Series on Israel Studies, initiated in 1988 and edited by Russell Stone, with dozens of books in print.[13]

Before moving forward in analyzing the factors that have contributed to the recent growth of this academic discipline, it is worth noting that the expansion has taken place in the context of controversy, a factor that outside commentators often dwell on. On one side are those who challenge the academic bona fides of Israel Studies altogether, charging that it is just a form of advocacy. On the other side are those who, arguing that practitioners in the field are as committed to observing academic standards as any other scholars, assert that the field fills an important pedagogical and scholarly niche and is no less legitimate than other fields that deal with complex subjects.

Media reporting on the matter has often focused on this debate, which at times mirrors aspects of the conflict that has engaged Israel since its establishment. For example, in June of 2005, at a time when the current growth in the field was first gaining traction and attracting significant attention, *The Chronicle of Higher Education* produced an extensive piece with the headline "The Politics of Israel Studies." In that article, Ali Banuazizi, a Professor of Psychology at Boston College and then the president of the Middle East Studies Association (which itself has at times been accused of anti-Israel partisanship), charged that people being hired to hold chairs in Israel Studies "would like . . . the academic study of Israel to be commensurate with the attention, special attention, that Israel receives in the United States, particularly in U.S. foreign policy." In contrast, Ronald Zweig, an Israeli who a short time before had been engaged to fill just such a chair at New York University, was cited as saying "that his own politics have nothing to do with his courses, and that he does not function as a classroom spokesman for the Israeli government. 'I don't consider presenting the Israeli perspective as part of my job,' he says."[14] Zweig had elsewhere declared that in accepting the chair he had "insisted that this job is not advocacy. . . . It's about scholarship."[15]

Taking its cue from what it called "a heated discussion" at the then just-completed annual meeting of the AIS held in Tucson, Arizona, the *Chronicle* article focused extensively on a somewhat related difference of opinion. Taking one side, Ian Lustick, a Professor of Political Science at the University of Pennsylvania, proclaimed that "Israel is now seen more as a function of the conflict than as the result of the Zionist blueprint," and he asserted that teaching should reflect that dynamic. The alternative position was presented by Kenneth Stein, Director of the Institute for the Study of Modern Israel at Emory University, who claimed that "the teaching of Israel's history has been hijacked" and went on to say: "We need to . . . put Israel . . . into the context of Jewish history."[16] Ilan Troen was also quoted in the article, saying, "Imagine if in America there were only people who studied Russia in terms of the Cold War or France and Germany only in terms of their conflict with each other. [That] would be a gross distortion of what those societies are really about." Echoing Stein's approach, Michael Stanislawski, Professor of History at Columbia University and head of a search committee filling the first chair in Israel Studies there, said, "In place of the sense of crisis, there should be recognition of a growing interest in Israel from the academic point of view."[17]

As philanthropic support for Israel Studies programs has expanded and gained attention, such debates have continued to preoccupy many of those reporting on the subject.[18] All the same, though, with a host of scholars on the scene and with more and more universities embracing the field, Israel Studies has taken its place as a solid academic discipline whose impressive growth can be attributed to a number of factors.

The first cause of the emergence of Israel Studies at this time has involved the post-Cold War world's growing sense of globalization, driven in part by a technological communications revolution that has brought about greater mutual dependency between countries. The need for understanding these developments and for enabling educated students to flourish within today's global environment has increasingly permeated academic life throughout North America and has been a major factor driving university administrators to introduce courses on international affairs into their curriculums, including courses on Israel.

Thus, Daniel Linzer, at the time Dean of Northwestern University's Weinberg College of Arts and Sciences, declared that "a priority for Northwestern and Weinberg College is expanding opportunities for students to learn about, and to participate in, international studies," as he described the university's establishment of an Israel Studies postdoctoral fellowship program in 2005, at the same time that a new offering in Turkish Studies was introduced there. Linzer went on to say, "Based on the vibrancy of our other international offerings, I expect that these new activities will find a ready audience."[19] In the same publication, Henry Bienen, then-president of Northwestern, was quoted as saying that "Northwestern students live in an increasingly interdependent world," and that "it is thus ever more important for Northwestern students to engage the world around them and to do this with a knowledge of cultures, languages, and the political economy of nations and peoples."[20]

Along with the advancement of a broad interest in international affairs, recent years have seen a particular rise in academic interest in the Middle East, long a region of cultural fascination and economic involvement for Americans. The region became especially central in the American consciousness following the terror attacks of September 11, 2001, and the subsequent invasion of Iraq. The interest has increased further with the evolution of American geopolitical and strategic involvements in the region and the drastic changes that have taken place there. The centrality of Israel as a key factor in much of that has been evident. This argument has also been stressed by university administrators.

Thus, when Eran Kaplan was recently named a Professor in Israel Studies at San Francisco State University, he expressed the hope to "show students how to move past the black and white of the issues involving Israel and invite them to apply what they learn to other global issues."[21] Similarly, in England, where new programs and chairs have also recently been established, *The Guardian* described the approach of Colin Shindler, Professor of Israeli Studies at the School of Oriental and African Studies at the University of London and soon-to-be chair of the newly created European Association of Israel Studies, by saying that "the decision to expand Israel Studies is a response to growing demand from students to know more about the political, cultural, social, and economic background to events in the Middle East and is an attempt to offer an academic alternative to what he [Shindler] terms 'the megaphone war.'"[22]

A second factor that has contributed to the dramatic growth in Israel Studies programs and chairs relates to funding. The above-noted developments have played out at a time of financial stress, and at most universities the urge to enlarge the curriculum with Israel-related material has not easily translated into a readiness or ability to provide their own funds to support the introduction of these courses. Much of that load has instead fallen upon outside donors. And here too, external trends at hand during the opening decade of the twenty-first century have played a significant part in the process, stimulating a readiness by Jewish donors to help make these programs feasible.

Jewish support for higher education is hardly a new phenomenon. Members of the Jewish community have long been generous in giving to their alma maters and to universities in their communities. Indeed, most of the fields supported by this largesse are unrelated to issues of particular Jewish communal interest, and many gifts reflect personal preferences, a sense of "paying back" by donors who have "made it" in fields of their own professional accomplishment, or in the case of the teaching hospital, a desire to make a contribution helpful in effecting cures in areas where loved ones have suffered.

One major area in which communal interests have helped to drive the readiness to support programs has been the field of Jewish Studies—a subject that developed significantly several decades earlier than did the growth of Israel Studies. While the broader subject of Jewish Studies is the focus of this entire volume, it is useful to reflect here on the intended purposes of that support, which reflect a somewhat different orientation from what has been manifested regarding Israel Studies.

Briefly put, it can be suggested that support for Jewish Studies in general has, for one thing, reflected pride in the academic endorsement of the entrance of Jewish history, learning, and thought into the mainstream of American intellectual life and a desire to advance academic treatment of those subjects. Additionally, at a time when research carried out by community organizations was showing that Jewish continuity was in jeopardy and that the level of young people's Jewish literacy was low, many in the community saw university courses as a way to fill a major communal gap. Meanwhile, a great deal of early donor backing for Jewish Studies was aimed at supporting Holocaust education, reflecting an urge to advance understanding and sustain knowledge of the Holocaust, particularly at a time when it was increasingly seen as "ancient history," with fewer and fewer survivors, eyewitnesses, and others for whom it was a personal experience still alive.

The motivation for advancing Israel Studies, it can be suggested, has come from similar but also different sources. In part, this urge was also driven by a desire to reach Jewish students—in this case, by connecting them with Israel as a means of enhancing their sense of Jewish identity. As Ilan Troen observed in commenting on the interests of members of the Jewish community in the mid-1990s: "The problem for them was less the status of the state of Israel and more the recognition of Israel as a vital component in building the Jewish identity of Jewish youth in the U.S."[23]

In the past decade, similar impulses and goals have led to the creation of the project known as Birthright Israel, through which the community provides free organized trips to Israel, which have been seen as offering highly positive experiences to Jewish youth.[24]

In part, the impetus for developing the field was also closely tied to developments in the region—and in this case the goal was not only to reach Jewish students. Russell A. Stone, a Professor Emeritus at American University and one of the founders of the Association for Israel Studies, has noted that the fiftieth anniversary of Israel's independence, commemorated in 1998, generated much interest in the field, along with the outbreak of the Second Intifada in 2000.[25] In fact, the collapse of the Oslo Peace Process in the fall of 2000 was accompanied by two unfolding sets of events which had a significant impact: the escalating terror war against Israeli civilians, which was embodied in the Second (or al-Aqsa) Intifada, and also a concomitant campaign aimed at challenging Israel's moral legitimacy and its right to exist as the nation-state of the Jewish people.

The terror war, though eventually contained, caused thousands of casualties and replaced the hope—held by many in the nineties—that peace was about to be achieved with a sense that Israel's physical security was at risk in ways it had not been thought to be for some time. Meanwhile, the anti-Israel war of words and images continued to grow in scope, creating a strong feeling of how much was at stake for Jewish communities and the sense that America itself—especially its college campuses—had to a certain extent become a battleground.

Many of Israel's supporters saw the intensifying anti-Israel political campaign as distorting historic and contemporary truths in advancing a polemical case driven by ideology and, in numerous instances, by bias. While activity of that sort has been more widespread in Europe than in the United States, its most congenial home in North America has been on university campuses, which in general have been more sympathetic to the Palestinian narrative and cause and more critical of Israel than the broader American population commonly is.

The campus-based agitation which has advanced this hostility—including pro-Palestinian demonstrations and street theater; vigorous promotion of boycotts, divestment, and sanctions; and disruptions of pro-Israel demonstrations and programs—has mostly been carried out by students, with some faculty involvement or support. But faculty-driven classroom activity has also raised concerns. This has pertained not only to courses with a specific Middle Eastern focus, but also to classes taught in a wide range of areas—including archeology, history, geography, sociology, and literature—where faculty members have exploited the classroom setting to convey messages that have been seen as factually questionable and hostile to Israel.

A groundbreaking study of the earlier development of these trends was Martin Kramer's 2001 book *Ivory Towers on Sand: The Failure of Middle Eastern Studies in America.*[26] The June 1967 war, Kramer asserts, was a turning point in the nature of Middle East Studies in the United States.[27] "From 1967," he writes, "the Arab-Israeli conflict made for a deepening politicization of the field, clouding the reputation for disinterested objectivity so important to the founders [of Middle East Studies]."[28]

A decade later, according to Kramer, "Middle Eastern Studies came under a take-no-prisoners assault, which rejected the idea of objective standards, disguised the vice of politicization as the virtue of commitment, and replaced proficiency with ideology. The text that inspired the movement was entitled *Orientalism,* and the revolution it unleashed has crippled Middle Eastern Studies to this day."[29]

The author of *Orientalism* was Edward Said, a well-known Palestinian American Professor of English at Columbia University in New York. Elaborating on the impact of his book 20 years after its publication in 1978, Kramer said, *"Orientalism* made it acceptable, even expected, for scholars to spell out their own political commitments as a preface to anything they wrote or did. More than that, it also enshrined an acceptable hierarchy of political commitments, with Palestine at the top, followed by the Arab nation and the Islamic world. They were the long-suffering victims of Western racism, American imperialism, and Israeli Zionism— the three legs of the Orientalist stool."[30] In this context, then, when Israel was taught, it was most often in the framework of the Israeli-Palestinian conflict—with the likelihood of the approach being sympathetic to the Palestinian side. For friends of Israel, not only was there a considerable and serious gap in the curriculum, but also when the subject of Israel was treated, it was not necessarily done according to strict academic standards.

This perceived slant of the Middle East Studies centers was seen as resulting from—or at least being made possible by—funding from Iran and oil-rich Arab Gulf countries that wanted to improve their images beginning in the mid-seventies, at a time when federal and foundation funding for Middle East Studies was drying up. A notable example, discussed by Kramer, was a major endowment that Georgetown University secured from Libya in 1977—and returned in 1981.[31] Such giving continued in the 1980s and the 1990s, including a 1986 donation of $5 million made by Saudi arms dealer Adnan Khashoggi to American University for a sports center and a 1998 gift from the Sultan bin Abdulaziz al Saud Foundation to the University of California at Berkeley's Arab and Islamic Studies Center.[32] Especially controversial was a gift from the president of the United Arab Emirates to Harvard Divinity School in 2000. It was returned in 2004 after it was disclosed that the donor had also supported a policy for engaging in discourse that "contradicted the principles of interfaith tolerance."[33]

Another burst of giving could be seen following the September 11, 2001, World Trade Center and Pentagon terror attacks, when Muslim countries were especially eager to advance a positive image of Islam. For example, in 2005, Harvard University and Georgetown University each announced $20 million gifts from the Saudi businessman and member of the Saudi royal family, Prince Alwaleed bin Talal bin Abdulaziz Alsaud. As *The New York Times* reported at the time, both gifts were made to support Islamic Studies, with the goal of advancing greater understanding of Islam.[34]

It was in this context, seeing a considerable gap in the curriculum, and believing that Israel, when included, was taught often in a fashion more appropriate to the realm of partisan debate, that members of several Jewish communities concluded that the playing field was not level. Resigned to the fact that most universities on their own were not going to remedy that condition, they considered it appropriate and desirable to play an ameliorative role. Some universities then came on board with matching funds.[35]

As the authors of a study produced in 2006 by the Israel on Campus Coalition wrote, "Conceptually, Middle East study centers are supposed to provide students and professors with the opportunity to examine the complexities of that region from a variety of perspectives and dimensions. Yet today, the approximately 125 Middle East study centers that exist across America tend to view Israel solely through the lens of the Arab-Israeli conflict or not at all. This situation, and the frequent complaints of hostility toward Israel within those departments, has stimulated the creation of Israel Studies programs and departments."[36]

Notwithstanding these factors, while the motivation for supporting the establishment of Israel Studies programs may have been driven in great part by a concern about Israel's image, administrators, faculty members teaching Israel Studies courses, and funders as well, by and large acted with recognition and respect for academic norms and principles.

Thus, for example, the *New York Times* column that focused on the

NYU appointment reported that "Professor Zweig assigns readings from Arab and Arab-American scholars like Rashid Khalidi, as well as dissident Israelis including Avi Shlaim."[37] Similarly, Ilan Troen is described by Liel Leibovitz as denying "the allegation that he, or any other endowed Israel Studies professor, was appointed as a foot-soldier in a war against pro-Palestinian scholarship. 'I don't agree with the notion of combat,' he said. 'It suggests propaganda. It suggests advocacy. I don't think that's what any of us are about. We're real academics . . . we're there to combat ignorance, not advocate a particular line."[38]

On that theme, Alex Joffe, a research scholar with the Institute for Jewish and Community Research, wrote: "American Jews are unquestionably dedicated to the ideals of the American university. . . . Donors to Israel Studies programs also know that their critics have knives sharpened and are ready to strike at the first sign of excessive enthusiasm. Therefore, intellectual leaders of Israel Studies have repeatedly emphasized that their goal is academic inquiry, not advocacy." Joffe concluded, "Israel Studies programs promise to represent Israel seriously rather than as a cartoon villain in a post-colonial morality play and to use the best intellectual tools to hearken back to nearly-vanished ideals of academic integrity."[39] Substantiating that kind of a claim, Yitzak Benhorin observed in 2010 that "whoever visits the University of Maryland campus could not possibly make the mistake of thinking that Israel Studies department is a mouthpiece for Israeli PR efforts."[40]

While the Lustick-Stein debate described in the *Chronicle of Higher Education* may have represented the prevailing situation in 2005, as Israel Studies has grown in the past half-dozen years, it is the Stein perspective that seems to have held greater sway. This is documented in the extensive January 2010 *Report on the Teaching of Israel on U.S. College Campuses 2008–09* carried out at Brandeis University. The authors, Annette Koren and Emily Einhorn, making a comparison to an earlier study of courses offered in 2005–6, noted that their current study "finds a 'normalization' of Israel study within the university curriculum. From course titles and descriptions, we see a move toward viewing Israel as a culture, society, political system, and historical entity rather than solely as a locus for international conflict."[41] Colin Shindler identified a similar trend in England on the occasion of the expansion of Israel Studies there. As *The Guardian* reported, "For Shindler, the increasing interest being shown by students in different aspects of Israel, from its politics to its art and films, is part of a drive to understand the country and people outside the context of the Israel/Palestine conflict."[42]

A third factor contributing to the current growth in Israel Studies, in this case by adding to the interest, has been a development in Israel itself that can be seen both in the cultural realm and in academia. The trend has expressed itself in a "turn inward" that has included a shifting of the focus of academic research from the traditional study of the history of Zionism, the establishment of the State of Israel, and Israel's conflict with its Arab neighbors, to a wider examination of the sociology, anthropology, politics, ethnicity, culture, literature, art, theater, and cinema of Israeli society. With the emergence of the "New Historians" in the late 1980s significantly contributing to this trend,[43] these developments within Israeli academia have added insights and data for those teaching these subjects in North America in a way that has made such coursework both deeper and more rounded. Meanwhile, as Israeli literary figures and visual artists have also turned inward for subject matter in their way, leading to greater personal introspection and to sharper focusing on personal relationships in their writings, art, and films, the resulting cultural products have become both more particular and at the same time more universal and thereby more accessible to audiences and students in the United States. At the same time, Israeli life, while retaining its particularity, has in certain ways also come to more greatly resemble the American condition, making the art that reflects this life more accessible in that way too. And so, for example, Israeli television shows have become virtual templates for such powerful, popular American television dramas as *In Treatment* and *Homeland.*

Returning to the practical realm, a fourth factor that has helped enable Israel Studies to grow in North America over the past decade has been the greater availability of Israeli academics. Given the belt-tightening policies adopted by Israeli universities and the decreasing number of employment opportunities in Israeli institutions of higher learning, a growing number of faculty members have taken leave from their positions in Israel and have responded to the demand in North America.

This availability has made it possible for a gap to be filled, since American universities have been far from able to produce a sufficient number of scholars and teachers in the field able to teach the many courses that have been added to the curriculum. There has thus been a fortunate confluence of circumstances where a newly created demand has been filled by visitors coming for limited timeframes or by professors taking long-term appointments, with many of the visitors brought to campuses around the country by the AICE with funding from the Charles and Lynn Schusterman Family Foundation, which in many ways has been a major force in advancing Israel Studies nationally. Meanwhile, some communities and schools have taken similar steps on their own, as exemplified by the programs carried out on four Illinois campuses thanks to the support of the Jewish Federation of Metropolitan Chicago, or the Younes and Soraya Nazarian Center for Israel Studies at UCLA, which represents another major community-supported effort.

Universities that have embraced the programs and courses that have brought about the growth in this field have struck a chord. The Israel Studies courses that have entered the curriculum at many institutions of higher learning have not only provided an academically sound alternative to treatments of the subject matter to those that previously prevailed in a number of places, but they have also filled a widespread vacuum elsewhere. This growth in Israel Studies has brought into many institutions' course listings an approach that is aimed at seeing Israel whole and as a member of the family of nations worthy of study and understanding in reference to its history, economy, sociology, political structure, culture, and other fields of inquiry that are regularly applied to other nations and regions. As Jan Jaben-Eilon notes, referencing an observation made by Russell Stone, "academic programs that revolve around Israel parallel other programs like Russian Studies or Latin American Studies, which are usually interdisciplinary programs."[44]

This overall development can be seen as paralleling a broader situation of the past decade as well, for it is occurring at a time when a range of activities in Israel have blossomed in ways that are fascinating in themselves, of global significance, and of interest to the North American university student population. We refer, in particular, to the burst of technological advances that has characterized the past several years in Israel; to the economic stability and growth that have been achieved in a time of economic difficulty throughout the world; and to a veritable renaissance in literature, film, theater, dance, and other creative arts, all of which are drawing increasing attention to the Israeli scene. The result has been an enriched curriculum responding to and generating student interest of a sort that has made these courses very popular on university campuses where they have been offered, with student enrollment and responsiveness demonstrating that the appeal of these courses is not at all limited to Jewish students.

Testimony to this fact is provided by the heads of three of the key programs in the field cited in Jan Jaben-Eilon's *Jerusalem Post* article "Studying Israel: Israel Has Finally Arrived."[45] Attributing the growth of the field in part to "academic interest by students," Arieh Saposnik,

Director of the Younes and Soraya Nazarian Center for Israel Studies at UCLA, is quoted as saying that "the Israel-Palestinian conflict is very hot," and Jaben-Eilon then paraphrases what he went on to say, adding that "ideally, students will develop an interest beyond the conflict and, in fact, all the Israel Studies programs offer a variety of courses." Jaben-Eilon goes on to say that, "according to [Ilan] Troen [at Brandeis], [Ron] Zweig [at NYU], and [Arieh] Saposnik [at UCLA], courses around the country are so oversubscribed that they must turn away students."[46]

In sum, the growth of Israel Studies at this time, and the way the field is being defined, is very much a result of conditions that have emerged during the past decade. A desire to address a burgeoning interest in international affairs has been joined by the identification of a gap in academically sound and wide-ranging instruction in a particular area of international studies. Donors have stepped forward with an interest in filling that gap, and suitable faculty members have been supplied to meet the demand for teaching experts in the field. The result has been that larger numbers of courses in Israel Studies are being offered, and they have been greeted by a strong response from the student population—which has, in turn, stimulated further growth in the field. Given the controversies and differences surrounding the Israeli-Palestinian conflict, not to mention the potential structural tension between community interests and academic values, this has not all happened without suspicion and criticism from some quarters. But university officials have been comfortable in validating the academic *bona fides* of these programs, and Israel Studies has emerged as a vigorous, still-growing, multifaceted field.

One question, however, remains to be answered. Where, in each university's structure, should these programs and courses be placed? While venues like the Middle East Studies centers established at many American universities in the 1980s and the 1990s might have seemed a logical choice, many of them were inhospitable to an unbiased and broadly based treatment of Israel. Those centers dealt with Israel mostly in connection with its conflict with Palestinians and often included faculty members with political leanings sympathetic to Palestinian positions on the conflict. Similar circumstances could be seen regarding many other Middle East programs. In light of that situation, as Israel Studies has grown as a discipline in the past decade, it has generally either been housed in Jewish Studies frameworks or established in stand-alone programs. As Liel Leibovitz observed, "discouraged by the risk of donating money to Middle East departments, some Jewish donors are opting to establish Israel chairs within a Jewish Studies department where they perceive faculty committees are more likely to be sympathetic to Israel."[47] However, while the decisions about where to place Israel Studies may have made sense, certain complexities have emerged.

As far as placement in Jewish Studies goes, there clearly is a natural alignment based on a number of factors, and the newer field of Israel Studies has been making its way into this broader field in recent years.[48] The affinity starts with modern Israel's geographical location on the land where the Jewish people lived and ruled in ancient times and where they had a continuous presence, albeit drastically reduced during most of the centuries of exile, and with which they felt a strong connection. Similarly, the history of Zionist thought and activity is tied to the history of Jews in Europe and elsewhere, while pre-state Zionist immigration and settlement, and then the establishment of the State of Israel, can be connected with the Holocaust and other aspects of Jewish experience in both early and mid-twentieth-century Europe, as well as with the experience of the Jews in Arab lands. The identification of Israel as a "Jewish state" provides further justification for placing Israel Studies in Jewish Studies. Meanwhile, a growing attention to the concept of Jewish peoplehood and to Israel-Diaspora relations bears appropriately on these matters. As Ilan Troen, Director of the Schusterman Center for Israel Studies at Brandeis University, has noted, "within 60 years, Israel's relative share of the Jewish world grew from 6 percent to 40 percent, and the specialists in Jewish Studies are beginning to realize that this is where the future is."[49]

All the same, many of these ways of looking at the subject need not necessarily be associated with Jewish Studies, and they certainly do not cover the totality of the Israel Studies curriculum. Furthermore, not only does Israel Studies not need to be subsumed under the broader heading of Jewish Studies, but there are even those who say that putting Israel Studies there leads to handling it in a limited fashion which might cut Israel Studies off from other profitable areas of study.

In a nutshell, placement in Jewish Studies can lead to a form of "ghettoization"—to the treatment of Israel not as a country in the world but merely as a manifestation of Jewish life, a tendency which could drive away examination by scholars in other fields and be off-putting for students. Rather than facilitating the study of Israel as a nation with a history and identity that, although greatly defined by Jewish-related themes, is not limited to them, placement in Jewish Studies can be counterproductive to the achievement of that goal.

Furthermore, as attendance at Jewish Studies conferences and conversations with Jewish Studies and Israel Studies faculty reveal, there is an element of tension involved here. In particular, a degree of protectiveness and even resentment has surfaced among some longstanding Jewish Studies faculty members as Israel Studies has emerged as a "growth area." In their eyes, Israel Studies is an upstart promoted by community members with nonacademic interests, and, when added to the curriculum, threatens to overwhelm less fashionable subjects while draining budgets needed to sustain more traditional Jewish Studies curriculum.

As Leonard Binder, a distinguished veteran in the field of Middle East Studies, said, "When framed by these well-established academic tracks [i.e. Middle East and Islamic Studies on the one hand and Jewish Studies on the other], Israel Studies are limited by the paradigms that channeled these alternative academic schemas."[50]

Different universities have found their own solutions to these issues. Where lone courses have been offered, either as permanent components of the curriculum or taught by visitors, they most often have been handled either through Jewish Studies programs or simply through the disciplines in which those specific courses fit (e.g. history, sociology, literature, etc.). When there has been enough magnitude to create a program in Israel Studies, those programs have tended to be established either as units within Jewish Studies or in a stand-alone fashion, with the scholars frequently appointed within the framework of their individual academic disciplines. This pattern has enabled the programs to avoid the strain of being part of Middle East Studies and the potential ghettoization of simply being part of Jewish Studies, while at the same enabling Israel Studies to achieve its own identity.

Exactly what it is that defines the field of Israel Studies is a matter still in flux. But what emerges from examination of the way the field is establishing itself is that Israel is today being studied internally as well as in a wider range of contexts. External approaches include looking at Israel in relationship to the history of the region and of the world; considering it within the framework of political, sociological, cultural, and economic developments in the region and of the world; and so on. When looked at internally, Israel becomes a more closed-in unit, to be studied intensely with in-depth reference to a single discipline or in a holistic, interdisciplinary fashion. This, for example, could mean considering the interlocking connections between Israel's literature, sociology, history, and political affairs, as well as other dimensions of the Israeli reality.

All in all, then, while continuing to evolve, Israel Studies has firmly taken its place in higher education as a serious academic field.

Given the factors that have led to the growth of Israel Studies over the past decade, it appears safe to predict that the field of Israel Studies will continue to grow and develop, rewarding scholarly investigation and stimulating increased student interest, along with cementing university and community support.

As this happens, one further development will probably grow increasingly essential: the expansion, growth, and advancement of degree-granting programs in Israel Studies throughout North America—programs producing PhD graduates in the field and creating academic positions to which those scholars may aspire on an increasing number of campuses.

The current abundance of Israel-trained scholars, as visitors to North American universities or with permanent appointments there, is something that will probably continue to be seen in the short as well as the long term. But with the field growing and its increasing professorial needs being met by other means as well, those scholars will inevitably cease to be the predominant holders of chairs in the field as they currently are.

In conclusion, like practically anything having to do with Israel in today's world, there are plenty of issues in play surrounding Israel Studies at North American universities. In addition—and also like so much having to do with Israel—the field is characterized by vibrancy, accomplishment, meaning, and value. As Israel takes its place among the nations of the world, Israel Studies is taking its place in the realm of academia.

NOTES

1. Ilan Troen, "Settlement and State in Eretz Israel," in Martin Goodman, Jeremy Cohen, and David Sorkin (eds), *The Oxford Handbook of Jewish Studies.* Oxford: Oxford University Press, 2002, p. 445.

2. Ilan Troen, interview with the authors, June 20, 2012.

3. www.aisisraelstudies.org/about.ehtml, last accessed June 15, 2012. All websites pertaining to Israel Studies that are cited in this article were last accessed on June 15, 2012.

4. When the Goodman Institute was founded, it was organized and managed under the Tauber Institute for the Study of European Jewry, which had been founded in 1980. When the Schusterman Center for Israel Studies was later created in 2007, the Goodman Institute was subsumed under its auspices. Sylvia Fuks Fried, email correspondence with the authors, June 25, 2012.

5. www.isime.org/about/mission-vision-goals/.

6. www.ismi.emory.edu/About.html.

7. Mitchell G. Bard, "Introducing Israel Studies in American Universities," *Jerusalem Center for Public Affairs,* December 23, 2008, last accessed June 15, 2012, http://jcpa.org/article/introducing-israel-studies-in-u-s-universities/. Information also provided by acting director of American University's Center for Israel Studies.

8. New York University, 2003; Columbia University, 2006; Brandeis and Yeshiva Universities, 2007; University of Nebraska Omaha, 2009; University of California, Los Angeles, 2010.

9. Gal Beckerman, "Israel Studies: Scholarly Pursuit or Public Diplomacy?" *The Forward,* May 26, 2010, http://forward.com/articles/128346/israel-studies-scholarly-pursuit-or-public-diplom/; also see Michael D. Colson, "Searching for the Study of Modern Israel," *Jerusalem Post,* January 13, 2010.

10. Yitzhak Benhorin, "Israel Studies Increasingly Popular in U.S.," *Ynetnews.com,* May 10, 2010.

11. Information provided by the Institute to the authors, May 30, 2012. The reports cited above deal with courses that may or may not be offered in the framework of formal Israel Studies programs.

12. Troen, "Settlement and State in Eretz Israel," p. 445.

13. Ibid.

14. Jennifer Jacobson, "The Politics of Israel Studies," *Chronicle of Higher Education,* June 20, 2005.

15. Samuel G. Freedman, "Separating Political Myths from Facts in Israel Studies," *The New York Times,* February 16, 2005.

16. Jacobson, "The Politics of Israel Studies."

17. Nathaniel Popper, "Israel Studies gain on Campus as Disputes Grow," *The Forward,* March 25, 2005.

18. For example, Beckerman, "Israel Studies: Scholarly Pursuit or Public Diplomacy?"

19. Northwestern University, "Widening the Global Path to and from Northwestern," *Crosscurrents* (Spring/Summer 2005): 10–12.

20. Ibid. The quotation from Linzer was also cited in the fall 2005 issue of *Northwestern,* the university alumni magazine. Demonstrating one aspect of the climate in which such Israel Studies programs have been established, the Northwestern University announcement evoked a hostile letter to the editor in the next issue of that publication from an alumnus who referred to Israel as "more of a pariah state in that part of the world than a true representative of the Middle East" and who charged that the Israeli postdoctoral fellows would "lecture Northwestern undergraduates insidiously" (Letter to the Editor, *Northwestern Magazine,* Winter 2005, www.northwestern.edu/magazine/winter2005/mailbox/mailbox_print.html). Similarly, an initiative to promote Israel Studies at the University of Illinois at Urbana-Champaign has been attacked several times by an individual who has described the program on that campus as having "nothing to do with

the serious study of Israel, and everything to do with promoting support for its criminal political behavior" (David Green, "Propaganda Disguised as Academic Inquiry at the University of Illinois," *The Electronic Intifada,* December 4, 2009, http://electronicintifada.net/content/propaganda-disguised-academic-inquiry-university-illinois/8564).

21. Denize Springer, "Eran Kaplan Was Named the Goldman Endowed Chair in Israel Studies," San Francisco State University, March 1, 2011, www.sfsu.edu/~news/2011/spring/18.html.

22. Harriet Swain, "SOAS Creates Two New Posts in Israel Studies," *The Guardian,* April 11, 2011.

23. Benhorin, "Israel Studies Increasingly Popular in U.S."

24. Leonard Saxe and Barry Chazan (2008), *Ten Days of Birthright Israel: A Journey in Young Adult Identity.* Waltham: Brandeis University.

25. Jan Jaben-Eilon, "Studying Israel: Israel Has Finally Arrived," *The Jerusalem Post,* September 7, 2011.

26. Martin Kramer, *Ivory Towers on Sand: The Failure of Middle Eastern Studies in America.* Washington, DC: Washington Institute for Near East Policy, 2001.

27. See similar comments by Howard Sachar, who considered the 1967 Six Day War between Israel and its Arab neighbors to be "the dramatic impetus" for the establishment of "more and more chairs devoted to the Arab-Israel problem in Middle East Studies centers and departments." Liel Leibovitz, "Battle of the Chairs: Arab Princes and Wealthy Jews Vie for Influence on American Campuses," *Moment Magazine,* February 2006, 16.

28. Kramer, *Ivory Towers on Sand,* p. 16.

29. Ibid., p. 22.

30. Ibid., p. 37.

31. See ibid., pp. 20–1, and the chapter notes on p. 26, especially note 64, which lists a number of articles that appeared on the subject between 1976 and 1984.

32. On that and for other examples see Julia Duin, "Saudis Give Big to U.S. Colleges," *The Washington Times,* December 10, 2007.

33. Stephanie Strom, "Arab's Gift to Be Returned by Harvard," *The New York Times,* July 28, 2004.

34. Karen W. Arenson, "Saudi Prince Gives Millions to Harvard and Georgetown," *The New York Times,* December 13, 2005.

35. For more examples of Arab giving and a perspective on this overall matter see Leibovitz, "Battle of the Chairs."

36. *In Search of Israel Studies: A Survey of Israel Studies on American College Campuses,* Israel on Campus Coalition (Boston, 2006).

[37.] Freedman, "Separating Political Myths from Facts in Israel Studies."

[38.] Leibovitz, "Battle of the Chairs," p. 18.

[39.] Alex Joffe, "Israel Studies 101," *Jewish Ideas Daily,* October 3, 2011.

[40.] Benhorin, "Israel Studies Increasingly Popular in U.S."

[41.] "Executive Summary," *Searching for the Study of Israel: A Report on the Teaching of Israel on U.S. College Campuses 2008–09.* Cohen Center for Modern Jewish Studies, Brandeis University, 2010, p. 1. The Brandeis University Summer Institute for Israel Studies, established in 2004, which enables faculty members in various fields to enhance their abilities to develop courses with Israel-related content, has itself contributed to this development.

[42.] Swain, "Soas Creates Two New Posts in Israel Studies."

[43.] Laurence Silberstein (2008), *Postzionism: A Reader. New Brunswick: Rutgers University Press.*

[44.] Jaben-Eilon, "Studying Israel: Israel Has Finally Arrived."

[45.] Ibid.

[46.] Ibid.

[47.] Leibovitz, "Battle of the Chairs."

[48.] See presentation by Alan Dowty, "Israel Studies—The International Dimension," Colloquium on Trends and Challenges in Studies of the State of Israel, Ben-Gurion University of the Negev, Beer-Sheva, Israel, June 4, 2008.

[49.] Amiram Barkat, "A Major in Israel," *Ha'aretz,* October 4, 2005.

[50.] Leonard Binder, "Perspectives on Israel Studies: A Personal View," originally in *Intersections,* the newsletter of the UCLA Center for Near Eastern Studies, 2006. Posted on the UCLA website.

Jews and Others:
Relationships with
African Americans and Catholics

During the period of time covered by this volume, American society underwent considerable change, and the relationship of Jews with others changed as well. While there previously were relatively permanent alliances of Jews and members of other groups, at least two of those relationships – with African Americans and with mainstream Protestants – became somewhat frayed, each for its own reasons. More broadly, the very notion of permanent alliances between any groups has waned, replaced by situational alliances on specific shared interests.

In my early years at the Federation, as Director of its Jewish Community Relations Council, I represented the organization – and by extension the Jewish community – at numerous events and participated in various kinds of dialogue groups. Several of us from different racial, religious, or ethnic backgrounds came together with some regularity, establishing a useful level of intimacy while jointly advancing intergroup relations in Chicago. Most of that is now long gone, with group representatives more often coming together only when they choose to deal with a situation of the moment or attempt to resolve particular differences between their groups. This, for example, has been done by Jewish leaders and key Presbyterians in Chicago as that religious denomination's national body has embarked on what has been seen as problematic activity regarding the Israel-Palestinian conflict.

The shift reflects a change in American society, whereby individuals on the whole are much more integrated with members of other racial, ethnic, or religious groups. It also reflects a change in Chicago, which has become less made up of ethnic-group-defined neighborhoods than it once was. Still, in Chicago at least, there have been two main types of intergroup relations that have continued to play out for the city's Jews, relations with which I have been directly involved as reflected in a number of pieces in this section of the volume.

First is the relationship between Jews and African Americans, whose historic ties are often called to mind. The breakdown of those ties decades ago reflected both the passage of time and developments in each of those communities. In Chicago, the break has been deliberately aggravated by Louis Farrakhan and by disciples of his who have come on the scene. One such person was Steve Cokely, who served as an aide to then-Mayor Eugene Sawyer and who gained attention as a purveyor of gross anti-Semitism in 1988, during the final months of my ADL tenure.

Despite Farrakhan's looming presence, there have also been attempts to repair the breach between Jews and blacks, and it shouldn't be thought that a relationship that was important during the Civil Rights era and the days of the Harold Washington mayoralty has no remaining traction at all. But as strong as nostalgia for the good old days may be for some, the relationship is not nearly what it once was.

In contrast, beginning, especially, in the era of Joseph Cardinal Bernardin, Chicago's Jews and Catholics have achieved and maintained a "model" interreligious relationship, certainly between those groups' respective leadership. While there may remain some unresolved issues, those are probed in the Scholars Dialogue framework that the Federation and Chicago Board of Rabbis maintain with the Archdiocese, a body which strives to advance mutual understanding and respect. Meanwhile, in another form of cooperation, the Archdiocese, under the leadership of Francis Cardinal George, came together with the Federation in a unique way to create and jointly support a computer literacy project in the Christian Arab village of Fassouta in the north of Israel – a project which reflected the interests in that country held by each group in its way and their comfort in acting jointly to address those interests.

Most of this section of the book deals with one or the other of the relationships I have just talked about, while the closing piece is something different. Based on a friendship first formed during my years in Israel, it deals with an interreligious, intergroup relationship of a personal sort.

Doing the Right Thing:
Reflections on Spike Lee's New Movie
and on the Cokely Affair One Year Later

JUF News, August 1989

• • •

Do the Right Thing, the powerful new movie by Spike Lee which deals with race relations in the inner city, has only one direct reference to Jews. It comes when a sequence of characters face the camera and spew out hate-filled phrases about members of other ethnic or racial groups. The anti-Semitic comments, surprisingly enough, are delivered by a Korean grocer.

The film also has a brief reference to Nation of Islam leader Louis Farrakhan, whose anti-Semitism, downplayed or ignored by many blacks, is regarded as highly significant by most Jews. Farrakhan's supporters include members of Public Enemy, a black rap group whose music plays an important role in *Do the Right Thing.* As it happens, the group's "Minister of Information," Richard Griffin, recently gave a bigotry-laced interview of his own. Holding Jews responsible for "the majority of wickedness that goes on across the globe," Griffin, who has a record of anti-Jewish hostility, asserted that "the Jews are wicked. And we can prove this." (The outcry which followed the interview, published first in *The Washington Times,* eventually led to Public Enemy's breakup).

As an apparently credible look into the black urban community, *Do the Right Thing* suggests that ordinary members of that community hardly are driven by anti-Jewish sentiments. But the Griffin interview, like last year's local crisis revolving around Steve Cokely (whose tape-recorded speeches were cited by Griffin as one of his authoritative sources), reveals how obsessed some blacks are by their hatred of Jews.

It was the first week in May 1988, when the virulent anti-Semitism of mayoral aide Cokely became public knowledge. Acting Mayor Eugene Sawyer waited to fire him, and some black spokesmen came out in support of Cokely, while most others remained silent. But it wasn't until the end of July that much of the rest of the country learned about the incident and about the continuing anti-Jewish sniping being carried out by some local blacks. Since then, black-Jewish relations in general, and the Chicago situation in particular, have been a subject of special interest in a number of ways, with the impact and implications of the incident continuing to reverberate.

The city's mayoral campaigns, played out in the wake of last year's events, showed how a candidate can be hurt by being seen as equivocating on bigotry and showed that the image of reaching out and building coalitions is important for getting elected in a multi-racial, multi-ethnic city like Chicago.

More recently, the 25th anniversaries of such major events in the history of the civil rights movement as the Schwerner-Goodman-Chaney murders and the passage of the Civil Rights Act have provided the occasion for remembering an era when Jews and blacks forged a coalition. And as the months since the Cokely affair have gone by, a number of encouraging things have been happening regarding black-Jewish relations, locally and nationally, with some Jews and some blacks coming together to try to better understand one another and to discover areas where they can jointly take action.

In late July 1988, Chicago's black-Jewish dialogue group issued a statement condemning the kind of anti-Semitism then being expressed in some quarters of the black community and the kind of racism manifested by the burning of a cross in front of a black home. During the mayoral campaigns, the group issued a statement proclaiming that anti-Semitism and racism should be kept out of the electioneering.

Despite these developments, though, there have also been troubling signs, suggesting that the lessons of last year's crisis have not been sufficiently learned. Indeed as time has gone by, a "revisionist" portrayal of what occurred during that first week in May 1988 has repeatedly surfaced. In the revisionist view, Cokely was the lone offender in the black community, with a number of black leaders speaking out against him and the media failing to report that. That simply is not what happened.

During the days while the mayor vacillated, some black voices were audibly raised defending Cokely. Most dramatic was that of political activist Lu Palmer, who on John Callaway's *Chicago Tonight* program on Channel 11, lent support to the most extreme and obscene of Cokely's anti-Semitic charges, including that Jewish doctors have deliberately injected the AIDS virus into blacks. This appearance alone, which provoked more irate phone calls to the station than any other segment of *Chicago Tonight* all year, considerably exacerbated the tensions prevailing in Chicago. Callaway himself later said that Palmer was the only black spokesman on the program that evening because none of the others who were invited were willing to go on the air to speak about the subject.

If responsible black leaders had wanted to be heard condemning the bigotry which Cokely espoused and to make clear that they saw no place in government for a person who held such positions, they had plenty of opportunities. But except for community leaders Nancy Jefferson and Bob Lucas, none did so until the end was clearly in sight. (Supporters of Ald. Tim Evans have since praised him for an early position he supposedly took, but according to press reports, he only expressed abhorrence for anti-Semitism in general and said that no prejudice should be tolerated but did not specifically refer to Cokely's remarks or call for Cokely's removal or any other form of discipline.)

A lengthy article on black-Jewish relations by Taylor Branch in the May 1989 issue of *Esquire* magazine, which focused on Chicago, provides an example of how the facts of what occurred here last year are being slighted. Though the piece contains extensive background on Cokely and has a full-page photo of him, it fails to deal with some of the most significant ramifications of the subject. Instead, beginning with a hyped-up title asserting the existence of an "uncivil war" between blacks and Jews, the article implicitly sees members of both groups as equally to blame for their conflict.

Though Cokely himself purports to be unhappy with the article and has talked about calling for a boycott of *Esquire's* advertisers because of it, it has helped him maintain the celebrity status which a number of media outlets have endowed him with since the controversy broke. Just a few weeks ago, he appeared for some two hours on WVON Radio in Chicago, a station with a primarily black audience, discussing the article and reiterating the conspiracy-haunted anti-Semitic rhetoric which had come to general public notice last year.

Readiness to buy into the revisionist view of what happened in Chicago, which discounts the extent of anti-Semitism in the black community and reduces the validity of concern and outrage in the Jewish community, is not limited to someone like Branch, an "outsider" who came to town to learn about the subject. According to reports on a black-Jewish conference at Dillard University in New Orleans, tensions developed there after a black participant from Chicago cited Cokely's fringe status in the community as an excuse for the lack of response by black leaders.

Even within the Jewish community itself, there have been efforts to side-step the issue. Over the past half year, the National Jewish Community Relations Advisory Council (NJCRAC) has been developing a proposition to be included in its "Joint Program Plan" which will be issued in September. The initial draft of the proposition – which balanced the responsibility for tensions between blacks and Jews – was regarded an unacceptable by Chicago's Jewish Community Relations Council (JCRC). Chicago introduced a successful motion at NJCRAC's February plenary session calling for rewriting of the proposition. While much of the rewrite was more satisfactory, Chicago's JCRC was still uncomfortable with a few passages in it, including a paragraph which described the Cokely affair. Chicago then proposed an alternative version of that paragraph, but the replacement was rejected by NJCRAC's Executive Committee with some opponents saying it was too inflammatory, particularly in light of the fact that the proposition is destined to be read by members of the black community.

The JCRC's stance on this issue is based on the belief that it is the profound obligation of the Jewish community and its leadership not to ignore or minimize any form of anti-Semitism. As much of a fringe figure as Cokely might be, he continues to be given opportunities to circulate vicious anti-Semitism and to gain the potential credibility that comes with visibility. And some of the other promoters of anti-Jewish hostility in the black community have even greater stature – such as Farrakhan, who finds ready platforms at college campuses around the country.

These people and the statements they make deserve to be taken seriously. Jews should not feel defensive or apologetic insisting, as our experience has tragically taught, that words are not only words; that rhetoric motivates people to act; that anti-Semitic myths maintain a life of their own and that the potential for their taking hold and spreading cannot be underestimated; and that, given our history and our minority status, a recognition of our potential vulnerability, even in pluralistic America, is not paranoia, but practical realism.

Many Jews react particularly strongly to revelations of anti-Semitism in the black community. There is a sense of betrayal in light of the record of Jewish tolerance and of Jewish support for black causes and given the memories of Jews and blacks working together to promote mutual interests. For many Jews there is also, I believe, a distressing shock in discovering anti-Semitism emanating from a people who have themselves suffered from prejudice so severely. Beneath it all may be a sense that if even blacks are not immune to expressions of the most extreme anti-Semitic notions, nobody is.

Jews cannot be blamed for feeling offended and becoming alienated when they are attacked. But for all the outrage which our community feels about anti-Semitism in the black community, for all of the need to stand up to it firmly, the fullness of our response does not necessarily end there. In *Do the Right Thing,* Sal, the Italian pizzeria owner, has an angry son named Pino who wants to turn his back on the black community and who even embraces anti-black racism. It would be more than unfortunate if, in reacting to anti-Semitism in the black community, members of the Jewish community would become like Pino.

The explosive ending of Spike Lee's movie shows that Radio Raheem's menacing assertiveness, Buggin Out's venom, Sal's loss of control and Mookie's cold destructiveness only harm others and bring no real good to any of them. Despite its disturbing conclusion, *Do the Right Thing,* with humor and tenderness along the way, provides a glimpse of the possibilities of interracial connection. It mostly leaves one sad about what is and wishing for what might be.

Out here in the "real" world beyond the film, Jews can play a part in trying to improve intergroup relations, as we have always done. Our expectations regarding Jews and blacks must be modest. When all is said and done, some of our two communities' interests are in conflict. The old civil rights coalition, especially as conceived of in memories tinged with romantic nostalgia, cannot be replicated in today's world. But surely, without compromising on anti-Semitism, we can, at least, try to bring our communities together to combat bigotry of all kinds, which so often targets each of our groups and which endangers us all, no matter who is the intended victim.

And something more. Spike Lee's movie explores the complexities of race relations in contemporary urban America – the proximity of prejudice, the suspicions and fears, the tenuousness of positive relations. But it also portrays the deprivation and sense of frustration of blacks in the inner city.

Jews are not to blame for the despairing conditions of the black underclass, and when demagogues make Jews scapegoats, they are not solving the prevailing problems and are making it less likely that Jews will be eager to play a part in the search for solutions. But must we write off an entire community, ignoring its problems and needs, because of the anti-Semitism of some of its members? Can we not, instead, strive to ensure that the lessons of an episode like the Cokely affair are clearly learned and not distorted or ignored and in that context try to help address the problems of the inner city?

There are no easy answers to any of this – including how the crisis of urban America can best be dealt with. In struggling to chart our own course of action we, like the characters in Spike Lee's movie, face the difficult challenge of doing the right thing.

The Jewish Community and the Domestic Agenda: An Alternative Perspective

*This essay was invited for a booklet on Jews and Race
in America published by The Susan and David Wilstein Institute
of Jewish Policy Studies (Spring 1992).
It was preceded by a piece by Gary E. Rubin
and followed by one by David M. Gordis.*

· · ·

Affirmative Action Not the Top Priority

For all of the problems tied up with the question of race in America today, I do not believe that Gary Rubin's thesis, that race has "emerged as the decisive domestic issue on the American Jewish agenda," holds up. That is, while the subject of race surely is out there, the attachment of overriding importance to the issue as of special Jewish concern is probably not shared by most members of the Jewish community, nor do I believe that Mr. Rubin proves it should be.

Mr. Rubin opens his essay by arguing that American Jews are increasingly divided on issues involving race. A prime example for him is the manner in which the American electorate at large has been split since the 1950's, with blacks driven toward the Democratic Party and whites toward the Republicans. In *Chain Reaction: The Impact of Race, Rights, and Taxes on American Politics,* Thomas Byrne Edsall and Mary D. Edsall analyze the national trend, noting the movement of Southern whites and Northern urban working- and lower-middle-class ethnics into Republican columns, in part on the basis of the issues listed in their book's subtitle. Although they point to the Canarsie neighborhood in New York to show how "once liberal Jews together with more conservative Italians shifted sharply to the right in the years leading up to the 1980 election," in general, Jews have remained relatively fixed in their political allegiance. When traditionally Democratic Jewish voters have gone Republican in Presidential elections, the reason has probably been tied to foreign policy more often than to domestic matters, and when the latter has counted, the issues have most likely been economic and not race-related.

The statistics are revealing. In 1976, 70-75 percent of Jews voted for Carter, up from 65 percent for McGovern in 1972. The ensuing drop to 45 percent for Carter in the 1980 election was doubtlessly greatly caused by the President's position on Israel, and 15 percent of the community's vote went not to the Republicans but to the third party candidate, John Anderson, making Jews his largest single bloc of voters. In 1984, when 66 percent of American Jews voted for Mondale, they were not far behind the 70 percent of those identified as "liberals" who supported him, according to *The New York Times/CBS News* polling; and the rate of support for Dukakis in 1988—64 percent of the Jewish vote—still contrasted with the 45 percent he received from the general population.

While I would not try to claim that no Jews have been vulnerable to the negative appeals of the politics of race, on the whole, they have been less attracted by that rhetoric than most other white Americans. It is often noted that in local elections Jews vote for black candidates at a higher rate than any other segment of the white electorate. On the national level, the discomfort which many Jews have felt about the presidential candidacies of Jesse Jackson surely had less to do with his race than with the insensitivity or worse of his "Hymietown" remark and of certain earlier comments, his association with Louis Farrakhan, and his positions on Israel. If fears of the Jackson influence on the Democratic Party made many Jews less comfortable there than they had formerly been, it is misleading to simply regard that as a "racial" response.

And so, for Jews, race has not been the kind of overriding issue impacting on voting choices that Mr. Rubin's essay suggests. Without a clearly racial basis for the readiness of substantial numbers of Jews to make the switch and vote Republican, and absent proof that Jewish interests are necessarily better served by all Jews being linked to African-Americans in the Democratic Party, Mr. Rubin's distress over the fact that a relatively small percentage of Jews have chosen to shift parties seems not to be justified. On the other hand, the argument can also be made that if some Jews are now ready to be found in the ranks of either of the major political parties, that may not be entirely bad for the community. There is advantage to having leverage in both parties; there is advantage in not being taken for granted by either.

All of this is not to say that race, brought back into the headlines and national consciousness by the explosive events in Los Angeles, does not remain a sensitive matter in America. Slavery and the segregation and discrimination which followed, along with the attitudes which have permitted and been engendered by those practices, have left America with unfinished business not to be ignored. Racial tensions permeate intergroup relations throughout the nation, and racism—albeit at levels evaluated differently by much of black America and much of white America—remains all too alive. At the same time, the misery of the African-American underclass is the shame of our cities today.

But these factors do not necessarily lead to the conclusion which Mr. Rubin seems to reach, namely, that support for affirmative action must be the Jewish community's top domestic policy priority. The debate about affirmative action has been going on for some time now, often focusing on the conflict of fairness versus equality which is central to Mr. Rubin's discussion. More recently, though, the efficacy of affirmative action in substantially alleviating poverty has been doubted. It is questioned whether race and poverty are necessarily bound together and suggested that even if there were widespread application of affirmative action policies, the profound problem of poverty in America, affecting a large number of blacks, would probably not be resolved. At the same time it has been increasingly noted that the racial thrust of affirmative action creates new social problems; black writers like Shelby Steele and Stephen Carter have described the damaging effect which affirmative action can have on African-Americans. Moreover, given prevailing realities, it is unlikely that the Jewish support for affirmative action which Mr. Rubin advocates would have all of the positive impact which he anticipates. Given Mr. Rubin's own acknowledgement that the areas of dispute regarding affirmative action are not very great within the Jewish community, it can be asked how much is left to be debated. The only cases he cites where Jewish organizations differ have to do with reserving university scholarships for minority students and the Federal Communications Commission's judging of applications for broadcast licenses. At issue seems to be not whether the Jewish community should support measures where quotas are involved, but how to evaluate specific practices on a case-by-case basis to decide whether or not the quota prohibition is violated. Even if the more "liberal" interpretations of the individual cases under dispute were to prevail in the Jewish community, it does not seem likely that national public policy-making would be so greatly affected, since Jewish opposition has hardly been the determining factor in the overall debate about affirmative action. And even if all Jewish organizations were 100 percent in sync with what Mr. Rubin calls for, that would turn out to be only a significantly limited support of affirmative action in the eyes of many African-American spokesmen. It is hard to see how this would serve to reinvigorate the black-Jewish alliance, an important side benefit which Mr. Rubin champions.

Mr. Rubin says that "in public policy debates among Jews, few domestic topics generate the interest or division aroused by race-related issues such as affirmative action, civil rights enforcement or minority scholarships." I am not so sure this is the case. In my community, there seem to be sharper disputes regarding public funding for parochial schools and reproductive choice. While debates about affirmative action may indeed proceed at the national organizational level, I wonder if they really are all that salient for the whole community. This is not to argue against the Jewish community's continued support for quota-free affirmative action measures, but it is meant to question seeing that as the community's top domestic priority.

The Dilemma of Diversity

Race is not the only prism to look through in considering the current social scene. An alternative approach would revolve around the dilemma of diversity as opposed to the dilemma of race. At issue is a dialectic in which both extremes have virtues and flaws—a dialectic in which the nation is now caught up, with serious, race-connected, ramifications for the Jewish community.

At one end of the spectrum is the ideal rendered by the image of the melting pot. This was the notion which held sway during the earlier decades of the century, when Jews and other immigrant groups swelled the nation's population. It conveyed a goal of all Americans becoming alike and assimilating into the overall society. There was much to recommend this objective for a nation of immigrants which, despite its theoretical embrace of newcomers, maintained both populist and elitist strains of intolerance which are being reasserted in current political contexts.

This concept, however, ignored certain facts. First, formal hurdles prevented segments of Americans from melting in, with blacks in particular denied full benefit of the melting pot. Second, what really happened in that pot was the creation not of an end product which took from all the parts, but rather one which reflected the dominant culture. Third, for all the virtues of forging a common culture in this new land, melting is costly not only for the individual groups which find their identities being melted away, but also for the overall society, which has less chance to benefit from the richness available through disparate ethnic sub-groups. With a group's history, language, beliefs, habits, and lifestyle creating identity for its members and giving meaning to their lives, the diminution of those sources of value is a loss not only to members of such a group but also to society at large.

For Jews, there wasn't really much blending into a new "Judeo-Christian" society, despite the flattering air of the phrase. Instead, many Jews simply became more like everybody else, not only shedding the distinctive clothing but also modifying or abandoning the religious customs and cultural habits brought from the old country. In the world of our fathers, large numbers of Jews from the cities and shtetls of Eastern Europe uncovered their heads, went to work on the Sabbath, ate un-kosher foods, and learned less about their past and their teachings. The very phrase "melting pot" comes from a 1908 play with that title, written by the English-Jewish writer Israel Zangwill, about a Jewish composer in New York who had the goal of creating a symphony expressing the harmonious merger of groups in America and who wished to act out his vision of America by marrying a Christian woman. While one could not entirely blame America for the willingness of some Jews to break from their past, and while adaptation was not necessarily total or an entirely negative response to modern conditions, such steps were reflective of an absorption of the American cultural ethos, and to a certain extent were an indication of what had to be given up to get ahead.

Coming to America brought European Jewry many benefits: greater safety than they had experienced abroad, not to mention refuge from the Holocaust which annihilated the communities left behind; opportunities to enhance their economic and physical well-being; and however breached at times, constitutional protection for their religious differences and the right to participate as equal citizens. But a price was paid for diving into the melting pot and is continuing to be paid in an era of increased religious tolerance, as has been documented by the 1990 National Jewish Population Survey of the Council of Jewish Federations. The survey shows that since 1985, around half of the marriages involving Jews have been to non-Jews and that three quarters of the children of such interfaith marriages are not raised as Jews. With increasing numbers in the community following the lead of Zangwill's hero, and the melting pot philosophy celebrated by Zangwill threatening the vibrancy and continuity of Jewish peoplehood in America, in recent decades many Jews have joined other Americans propelled toward the alternative pole of the "diversity" dialectic. This pole celebrates not sameness but difference. Rather than responding to a feeling of shame which leads to differences being hidden or shed, this philosophy calls for the dignified assertion of such differences. It developed along with the surfacing of "black pride" in the 1960's. More recently, the flow into the country of members of Latino and Asian groups hoping to maintain their ethnic identity has intensified the trend. At the same time, the expression of group identification based on such factors as gender or sexual preference has also increased. For Jews, the movement toward this pole of the dialectic has seen increased Jewish identification, with factors like the growth of the day school movement as both effect and cause. There has been an increased familiarity with Jewish history, including the Holocaust era and, often in nostalgic fashion, the shtetl experience in Eastern Europe which preceded it. There has been an apparent increase in religious observance. And there has been a heightening of ties with Jews abroad, in the Soviet Union and in Israel. The intense relationship with the Jewish state has been an especially significant factor in the shaping of the identification of contemporary American Jewry, particularly since the Six-Day War in June of 1967.

For all of the virtues of this pole of the dialectic, it too, in the extreme form which it increasingly seems to be taking in the 1990's, has its dangers and flaws. The problem emerges when people see themselves only as members of their sub-groups rather than as parts of a greater whole, and when they regard their group not as striving to be in harmony with others, but as inevitably in conflict with them. Interethnic strife is the order of the day on the international scene, with much of Eastern Europe returning to the pre-World War I condition which gave birth to the term Balkanization. In America, too, we are seeing a tendency toward fragmentation, tribalism, and our own form of Balkanization. If the homogenizing extreme of the melting pot is a threat to the continuity of America's various subgroups and undesirable in its way, this extreme pits the groups against one another, creating an overall atmosphere of tension and lessening the chances of the groups working together to pursue shared policy goals. The result is unhealthy warfare, in which each group tends to define itself in reference to its true or imagined victimization at the hands of others, and to think of itself in terms of its supposed cultural superiority over the others. Even as the assimilationist magnet of the melting pot point of view continues to exert a pull, this end of the spectrum is increasingly strengthened, threatening the overall society in its way and bringing particular problems to Jews, some in a racial context.

Jews, like members of other groups, can be hurt by the excessive turning inward and isolation which go with tribalism. Jews are as vulnerable as anyone else to the psychology of victimization, to seeing everyone else as their enemy. Given Jewish history and the tenacity of anti-Semitism, that may be understandable, but it is not based on an entirely accurate reading of contemporary reality, and it threatens to cut Jews off from friends and potential allies. Meanwhile, Americans in general and Jews in an additional way are endangered by the rising influence of the set of attitudes surrounding the "difference" pole of the diversity spectrum, by the ideology of multiculturalism as that term has come to be used.

Writing in *The American Scholar* in 1990 and using the label "particularistic multiculturalism," Diane Ravitch has said, "Particularism is a bad idea whose time has come. It is also a fashion spreading like wildfire through the education system, actively promoted by organizations and individuals with a political and professional interest in strengthening ethnic power bases in the university, in the education profession, and in society itself." In *The Disuniting of America: Reflections on a Multicultural Society,* Arthur Schlesinger Jr. adds, "The ethnic revolt against the melting pot has reached the point, in rhetoric at least, though not I think in reality, of a denial of the idea of a common culture and a single society. If large numbers of people really accept this, the republic would be in serious trouble."

In a pluralistic multicultural framework, members of minority groups have cultures and values to be reciprocally understood and respected by others, and they are seen having equal rights with others. From the perspective of the ideology of particularistic multiculturalism, however, the focus is on "people of color," often along with women, gays, and lesbians, who are regarded as oppressed victims of an evil and inferior Western culture. Jews, in a perversely ironic twist given their history and the continued virulence of anti-Semitism on the world scene, are not regarded as fellow minority victims of that Western culture. Rather, via an appropriation of the very anti-Semitism which Western culture spawned and sustained, they are seen as undifferentiated members of that culture at best, and as conspiratorial manipulators of it at worst. Israel, in turn, is regarded not as the proud expression of Jewish nationalism and the vehicle of Jewish liberation, but rather as a racist embodiment of Jewish values, and as the imperialist oppressor of innocent Palestinians.

A key aspect of the particularist multicultural trend has been the Afrocentrist movement, which has at its core the assertion that, as Schlesinger puts it, "black Africa [which supposedly included ancient Egypt] is the birthplace of science, philosophy, religion, medicine, technology, of the great achievements that have been wrongly ascribed to Western civilization." Schlesinger describes the role taken in this movement by Leonard Jeffries, chairman of the Afro-American Studies Department at the City College of New York. As consultant on African-American culture for a 1989 Task Force on Minorities, Jeffries found "deep-seated pathologies of racial hatred" in New York State's ethnically-sensitive 1987 curriculum.

Jeffries himself has his own racist point of view, laced with anti-Semitic venom. He has gained notoriety for his description of Europeans as selfish "ice-people" and Africans as superior "sun-people," for claiming that "rich Jews" were responsible for history's greatest sin against black people by financing the slave trade, and for asserting that Jews in Hollywood were involved with the Mafia in "a financial system of destruction of black people."

The attribution of guilt for slavery to Jews is elaborated on in a recent publication from the Historical and Research Department of Louis Farrakhan's Nation of Islam called *The Secret Relationship Between Blacks and Jews.* Volume One, which was released last fall, develops the assertion that "Jews have been conclusively linked to the greatest criminal endeavor ever undertaken against an entire race of people—a crime against humanity—The Black African Holocaust." The Afrocentrist assertion that Africa, not Europe, was the source of civilization, is echoed in Farrakhan's theology by the belief that blacks, not Jews, are the true chosen people, leaving Jews as impostors or worse, as well as perpetrators, rather than victims, of Holocaust-like suffering. While the Afrocentric instruction which is being promoted in school systems throughout the country is justified as a means of inculcating self-esteem in young blacks, its potential in achieving that purpose is highly questionable. Moreover, it promotes a world view which sees whites in general, and, for some of its foremost advocates, Jews in particular, as blacks' evil adversaries.

Farrakhan's philosophy is propelled toward separation as a goal, and Afrocentrism seems headed that way as well. Comparison can be made with the nation's white supremacist organizations, which are anti-black and hostile to Asian and Latino immigrant groups on the one hand, but anti-Semitic in a theological and paranoid manner that parallels Farrakhan's on the other. These two strains in current social tribalism have taken particularism to a separatist conclusion. Even without going that far, however, particularist versions of multiculturalism can be seen as a danger, not only in their potential impact on Jews. As Arthur Schlesinger says, "I am constrained to feel that the cult of ethnicity in general and the Afrocentric campaign in particular do not bode well either for American education or for the future of the republic."

While the extreme of assimilation can posit a disrespect for cultural differences which can rightfully be abhorred by African-Americans along with members of other sub-groups striving for or championing group identity, that is not the only alternative to Balkanizing multiculturalism. That is not what integration must mean. There is a middle ground which takes from the best of the two poles of the dialectic. As Schlesinger puts it, "The question America confronts as a pluralistic society is how to vindicate cherished cultures and traditions without breaking the bonds of cohesion—common ideals, common political institutions, common language, common culture, common fate—that hold the republic together." Between the Scylla of the stultifying homogeneity of the melting pot and the seething Charybdis of extreme Balkanization lies a pluralistic society in which individuals have the opportunity to identify themselves with particular groups and to be enriched by being parts of them, while at the same time living together with mutual respect. Multiculturalism may have become the battle cry for a militant zero-sum approach which challenges the value of America's traditional Eurocentric culture. But for all of its flaws and limitations, it is in fact that culture, in its promotion of democratic norms and its protection of individual rights and group differences, which offers a solution to the dilemma of diversity. The need to assert the worth of such a middle ground position and to find a way to get there must rank, I believe, very high indeed on the nation's and the Jewish community's current domestic agenda.

Protecting Ourselves While Caring About Others

Mr. Rubin touches on the subject of multiculturalism in his list of areas where American Jews are dividing themselves on the question of race. "Will Jews," he asks, "become alienated from the universities, or at least from certain disciplines within them, because of our fears of the impact of multi-culturalism, another race-oriented issue? Or will we see in this movement possibilities for advancing Jewish interests and values on campus?" Surely he is right in that, where possible, an attempt should be made to advance Jewish interests and values on the nation's campuses through the multicultural framework. More than that, though, it will be important to see where the whole multicultural movement goes and what role Jews might be able to play in moving it in a positive direction. For if Jews do have "fears of the impact of multi- culturalism," that is, as I have attempted to show, for very good reason. Though Mr. Rubin here merely calls multiculturalism a "race-oriented issue" and not a new vehicle for the expression of anti-Jewish hostility by African-Americans, in raising the question of whether concern about black anti-Semitism will lead

Jews to take steps which are contrary to Jewish values and detrimental to Jewish interests he is more blunt about what is involved. Overall, Mr. Rubin does not play down the nature or threat of anti-Semitism in the black community, referring to the Crown Heights affair and the Leonard Jeffries matter as possibly bringing the issue of black anti-Semitism to a new stage. But the problem still, I believe, goes further than his discussion takes it.

This is a time when the music of super-popular African-American rap artists has been laced with anti-Semitic lyrics echoed by comments of theirs in media interviews. Meanwhile, on campuses around the country these days the academic calendar is regularly punctuated by crises revolving around visits by such merchants of anti-Semitica as Jeffries, the former Stokely Carmichael (now an apostle of militantly anti-Zionist third-worldism), and Chicago's Steve Cokely, who achieved his 15 minutes of fame in 1988 while spending several days holding on to a position at City Hall even after it was publicly disclosed that he had charged that Jewish doctors were deliberately infecting blacks with the AIDS virus.

Chicago has also given the nation Gus Savage, a black U.S. Congressman notorious for his use of racist invective, who two years ago created a scandal by baiting his opponent for having Jewish supporters. In the March 1992 primary campaign, Mr. Savage once again invoked the politics of fear and animosity, charging that the African- American community faces a "danger of genocide," and that "the Jewish population is contributing to this pending disaster." Mr. Savage received a standing ovation at the candidates' forum where he offered such remarks, and several black public officials were at his side when he called a press conference to defend himself against subsequent criticism and referred to supporters of Israel as "un-American."

Jews generally find the anti-Semitism which comes from within the black community a particular source of anger and anguish. There is a sense of betrayal in light of the history of shared involvement in the civil rights movement and given the feeling, sometimes crudely expressed, that Jews played a special role in ensuring black rights. I suspect there is also a less-conscious sense of dismay that if even African-Americans, with their own history of suffering from prejudice, are vulnerable to gutter-level anti-Semitism, then no one can be thought to be free from possibly succumbing to it. The claim made by some ideologues that it is impossible for blacks, as victims of prejudice, to be prejudiced, since they are powerless to inflict suffering on others, rings hollow. Jews too well know that circulation of the rhetoric of anti- Semitism, from whatever source, has the potential of spreading like a poison through both the immediate audience and the broader society. And if African-Americans do not have the social power to oppress Jews, it does not take baseless paranoia to deeply trouble Jewish witnesses to the crowd-pleasing Jew bashing of a Louis Farrakhan and his like. In that regard, the Crown Heights violence which followed rabble rousing on the streets, accompanied by the chanting of anti-Semitic slogans, and which included the murder of a Jewish young man, was ominous.

While there apparently is no conclusive basis for believing that anti-Semitism in the general black community is appreciably greater than in the overall non-Jewish American population, that is little comfort for most Jews. The issue is more than mere perception. The trouble is that too many putative African-American leaders in academia, in the political realm or public life, and on the streets, seem either to be possessed by conspiracy-haunted images of Jews or to find the scapegoating of Jews for black problems to be useful. A further part of the problem is that they seem to be getting away with it. As Tom Smith, director of the General Social Survey of the National Opinion Research Center, has recently pointed out, the only figures who have been able to maintain leadership status in their communities in America despite expressing anti-Semitic feelings are African-Americans.

No wonder, then, that many Jews are troubled, and some even question the point of pursuing positive black/Jewish relations and of supporting efforts to alleviate the condition of African-Americans in the inner cities. More and more Jews seem disinclined to just swallow hard and go on doing what they have done. This is certainly not to claim that all Jews are themselves free of racist inclinations and altruistically motivated. But while a Michael Levin may exist, he cannot be said to have the stature to command anywhere near the following of a Leonard Jeffries. The Louis Farrakhans and company are without counterpart in the Jewish community, nor would anybody be likely to last at that level of leadership who preached an equivalent racist creed. Concern with the ability of some black leaders to express anti- Semitism and maintain legitimacy goes beyond conservatives in the Jewish community. In a recent issue of *Tikkun*, for example, author and journalist Jim Sleeper argues powerfully on the need for race-baiting black demagogues to be denied stature by others in their community. "The time has come," he writes, "for black activists and all who support civil-rights struggles to face up to a...dismaying mission: that of isolating and defeating much of what now passes for black protest leadership in New York City and some other parts of America." Writing from a "progressive" point of view in support of a "movement for social justice," Sleeper argues that "the more the theatrics of a debased identity politics like [Al] Sharpton's and [Sonny] Carson's chill internal debate among blacks and alienate other groups, the more isolated the black community will become from this larger national and global project." Mr. Rubin talks about Jewish "liberals pushing for a continued positive relationship with blacks and conservatives advocating a more confrontational approach." But this is not an issue simply to be resolved by Jews. A confrontational approach may sound objectionable, and for Jews to be lecturing blacks on how their leaders should behave or how they should relate to their leaders smacks of a control and paternalism which, from the black point of view, is precisely part of the problem. Still, to exonerate black leaders from the responsibility of making anti-Semitic expression unacceptable is to maintain a posture which is not only perilous but also condescending in its own way. The current Jewish drift from the African-American community, as detrimental as it may be to Jewish interests, is likely to continue until there are some visible changes among blacks.

Even at this point there are leaders in the black community ready to do and say the right thing. As Mr. Rubin points out, while too many black leaders were silent on Crown Heights and have been silent on Jeffries, important voices of condemnation have been raised in the African-American community, if often ignored by the media. Meanwhile, in Chicago, the city's main black/Jewish dialogue group, participated in by clergy, organizational officials, and academics, itself issued a statement on the Crown Heights affair initiated by one of its black members. I had the opportunity of co-drafting it with the black executive director of an organization called Project Equality. The statement explicitly condemns "those who exploited the situation by choosing inflammatory words to incite violent deeds" and "by promoting hatred rather than reconciliation;" it draws the lesson that "leadership cannot be left to demagogues." At the same time, two theater companies in Chicago and Washington, D.C., recently premiered a black playwright's sensitive dramatization of the experiences of two Jewish athletes in the 1936 Olympics, victims of prejudice in their own way, who come together with their black teammates in a transcendent friendship.

Especially encouraging was the result of the recent primary election in which Gus Savage was defeated by Mel Reynolds, a black candidate who rejected the politics of divisiveness and bluntly said, three days before the election, that "the black community in Chicago is in danger of losing its moral authority on the issue of race if it allows Gus Savage to use hate to get elected." Savage had told his followers that the election should turn on "how you feel about Jews rather than how you feel about blacks." In the end it was voters not only from the suburban area newly drawn into the district, but also from urban areas previously supportive of Savage, who made Reynolds the winner. Unbowed, in acknowledging defeat Savage lashed out at "the white racist media and racist reactionary Jewish misleaders," but the electorate, black and white, had spoken.

In order for blacks and Jews to maintain a proper relationship, the former need to take several steps, including recognizing that Jews too have been victims of horrifying bigotry and remain endangered by it, denouncing instances of anti-Semitism, and denying stature to those black leaders who would express and exploit anti-Semitism either because they truly embrace it or because they choose it as a cynical means of furthering their own goals. Anti-Semitism is both evil and harmful. For Jews to insist on these steps is not simply to be "confrontational" and hung up on "Jewish dignity." It is rather to be appropriately asserting a posture right for Jews on both a moral and pragmatic basis and (however this might sound) to be pointing the African-American community in a direction which is in its own best interest as well. At the same time, if black/Jewish relations are to become less tense, African-Americans committed to affirmative action must be prepared to acknowledge that Jewish opposition to quotas, based on principle and strengthened by historic Jewish exclusion, is not equivalent to black anti-Semitism.

That much said, I nevertheless believe Mr. Rubin is right in arguing that Jews should not turn their backs on the black community. We have a parallel and shared destiny as the two most wounded victims of irrational prejudice, to this day being twin targets of neo-Nazis, Klansmen and their ilk. We have a history brightened by episodes of working together, and we both have much to gain by coming together in coalition in today's world—though it is unrealistic to hope for a simple return to something like the civil rights movement, especially as it is nostalgically recalled. And for all of the provocations of some black leaders, members of the Jewish community would be wrong to become insensitive to the continuing need to combat racism and to become uncaring about the anguish of the black underclass in urban America.

At the most practical level, our ability to advocate for our special interests is enhanced when we have allies to join us. An overwhelming absorption into Jewish particularism paradoxically makes us less effective even in promoting such specifically Jewish causes as American support for Israel. In the same vein, not only is racism bad in itself, but as it is allowed to prevail the climate for increased anti-Semitism is enhanced. Furthermore, an America in which the devastation of the inner city continues to fester is an America in which conditions detrimental to the well-being of Jews, along with all other Americans, are likely to intensify.

More than that, though, it is simply the right thing to do and in tune with its traditional social behavior for the Jewish community to feel impelled to combat the poverty which too many Americans, a disproportionate number of them black, suffer from. While support for the general goal of fighting poverty does not necessarily translate into endorsement of all of the policy measures which Mr. Rubin might call for regarding affirmative action measures, other courses of action are available as well. In fact, elements of the Jewish "establishment" have already been following them. In Illinois, for example, the Government Affairs Program of the Jewish Federation of Metropolitan Chicago, working with Jewish state senators, has been the chief advocate for a new line item for homeless shelters in the state government budget under the Department of Public Aid, and it has been a primary advocate for the state's two last welfare grant increases, with important education funding spinoff. Advocacy in the health care area has also been pronounced, as it increasingly is nationally. There should be no illusion that by fighting poverty we are automatically lessening the hold of the demagogues and reducing anti-Semitism in the black community. But nor should the expression of anti-Semitism from some quarters there allow us to accept racism and the suffering of poverty.

We need, in other words, to be active on two fronts. Rather than rendering a series of either/or directions for a split Jewish community to choose between, most areas of division listed by Mr. Rubin can be seen as describing alternative impulses to be reconciled by the community. We need to challenge blacks about the sources of our dismay, which is best done in a dialogue framework where trust and respect have been established, and we need to attempt to develop positive relationships, but not by selling ourselves out. We need to pursue our own interests, but we also need to cultivate and work with coalition partners whom we can support and who will support us. We need to protect ourselves and to care about others.

We need, then, to live in tune with the often cited but still profound vision of Hillel. *The Ethics of Our Fathers* tells us that Hillel used to say, "If I am not for myself, who will be for me?"—a statement which can be seen as making the case for the Jewish pursuit of Jewish interests. But Hillel added, "And if I am only for myself, what am I?"—which can be taken as implying the limitations of a narrow, self-centered perspective. The fulfillment of Hillel's two-sided dictum in today's race-troubled America, where Jews and blacks have their own problems and have an uneasy relationship with one another, may not be easy. Lest, however, we be tempted to just sit back and wait for better times, we should observe that Hillel ended this reflection by saying, "And if not now, when?"

Legacy of Black Writer
May Help Black-Jewish Relations
JUF News, August 1994

. . .

L earning with sadness of the death of Ralph Ellison earlier this spring, my mind flashed back to a classroom at the University of Chicago over 30 years ago when, as an undergraduate student, I was privileged to have the famous writer as a teacher.

I remembered the lilt in his voice and the manner in which he conveyed his love of jazz. I remembered the twinkle in his eye and recalled the day when, talking about *The Adventures of Augie March,* he suggested that while writing about Jewish characters and experiences Saul Bellow had captured an aspect of Jewishness in the very language of his text.

I also remembered how Ellison himself, whose *Invisible Man* had rendered the nature of the black experience in America more profoundly than any novel to date, and who was himself both a product and devotee of black culture, at the same time believed in the reality and value of a shared American experience.

And my sadness at his death was compounded as I reflected on the state of affairs in which we presently find ourselves in America regarding race relations in general and black-Jewish relations in particular. The ugly underside of that was manifest in a C-Span broadcast of an anti-Semitic hate-fest on the Howard University campus featuring Khalid Abdul Muhammad, Leonard Jeffries, and others (including Chicagoan Steve Cokely) which occurred at about the same time.

The name of the course taught by Ellison was "The Civil War and American Literature." On a hunch, a couple of days after his death I scrounged through some cartons in our basement and there, sure enough, was my notebook from the class, a rare memento saved from my college days. Ellison's thesis, my notes reminded me, was that the Civil War had brought to the fore certain basic American conflicts without resolving them, and that American writers since then had created fiction steeped in the issues of that war in an attempt to give meaning to the American experience.

The basic issues, he had said, involved conflicts between individual freedom and group responsibility and between idealized self-images and reality. For Ellison these themes obtained whether a writer was black like himself and Richard Wright, Jewish like Bellow, or one of the classic American novelists. (This was the era before "political correctness," and Ellison had no trouble in assigning a reading list which, in addition to Wright and Bellow, consisted of Melville, Twain, James, Crane, Fitzgerald, Hemingway, and Faulkner.)

As sensitive as Ellison was to cultural differences, he maintained a belief not only in the commonality of the American experience but also in a broader commonality. In an interview published in the *Chicago Maroon* at the time, he said of his own work, "What I'm trying to do is what the novel has often tried to do, to strip essentials and determine what really constitutes human qualities and what it is that really makes us human."

Writing about Ellison in an article in *The New Republic* shortly after the author's death, Stanley Crouch described the opposition he long faced from black nationalists in the light of such attitudes. In fact, it is precisely those forces which seem to be in the ascendancy these days, attempting to impose their ideology and their prejudices on the overall black community. As the exponents of such attitudes have received visibility through the media and garnered applause on college campuses, the core of the current distress in black-Jewish relations has been both revealed and exacerbated.

Over the past number of years there have been several episodes regarded as crises in black-Jewish relations. One can think, for example, of the so-called Andrew Young affair, when the black ambassador to the United Nations was forced to resign for unauthorized meetings with the PLO, or of the developments that followed Jesse Jackson's description of New York as "Hymietown" while campaigning for president. Those crises and others like them eventually passed, even though they occurred in the context of tensions triggered by differing agendas for the two communities.

Today, however, we seem to have entered a new stage in the relationship itself, a condition characterized in part by the fact that certain black leaders and spokesmen – Louis Farrakhan and others linked to the Nation of Islam being the most prominent and influential – whose belief system, reflected in their rhetoric, is at its core anti-Semitic, have been gaining increasing acceptability within some segments of the black community and increasing national visibility through the media.

A slew of examples could be given, ranging from Farrakhan's meeting with the Congressional Black Caucus to Khalid Abdul Muhammad's campus appearances to extended interviews with one or the other of them on *The Arsenio Hall Show*, on *20/20* with Barbara Walters, on Phil Donahue's show, and more. Most recently, there was Farrakhan's participation in an African American leadership summit convened by the NAACP, once regarded as the epitome of a mainstream black organization.

As recently as a year or so ago, when this phenomenon began to emerge, it could be hoped that Louis Farrakhan would not be able to set the terms of black-Jewish relations. But as the ensuing developments have followed, that has become increasingly difficult to avoid.

Ironically, this is all happening at a time when at least two of the major earlier subjects of dispute between the communities – Israel-Palestinian relations and affairs in South Africa – have in effect been taken off the agenda of the black-Jewish dialogue due to the changes which have taken place in both areas. In their stead have come new issues essentially created by Louis Farrakhan and other Afrocentric black nationalists, such as the role played by Jews in the history of slavery; the Holocaust and the relative degree of pain suffered by blacks through slavery and by the Jewish people through the Holocaust; the very identity of the Jewish people; and the origin of man. And along with the emergence of these areas of dispute, Farrakhan himself has become a key object of tension.

Jewish leaders and organizations have appropriately spoken out against the bigoted anti-Semitic perspective which drives the world view of Louis Farrakhan and his followers. But the first voice to nationally condemn Khalid Abdul Muhammad's notorious Kean College speech and the silence about it from other blacks was himself a black professor, in a column in *The New York Times*. The anti-Semitic content of a Malcolm X mural at San Francisco State University was painted over by a black professor there. And it was the black leader Julian Bond whose column in the *Baltimore Sun* protested the inclusion of Louis Farrakhan in the NAACP's African American leadership summit which took place in that city.

While the implied legitimization of the bigotry of a Farrakhan which goes along with his becoming more acceptable is deeply troubling, in fact the mainstream organized Jewish community chose not to publicly protest his presence at that summit. Whatever impression the media may have given, there was only a modest number of Jewish demonstrators in Baltimore, from the left and the right, none of them representative of any of the mainstream organizations.

But still, then as otherwise, Jews have become increasingly charged with interfering in the efforts of blacks and, by implication, blocking black progress. And supposed defiance of the Jewish community, a posture patented by Farrakhan in his public speeches over recent years, has become a further mode of black demagoguery.

That the issues of the day are for the most part manufactured leads to a crucial point in understanding the current dynamic. For however much impact these developments may have on black-Jewish relations, their origins in fact have practically nothing to do with the ways Jews and blacks, individually or collectively, interact with one another. Instead, they derive from a struggle within the black community itself regarding leadership and direction.

On one side of the struggle are those of the Ralph Ellison mode who, while tied to their own group's culture and identity, also believe in a common culture, who support both pluralism and integration along with a sense of shared humanity. On the other side are those driven by an ideology which stresses difference and separation, which dwells on the unique victimization of black people and which insists on their overall superiority. Given the anti-Semitic beliefs and rhetoric of members of the latter group, as they gain enhanced influence and visibility the situation becomes more and more of a black-Jewish issue whatever the nature of its beginnings.

As the aforementioned struggle plays out in the black community, there are those who, claiming that unity could help solve the enormous problems of the inner cities, ignore or attempt to explain away the anti-Semitism of Louis Farrakhan in inviting him inside their tent. While Jews should indeed be sensitive to the claims that blacks, like anyone else, have a right to choose their leaders and the people with whom they want to sit down and talk, it is hard to see how people with such disparate philosophies as tolerant bridge-builders and scapegoating separatists might in fact be effectively yoked together.

And it should be pointed out that several black analysts have been saying that by turning a blind eye to the bigotry of some of those whom they would bring into their camp, some black leaders are squandering the moral capital accumulated by their people while maintaining high principles in facing their persecution.

It was, in a way, an age of innocence, personal and national, back when I sat in that University of Chicago classroom. The civil rights era was yet to come, when Jews and blacks would march, and even die, together, transforming America. As Ralph Ellison pointed out, we need to be leery of the national trait which involves being possessed by false images, and it is important not to let nostalgia cloud our memory of that era, leading us to overstate the scope of the relationship then. But neither should we be comfortable with attempts to deny the reality of what truly was.

Since then, the nation has continued to change. Some of the problems faced today, including those of the cities, are immense, and a reconstructed civil rights movement seems neither available nor the best vehicle for confronting today's quandaries. But the pull toward tribalism which besets America today is not a means to the solution of anyone's difficulties. It is part of the problem, and some black leaders, along with columnists like Clarence Page, Salim Muwakkil and William Raspberry well recognize that. In the tradition of a Ralph Ellison, they resist the tide of Balkanization, asserting that impulse is bad for their community and bad for the country.

As for the organized Jewish community, distressed by the gains of Louis Farrakhan and others, it tries to go about its business in this area, combatting anti-Semitism and the efforts of those who promulgate it; engaging in rational dialogue where available; and looking for opportunities to work with friends in serving the interests of each of our communities as well as the broader society.

Meanwhile, I, with others I am sure, look forward to the anticipated publication, sadly now to be posthumous, of the long-awaited second novel of Ralph Ellison. It will be especially interesting to see how he applied his art and wisdom to render and illuminate the condition of his people, our nation, and mankind at this troubled and troubling time.

Reflections on a Journey to Israel
with Joseph Cardinal Bernardin
JUF News, May 1995

• • •

On December 24, 1975, I found myself in Bethlehem wearing the uniform of the Israel Defense Forces, along with my reserve unit. Our assignment was to stay up all night in the fields surrounding the city, protecting its inhabitants and visitors against possible attacks aimed at disrupting the Christmas Eve observances in the Church of the Nativity and in Manger Square.

It was a strange experience for a "nice Jewish boy" from West Rogers Park. I thought back to my childhood and speculated how unlikely it would have seemed to have been told some 20 years earlier how I was going to be spending that night.

I would have been equally incredulous had I been told then that some 20 years later I would be coming to Bethlehem in the company of the Archbishop of Chicago and a group of local Jews and Catholics.

That recent stop was part of a voyage across the ocean which for me turned into a journey inward as well, into an exploration of how I came to be there. And it was a trip which frequently reverberated with epiphanies of the once-unexpected, with signs of how much certain things have changed in ways that have meaning not just for me personally but also for the Jewish community of Chicago and for the Jewish people.

Another occasion when I imagined how unlikely a current experience might once have seemed came when our group visited the Western Wall. What, I wondered, might my grandfather have made of this from the vantage point of early-20th century Poland, a time and place when, it is said, Jews would cross the street rather than even walk alongside a church. An owner of Hebrew books both sacred and secular that have been passed on to me, with a family album which had on its first page a photograph not of a relative but of Theodor Herzl, he might have dreamed but could little have anticipated that someday his namesake would be standing in prayer before this venerated site, now in a sovereign Jewish state, alongside a prince of the church.

As incongruous and unexpected as many of these experiences may have been in reference to the past, they didn't come out of the blue. Most of the Catholic and Jewish participants in the trip had grown close to one another in dialogue and friendship for several years. And the person at the center of the trip, Joseph Cardinal Bernardin – fulfilling the dictates of the Second Vatican Council of 1965, following the Pope's lead, perhaps above all driven by his own values and predilections – had made outreach toward the Jewish community and reconciliation between Catholics and Jews a signature of his ministry. That priority reached a zenith on this trip, with a significance that I believe transcended even the lofty hopes and expectations that many of us had as we set out on it.

In the Church of the Holy Sepulchre on a Friday morning, celebrating his first pubic mass in Israel, the Cardinal chose to refer to the Chicago Catholic-Jewish experience in his homily. "While authentic dialogue is never easy," he said, "and there are many differences among us, mutual trust and honesty will help us discover what we have in common." Moving to a broader framework of reconciliation while referring to religious texts, he closed by saying, "Let us ask God to help us remove from our minds and hearts the obstacles that remain in our relationships so that we can more fully love God with all our being and our neighbor as ourself."

The centerpiece of the trip was the speech given by the Cardinal at the Hebrew University entitled "Anti-Semitism: The Historical Legacy and the Continuing Challenge for Christians." In focusing on its subject, the address treated two topics central to Jewish experience in the 20th century which are central to ongoing Catholic-Jewish dialogue as they were to our trip: the Holocaust and the State of Israel.

Closing his speech by describing what he called "future possibilities," the Cardinal proclaimed, "Above all, in light of the history of anti-Semitism and the Holocaust, the church needs to engage in public repentance." Associating himself with a statement recently issued by German bishops in acknowledging that "Christians did not offer due resistance to racial anti-Semitism [and that] many times there was failure and guilt among Catholics," the Cardinal recalled our group's visit to Yad Vashem that morning.

It was an extraordinary stop. After walking along the Avenue of the Righteous Gentiles and then visiting the museum documenting the Nazi evil, we held a service recalling the six million victims of the Shoah, with the Cardinal laying a wreath in their memory. Next we entered the overpowering children's memorial, where lights flicker in a backdrop of infinite darkness and names are recited of innocents prematurely and cruelly sent to the confines of the eternal.

Exiting that hall, the Cardinal, visibly moved, issued a brief statement and faced the press. Asked for his reaction to the charge that the church had not done enough to oppose the Nazis, the Cardinal responded that while some things had been done, those charges on the whole were valid; not enough had been done, he said, for which, he concluded, "we must convey our sorrow and beg forgiveness."

Our visit to Yad Vashem ended with a walk through the Valley of the Destroyed Communities, powerful in its way and a reminder that it was not only six million individuals, not only the children, but whole communities, indeed, a civilization that were wiped out.

The group's morning began with a presentation by Professor Emil Fackenheim, who offered profound insights not only into the implications of Yad Vashem but into the entire visit to Israel. Drawing upon his own experiences during the Holocaust and after and citing language from the Book of Ezekiel and the anthem "Hatikvah," he said that while hope had been killed in Auschwitz it had been reborn in Israel.

Fackenheim's ideas about Jewish death and rebirth in the 20th century and about the place of the Holocaust experience in Israeli consciousness were to come to mind throughout the trip. There were reminders of those thoughts during our meeting with the Ashkenazic Chief Rabbi, Yisrael Meir Lau, himself a survivor; when the Agam memorial to the victims of the Holocaust was seen through a drizzling rain as we approached the Western Wall; and at many other times.

In the Cardinal's remarks on the Holocaust, planned and spontaneous, as well as in his actions, signs of a new stage in the relationship between Catholics and Jews were rendered throughout the trip, with guilt for anti-Semitism acknowledged, repentance expressed, and reconciliation promoted. That this was done in the company of Catholics and Jews in the State of Israel added relevance. And specific statements which were made regarding the meaning of Israel to the Jewish people added still another layer of significance to all of this.

In his Hebrew University address, the Cardinal declared, "I recognize that for the vast majority of Jews, Israel signifies their ultimate tie to Jewish peoplehood, their central point of self-identity." Building on the theological dimension of such a statement, the Cardinal also said, "The Holy See's action in formally recognizing Israel...represents a final seal on the process begun at the Second Vatican Council to rid Catholicism of all vestiges of 'displacement theology' and the implied notion of perpetual Jewish homelessness. The Accords represent the Catholic Church's full and final acknowledgment of Jews as a people, not merely as individuals." Our trip to Israel was in many ways a celebration not just of the accomplishments of Catholic-Jewish dialogue in Chicago but of the turning of that corner in global Catholic-Jewish relations.

Off the table of the Catholic-Jewish exchange for the past year or so has been what until then was a longstanding tension created by the Vatican's failure to formally recognize the State of Israel. The change which that recognition brought was dramatically called to mind during what I unexpectedly found to be one of the most moving experiences of the trip: a luncheon with Monsignor Andrea Cordero Lanza di Montezemolo, Papal Nuncio to Israel. A warm and impressive man, the Nuncio described his effort in promoting the Vatican-Israel ties and the Pope's effusive praise of him for his accomplishments. He also countered possible concerns about Vatican attempts to impose itself into the peace negotiations. In a media interview he made clear his posture on certain current developments, saying that while the church holds that religious rights must be assured, it does not see itself as having a role in political affairs, which are to be directly negotiated by Israel and the Palestinians. That position, he asserted, applies as much to Jerusalem as to other outstanding issues, with the question of sovereignty implicitly thus not being regarded as the business of the Vatican. Such ideas were echoed time and again by Cardinal Bernardin, in both private meetings with various officials and in public statements to the press.

These comments were not made in a vacuum. Just two weeks before our group set out for Israel a statement directed at President Clinton was issued by eight Christian leaders in America, one of them being William Cardinal Keeler, the current President of the National Council of Catholic Bishops, who later qualified what he called its intent. The statement criticized Israel's behavior in Jerusalem, challenged Israel's reference to the city as its eternal and undivided capital, and seemed to imply that the religious community should have a role to play in determining Jerusalem's ultimate political status. Contrary to common practice in the Catholic-Jewish dialogue, Cardinal Keeler had signed the statement without consulting with or even informing the Jewish community.

The American statement itself followed one issued in November by the heads of Christian communities in Jerusalem, including the Latin Patriarch Michel Sabbah, which announced the need to provide "a special judicial and political statute for Jerusalem which reflects the universal importance and significance of the city." Alluding to the November document during our group's meeting with him and in later comments to the press, Sabbah asserted that Jerusalem, "should be a capital for everyone," with a "special status."

There are several related issues, not likely to go away soon, which may well define an area of tension in Christian-Jewish relations in the months ahead. They include the shrinking size of the Christian population in Jerusalem and the West Bank (which actually began before Israel gained control of those locations in 1967 and which is at least in part stimulated by trepidation regarding the impact of Islamic fundamentalism); the problem of access to Jerusalem in light of security measures which Israel needs to take in response to terrorist activity; and the ultimate status of Jerusalem. In that framework Cardinal Bernardin, while sympathetic to the feelings of Christians in the region, has exerted important ameliorating leadership by joining the Papal Nuncio in declaring that the only legitimate way to resolve outstanding local questions, including those involving Jerusalem, is through direct negotiations between Israel and the Palestinians. And he has done so with an ongoing commitment to maintaining an open dialogue with the Jewish community on these subjects.

Stated goals of the trip were to celebrate and enhance Catholic-Jewish dialogue in Chicago; to spread the message of what has been accomplished at the institutional and leadership levels more broadly within our communities; and to present ourselves as a sort of model for fruitful intergroup relations. From the perspective of the Jewish participants there was also a desire to communicate the meaning and importance which Israel has for us.

Besides the official visits with President Ezer Weizman, Prime Minister Yitzhak Rabin, and Foreign Minister Shimon Peres, there were also stops at places able to render both everyday life in Israel and its deeper reality. One was at the Absorption Center in Mevasseret Zion, where we heard from new olim from Sarajevo and Syria. It was a touching source of pride to learn how they were helped in overcoming their suffering and brought to Israel by the Jewish Agency and the American Jewish Joint Distribution Committee – organizations which, as both longtime JUF leader Maynard Wishner and the Chicago-born spokesman of the Jewish Agency explained to the Cardinal and to our group, are supported by the American Jewish community in general and the Jewish United Fund of Metropolitan Chicago in particular.

To visit children from all over the world at this Absorption Center, seeing them learning Hebrew and becoming Israelis, was to be able to feel on one's pulse the continued relevance of the Zionist dream and to witness in human terms the rebirth and continuity of the Jewish people in their own homeland. And to visit Petach Tikva, Chicago's sister city, and to see the community center which grew out of the Project Renewal effort engaged in by the JUF there, was to have further graphic demonstration of the partnership between our community and the people of Israel.

From the perspective of the Cardinal, a first-time visitor, there was also the important sense of being on a pilgrimage to what Christians regard as the Holy Land. In a discussion held before our departure, participants in the trip took note of potential awkwardness that might arise when the Catholic members of the group were engaged in religious devotion, with the Jewish member of the group observing. As it happened, for me those moments – particularly the walk through the Stations of the Cross and the church masses in Jerusalem – proved to be occasions powerfully demonstrating the complexity of interreligious dialogue. For as much as some of our experiences together have made clear our common humanity and even some similarities in our religious traditions, the dialogue has also revealed deep and abiding differences. And that, I believe, is as it should be.

This is a matter that Rabbi David Hartman rendered at the philosophical level in a scintillating presentation to the group which had continuing impact. For me, watching the Catholics engage in religious ceremonies so intensely meaningful to them led to a sense not of a meltdown of essential differences between our religions but to an intensification of my sense of Jewish identity. And so it was important to show our Catholic friends how in our tradition we welcome the Shabbat with Kiddush and songs like "L'cha Dodi" and end it with Havdalah during the trip.

And so it was that, for me, the framing close of this trip came not with our final meal together (which was indeed special in its way) nor with the long flight home. Instead, it came the following Shabbat, in my synagogue, when I received an aliyah. As it happens, I found myself standing on the bimah with none other than Elie Wiesel, an annual visitor to the congregation who, our guide at Yad Vashem had told us, once identified his face in a photo of Auschwitz inmates exhibited there. He was a person who, I felt sure, could well recognize the multi-faceted significance to the Jewish community of the remarkable journey from which I had just returned.

NOTE ADDED IN 2014: The itinerary also included a meeting with Yasser Arafat at his Gaza City headquarters which was bizarre in a number of ways. An uncomfortable tone was established quickly, when Arafat objected to the gift that the Cardinal presented to him at the opening of the session, as he did for each dignitary we met with – an engraved piece of glass commemorating this Catholic/Jewish trip. Arafat's complaint was about the absence of reference to the Muslim religion. Most troubling, however, was the shocking assertion he made during the meeting that a lethal terrorist attack which had occurred in Israel a short time before – at a bus stop close to the army base where I used to report for my own reserve duty, where soldiers on leave regularly lined up to hitch rides – was carried out by the Israelis themselves. Arafat was to continue to make that charge in a number of settings, but it was very disconcerting for us to hear it for the first time.

Bernardin Navigated Life by Word and Example

This piece appeared in the Chicago Tribune on November 15, 1996,
one day after the death of Cardinal Bernardin

• • •

A s he approached his death with faith, courage and serenity, Cardinal Joseph Bernardin brought Chicagoans together in sadness and in admiration. Indeed, for all of the 14 years that he served as archbishop of Chicago, he was a driving force for reconciliation--by word and example.

Bernardin was open about his fatal illness, saying that in such a crisis it is natural to reach out to "family." The ties intensified after he came here in 1982 and introduced himself to us as "Joseph, your brother." They became particularly strong during the past three years as he demonstrated the depth of his humanity and his unique gifts.

Enduring baseless charges of sexual abuse made by a former seminarian in Cincinnati, where he served as archbishop before his move here, he showed compassion and forgiveness toward his accuser, which crystallized his devotion to reconciliation. That devotion was expressed again one year after he was vindicated, in March of 1995, when he went to Israel with representatives of Chicago's Catholic and Jewish communities.

Catholic-Jewish relations meant much to Bernardin, and he was adamant that his first visit to this land, holy to both religions, would be carried out in a fashion unprecedented for a cardinal of the Roman Catholic Church. Many moments of the trip touched on core aspects of the relationship, some of them sensitive. There was a lunch with Monsignor Andrea Cordero Lanza di Montezemolo, who had negotiated the Vatican's long-delayed formal recognition of Israel. ("You are a historic nuncio," Montezemolo told us the pope said to him.) There was Bernardin's unflinching speech on Christianity's centuries-long record of anti-Semitism, delivered at the Hebrew University in Jerusalem after an emotional visit to Yad Vashem. (A striking photo of Bernardin taken at Israel's Holocaust memorial museum provides the cover for a collection of his writings on Catholic-Jewish relations, which is being speeded toward publication.)

And there was a meeting, especially poignant in retrospect, with the late Yitzhak Rabin. When the cardinal attempted to open it, as he did all the other sessions, Rabin interrupted to say that he was the host and he

302 On the Front Lines in a Changing Jewish World

would speak first. However, when a half hour had gone by and an aide signaled that there was a schedule to keep, the prime minister waved him off to keep the conversation going with the cardinal.

Differ as they did in many ways, Bernardin and Rabin also had much in common, and they seemed to recognize that. Neither, however, could have known how little time each had left to accomplish their objectives.

The cardinal's cancer was first diagnosed three months after his return from Israel. After recovering from his surgery, Bernardin made his first local public appearance at the annual meeting of the Jewish Federation of Metropolitan Chicago, and he announced, as an outgrowth of his Hebrew University speech, the establishment of an annual guest lectureship in Chicago on theological issues affecting Catholic-Jewish relations. Called the Joseph Cardinal Bernardin Jerusalem Lecture, the first of these programs took place in April.

Before his cancer returned, the cardinal also announced the establishment of one more effort aimed at reconciliation, a framework for bringing together disparate voices within American Catholicism called the Catholic Common Ground Project. Participants in this project met in October for the first time and the cardinal gave a keynote address endorsing what he called "legitimate" dissent within the church while insisting that it be expressed in a respectful manner.

Bernardin has been described as a "radical centrist," a person who abjures the comfort and ease of taking a position tending toward either of the extremes and instead looks for a way to bring ideas and people together. In that and in his behavior in general, he embodied much which is contrary both to the image of Chicago and to many aspects of contemporary American culture.

His charisma was quiet and warm, not loud and flashy. In a country where everything needs to be "new," he reached out to the eternal. In a materialistic age, he offered an intimation of the transcendent.

Admitting his own fears, this 68-year-old spiritual leader spoke of death as a "friend" and offered comfort to those who would survive him. Not all Chicagoans, of course, shared his particular religious perspective, nor his belief in the afterlife. But there was something in his honesty, his goodness, his readiness to face the quotidian reality of death, which, in its paradoxical way, projected an enhanced sense of life.

The citizens of Carl Sandburg's "City of Big Shoulders" and Nelson Algren's "City on the Make" now sense that our hometown was blessed by the presence of a man of faith who faced his own autumn with resonating dignity and grace.

The Catholic-Jewish Scholars Dialogue of Chicago: A Model of Interreligious Dialogue

Presented at a conference on Nostra Aetate Today:
Reflections 40 Years after Its Call for a New Era of Interreligious Relationships,
at The Institute for the Study of Religions and Cultures, Pontifical Gregorian
University, Rome, Italy, September 26, 2005

• • •

Issued by the Second Vatican Council 40 years ago, the document known as *Nostra Aetate* declares, "Since Christians and Jews have a common spiritual heritage, this Sacred Council wishes to encourage and further mutual understanding and appreciation. This can be achieved, especially, by way of biblical and theological inquiry and through friendly discussions." For over 20 years, the Catholic-Jewish Scholars Dialogue of Chicago has dedicated itself to fulfilling those goals.

In March of 1983, eight months after Joseph Bernardin arrived in Chicago as Archbishop and one month after he was created Cardinal, he addressed the Chicago Board of Rabbis and the Jewish Federation of Metropolitan Chicago, declaring that he came "as your brother, Joseph." Attributing significance to the fact that this first meeting with Chicago's Jewish community took place during the twentieth anniversary year of the convening of the Second Vatican Council, which produced *Nostra Aetate,* Bernardin said, "I wish to personally endorse the efforts to promote better Jewish-Christian relations, and I pray that there might be a greater level of interaction here in the Chicago area."

"We teach in a number of ways," Bernardin was later to write, one of them being "by the programs and institutions we create." Among the several structures for furthering the goals of *Nostra Aetate* that were created in the Chicago area under his auspices was the Catholic-Jewish Scholars Dialogue. It grew out of a committee of six Catholics and six Jews that first met on July 20, 1983, after the Board of Rabbis responded to his speech by asking him to establish a formal framework to realize his vision of interfaith encounter. (Though the Archdiocese declared an intent to begin without publicity, the committee's first meeting was reported on by the *Chicago Sun-Times,* which labeled it "historic.")

Partnering with the Archdiocese in establishing and sponsoring the

Scholars Dialogue as it ultimately took shape were those two local Jewish communal entities the Cardinal had addressed, the Board of Rabbis and the Jewish Federation. They and the Spertus Institute of Jewish Studies have continued to appoint the Jewish participants in the Dialogue, while the Catholic participants have been named by the Archdiocese.

The Dialogue is made up of institutional officials and academics, parish priests and congregational rabbis. From its early years it has been strengthened by the involvement of a number of longtime practitioners of interfaith outreach, including Rabbis Herman Schaalman, Herbert Bronstein, and the late Hayim Perelmuter, and Father John Pawlikowski, Sister Carol Frances Jegen, and Professor Jon Nilson. It has also benefited from the local presence of academic institutions like Mundelein College, Loyola University, the Catholic Theological Union and the Spertus Institute for Jewish Studies.

The Scholars Dialogue has been administered by the Federation's community relations arm, the Jewish Community Relations Council, working in concert with the Archdiocese Office of Ecumenical and Interreligious Affairs, with Sister Joan McGuire, Father Dan Montalbano, and Father Tom Baima playing important roles out of that office. The director of the JCRC when the Dialogue was established was Peggy Norton.

The earliest record of the group's activities in the JCRC files appears in a memorandum dated December 1985 that summarizes the subjects treated by the group in the previous year. The topics are instructive. They included similarities and differences in the two faith traditions, speeches given by Cardinal Bernardin, and statements issued by the Vatican. The group also focused on such matters of current concern as the Vatican's failure to recognize the State of Israel, the anti-Semitism then being circulated in Chicago by Rev. Louis Farrakhan, and issues surrounding public displays of crèches and menorahs. Topics raised for the coming year included consideration of the film *Shoah* and the view of salvation for Jews in the Christian scheme of things.

A look at the topics addressed by the group in its subsequent years reveals a similar pattern. With sessions often introduced by papers presented by members of the group or guests, meetings have examined parallel and differentiating approaches of the two faith traditions to subjects such as prayer, the role of women, messianism, euthanasia, illness and faith, mysticism, spirituality, repentance and forgiveness, and Shavuot, Pentecost and revelation. We have explored the contrasting ways the two traditions read the same biblical texts (with our joint exploration of opening passages from Genesis including a presentation by Sister Dianne Bergant of CTU, who had just appeared in a multi-part program on the Bible carried on National Public Television). In advancing an understanding of Jews as we regard ourselves, the group has discussed the nature of Jewish peoplehood and ties to the land of Israel, and has contrasted that with the Christian view of the land. We have looked closely at Catholic-Jewish relations themselves and have jointly examined texts relevant to those relations ranging from Vatican statements to *Dabru Emet.*

These various topics have often evoked rich conversations, sometimes carried over to subsequent meetings. In tune with the goals and spirit of *Nostra Aetate,* they have enabled us to not only better understand the beliefs and practices of the "other," but also to better understand our own traditions, sometimes profoundly so. And they have enabled us to develop close personal connections based on familiarity and respect.

The deepening of the relationships has enabled us to have frank and open conversations about other sets of topics that have been addressed by our group as well. These have included consideration of subjects stimulated by events of the day and pertinent to one or the other of our groups or to Catholic-Jewish relations overall. In its early years the group talked about a visit to Israel by New York's Cardinal O'Connor that sparked controversy and about a visit of the Pope to Miami. It considered the implications of developments at the close of the Cold War in Europe for religious life there. With the outbreak of the Persian Gulf War in 1991, it discussed the views of war and violence held by our two faiths, then convened a public program on that topic. That subject was revisited at the time of the second Gulf War ten years later, when we discussed "Theological and Religious Ideas Regarding Armies, Power and Powerlessness, and Nationhood."

When the Parliament of the World's Religions convened a meeting in Chicago commemorating the previous time it had done that, one hundred years before, members of the group considered the ways their two traditions look at non-Jewish and non-Christian religions. This was followed by a session on Christianity and Islam and another on Islam's roots in Judaism and Christianity. At the time of the conflict in Bosnia, the group discussed that event's meaning to each of their faiths and subsequently devoted a session to focusing on the role of communities of faith in international affairs overall. More recently, the group has discussed topics ranging from breakthroughs in stem cell research to Mel Gibson's *The Passion of the Christ.*

Two areas of consideration have been of special interest to the group:

ones revolving around the Holocaust and ones dealing with the State of Israel. In 1988 the group reflected on a program held in Chicago on the 50th anniversary of *Kristallnacht,* and then, one year later, the controversy surrounding the Carmelite convent at Auschwitz triggered intense concerns. Related to that was a proposed visit to Chicago by Poland's Cardinal Glemp in 1989 and visits that he did pay in 1991 and 1998. The latter year was also notable for the Vatican's issuing of *We Remember,* which evoked extensive consideration by the group. One year later the group went *en masse* to Washington for a day-long visit to the U.S. Holocaust Memorial Museum that included a Dialogue meeting *in situ* where it considered the subject of "The Holocaust as Crux in Catholic-Jewish Relations." At a session there addressed by Eugene Fisher, Associate Director of the Secretariat for Ecumenical and Interreligious Affairs of the United States Conference of Catholic Bishops, it reviewed "Christian-Jewish Relations in America Today."

As for Israel, it too has been approached in a number of ways, including via discussions first about the Vatican's non-recognition of Israel then later about the significance of the recognition. Other sessions have focused on Jerusalem in Jewish history and on the meaning of Jerusalem to the two faith traditions, and the group reacted to a statement on the significance of Jerusalem to Christians issued by the Patriarchs and heads of Christian communities in Jerusalem. A trip to Israel led by Cardinal Bernardin in which many members of the Dialogue participated, about which more later, was discussed by the Dialogue group, as was a talk given in Chicago by Michel Sabah, the Latin Patriarch, and later, the dramatic visit to Israel of Pope John Paul II. The group has repeatedly held discussions revolving around whatever have been the latest developments in Israel, often with reference to positions taken by the Church and other Christian bodies. Over the past few years, we have also talked about the rise of a new form of anti-Semitism in this context -- one that uses traditional tropes but is greatly generated in the Arab and Muslim worlds and has an anti-Israel and anti-Zionist thrust at its core.

Besides contributing significantly to the subject matter addressed at Dialogue meetings and advancing understanding of the meaning of Israel to the Jewish community, visits to Israel have had a strong effect in deepening relations between members of the group, especially when that has involved joint travel. The Federation has long organized and sponsored visits to Israel for non-Jewish community leaders, and it maintained a travel program for Christian leadership with the American Jewish Committee through the 1990s. A majority of the Catholic participants in the Dialogue have gone on such trips to Israel with Federation officials, some of them for their first time. The success of those visits was helpful in planning the 1995 trip in which Cardinal Bernardin himself led a joint delegation of Chicago Catholics and Jews to Israel, the first time a Cardinal of the Church had visited Israel with such a delegation.

The trip was planned by representatives of the Federation, the American Jewish Committee, and the Archdiocese, and the delegation accompanying the Cardinal consisted of representatives of those three institutions plus the Chicago Board of Rabbis and the Spertus Institute of Jewish Studies. It marked a high point for the Dialogue and represented a fulfillment of the various programs maintained by the Archdiocese in conjunction with each of these Jewish communal organizations.

The Bernardin-led group traveled to Israel shortly after formal ties had been established between the Holy See and Israel. With that source of tension off the table, and at a time when the Oslo Process seemed to offer the possibility of peace and reconciliation between Israel and the Palestinians, spirits were high. The visit included a moving lunch with the Papal Nuncio who had negotiated the agreement between the Vatican and Israel and meetings with Prime Minister Yitzhak Rabin in Jerusalem and Chairman Yasser Arafat in Gaza. Highlights included a visit to Yad Vashem and religious experiences for one or the other of the groups at the Western Wall, the Via Dolorosa, and the Mount of Beatitudes. The delegation was accompanied by reporters and cameramen representing both of Chicago's newspapers and all of the city's major television stations. That helped make the trip an unequaled opportunity for modeling the positive interfaith relations that had developed out of our Dialogue group and out of other programs back home.

The cornerstone of the visit was the address that Bernardin delivered at the Hebrew University in Jerusalem on the subject "Antisemitism: The Historical Legacy and the Continuing Challenge for Christians." Not long after returning from the trip Cardinal Bernardin learned of the cancer that was ultimately to take his life. The disease was in remission at the time the Federation held its annual meeting the following fall, when, as guest speaker, he announced his intention to further advance the goals of the trip and to extend the impact of his Hebrew University address by establishing an annual lectureship on Catholic-Jewish relations in Chicago. Named the Joseph Cardinal Bernardin Jerusalem Lecture, it has been maintained on an annual basis, alternating between Catholic and Jewish speakers.

Second in the series was Professor Emil Fackenheim, with whom the group had met in Israel, whose topic was "Jewish-Christian Relations after the Holocaust: Toward Post-Holocaust Theological Thought." The following year Edward Cardinal Cassidy, then President of the Vatican's Commission for Religious Relations with the Jews, came to speak on "Catholic-Jewish Relations: A New Agenda?" While he was in Chicago, he met with the Scholars Dialogue and he closed the session by saying that he wasn't sure how much he had to teach the group. He followed his visit with a letter to the Dialogue saying, "We are greatly encouraged by the way Jewish-Catholic relations have developed in Chicago and trust that you will continue to be an example that others can fruitfully follow."

The most recent address in the Jerusalem Lecture series, commemorating the tenth anniversary of the program, was delivered this past February by Francis Cardinal George. In succeeding Cardinal Bernardin as the Archbishop of Chicago, Cardinal George has maintained strong support for Catholic-Jewish relations, and he has spoken out forcefully on issues that have engaged the Dialogue group. When Mel Gibson's *The Passion of the Christ* threatened to revive the deicide charge discredited by *Nostra Aetate,* he met with a Jewish and Catholic delegation, then used his regular column in the newspaper of the Archdiocese to say, "Popular presentations of Christ's Passion over the centuries have been the occasion for outbreaks of verbal and physical violence to Jews, and these incidents are part of the memory of the Jewish people. We should, I believe, not only honor these memories but also try to see the film itself with them in mind. As Christian believers, we must be moved to our very depths in seeing the Passion of Jesus presented so graphically; but as Christian believers who share this society with Jews, we should also be moved by their concerns. As Christian believers, we condemn anti-Semitism as a sin; the sin of hatred for the Jewish people is therefore part of the history of human sinfulness which brought Jesus to the cross.»

The Cardinal's address in the Jerusalem Lecture series, which was heard by 700 members of Chicago's Catholic and Jewish communities, was called "Catholics, Jews, and American Culture." In it he proposed "that we commit ourselves to a new engagement in Interreligious dialogue." He subsequently made an excerpt from the talk, headed "Four 'Rules' for Interreligious Engagement," available to the Catholic-Jewish Scholars dialogue for its March meeting. Those four rules -- calling for "a commitment to faith," "a commitment to the common," "a commitment to the truth," and "a commitment to action" -- reflect principles valued by the group.

As much as the Dialogue has been an assembly of "scholars," in anticipating the fourth of the Cardinal's rules, its activities have not been merely academic. It has entered the public arena on a number of occasions, at times with significant impact while gaining local and even national attention.

Probably the most important public action the group has taken was through a 1989 statement that grew out of Dialogue sessions about the controversy surrounding the Carmelite convent then being built at Auschwitz. The statement declared that "the controversy threatens to engulf constructive work towards Christian-Jewish reconciliation throughout the world." Members of the Dialogue urged "that the necessary steps be taken to expedite the movement of the convent from the camp site." They went on to say, "We deem it imperative for leaders in both faith communities to take immediate, positive steps to diffuse some of the present tensions and rebuild confidence."

The statement appeared simultaneously in the community newspapers published by the Archdiocese and Federation, and a delegation from the Jewish community led by the Chairman of the Dialogue group met with Cardinal Bernardin and Archdiocese officials as this crisis was unfolding. At that meeting, the Cardinal endorsed the Dialogue's statement; his support was subsequently reported on publicly and had definite impact. In a speech he gave to the Board of Rabbis shortly afterwards, Bernardin said: "I have little doubt that this statement -- which attracted national coverage -- and the support it received from our summer meeting contributed to the ultimate resolution of the conflict."

As the convent controversy was playing out, it was exacerbated by an inflammatory homily delivered by Jozef Cardinal Glemp, the Primate of Poland, that expressed traditional anti-Semitic notions. Glemp was scheduled to visit Chicago, and concerns about that visit were also expressed at the aforementioned meeting with Cardinal Bernardin, who indicated that he had written to Glemp. One day later, Glemp's secretary announced that he was postponing his visit "because of circumstances unfavorable for the pastoral good."

After the controversy was settled, Glemp did visit Chicago as part of a trip to the U.S. in 1991, when he made a private appearance to which several members of the Dialogue were invited at the Spertus Institute of Jewish Studies. Not long before, a seminar on Judaism for Polish priests and seminary professors had been hosted there. In 1998, Cardinal Glemp was in Chicago again, and this time there was a special meeting of the entire Dialogue group with him on the Loyola University campus. He wished to talk with the group about the establishment of a "Day of Judaism" in Poland and about related developments, and the group used the opportunity to express itself about recent manifestations of anti-Semitism in Poland.

The Dialogue has expressed itself publicly on other subjects as well. In 1991, it spoke out as steps were being taken to beatify Queen Isabella I of Spain, a possibility which was ultimately averted by a resolution from the Pontifical Council for Christian Unity, a body on which Cardinal Bernardin served. On this matter too, the Cardinal was in contact with representatives of the Dialogue, and the Dialogue's action on this subject was also reported on nationally.

On another matter, in 1992, following a Dialogue session where the differing positions of the two faith traditions on abortion were carefully examined, the group issued a statement released at a press conference at the Archdiocese and printed simultaneously by the communal newspapers published by the Archdiocese and the Jewish Federation respectively. This statement expressed concern about the way in which "the public debate on abortion . . . has harmfully polarized our society," and it condemned the "stereotyping of religious traditions and attacks upon the integrity of those who hold different views." Describing the issue as involving "a complex ethical dilemma about which honest and thoughtful people can and do differ," the group's members said they "call upon all to proceed with sensitivity and dignity in their public discourse and action on this subject." They closed by saying, "As Catholics and as Jews, we call upon all to proceed with compassion, caring, and charity, in our joint calling to build a more just and more holy world for all." This statement received widespread local and national media attention and was welcomed by other communities interested in taking a similar stance.

The group also issued a statement of concern regarding anti-foreigner violence in Germany in 1992 and applauded the establishment of Vatican-Israel relations in 1993. In 1998, the group sent a detailed four-page letter to Cardinal Cassidy, in his capacity as President of the Vatican's Commission for Religious Relations with the Jews, following the release of *We Remember: A Reflection on the Shoah*. This letter, meant for his consideration and not public distribution, noted what it described as a "sea change within the Church and in its relation to Judaism and the Jewish people" and pointed to several positive aspects of the statement, then conveyed several concerns about it. The letter expressed the view that "the document does not go far enough in reckoning with the complete experience of the Jewish people and Judaism with the Church over the past 2,000 years," and it noted a number of historic details that the members of the Dialogue thought merited greater scrutiny. It also expressed the view that "though Nazism was not merely the final and most gruesome chapter in the long history of Christian anti-Semitism, neither was it totally disconnected from that tradition." Finally, the letter supported a call issued by Cardinal Bernardin in his Jerusalem Lecture "urging the Church to submit its World War II record to a thorough scrutinizing by respected scholars" as a means of clarifying the wartime practices and policies of Pope Pius XII. In sum, the letter, with regret, expressed the view that *We Remember* was "an incomplete statement." In his reply, Cardinal Cassidy conveyed appreciation for the letter and the hope that its ideas "will contribute to a continued dialogue between Christians and Jews."

The group has also frequently corresponded with Cardinal Keeler, the lead American cardinal regarding Catholic-Jewish relations. When it wrote him in 2001 expressing concerns regarding remarks made by President Bashar al-Assad of Syria in the presence of Pope John Paul II, he responded by observing that "combating the deicide charge on all levels of Christian life where its vestiges may linger is as urgent as any task facing the Church today, 36 years after *Nostra Aetate* just as it was in 1965."

Looking forward, it is likely that the Dialogue group will continue to devote considerable attention to Israel-related matters. Israel is central to contemporary Jewish identity and life and the conflict between Israel and the Palestinians remains unresolved, with some Christian circles providing sympathetic hearings to individuals and groups that implicitly challenge Israel's very legitimacy. Difficulties between Jerusalem and Rome may arise from time to time, and the fundamental agreement between Israel and the Holy See is yet to be fully resolved. And yet, with formal recognition and normal relations in place, with the theological implications of that recognition implicit, and with channels open for resolving differences, the relationship between Israel and the Holy See is essentially friendly. That positive tone permeates the discussions that transpire within our Dialogue group.

Much the same can be said about our group's conversations surrounding ongoing manifestations of anti-Semitism, where the concerns raised by Jewish participants are noted with understanding by their Catholic counterparts. When it comes to the Holocaust, however, though our own group is generally of one mind regarding the subject, the kinds of conversations we continue to have demonstrate that, despite *Nostra Aetate* and the years that have gone by since its adoption, some serious issues surrounding the Shoah and the way it has been addressed by the Church remain unresolved.

Now over twenty years old, Chicago's Catholic-Jewish Scholars Dialogue has taken shape in the framework of the principles of *Nostra Aetate,* but with a number of other influences coming into play as well. Many of its members remember an earlier era of Christian-Jewish relations, when Church teachings and the Church played a very different role. Indeed, some of the early members of the group themselves came from and recollected conditions in Nazi Europe. The late Rabbi William Frankel, for example, from time to time would recall seeing the Archbishop of Vienna publicly welcoming the Nazis into that city. A veteran member of the group, Maynard Wishner, has spoken of his experiences growing up in Chicago and facing neighborhood bullies accusing him being a "Christ killer." Catholic members have remembered the anti-Semitic radio broadcasts of Father Coughlin. Others of us, though we may not have had such experiences ourselves, know of that past from parents and other relatives. But it is apparent and significant that our Dialogue group meets at a time and in a place when Jews are seen not as those who killed Christ and rejected his teachings, nor as practitioners of a fossilized religion, but as a people from whom Jesus himself came, and as proponents of a faith with a continuing vitality.

And there is something else. *Nostra Aetate* grew out of the European experience, and many of our communal memories come out of that context as well. The American experience, in contrast, has been a much more benign and tolerant one, embracing pluralism, and a Dialogue like our own has greatly benefited from that reality. Finally, the Dialogue has taken root in Chicago, and that factor merits recognition as well. The ancestors of many of the Catholics and Jews in Chicago came there a century ago, establishing an urban center where the two communities lived side by side, not always without animosity, not always free of Old World prejudices, but still getting to know one another as neighbors and learning to live together and to find common ground. A Dialogue like ours benefits greatly from the environment that that shared experience created.

In that overall context, and grounded in an institutionally-mandated wish to work to make things better, the Catholic-Jewish encounter in Chicago has emerged as the city's leading example of positive intergroup relations. And the Catholic-Jewish Scholars Dialogue has been the epitome of that. All the same, despite attempts to give visibility to our work and to project ourselves as a model, in the general population wounds continue to fester and memories of the past continue to have an impact on many people's sense of the current state of affairs. Most in the Jewish community have limited knowledge of how far things have come, and some are inclined to talk about what has happened as too little and too late. At the same time, on the Catholic side there are those inclined to think, "Haven't we done enough, and why do we have to continue to be the ones to make the overtures, to hear the complaints, to be told about the steps that we need to take." Even as Cardinal George and others talk of strengthening the Dialogue, one can't help wondering how many people there are out there of a generation formed in the post-*Nostra Aetate* era who recognize and appreciate the nature and the importance of sustaining such work.

Finally, one more set of observations and questions needs to be considered, I believe, and though this is the focus of other sessions at this conference, I raise it here in the context of this paper. I am referring to relations involving the third of the Abrahamic faiths, Islam.

Over the past number of years, and in the U.S. especially since September 11, 2001, there has been increasing outreach to the Muslim community, sometimes in the bilateral framework of Catholics and Muslims or Jews and Muslims, sometimes in a trilateral framework revolving around all three groups. In reflecting a desire to advance interfaith understanding and respect, such outreach certainly is desirable, and as I have mentioned, our Dialogue group has engaged in sessions where we have together attempted to learn more about Islam. The caution I would raise is that as positive and even necessary as dialogue with Islam may be in today's world, it cannot simply be overlaid on the Catholic-Jewish dialogue template and must not take the place of Catholic-Jewish dialogue. The relationships between Christianity and Judaism on the one hand, and Christianity and Islam on the other, have very different historic and theological contents, and if that is lost sight of or distorted, the Catholic-Jewish encounter which has been of such value since *Nostra Aetate* will lose an essential aspect of its meaning.

Jewish-Christian history, particularly in Europe, provides a complex context for the Jewish-Catholic encounter, and the development of our dialogic relationship has reflected decades of effort and evolution. To lose sight of that and imagine that either of us could at once have the same kind of relationship with the Muslim world, or that we could quickly establish the same levels of trust, is to set up ourselves, and them, for disappointment. There is much to do in recognizing our common humanity, in strengthening the bonds of communities of faith, in unburdening ourselves of stereotypes about the other, and in modeling positive relationships in this area, where they are especially needed. And yet, as far as interfaith dialogue goes, there needs, I believe, to be caution. And so, even as outreach to the Islamic world and Muslim community is pursued, let that not be in the framework of a structure that might lead to the weakening or abandonment of the Catholic-Jewish dialogue set in motion by *Nostra Aetate.*

With the symbolism of Pope Benedict XVI's Cologne synagogue visit setting the tone, there is good reason to consider ourselves living in an era during which Catholic-Jewish relations are likely to continue to evolve, an era when a Dialogue group like the one that has been maintained in Chicago can continue to thrive, enriching its participants, benefiting their communities, and serving as a model for interfaith relations in Chicago and beyond.

Facing the Unresolved Issue
in Interfaith Dialogue
The Forward, October 28, 2005

. . .

Built in the year 81 C.E., the Arch of Titus stands dramatically in the Roman Forum, commemorating Titus's military triumph over the Jews and the destruction of the Temple in Jerusalem 11 years earlier. A bas-relief on the inside of the arch depicting Roman soldiers carrying the spoils of victory highlights the massive menorah.

Contemplating this monument to the past while in Rome recently for a conference on the seminal Vatican document *Nostra Aetate,* I was struck by an apparent irony: As radically improved as Catholic-Jewish relations have been since *Nostra Aetate* was issued 40 years ago this week, the church has yet to fully take into account the complex interlocking of peoplehood, faith and attachment to land that characterizes Judaism and is represented graphically on this arch.

In *Nostra Aetate,* the Second Vatican Council repudiated nearly two millennia of Christian instruction proclaiming that the Jewish people had been punished with humiliating exile for crucifying Jesus and refusing to accept him as the messiah. While *Nostra Aetate* declared that "it is true that the Church is the new people of God," it went on to instruct that "the Jews should not be spoken of as rejected or accursed as if this followed from Holy Scripture."

The document called for a new relationship with the Jews, advancing "mutual understanding and appreciation." Through the years that have followed, liturgy referring to the Jews and instruction about them have been significantly changed. The Jewish Bible and the Gospels have been interpreted in new ways, the Church has respectfully explored Christianity's origins in Judaism and anti-Semitism has been branded a sin.

Before Vatican II, the Church had taught that God's covenant with the Jews was abrogated by a new covenant with the believers in Jesus. Presentations delivered at the conference I attended at the Pontifical Gregorian University made clear just how far Catholics and Jews have come since *Nostra Aetate* was issued in dealing with theological issues revolving around the question of covenant, as well as in other areas. The good will and collegiality fostered by four decades of outreach and dialogue between clergy, scholars and organizational officials was palpable.

But at the same time, several Jewish participants at the conference, beginning with Ruth Langer of Boston College, made clear that from their perspective there is another issue yet to be resolved: the Jewish people's connection with the land and the State of Israel.

The Holy See formally recognized Israel in 1993 — 45 years after its establishment — a delayed but nonetheless important step in many ways. With the Vatican's action affirming the Jewish people's re-establishment of sovereignty in their ancient homeland, the notion that exile was a permanent and necessary condition was definitively undercut, making the formal establishment of relations between the Holy See and Israel a practical act that followed from and complemented the assertions of *Nostra Aetate.*

Still, from that time until today the Vatican has maintained a two-track approach, relating to Jews as a religion through dialogue while seeing its relations with Israel purely in a political framework. The Vatican even deals with the two matters through different offices. This mindset can be seen in other situations, as well.

While in Rome, I joined a delegation from the Catholic Theological Union of Chicago in Saint Peter's Square at a general audience with Pope Benedict XVI. Coincidentally, as the text for his homily that day, the pope chose a passage from the Psalms that references God's bringing his people back to the "Promised Land." In his reflection, the pope emphasized the way that God works in history and described the return of the Jewish people to the Land of Israel and their redemption as prefiguring individual salvation.

By speaking in generic terms while interpreting this Old Testament text, he avoided the supersessionist, sectarian triumphalism of an earlier age. All the same, he treated the passage from the Jewish Bible referencing the connection of the Jewish people with the Land of Israel in universal and symbolic terms only, taking no notice of the particular way that such a passage resonates for the Jewish people themselves.

As the pope's homily implied, what remains absent from the post-*Nostra Aetate* encounter of Jews and Catholics — especially with the Vatican — is full-blown recognition of the fact that Jews are not simply practitioners of their religion, and that their connection with Israel is not just a political matter. Jews are members of a people whose connection to Israel is essential to their identity and sense of self. For Jews, peoplehood and faith are intertwined existentially.

Talking about the obligation to pursue "a better mutual understanding and renewed mutual esteem," the guidelines for implementing *Nostra Aetate* issued by the Vatican in 1974 say, "On the practical level in particular, Christians must therefore strive... to learn by what essential traits the Jews define themselves in the light of their own religious experience." The practice of maintaining a dialogue with the Jews that focuses purely on religious matters while seeing anything having to do with Israel as existing merely in the political realm fails to relate fully to Jews as Jews regard themselves. While many Catholics and Jews engaged in dialogue have advanced that kind of understanding, similar work needs to be done by others, as well.

The Arch of Titus, weatherworn and crumbling, is surrounded by the ruins of an empire that is no more. No longer the triumphant gateway it was built to be, it has become a curiosity for the visiting tourist.

But as I concluded while gazing at the scene that the arch portrays, the very menorah that had been looted from the destroyed Temple of Jerusalem and that was displayed as an icon of the defeated, exiled and humiliated Jews has been symbolically reclaimed by the Jewish people. It has been returned to their land as the emblem of the State of Israel, through which nearly 2,000 years of exile have been reversed. That menorah encapsulates the amalgam of religious traditions and practices, historic experiences, language, culture and attachment to a particular land that defines Jewish peoplehood.

As the 40th anniversary of the historic issuing of *Nostra Aetate* is widely commemorated this week, a challenge still facing the Catholic-Jewish encounter set in motion by the document is for the Catholic participants to better understand and relate to the Jews as we are — and as we understand ourselves in our time. And that means dealing with our sense of connection to Israel as a central aspect of our totality.

Religion And The Press:
A Jewish Community Perspective
Delivered at a Symposium Co-Sponsored by the
Medill School of Journalism and Sheil Catholic Center
Northwestern University
July 25, 2005

. . .

Religion is in the news. Religion is news. The problem is that it is often treated within the realm of other subjects and with limited attention to its own values. And thus, news about Evangelicals these days is often linked with politics and public affairs; news about Catholics has recently emphasized scandal and, in this era of celebrity, spectacle, and competition, fascination with the passing of one Pope and selection of another; and Muslims have been reported on through the prism of national and international developments revolving around immigration and its impact on the changing face of Western societies on the one hand, and around global terrorism on the other.

Jews and Judaism have been part of almost all of these "stories" and of some of our own in ways I will shortly attempt to illustrate. But first I would like to suggest that, for all of our faith communities — and for others that are not represented today like the Christian Orthodox religions which have substantial numbers here in Chicago and the Asian religions that are growing as well, not to mention the mainline Protestants — there is an overriding sense that we are simply not represented in our own terms; that there is insufficient serious attention focused on the religious history, traditions, and values that define each of us for what we are; and that there is little sophisticated recognition of the distinctiveness that differentiates us.

At the same time, the faith communities, I would suggest, need to recognize the challenges faced by the news industry whose work we are so quick to critique. We need to be understanding of the press and we need to acknowledge the professionalism of many of its practitioners. Hopefully a forum like today's, by putting some of these issues on the table and examining them honestly, can help improve matters in a fashion that is fair to serious print and electronic journalists while advancing results that serve broader societal needs.

And now to my remarks about the faith community I am representing, one that has been regarded as a "mainstream" religion in America since the 1950s. While Judaism has thus received a relatively goodly amount of exposure in the U.S., and while that has helped it gain a degree of understanding in the country, there have been downsides in the manner in which Judaism has been treated. Regarded as "familiar" and not necessarily all that different from Christianity, it has often been handled from a Christian perspective. Thus, for example, the winter holiday of Chanukah, which gets a lot of attention, has been portrayed as equivalent to Christmas both in its nature and its importance for Jews, whereas it is in many ways very different and is in fact one of the minor holidays on the Jewish calendar. So too Jewish houses of worship have often been thought of as not that different from churches, with few attempts being made to see them on their own terms.

In fact, Judaism is a minority religion, practiced by a relatively small percentage of Americans, and many non-Jewish reporters have only a limited knowledge of its nature, principles, or practices, with that knowledge frequently coming in a superficial fashion. One result has been that much which is central to Judaism has been pretty much ignored by the mainstream media, which as a result often simply keeps stereotypes alive. Meanwhile, given the media's general interest in what is photogenic and exotic, some less-than-common aspects of Judaism often get inordinate media exposure. For example, television and newspaper photographers often seem drawn to ultra-Orthodox Jews, with their beards, dark clothing, and hats, whereas that sort of garb is adopted only by some of the Orthodox, who themselves represent a minority stream in American Judaism.

I think of the occasion last winter when, as we regularly do in an effort to provide an instructive aspect to a story we know they wish to report on, we invited the media to cover the ceremony held in the lobby of the Federation building that brings our staff together for the lighting of the first candle of Chanukah. The ceremony was filmed, photographed, and finished, and most of my colleagues had gone back to their offices. One of them, who happens to be ultra-orthodox and looks it, was still in the area. Seeing that, a newspaper photographer who was packing up his equipment, whipped out his camera. He would have made that his shot, but my colleague said we were done with the ceremony and asked him not to take that picture. At the other end of the spectrum, there is also a fascination with fringe groups, even with groups like so-called Messianic

Jews, who were misleadingly portrayed by the *Daily Herald* a few months ago, though members of that particular kind of group are not even considered to be Jewish by the community.

There is a long history of stereotyping of Jews and Judaism in Western civilization which news coverage often picks up on and sustains. Much of this stereotyping has, through the centuries, been very negative and often terribly destructive — sometimes deliberately so. In today's mainstream press, such negative qualities are no doubt not usually evoked deliberately. But whatever the motivation, the media sometimes continue to present Jews in accordance with images devised by the Jewish people's worst enemies, giving continued life to some of the worst and most misleading stereotypes.

A striking example could be seen in the cartoon that appeared in the Chicago Tribune a couple of years ago, in which Israel's Prime Minister Ariel Sharon, labeled with a Jewish star, was portrayed in the fashion of *The Protocols of the Elders of Zionism* and Nazi iconography, hooked nose and all, wielding inordinate power over George Bush and being driven by a lust for money. In a subsequent editorial, the *Tribune* acknowledged the anti-Semitic content of the cartoon and expressed regret for having published it. But the fact that the cartoon had appeared in the first place was revealing. With their oversimplifications and deliberate attempts to be provocative, cartoons, I might add, are often especially problematic in the ways they treat Jews as well as members of other religious communities.

In contrast to a treatment of this sort, stories about Jews and the Holocaust can be especially sympathetic. An extensive *Tribune* article in which Howard Reich portrayed his mother's Holocaust-induced posttraumatic stress syndrome was probably the longest Jewish-community-linked story in the local press in years. However, even sympathetic stories focusing on Jewish suffering run the risk of providing an image of the Jew *only* as victim, something which creates a distorted impression of the totality of Jewish experience.

The media's fascination with the Holocaust, while providing meaningful exposure to this horrifying chapter in Jewish history, also creates frustration in that there are many "positive" Jewish experiences which attract far less coverage. The extent to which this phenomenon prevails cannot be exaggerated. The Federation's Communications Department and our agencies can send out media alerts on all kinds of subjects, touting all sorts of communal programs, projects, and developments that we think are newsworthy and that project a multi-faceted image of Jews and Judaism in Chicago. Some indeed do get attention. Many, however, don't — though you can be sure that practically any program that is connected with the Holocaust will immediately attract media interest. Even a community forum on as current a topic as terrorism and global anti-Semitism, with world-renowned experts from England, Sri Lanka, Israel, and the U.S., that attracted over 600 attendees on April 10, could not attract any media coverage, though the same month saw plenty of coverage of the community's annual Holocaust memorial observances. Then there is the matter of the community's ties to Israel.

Jews are bound to each other not only as practitioners of a particular belief system and heirs to a shared history and culture but also through ties of peoplehood and through connections with the land of Israel. These are complicated and somewhat uncommon matters not always fully comprehended by the public or accurately captured by the media. For all of what might seem like a great deal of attention to the "Israel story" in the press, the dimension of it I am talking about is rarely illuminated. While the press seems especially eager to provide coverage of Holocaust-connected aspects of contemporary Jewish experience, it seems relatively uninterested in providing exposure to the community's connection with Israel. Only in recent years, for example, has the Jewish community's annual celebration of Israel's Independence Day been covered locally. Furthermore, when the subject is covered, disproportionate attention is often paid to opposition voices. Especially striking but far from unique was the occasion in the fall of 2000 when, shortly after terror attacks against Israelis escalated, the community held a solidarity rally at the Hyatt Hotel that attracted thousands of participants. Outdoors there were around a dozen protestors — but the *Tribune's* coverage the next day ran photos of the demonstrators and of a handful of participants confronting them as though the two sides were equivalent and their conflict was the "story."

As Cardinal George has said, conflict is of course at the core of much news coverage, no doubt driven by a sense of what readers, listeners, and viewers are interested in. But the emphasis on conflict can create distorted, even inflammatory, coverage. Today, as a result of Israel's situation, Jews are often regarded as in basic conflict with members of another religious group, namely Muslims, though the images of Judaism and of Islam which emerge from this kind of treatment can render inaccurate portrayals of both religions.

A striking example of the distorted and even provocative fashion in which the media sometimes play up and even potentially stimulate Muslim-Jewish conflict could be seen in the *Tribune's* coverage of the announcement that, as the opening of its story last August 24 said, "The U.S. Department of Homeland Security . . . revoked a visa granted to Tariq Ramadan . . . effectively barring him from a teaching post he was to begin this week at the University of Notre Dame." The middle of that sentence described Ramadan as "a renowned Islamic scholar who is accused by some Jewish groups of being a Muslim extremist," though the article itself provided absolutely no support for that assertion about Jewish groups while ignoring the fact that non-Jewish scholars and government officials in Europe had indeed taken that position about him. The article cited an American professor and other "scholars" whom, it claimed, "said they suspected the government's decision to bar Ramadan could have been influenced by some Jewish groups that have waged a campaign against scholars and public intellectuals whose views on Islam and the Middle East conflict with their own." There and in a number of other places the article framed the story as revolving around a Jewish/Muslim conflict far more than the facts it presented — or, I would suggest, the facts that existed — warranted. In so doing, I might add, it also created an impression of Jewish power and influence like that which is of course at the core of anti-Semitic stereotypes, old and new.

It is in such a way that Jews figure in the news media's treatment of Muslims. Similarly, a possible Jewish-Christian conflict came into play in one of the biggest national religion stories of the past couple of years, namely the controversy surrounding the opening of Mel Gibson's "The Passion of the Christ." Purported initial Jewish opposition to that film was an essential part of the early coverage, with the media serving as a vehicle for promoting the film rather than accurately describing the reality of the situation. Once again a false image of Jewish power, or at least of an attempt to use power, was created, though Jewish groups were neither engaged in attempts to block distribution of the film as was charged nor hostile to Christian beliefs as was implied. In fact, the critique of the film that emerged came from Jews and Christians alike, who were jointly alarmed by its evocation of anti-Semitic stereotypes and its resurrection of deicide charges rejected by the Catholic Church and other denominations decades ago.

This is not to say that the news media alone are to blame for projecting images of interfaith conflict or for manufacturing stereotypical images of nefarious Jewish influence. As criminal and civil actions have been brought against several Chicago-based groups and individuals accused of aiding international terrorist activities, the defendants, their attorneys, and other supporters of theirs have routinely scapegoated Jews and the

State of Israel. For example, two months before the government froze the assets of three local groups for engaging in such a practice, the attorney for one of them was quoted in the Tribune blaming the government scrutiny and the media coverage on "Zionist forces in the U.S." In this case, the Tribune was reporting but not endorsing the charge, inflammatory as it itself was.

Similarly, there are print and electronic news editors and reporters who evidence sensitivity to the kinds of concerns I am raising. When Cardinal Ratzinger was elected Pope and it became known that he had connections with the Nazi youth organization as a young man, the assignment editor at a local television station called to ask if we had concerns we wanted to convey. We said that we lacked complete details, but based on what we did know, did not see this as a subject meriting a Jewish community response beyond what some others had already said. The station was understanding and avoided a new occasion to create an image of Jewish-Catholic conflict — though there were national media outlets which, of course, did see this as an area of apparent conflict to highlight.

While many editors and reporters thus indeed do exhibit professional seriousness and responsibility in covering the subject of religion, and while haphazard media bashing is unwarranted and unhelpful, there certainly are problems, as my remarks and those of my fellow presenters have shown. In sum, perhaps the greatest cause of differences between the religious communities and the news media is that the media are by and large motivated by a desire to tell a story they think will be of interest to their audience, while the religious communities wish they would do more to report on developments we think are newsworthy or important and would do more to illuminate the nature of our communities and of the religious values and practices that define them. In our view, these qualities get limited attention of a probing and differentiating nature, and they are often dealt with, if at all, in a superficial fashion, sometimes by reporters altogether new to the religion beat who are often drawn to the exotic or unusual and who frequently impose a standard "news" template emphasizing conflict.

Given the important role that the news media play in shaping the public's understanding of our various communities in today's diversified, pluralistic society and of the nature and role of religion in contemporary American life, this is not a matter to be taken lightly. I thus applaud and thank the organizers of today's symposium for bringing together representatives of several religious communities and the press to explore these matters together; to learn from one another; and, let us hope, to advance accurate, illuminating news coverage of religion in American life today.

Afterword to A Legacy
of Catholic-Jewish Dialogue:
The Joseph Cardinal Bernardin Lectures
Archdiocese of Chicago: Liturgy Training Publications, 2012

• • •

I am grateful to the Rev. Thomas Baima for asking me to prepare this Afterword.

When I began to think of what would be an appropriate approach to take in it, I found the material at hand evoking several poignant memories.

My first recollection has to do with the travels that got this project started. As Father Baima indicated in his Acknowledgments to this volume and as he notes in his Introduction, the Joseph Cardinal Bernardin Jerusalem Lecture, which is now an annual event in Chicago, originates from a lecture on "Antisemitism: The Historical Legacy and the Challenge for Christians" given by the late Cardinal himself in Jerusalem during the 1995 Catholic-Jewish trip which he led. That visit took place shortly after the Vatican established formal ties with the State of Israel, a historic event in Catholic-Jewish relations, and it grew out of the interfaith dialogue that had developed in Chicago over a number of years, greatly inspired by Bernardin's vision and sense of his vocation.

Traveling together in a land of central religious significance for each of our communities – and in a country of particular meaning for the individual and group identity of the Jewish members of the delegation – we were able to fulfill the traditional goals of interreligious dialogue by enhancing our respect for the "other" while intensifying our sense of self. For me, that dual effect was experienced with particular power the day we walked down the Via Dolorosa.

The impact of the location on the Cardinal was palpable. His very demeanor conveyed deep spirituality, expressing the profound meaning his religion had for him and strengthening the respect that I already had for him as a man of faith. At the same time, that Old City setting and its surroundings had very different resonance for me, heightening my sense of difference from him as I became all the more aware of my identity as a Jew with a particular history, set of traditions, tie to peoplehood, and connections with the place where we were.

Cardinal Bernardin was a great believer in setting an example. He wished to lead what we were told was the first-ever trip to Israel in which a Cardinal headed a Catholic-Jewish delegation not only for the enriching experiences it would provide but also for the way that, in acting out this interfaith engagement, we would be modeling interreligious experience for others. Those others included the Jews, Christians, and Muslims with whom we interacted on the trip on the one hand, and the people of Chicago on the other. The wall-to-wall Chicago media attention we received, also described by Father Baima in his Acknowledgments, was a vehicle for projecting that modeling image back home.

"We teach in a number of ways," Bernardin once wrote, including "by the programs and institutions we create." That observation leads me to another memory, this one stained with sadness. During our visit to Israel, I and Maynard Wishner, a prominent lay leader of the Federation, invited the Cardinal to deliver the keynote address at the Federation's annual meeting, which was scheduled for six months later. He agreed, not knowing that in between those two dates he would be diagnosed with cancer and would have to undergo difficult treatment for the disease.

When the scheduled date came he kept his commitment to speak, making that one of his first public appearances during the period when his cancer was in remission. My memory here is of greeting him at the entrance to the hotel meeting room, where hundreds of lunchtime guests awaited him, and of hearing him, with a familiar twinkle in the eye but with a now-drawn visage say, "Michael, I have something to announce in my speech that you are going to like." The "something" was his declaration that the Archdiocese was committing itself to working with its Jewish organizational partners from the trip to organize an annual lecture to sustain and advance the trip's impact on Catholic-Jewish relations. That event, building on what the Cardinal himself had done in Jerusalem, is what came to be called the Joseph Cardinal Bernardin Jerusalem Lecture.

In its earliest years, the lecture series was tied to the Israel trip in another way as well, for the initial Jewish speakers – Professor Emil Fackenheim, who gave the first of the lectures in Chicago, and Rabbi David Hartman, who gave the third – had provided especially powerful experiences when the group met with each of them in Israel. Their Chicago presentations, along with the second lecture in the series, "Catholic-Jewish Relations: A New Agenda?" delivered by Edward Cardinal Cassidy, then the President of the Pontifical Commission for Religious Relations with the Jews, set a high standard for the lectures, one which subsequent speakers have fully lived up to.

326 On the Front Lines in a Changing Jewish World

Sadly, Cardinal Bernardin lived long enough to hear only the first lecture. He was succeeded as Archbishop of Chicago by Francis Cardinal George, who has presided over each of the subsequent lectures in the series with his own sense of commitment to its purposes. While Cardinal Bernardin institutionalized the lecture series, Cardinal George, as Father Baima points out in his Introduction, advanced Israel-linked Jewish-Catholic cooperation of another sort by leading the Archdiocese to partner with the Jewish Federation in establishing a computer literacy project in the Israeli Christian Arab village of Fassouta. And while Cardinal Bernardin's lecture in Jerusalem was the progenitor of the Jerusalem Lecture series, Cardinal George provided the closing frame for the first decade of the series by being the guest speaker ten years later, on the topic "Catholics, Jews and American Culture."

Interestingly enough, whereas both Cardinals spoke to the future, Cardinal Bernardin's lecture for the most part looked backward and talked about attitudes and behavior that were profoundly detrimental to the achievement of positive Jewish-Catholic relations, while Cardinal George looked greatly at the present moment and put the two religious groups together on one side of a divide that has secularism on the other side. As Cardinal George put it, they are two "pre-modern faiths in a post-modern culture." He closed his lecture by saying:

> This, I believe, is the challenge and possibility that confronts us as we come to the tenth year of the Jerusalem Lecture series. If we are to make a contribution to the development of a new culture here, the biblical religions must find their respective voices and claim a new visibility. We must be heard and seen in the public square precisely as men and women of faith, eager to dialogue with all others, even secularists, as we have dialogued with one another.

Though much happened in the world in the ten years between the two Cardinals' lectures, and though there have been additional developments in the dominant areas in which Jews and Catholics engage in the five years since Cardinal George gave his talk, some things remain the same, or nearly so. One of the most touching meetings held during the Israel trip with Cardinal Bernardin was a session with Prime Minister Yitzhak Rabin. It was a time when Israel was participating in the Oslo Peace Process, when there was hope that reconciliation and peace between Israel and the Palestinians were on the horizon. But peace today seems no closer than it did then – perhaps even further away. And at the same time, although during the trip we had celebrated the establishment of Israel-Vatican ties at a lunch in Jerusalem with the Papal Nuncio, Andrea Cardinal Cordero Lanza di Montezemolo, the final details of the Israel-Vatican agreement have yet to be resolved. Furthermore, Cardinal Bernardin's call for the Vatican to open its Holocaust-era archives remains unrealized, and issues revolving around the Holocaust continue to surface from time to time in a way that affects Catholic-Jewish relations.

Meanwhile, the first decade of the series has by now been followed by another half decade of lectures, and the series goes on. It is always a high point on the interfaith calendar in Chicago, drawing significant audiences of people from both communities who invariably convey their appreciation for the opportunity to come together in that way.

Finally, then, while the delivery of each of these lectures has played an important part in advancing understanding and awareness of one another for Chicago's Catholics and Jews, thereby enhancing their relationship, this collection of the first ten years' worth of lectures will both expand the audience and keep those lectures alive, advancing the goals of dialogue in a different format. It is a result that we who have been partners in this enterprise locally hope will bring benefits both in Chicago and beyond.

Remembering Jamil Abu Toameh, a True Teacher

The Jerusalem Post, October 30, 2009

• • •

When Jamil Abu Toameh died suddenly last week, Israel and the Middle East lost a man of a type all too rare in today's world. And I lost someone who, as I was growing up in Chicago years ago, it would not have occurred to me to be likely to have as a future friend.

I first got to know Jamil after I came to Israel in 1968 to join the English Department faculty at Tel Aviv University. Most of the students who entered my classrooms then were different from their counterparts who I had previously been teaching in the States, but none more so than Jamil.

Older than me by a few years, he was an Israeli Arab who, I learned, had been doing translation work in the Gulf States before he returned to Israel and undertook studies leading to a degree at the university. He was a standout, serious student with flawless English and engaging graciousness, and over time the relationship of teacher and student evolved into one of friends.

I suppose it is a cliché to talk about teachers learning from their students, but once we got out of the classroom it was Jamil who in many ways became the teacher and I the student. The subject matter involved a segment of the Israeli population about which I otherwise knew very little.

Jamil came from a leading family of the Arab village of Baka al-Gharbiyeh, in the Triangle area in the north. It was, by then, the early '70s. I had two small children who were born in Israel, and thanks to invitations from Jamil, my family and I visited him and his family in Baka.

The first visit, as I recall, was the day of a festive local wedding. With pride in his heritage and warm hospitality, Jamil wanted us to know about and experience the culture from which he came and which was maintained in this Israeli village. It was interreligious relations in its purest form, the epitome of which involves understanding of and respect for the other accompanied by a deepening sense of one's own identity.

My family and I returned to the States in 1979, with a hand-painted *nargilah* as a farewell gift from Jamil in hand. I next "saw" him in a most unexpected way.

In Chicago in the early '80s, my wife and I attended the screening of a film based on interviews with Israeli Muslims and Jews, *in situ,* talking about the ways their faith traditions present the story of Abraham. There, to my surprise, was Jamil, eloquently illuminating the Muslim approach to the patriarch of the world's three major monotheistic religions. I was later to learn that he had become active in a Muslim-Jewish dialogue group, and his participation in the film was in part an extension of that involvement.

That was one of the things that Jamil and I talked about when we re-connected during a subsequent visit of mine to Israel. Though his brother Jalal, now deceased himself not so long ago, had remained in Baka al-Gharbiyeh and would become its mayor, Jamil and his family were by then living in Jerusalem, where he was practicing the professional role which, in many ways, defined him: that of educator.

For him, I believe, education was not just a profession but a calling. A shared love of literature and interest in ideas had first brought us to-gether, and that was something he wished to convey to others as well. He was also driven by a sense that through education individuals can enrich, advance, and fulfill themselves — and his people could fulfill themselves as a group — and he became principal of a girls' high school in east Jerusalem to advance that cause.

One of my most illuminating yet painful memories of talking with Jamil relates to his experiences as a principal. It comes from a conversa-tion we had at a time when I visited Israel during the first intifada. There he sat, this large man of great dignity, by then his hair turned white, talk-ing about what he described as young thugs, still children, and the way they had threatened him with the consequences that would follow were he not to dismiss his pupils from school so that they could go out into the streets and riot. His answer to them was that it was through educa-tion, not anarchic violence, that a better future for their people lay. Visibly shaken, he told me of how he resisted those threats.

In the '90s Jamil was able to further advance his pedagogical vision when he was named director of education for the Jerusalem Municipality. Now we could sit in his fine office in the new municipality building complex and talk about life, books, and the Israeli national spectator sport, politics.

He told me how he was working on an Arabic translation of George

Orwell's *Animal Farm,* a book which, he believed, offered a parable of current Palestinian political life. He rued the absence of a Palestinian leadership ready to sincerely and effectively work toward resolution of the Israeli-Palestinian conflict and was embittered by the corruption and mendacity he saw in Yasser Arafat and many around him.

Neither an Uncle Tom nor naive, he recognized the challenges faced by Israeli Arabs and the complexity of the Israeli-Palestinian impasse. And yet he sustained a vision of Jews and Arabs living together in friendship in the State of Israel and of Israel and its Palestinian neighbors living together in peace, and he taught by example how that could come about. He was a person of wisdom, tolerance, and courage, who softened life's blows with a gentle sense of humor. He loved his family and was proud of his children. A true teacher, he brought powerful lessons to all who were near him and ready to learn.

If only there could be more people like my friend Jamil Abu Toameh, especially at a time like this. He will surely be missed.

Framing the Communal Agenda
and Advancing Jewish Peoplehood

The agenda of the organized American Jewish community has evolved in a number of ways during the period of time this book covers, reflecting changes in American society and changes within the community itself.

The longest piece in this section focuses on the history and nature of Jewish Community Relations Councils and their national structure. It first appeared in 2002, in a volume to which I had been invited to contribute by Daniel Elazar, who is memorialized in a piece that is also included in this section. That longer article focuses on trends that continue to be pertinent in the framing of the communal agenda, particularly issues that revolve around the principles of universalism and particularism which I spoke about in introducing this volume. The other pieces in this section focus, to a greater or lesser extent, on the importance of maintaining a sense of Jewish peoplehood in an individualistic society. I pointed to this issue in that introductory essay as well. It is one that will surely remain high on the community's agenda as its institutions struggle to find solutions that will both sustain community and allow space for the young people of today to find fulfillment on the paths that they are taking.

Remembering Daniel Elazar

JUF News, January 2000

. . .

With the death of Daniel Elazar in Israel on Dec. 1, the Jewish world lost one of its foremost thinkers at the age of 65.

Born in Minneapolis and raised in Detroit, Elazar had many Chicago connections. He became a good friend to a number of Chicagoans when, in the early '50s, he served on the staff of Camp Ramah in Wisconsin. Those friendships were intensified and enlarged when he came to do graduate studies at the University of Chicago in the mid-'50s.

My own acquaintance with Danny goes back to that period. Here, in the heartland, in mid-century America, he and his friends combined intellectual flair and Jewish commitment. That combination was to characterize Elazar throughout his life and to inform his exceptional career.

He participated in the Jewish Agency's Summer Institute in Israel in 1953, when he contracted polio. As the years went by, he was afflicted increasingly by the impact of that handicap and other ailments. Still, he kept up a pace that few could replicate—maintaining a distinguished international presence; establishing and directing a series of notable projects; teaching and mentoring a long list of students with stellar accomplishments of their own; and producing a massive body of work.

As a student he focused his attention on the subject of American federalism. After receiving his master's and doctorate at the University of Chicago, he went to work at the University of Illinois in Champaign-Urbana. His next stop was in Minneapolis, where he served on the University of Minnesota faculty and where our own paths crossed once more. He soon moved to Temple University in Philadelphia, where he founded and directed the Center for the Study of Federalism. While maintaining his association with Temple, he made aliyah to Israel where he joined the faculty of Bar-Ilan University and headed the Institute for Local Government. In 1976, he founded and began directing the Jerusalem Center for Public Affairs.

That same year saw the publication of one of Elazar's most important books, *Community and Polity: The Organizational Dynamics of American Jewry*. Put together, those two landmarks encapsulate his emergence as a .

top expert on the Jewish community of North America and a pathfinder in the development of political theory in Israel. His institute took its place as a leading Israeli and international Jewish think tank, while his own work continued at full throttle. By the end, he had authored, co-authored, or edited some 80 books.

Our relationship picked up again in the '70s, when both of us were living in Israel, then again this last decade, through his connections with the American federation system in general and Chicago's federation in particular. With Israel-Diaspora relations moving into a new stage, Elazar brought a profound understanding of each of the communities to the subject and had a unique ability to put the relationship in context. He conveyed his ideas through his writings and through his regular participation in forums such as those at the annual General Assembly of the then-Council of Jewish Federations (now United Jewish Communities).

Happy to keep in touch with our local community, he always made himself available for briefings with delegations of political leaders brought to Israel by the Federation. In those briefings, he demonstrated unequaled knowledge of Chicago and Illinois politics, knowledge that he used to help the visitors understand political life in Israel. He also recounted some of his rich and rare first-hand experiences. In the summer of 1995, he established a special rapport with Congressman Bobby Rush, who had recently been in South Africa for the inauguration of Nelson Mandela, by describing the role he himself had played in assisting in the writing of the new constitution of that country. Two years later, in a session in Jerusalem with Congressmen Jerry Costello and Danny Davis along with members of the Illinois General Assembly, he cited his experience of visiting every county in the state when at the University of Illinois decades earlier. He dazzled Rep. Costello as he spoke knowingly about politicians from the congressman's home county in the southern tip of the state.

The aggressively virulent illness that took Elazar's life moved quickly in the few months following its diagnosis, but he remained active. In his home he met with one more delegation from Illinois, made up of members of the state's General Assembly on a trip organized by the Federation. That was perhaps the last such meeting in which he took part, but he continued to work on, among other things, a project on Jews in the American Public Square which he had been commissioned to put together by the Pew Charitable Trusts. Only three days before his death, he was still being quoted on Israeli affairs in an Associated Press story.

The ties with Chicago had continued last spring, when he and his wife, Harriet, a former South Sider to whom he was married at Rodfei

Zedek Congregation in Hyde Park in 1961, spent several months here. Elazar served as a visiting professor at the University of Chicago and made a number of appearances in the community. He provided a chapter on the link between American Jewish federations and the European structure of kehillah for the catalog of an exhibit commemorating this federation's Centennial, which will open at the Spertus Institute of Jewish Studies in mid-January. While here, he offered to prepare a study of the history of this federation as only he would have been able to do it. That, alas, is one of the many projects that he did not live to complete.

As prodigious as his achievements were, had his life not ended so suddenly, he surely would have accomplished even more, at a time when there is great need for the depth and breadth of understanding that he was able to bring to the evolving subject of Jewish public affairs and the lucidity with which he expressed his ideas.

The Jewish people have a tradition of honoring the scholars and teachers in our midst. Few in our own time have been as deserving of such honor from world Jewry as Daniel Elazar, a brilliant thinker devoted to his family, his friends, and his people. May his memory be for a blessing.

Local Community Relations Councils and Their National Body

In Jewish Polity and American Civil Society,
Boston: Rowman P. Littlefield, 2002

Introduction

Well over 100 Jewish Community Relations Councils (JCRCs) (some of them with different names) are found in American cities throughout the country. Some are committees of federations, some are federation departments, and some are freestanding organizations. For some of them, the constituents are individuals from the community serving on a Board of Directors; for some of them, the constituents are representatives of local organizations or of the local chapters of national organizations; and for some of them the constituency is a hybrid. Though in the past some of these bodies served jointly as CRCs and regional offices of national organizations, today that is rare. The key to the uniqueness of the JCRCs is that they are locally-based bodies. While benefiting from the possibility of drawing upon the expertise of national organizations, they frame positions expressive of the perspectives of their constituents and they carry out action agendas on behalf of and in the name of the local Jewish communities.

The importance of the CRCs is emphasized by Daniel Elazar: "From the 1950s on, the emergence of the Jewish Community Relations Councils attached to the federations established a core that, with federation backing, could not easily be ignored. These JCRCs, with the Jewish Council for Public Affairs and the federations, play the largest role in Jewish representation today, although they draw the least publicity."[1] With many of the issues revolving around the subject of Jews and the American public square being carried out in the local arena, Jewish Community Relations Councils are indeed significant players, and their importance has increased over recent years as Jewish organizational life, along with national life in general, has become more and more decentralized.

Community Relations Councils began to come into being in the 1930s. According to Jerome Chanes, their purpose was "to provide a means for coordination of defense activity within a community" since "communities were no longer content to leave activity entirely to national organizations who rarely consulted with one another or with local leadership." They were also meant "to serve as forums for the discussion of varied views."[2] Like the three community relations "defense" organizations — the American Jewish Committee, the American Jewish Congress, and the Anti-Defamation League of B'nai B'rith — CRCs primarily focused on combating anti-Semitism.

Chanes questions the generally-received view that at their inception CRCs were a product of the federations in the various communities. But he acknowledges that even if that was not the case originally, after the Council of Jewish Federations brought fourteen CRCs and four national agencies (the aforementioned defense organizations plus the Jewish Labor Committee) together to form the National Community Relations Advisory Council (NCRAC) in 1944, the federation world became the prime mover for the establishment of CRCs throughout the country.

By 1950, when Professor R. M. MacIver was engaged by the NCRAC system to prepare a *Report on the Jewish Community Relations Agencies,* the numbers of CRCs had grown considerably. In his report, published in 1951, MacIver declared that "one of the healthier developments in the complicated skein of Jewish organizational activity has been the formation of integrative community councils and particularly, from our present viewpoint, of community relations committees. . . . These bodies have gradually been taking hold, increasing in number and status and setting an example of unified action that furnishes a significant contrast to the operation of the jealously separatist national Agencies."[3]

While preparing his study, MacIver was able to observe a shift in the agenda of the community relations world from the time the earliest CRCs were created. Though the need to protect Jewish security and maintain Jewish rights had remained central to the community relations agenda, in the post-World War II environment anti-discrimination efforts had broadened. Anti-Semitism was made less legitimate in America by the impact of the Holocaust and by efforts to counter anti-Jewish bigotry, though discrimination lingered in areas such as employment, housing, and educational opportunity. As that point, the community relations field enunciated as a cornerstone of its activities the premise that the security and well-being of the American Jewish community was directly tied up with guarantees of equality for all Americans. In so doing, the field became an active player in the nation's civil rights movement, working in coalition with like-minded bodies.

While Abraham Joshua Heschel and local rabbis may have brought religion-based convictions into the civil rights struggle, community relations activities at this time were generally less tied to an overt expression of Jewish concepts than was to become the case later. Insofar as the community relations organizations were operating with a self-conscious sense of Jewish principles and with the aim of projecting Jewish values into the public square, their sources and vision for the most part derived from what is commonly referred to as the "prophetic tradision."[4] Their goals, to a great extent, were universalistic. That was to change in the coming years.

A turning point came in the late 1960s and the early 1970s, in the context of several other developments. It was at that time that identity politics began pitting one group against another in America, and many Jews were made to feel less at home in the civil rights movement. At the same time, like others, Jews developed their own intensifying sense of group identity. Especially significant for the Jewish community was the impact of the Six-Day War, which occurred in June 1967, when Israel had to defend itself against Arab neighbors in a military conflict preceded by a period of great tension.

In a recent book which takes an acerbic approach to the organized Jewish community, Peter Novick asserts that Israel was not really in serious danger at that time, and he implies that Jewish leaders deliberately exaggerated the threat and stoked people's fears of the coming of another Holocaust in order to promote sympathy and support for Israel.[5] A more accurate and fair-minded accounting of that period would assert that however strong Israel's military may have been, the prewar fears were based on a realistic understanding of what was at stake. Though most American Jews may have believed that Jewish security had been assured after 1948, they suddenly faced the shocking recognition that the very place which they had regarded as safeguarding Jewish lives and guaranteeing that the horror of a new Holocaust could not occur was itself at risk. Israel's swift and decisive military victory did not erase the realization that Jewish survival was more tenuous than had been believed, and many Jewish organizations became far more focused on efforts to strengthen American support for Israel's security than they had been. At the same time, the victory also evoked a sense of pride, dignity, and assertiveness from American Jews.

Thus, at a time when the American intergroup relations landscape was itself being transformed, American Jews more than ever before linked their identity and their destiny to the State of Israel and to their brothers and sisters there. Israel and other explicitly "Jewish" subjects increasingly came to the fore on the community relations agenda, with ties to Jewish tradition becoming increasingly more pronounced, and a more assertive, stand-up-for-yourself style began to be demonstrated in the public arena on behalf of these priorities.

Stimulated in great part by the same historic event, many Jews in the Soviet Union were inspired by the Six-Day War to return to their Jewish roots with pride and to pursue the right to practice their religion and the right to emigrate to Israel. Activity on behalf of Soviet Jewry, which was already underway, received an added boost, and the American Jewish community relations world had another top priority added to its agenda in these years. At the same time, with consciousness of the Holocaust coming to the fore and with survivors more and more willing to speak about their experiences, that catastrophic event, seen increasingly in a "Jewish" way, also began to form a greater part of the transformed communal agenda.

Different as this more particularist agenda was from the more universalistic one which preceded it, it was not as though the old priorities were altogether replaced, but rather that these new ones were layered on top of them. The old civil rights and civil liberties agenda was maintained in the framework of what often became spoken about as a social justice agenda, while the new priorities clearly began to dominate community relations activities. This continued for over two decades, when a modulating process began which is still unfolding.

Focusing on a single community relations council to illustrate these trends, the next part of this chapter traces the past thirty years of work by the Jewish Community Relations Council of the Jewish United Fund of Metropolitan Chicago, which offers a paradigmatic illustration of the activity characteristic of that period. The chapter then looks at the fashion in which the national body which was established in 1944 as the National Community Relations Advisory Council has itself evolved, a body which is attempting to define the role it will play in the public square today and in the years ahead.

I

The establishment of Chicago's JCRC may be traced to the February 28, 1970 visit to Chicago by French President Georges Pompidou. His country had just refused to sell supersonic jets to Israel after supplying over 100 of them to Libya, an implacable enemy of the Jewish state. In an incident reported prominently by the local media, some 15,000 members of Chicago's Jewish community demonstrated against that policy, disrupting the calm of Pompidou's visit to the city. The protest was organized by what was called the Ad Hoc Committee on International Affairs, made up of grassroots leadership as well as leaders of the Jewish Federation and Jewish Welfare Fund of Metropolitan Chicago. One result of the protest was an impetus for establishing something more permanent in the federation framework. In 1971, the Welfare Fund thus formed an exploratory Public Affairs Committee (PAC). In January 1972, after it was determined where in the federation family the new entity would best fit, that committee was reorganized under the Jewish United Fund and began to function.

Observing the anomaly presented by the fact that neither Chicago nor New York had a JCRC in 1951, R. M. MacIver had said then, "While we are reluctant to suggest any addition to the already over-elaborate structure of Jewish community relations agencies, we nevertheless believe that, were effective steps taken to establish a CRC for each of the two greatest metropolitan areas, the effect would be salutary." He suggested that the reason these cities lacked CRCs may have resulted from the "presence in these areas of headquarters of national agencies."[6] Local observers recall that the objections of the branch offices of the national organizations (one of which, the ADL, had even had its national headquarters in the city until the late 1940s) had indeed played a part in preventing a CRC from being established any sooner in Chicago. Particularly instrumental in getting such an entity formed in Chicago was Philip Klutznick.

A former U.S. ambassador to the United Nations and future secretary of commerce, Klutznick was a major force in national Jewish communal life as well, having served as national president of B'nai B'rith and having been a key player in the Conference of Presidents of Major Jewish Organizations during its early years. Locally, he had helped bring the federation's fund-raising efforts together after the Six-Day War. Once he applied his powers of persuasion in this area, the Chicago offices of the national agencies were ready to join a number of local organizations within the framework of a federation-sponsored community relations council called the Public Affairs Committee, with Klutznick as its first chairman.

Constituents of this body, in addition to the local offices of the national defense organizations and the federation itself, comprised a broad range of religious, Zionist, and social action groups, each of which had veto power in the decision-making process. As laid out in a "statement of purpose, interest, and function," issued in June 1972, the "areas of concern" of the Public Affairs Committee consisted of "events and issues affecting Jews in Israel, in the Middle East, in the USSR, and wherever the status and welfare of Jews may be affected." In dealing with "the creative survival of American Jewry as a flourishing community dedicated to the preservation of Jewish values and the traditions of American democracy," the committee addressed a range of topics grouped under "individual liberty and Jewish security; . . . church-state relations; . . . and urban problems as they affect Jews living in an urban society." As it moved forward, the PAC was guided by Klutznick's assertion at its first meeting that "the committee was not expected to be just a debating society but rather a means for common planning and action."[7]

From that first meeting in March 1972, which focused largely on participation in a National Solidarity Day for Soviet Jewry on April 30, the issue of Soviet Jewry continued to be one of the dominant subjects for Chicago's Public Affairs Committee. The group's agenda revolved around demonstrations, meetings with elected officials, petition campaigns, interfaith prayer efforts, involvement in national planning, and more.

Israel was also a staple of the agenda. Almost immediately after the PAC was founded it began conversations about community-wide planning for Israel's twenty-fifth anniversary year. The group also quickly became involved in monitoring the treatment of Israel in the media and in local museum exhibits, as well as reacting to terrorist incidents directed against Israel. Attention then leaped forward following the Yom Kippur War in October 1973, with concerns expressed regarding the treatment of Israelis held prisoner in Syria, continuing U.S. aid to Israel, and related matters. At the time, the PAC's Committee on Scope, Structure, Planning, and Membership urged the federation to add an additional staff slot to the PAC to deal with those matters. A report from that committee specifically said, "The overriding priority is and must be the Middle East," with committee meetings scheduled to take place weekly. At the same time, Soviet Jewry was not to be neglected.

Various pro-Israel steps were taken through the 1970s. These included opposition to the Arab boycott; measures to counter anti-Israeli activities, often seen on local campuses; confrontation with U.S. Senator Charles Percy as his activities regarding the Middle East took a troubling turn; and coordination of communitywide Israel Independence Day observances on an annual basis. When the third chairman of the PAC was installed in 1977, the PAC's executive was quoted in the organization's minutes stressing that, like Chicago's, "most CRCs' priorities have been Israel and Soviet Jewry." When Egypt's Anwar Sadat came to Israel that year and set in motion an intensified peace process involving Israel and Egypt, the PAC's attention to Israel-related matters intensified even more. Meanwhile, in 1982 the Chicago Conference on Soviet Jewry was established within the PAC framework to coordinate and advance ongoing local efforts in that area.

Some domestic issues also attracted the attention of the PAC in the early years. According to PAC minutes, following a report by a spokesman of the ADL at its December 1974 meeting, "the feeling was expressed that the Public Affairs Committee is not devoting enough time to effectively deal with domestic affairs." The report had focused on the way that General George Brown had used disparaging stereotypes about Jews when speaking at Duke Law School. Thus, the effort to combat anti-Semitism and the wish to participate in intergroup activities to assist in that effort and promote other communal interests, a goal of other CRCs from their establishment in the 1930s, can also be seen as forming the core of the domestic agenda of Chicago's PAC.

At the PAC's early meetings there was talk about taking action against vandalism and swastika smearings that had occurred at the time in the community. At one of the meetings, a speaker from the American Jewish Congress addressed the question: "What are we doing about discrimination against Jews?" As the decade of the 1970s moved forward, increasing attention was given to an upsurge in local neo-Nazi activity, mostly revealed in public demonstrations.

By 1977 and 1978, neo-Nazi activity had increased dramatically in Chicago, and one particular sequence of events, which the PAC played a key role in addressing, virtually put a Chicago suburb on the national map. Well aware of the advantages which could accrue to them from publicity and of their power to inflict psychic damage, Chicago's band of neo-Nazis, headed by Frank Collin, announced that they were taking their show out of Chicago's southwest side and into the northern suburb of Skokie, with its large Holocaust survivor population. They got the reaction they sought. As limited as their ability to do physical damage may have been, by reminding Skokie's citizens and Chicago's Jewish community of the horrors wrought by Hitler and his swastika-wearing henchmen, Chicago's neo-Nazis set in motion a strong communal response intended first and foremost to keep them out of Skokie.

The community's reaction, involving several organizations, was coordinated by the PAC, with Sol Goldstein, a survivor leader and member of the federation board who chaired the PAC's Committee on Individual Liberty, spearheading the effort. (When Hollywood later made a movie about this episode called "Skokie," the Sol Goldstein part was played by the movie's leading actor, Danny Kaye.) Though the courts which heard the case rejected the legal attempts to stop the Nazis from marching in Skokie, in the end Collin and his followers chose to demonstrate in Chicago's Marquette Park instead, where they were met by a PAC-organized counterdemonstration.

Among the results of this episode was the discovery by many members of the Jewish community that there were limits to their support of the tenets of the American Civil Liberties Union; for them, when emotions were high and the perceived interests of the Jewish community were at stake, these interests would hold sway. In a way, then, this episode can thus be seen as a marker demonstrating a shift from the organized Jewish community's behavior in the public square in the 1960s, when it was largely driven by a universalist civil rights/civil liberties agenda, to the way it acted in the 1970s and beyond, when a more particularist approach began to take hold. Furthermore, the episode occurred concurrent with — and locally contributed to — the addition of another "Jewish" priority to the communal agenda: the Holocaust.

On the national scene, the late 1970s saw the screening of the television mini-series *The Holocaust;* the rise of the Holocaust denial movement — which had an early and highly visible local proponent in the person of Arthur Butz, a professor of electrical engineering at Northwestern University who authored *The Hoax of the 20th Century*; the establishment of an Office of Special Investigation in the Justice Department to pursue war criminals who had illegally made their way into the United States; and an increased readiness by survivors themselves to talk about their experiences. In the Chicago area, the Skokie episode was followed by the establishment of a survivors group, which pushed for the nation's first statewide legislation mandating the teaching of the Holocaust in the classroom, and by the efforts of another group, which led to the construction of a memorial in Skokie. With Goldstein staying involved, the PAC itself continued focusing on Holocaust-related matters.

Israel, Soviet Jewry, anti-Semitism, and Holocaust-related matters formed the core of the PAC agenda at the time. A special meeting held in October 1979 demonstrated how far matters had evolved from the 1960s when much of the nation's community relations attention was devoted to civil rights. The issue of concern at the meeting centered around tensions that had surfaced in black-Jewish relations, in part as a result of Andrew

Young's having to resign from his post as ambassador to the United Nations for holding an unauthorized meeting with the PLO. The issue had a local dimension due to the Chicago presence of black community leader Jesse Jackson. Discussion revolved around anti-Israel and anti-Semitic attitudes expressed in segments of the black community, and the PAC director urged the "beginning" of a dialogue to address such matters locally. The close coalitional partnership that had prevailed between Jews and blacks in the previous decade had become a thing of the past. Now, threats to the Jewish community and its interests were seen to reside within the ranks of that erstwhile partner in the fight against discrimination — a factor that was to intensify in the 1980s, particularly in Chicago, home of Louis Farrakhan and the Nation of Islam.

The community relations agenda forged in the late 1960s and maintained in Chicago as well as elsewhere in the 1970s remained largely intact throughout the 1980s. Church-state issues also received increasing attention, and strict separation was supported locally as well as nationally. Revealingly, in December 1987, the Chicago organization (which a year previously had been renamed the Jewish Community Relations Council) opposed the erection of both a crèche and a Chanukah menorah at the Daley Plaza in Chicago, even though it was a Jewish organization (albeit not a member of the JCRC) that had erected the menorah. In other areas, support for Israel became complicated by the incursion into Lebanon and discomfort with Israel's settlement policy in some quarters; changes were obviously afoot in the Soviet Union; the community was doing more to memorialize the victims of the Holocaust; but, by and large, the trends established earlier remained intact.

At the end of the 1980s, a new period in community relations affairs began to reveal itself. One of the propellants of change was a "religious revival" which could be seen having an impact on American life in general during this period. In the Jewish community, the trend toward increasing attachment to religious activities and values was compounded by developments highlighted in a population study issued by the Council of Jewish Federations in 1991. Tracking statistics regarding assimilation and intermarriage, this study awakened the view that the greatest threat to the future of the American Jewish community was not from enemies outside but from community members' lack of connection with their own roots. The result of this confluence of influences was a greater overall emphasis on what became known as "continuity." This included a more self-conscious turning to Jewish traditions, texts, and modes of behavior. In some cities, activity in the JCRC began to be promoted as offering a point of entry into overall Jewish communal life. In Chicago, the deepening attachment to tradition was demonstrated by the introduction at the beginning of each JCRC meeting of a d'var Torah, in which delegates to the JCRC, rabbinic and lay alike, take turns in offering reflections on the Torah portion of the week, frequently finding rationale in these Jewish sources for community relations activity practiced by the JCRC.

A particularly striking way in which the "continuity" agenda has had an impact on community relations is seen in the changing attitudes to public funding for religious day school education in the form of vouchers. In Chicago, a majority of the JCRC membership holds firm in opposition to vouchers, largely for church-state reasons. But a minority would favor making vouchers available, mostly because of the assistance which might be provided to parents of day school students. Given these division, the JCRC has remained without a position on this issue.

As significant as the "continuity" thrust of the 1990s may have been in effecting changes in the agendas of some CRCs, developments set in motion by the collapse of the Soviet Union and the end of the Cold War have had at least as great an impact on the overall community relations agenda. At the time following the end of that international engagement, when much of America began turning inward, the Jewish community followed suit to an extent, but the community's involvement in and concern about international matters remained greater than that of Americans in general. Still, though the community stayed involved, there were significant differences in the nature of its involvement, given the dramatic changes which were taking place in the world.

For one thing, the fall of the Soviet Union, which opened the gates to free emigration and allowed Jews who remained in that region of the world to reconnect with their origins and traditions, greatly transformed the Soviet Jewry agenda. Beyond that, the disappearance of the support which the Soviet Union had provided to its Arab allies and the end of the flow of arms to them enhanced Israel's security and made possible the breakthroughs in the peace process that came early in the 1990s. So the community did not sense as great a need as it had before to act to ensure Israel's safety. At the same time, internal issues that were turned loose in Israel during the decade led some members of the American Jewish community to get involved in those matters, and some others to feel less connected. Finally, Holocaust-related affairs became even more central to the community's agenda as information involving the Holocaust era, which was previously inaccessible behind the Iron Curtain, suddenly became available and triggered various responses,

It is not so much that the community relations field moved on to other areas of concern as that it transformed the fashion in which it deals with its longstanding agenda items. With less need for external advocacy in these areas, many Community Relations Councils began to become more and more involved in activities within and for the Jewish community itself, albeit with an occasional or partial outward thrust.

Thus, since there are still realistic concerns about the fashion in which instability and economic difficulty can put Jews at risk in a traditionally anti-Semitic and increasingly nationalistic Russia, and since there is lingering nervousness about free emigration, activity to address those kinds of problems has continued. But this goes on at a reduced level, and it has been joined by a more "hands-on," project-centered type of activity. So Chicago's JCRC spearheaded a local "Cans for Kiev" project and, in a framework being established by the federation, organized a kehilla-type relationship with that Ukrainian community involving various forms of partnering. Other JCRCs, such as those in Baltimore, Boston, and Cincinnati, have also moved forward significantly with such twinning relationships with communities in the former Soviet Union.

As far as Israel is concerned, the institutionalization of community wide Israel Independence Day programming, introduced some years ago, continued as a central part of the local agenda in Chicago, with the large-scale celebration of Israel's fiftieth anniversary replicated in different ways around the country having highlighted that activity. In addition, the JCRC and federation were able, within a day, to bring 5,000 members of Chicago's Jewish community together following the tragic assassination of Prime Minister Rabin. In dealing with Israel in the 1990s, JCRCs continued to carry out some of the "old-style" activity – still advocating for a strong American-Israel relationship; still working with the media to ensure fair and accurate treatment of Israel; still reaching out to the non-Jewish community to enhance understanding of Israel; still taking steps to blunt the efforts of Israel's proclaimed enemies, steps which began to include opposing terrorist activity of a new sort, tied not so much to states or ideology as to extremist religious impulses. (Chicago's JCRC drafted and advocated statewide legislation to outlaw the raising of funds intended to support international terrorist activity. The first of its kind in the country when it became law in 1996, the legislation served as a model for other JCRCs.) At the same time, there began to be a new dimension to this activity, which in great part focused on helping the Jewish community itself to better understand what was going on in the peace process as the Israel government demonstrated a willingness to talk to one-time mortal enemies and to take risks in an attempt to bring about peace. That new kind of activity also involved working along with federations to help American Jews and Israelis develop enhanced understanding of each other and to prevent the religious diversity issue in Israel from causing a breach between the two communities. With the collapse of the Oslo process in the fall of 2000, JCRCs found themselves both returning to their "old style" advocacy in some ways and working within the community to enhance solidarity with Israel.

In the 1990s, JCRCs such as Chicago's found themselves becoming more and more involved with Holocaust-related matters — promoting Holocaust education; having more of a role to play at Holocaust memorials as the survivors themselves increasingly disappear from the scene; and providing support to the Office of Special Investigations, whose efforts accelerated with the availability of previously inaccessible data. Most of all, JCRC offices in Chicago and several other cities have found that a major addition to their work beginning in the 1990s has been providing assistance to survivors and their families in exploring their rights and pursuing the possibility of retrieving some of those Holocaust-era assets which have been shaken loose through various steps taken during recent years. In Chicago this has included offering extensive person-to-person assistance; organizing day-long information sessions with the state's Department of Insurance; putting together a day-long conference with Northwestern Law School; and serving as the advocacy arm in a multi-agency support structure for survivors.

The JCRC's domestic agenda also changed in the 1990s, here, too, in part, because of change on the world scene. No longer driven by fear of a communist threat, domestic hate groups now have their paranoia stimulated by imagined plans for a "new world order" driven by an international conspiracy aimed at undermining America. As usual when conspiracies come into play, it is the Jew who is demonized as the primary villain. So, while anti-Semitic attitudes have lessened on the national scene, those that still prevail can have the power to drive members of extremist groups who are inclined to violence over the edge. That happened during the weekend of July 4, 1999, when Benjamin Smith, a disciple of an extremist group leader, went on a shooting rampage which was first directed at Jews on their way home from synagogue in Chicago, and which ultimately took the lives of a well-known African-American figure in nearby Evanston and an Asian student in Indiana. In a contemporary way, the need to combat anti-Semitism and its effect thus remains high on the community relations agenda.

In the decade of the 1990s, the nature of relations between the Jewish community and other communities underwent certain changes. Relations with Poles and members of other Eastern European ethnic groups were strained as Holocaust-related issues increasingly came to the fore. Louis Farrakhan's ascendance created a hurdle to be overcome before dialogue and relationships could go forward with the African-American community, though there were ways in which positive relationships between blacks and Jews were maintained during the decade. The Jewish community also saw itself forging new relations with America's growing ethnic minorities, particularly Asian-Americans and Latino-Americans. (The possibility of forming closer relations with Muslims, something which might have seemed to be enhanced by the steps taken to resolve the conflict between Israel and its Arab neighbors earlier in the decade, faced handicaps. For one thing, Jews and Muslims had limited shared history in the United States, and for another, numbers of Muslim activists in America separated themselves from Yasser Arafat's moves toward reconciliation with Israel and maintained ties with the Palestinian rejectionist camp.)

In today's transformed community relations world, the Jewish community is, in general, less tied to long-term coalition partners with whom it shared a multifaceted, ongoing agenda than it once was. Instead, partnerships are formed mostly on a situational basis, depending on the subject. If the issue is hate crimes, then there are partners to be found in various minority communities. If the issue involves religious rights, then other kinds of partnerships may be forged. Thus, the JCRC and other Jewish organizations in Illinois have found themselves standing behind the barricades with members of the Evangelical community in promoting a statewide religious freedom restoration act. Meanwhile, drawing upon their longer-standing experience in the public arena, JCRCs have also provided advice and assistance to newer groups as they organize themselves to promote communal interests and to reach out to the media and the public in general.

The intergroup climate in which these activities have taken place is one in which the watchword is diversity. In a world where balkanization has become not just a metaphor but a description of the bloody and awful direction in which intergroup conflict and hatred can go, America has had its own problems in dealing with intergroup issues. At times that has meant seeing various groups following the path of a negative multiculturalism by circling the wagons, regarding others only as enemies, and being driven by a psychology of victimization. Certain racial and ethnic groups have acted out this form of multiculturalism in a fashion detrimental to the Jewish community, segments of which have themselves at times been drawn to such a mode of behavior. But as destructive as such domestic tribalism can be, full-scale implementation of the old-time notion of a melting pot would endanger the traditions and values that give positive identity and meaning to the lives of members of many religious, ethnic, and racial groups, Jews included. The challenge is to build a society where pluralism and diversity can flourish, a society made up of groups which maintain their own specialness, understand and respect others' differences, and join together with shared belief in the common humanity of all people and a shared commitment to basic American principles. In Chicago, a city greatly defined by its ethnic, racial, and religious mix, a model for this kind of positive intergroup relationship has been established in the relationship between Jews and Catholics, in which the JCRC has played a significant role.

One of the institutional frameworks in which leaders of the two religious communities come together in Chicago is a structure called the Catholic-Jewish Scholars Dialogue. It was organized at the initiative of the late Joseph Cardinal Bernardin shortly after he came to Chicago in the early 1980s. Its partners are the Archdiocese of Chicago, on the one hand, and the Jewish Federation and Chicago Board of Rabbis, on the other, with the JCRC office serving as facilitator. Over the years, the dialogue has regularly brought its members together every other month for presentations and discussions that have given members of each group deeper understanding and appreciation of the traditions and beliefs of the other community, and a framework for dealing together with particularly sensitive issues of the day. A statement that the Dialogue issued regarding the convent at Auschwitz, endorsed by Cardinal Bernardin, was said to have had a direct impact on the decision of the Vatican to intervene in the crisis which had surrounded that issue. Another statement, which gained national attention, acknowledged differences in the way each of the groups' traditions deal with abortion and called for dealing with the subject with civility and respect for alternative points of view.

A climactic moment for the Dialogue, which its efforts helped make possible, was a 1995 mission to Israel led by Cardinal Bernardin during which he gave a groundbreaking speech on "Antisemitism: The Historical Legacy and the Continuing Challenge for Christians." The trip was described as the first-ever interfaith mission to Israel led by a cardinal, and, through virtually nonstop local media coverage, it brought to Chicagoans of all backgrounds a powerful image of meaningful intergroup relations in action. Bernardin's successor, Francis Cardinal George, has made clear his own commitment to sustaining this relationship, which continues to flourish in Chicago.

Significantly, this prototype for successful contemporary intergroup relations functions in a religious framework, with the participants seeing themselves as representing two "faith communities." As the members of the Dialogue study scriptural texts and discuss subjects like repentance, prayer, implications of the new millennium, and such staples of the Jewish community relations agenda as Israel and the Holocaust, they do so with specific reference to their religious identities and religious traditions. In its nature, this kind of intergroup framework can be seen as symbolic for the current era.

Overall, then, in ways both profound and simple, as the Jewish community has forged its agenda in the public square over the past three decades, it has done so in a fashion increasingly tied to its past, its sense of peoplehood, and its traditions. The annual calendar of the organized community's programming has far more to do with observance and anniversaries derived from Jewish experience than it once did, and respect for Shabbat and various holidays during the year is also more manifest than it once was. More principles of action are linked to concepts enunciated in the traditional religious sources. More words in the working vocabulary are taken from Hebrew, the ancient language of scripture and prayer and the living language of the modern State of Israel. Increasing use of the term *Shoah* instead of Holocaust may annoy a critic of the organized community such as Peter Novick,[8] but it is exemplary of this trend, as is reference to Israel's Independence Day as Yom Ha'Atzmaut. The fact that the Vatican, in issuing its statement on the Holocaust in 1998, used the word *Shoah* and described its own movement toward repentance with the Hebrew term *t'shuvah* demonstrates the impact of the Jewish community's use of this language. Even those most tied to a universalistic social justice agenda have taken to basing their behavior on a concept presented by the Hebrew phrase *tikkun olam* (repair of the world). Although, as Mordecai Lee, a former CRC director, has observed, this term makes few appearances in the sources and the way it is being used today may be questionable from a traditionalist point of view, the impulse for using it is consistent with the current trends.[9]

As in the use of terminology, one can see a shift to ever more self-consciously promoting what are defined as Jewish communal interests in various aspects of the community relations universe. At a time of burgeoning social service demands, for some JCRCs that has meant using techniques and contacts garnered from advocating on behalf of Israel,

Soviet Jewry, and other issues to advocate on behalf of communal needs addressed by federations and their agencies. (In Chicago, that role is handled by the federation's Government Affairs Program. Conversely, the federation's Government Affairs Offices in Washington, D.C., and at the state capital in Springfield serve as arms of the JCRC on community relations issues, as does the federation's Israel office.) At the same time, the "continuity" agenda and world events have caused JCRCs, the ambassadors of their communities to the outer world and the state departments of the federations in their cities, to become increasingly involved with the relations between members of their own community. In the current environment, that form of activity has taken on special significance. With denominational, political, and other differences between segments of the community becoming ever more strident, the JCRC has emerged as a rare entity which offers a table where all groups in the community can come together to find common denominators and pursue common interests. Whereas Philip Klutznick had told Chicago's Public Affairs Committee, meeting in May 1972, that "at no time have there been fewer issues of controversy in the Jewish community than today," that is not something which could be so easily asserted today. Now, the JCRCs serve the crucial role of promoting communal unity, thereby preserving ties of Jewish peoplehood while continuing to represent the community in the public square.

Besides functioning in their individual communities, today 122 community relations councils join together along with thirteen national organizations in a national body. The following section reviews the history of that body and examines issues surrounding its current status.

II

What is now called the Jewish Council for Public Affairs (JCPA) was formed by the Council of Jewish Federations and Welfare Funds in 1944 as the National Community Relations Advisory Council (NCRAC). It initially brought together fourteen community relations councils from around the country and four national organizations: the American Jewish Committee, the American Jewish Congress, B'nai B'rith's Anti-Defamation League, and the Jewish Labor Committee.

Those four national bodies had previously joined in an entity called the General Jewish Council, but the notion of bringing them together with

CRCs in an attempt to coordinate community relations activity nation-wide was something new. The triggering impetus was a desire to forge a unified front against anti-Semitism. In an analysis of the early years, Walter A. Lurie has noted the importance attached to combating discrimination in war industries, and he has observed that employment discrimination in general quickly became a top priority for the organization.[10]

In 1952, two major defense organizations, the ADL and the AJCommittee, withdrew from NCRAC in reaction to the report issued by Professor R.M. MacIver the year before, unhappy about what they saw as a threat to their autonomy in the report's recommendations, including its call for a realignment of the national defense agencies. They were not to rejoin the national body until 1965. Nevertheless, with a structure augmented by other national organizations and additional CRCs, NCRAC continued to deal with security, discrimination, and other such issues on its early agenda. But then, with the social climate in America transformed following the war, the role played in the public square by the organized Jewish community, both locally and nationally, underwent significant change.

Introducing a 1981 collection of papers on "Jewish Communal Services in America 1958-78," Earl Raab spoke of "three 'periods' in the field of Jewish Community Relations. The First Period was dominated by the grim fight against overt anti-Semitism, here and abroad, plain and simple. The Second Period was marked by the post-World War II surge in American prosperity and idealism, and in American-Jewish integration; it was dominated by activity on behalf of a democratic and pluralistic America, the by-words being civil rights and civil liberties. The theme was also relatively plain and simple: the security of the Jew depended on such an American society."[11]

NCRAC, which was born at the very end of Raab's first period, came of age during the postwar period. Led by its first executive director, Isaiah Minkoff, NCRAC distinguished itself in the civil rights struggle that was taking shape at the time. With the organization's deputy director, Arnold Aronson, staffing what became the Leadership Conference on Civil Rights, NCRAC assumed a significant national profile on this issue. At the same time, it provided an early forum for the community to debate efforts to advance the separation of church and state. As tracked by Gregg Ivers in *To Build a Wall: American Jews and the Separation of Church and State,* those debates pitted the more aggressive and litigious AJCongress, represented and led in this area by Leo Pfeffer, against the AJCommittee and ADL. With the former group ultimately carrying the day despite the others' greater caution about the impact on intergroup relations and local concerns, the community relations field became a strong supporter of the principle of strict separation.[12]

As Raab and others emphasize, priorities changed beginning in the late 1960s. In describing the Six-Day War of 1967, the impact of which he called a "watershed," Raab wrote in his 1981 piece, "The public defense of Israel, which had been a negligible part of the Jewish community relations agenda in the Second Period, has come to dominate that agenda in the Third Period." Looking at other events of the time, Raab went on to say:

> One of the results of these developments was a burgeoning of the Jewish community relations field. At the beginning of this period about three dozen local community relations councils or committees were affiliated with the National Jewish Community Relations Council. At the end of the period, about a hundred such local agencies were affiliated. . . .By the same token, as a result of these developments, the American Jewish public affairs agenda seemed to 'turn inwards,' as some put it, away from the Second Period preoccupation with the internal nature of the American society.[13]

It was in 1969, in the increasingly more self-consciously "Jewish" environment of the times and, as Walter Lurie has put it, "as a response to shifts since 1944 in Jewish and general acceptance of public group identification,"[14] that NCRAC added a word and changed its name to the National Jewish Community Relations Advisory Council (NJCRAC). With Israel and the cause of Soviet Jewry coming to dominate the field's agenda, NJCRAC played an important coordinating role. In November 1973, three weeks after the Yom Kippur War, the General Assembly of the Council of Jewish Federations voted to fund the activities of a special task force on Israel to be operated out of the NJCRAC offices. As early as 1964, NCRAC had taken a turn in coordinating the recently-created American Jewish Council for Soviet Jewry, a role taken over shortly after that on a permanent basis by NCRAC staffers, first Albert Chernin, then Abraham Bayer, until 1971, when the AJCSJ became the National Conference on Soviet Jewry.[15]

Despite NJCRAC's involvement and the focus of some of its staff members and organizational constituents on the more specifically "Jewish" communal agenda, during the 1970s and 1980s and into the

1990s segments of NJCRAC's leadership and constituency remained committed to the kind of universalistic emphasis on civil rights and civil liberties which had held sway during the earlier era. Exemplifying an emerging debate as it was to take shape in the last decade of the century were two 1991 articles in the *Journal of Jewish Communal Service,* in a forum on "The Jewish Agenda and Public Policy: Directions for the 1990s." In one article, Murray Friedman, executive director of the American Jewish Committee's Philadelphia office, expressed his concern for what he saw as "the difficulties that our Jewish communal agencies have had in dealing with . . . the transformation of the civil rights movement, the breakdown of traditional norms, and the erosion of support for Israel." Arguing that "it is no contribution to inter-group relations if our involvement means we back away from guarding direct Jewish interests and concerns," he called for "a redefinition of an older liberalism about which we can be very proud and the conversion of it to a more realistic understanding of Jewish and American interests and public policies as we move into the 1990s."[16] In contrast, in the same issue of that publication, Albert Chernin, by then executive vice chairman emeritus of NJCRAC, harkened back to the era when "the premise underlying the community relations field's activities was that the security of American Jews was directly linked to the strength of the American democratic society." Addressing the present moment, he proclaimed that "the same assumptions that guided the development of our policies and goals in 1945 still should continue to guide us in 1990."[17]

The tension between these two organizational trends can be examined from a structural perspective. Not only were the ADL and the AJCommittee absent from the National Community Relations Advisory Council lineup from 1952 until 1965, but so were such major communities as New York and Chicago. As MacIver noted with chagrin in his report, neither of those cities yet had a CRC. When they did form such bodies and join NJCRAC in the 1970s, it was with strong support for the Israel-connected aspects of the communal agenda. Furthermore, in representing what, until Los Angles passed Chicago in population, were the country's two largest cities, they significantly affected the balance of power within NJCRAC. (New York was and has remained, by far, home to the largest Jewish community in the country. Though Chicago lost its status as number two some time ago, the strength of its community continues to manifest itself through a very successful annual federation campaign, second largest in the country, in addition to the production of key national leadership and other means.)

For many of the old guard who had long been active in NJCRAC, along with others who entered Jewish communal life later but had begun their personal involvement in the public square in the early 1960s, the civil rights era was seen as a "golden age" which provided a defining context for the organization. With the bloom somewhat off the Israel rose following the incursion into Lebanon in the early 1980s, and with the hard-line policies of Israel's Likud government seeming to some to hold back progress on peace, segments within NJCRAC were ready to break ranks with those who maintained the traditional position of the organized community that decisions about peace and security were to be made by the democratically-elected government of Israel, with diaspora Jewry having no public role in that process. Urging the organization to publicly criticize the government's settlements policy, this grouping within NJCRAC was headed by activists associated with AJCongress, a charter member of NCRAC, and the Union of American Hebrew Congregations, which had joined the national body almost immediately after NCRAC's founding. The other side, which carried the day in national debates, was led by the New York and Chicago JCRCs and the ADL, none of which were part of NCRAC during the civil rights era, along with other communities and national organizations.

Israel-linked activity continued to be coordinated by NJCRAC's Israel Task Force, and one of the organization's finest hours came in 1991 when NJCRAC helped organize the national day of advocacy in Washington on behalf of loan guarantees for Israel, which provoked President George Bush's notorious outburst against "some powerful political forces" represented by "something like a thousand lobbyists on the Hill." Still, following the breakthrough in the Middle East peace process in the early 1990s which was touched off by the Oslo agreement, there was an increased tendency in some NJCRAC circles to talk of reducing significant involvement with Israel-related issues. (Complicating matters further, by now there were rightist segments of the community outside of the NJCRAC orbit ready to publicly demonstrate and to take to Capitol Hill in direct opposition to the peace policies of the Israeli government – but that is another story.) Similarly, while NJCRAC had played a key role in bringing the communities together for a massive Soviet Jewry rally in Washington in December 1987, by the 1990s core activity regarding Jews in the Soviet Union – direction for which in any event had long been passed on to the National Conference on Soviet Jewry by NJCRAC – was reduced further. Since it could be claimed that less attention would need to be directed to overall overseas concerns in the new global environment, the notion of returning to a predominantly domestic agenda was encouraged by some NJCRAC leaders.

Still, as much as these circles within NJCRAC may have wished the organization to act in the 1990s as it had during the civil rights era, the milieu was different. Not only was the particularistic Jewish agenda still around, but for many the need for that kind of approach had intensified as a result of their fear that increasing assimilation, as measured by the national population study conducted by the Council of Jewish Federations, was the true emerging threat to the future of the American Jewish community. Furthermore, though the Middle East peace process and the fall of the Soviet Union had created new realities, that did not mean that the Jewish community's interests in those areas of involvement had evaporated. Indeed, rather than clearing the decks for a return to the agenda of Raab's second period, developments at the turn of the decade set in motion what may be seen as a fourth period in community relations affairs. The institutional tension which became heightened at this moment of transition was aggravated by the fact that some NJCRAC activists failed to recognize that a changed context for community relations activity was beginning which called for an appropriately altered kind of behavior from the Jewish community. Instead, they were driven by the urge to return to a posture more suitable to an earlier era.

As it happens, at the very time of this tension between those who would respond to the current conditions by stressing the social justice attitudes of the 1960s and those looking for ways to adapt to the emerging realities of the early 1990s, NJCRAC undertook a strategic planning process to examine the mission, structure, and function of the agency. Ironically enough, while the national agencies had had problems with recommendations in the MacIver Report issued over four decades earlier which had aimed at limiting organizational duplication, now it was they who had a problem with duplication, objecting to the possibility that NJCRAC might become more like them. Indeed, this time around, while there was no threat to their autonomy, the restructuring took away from these national bodies the veto power which gave them particular clout in NJCRAC. It also established a NJCRAC presence in Washington, which they had long opposed, charging that it would make NJCRAC a functional agency like them. And it gave the organization a new name and other trappings of its own autonomy, including an executive committee renamed a board of directors. Still, except for those denominational movements which successfully insisted on the retention of a veto on religious issues, the national organizations ultimately held their fire for the most part, tempering their criticism and going along with the changes. On the other hand, this time it was from the ranks of the communities, to which NJCRAC would presumably be thought to be the closest, led by Chicago and New York, that the greatest expressions of concern with the restructuring came. These concerns especially revolved around issues of governance and the organization's role in serving its communal constituents.

As the strategic plan was debated, voices were raised in certain communities arguing for the need for NJCRAC's procedures to reflect its constituency-driven nature. To advance that goal, it was asserted, there needed to be a way that the communities would be represented in a fashion more or less commensurate with their size. In response to language proposed for the new by-laws, which talked of members of the board of directors acting in an *ad personum* fashion, it was stressed that delegates to the annual plenum and to the board of directors meetings should be representatives of their communities and organizations, to which they would be accountable.

While the final language of the plan was modified to take these objections into account, concerns continued as the strategic plan began to be implemented. A key concern dealt with the focus of the organization, as implied by its name. A large number of constituents had expressed a preference for calling the group the National Jewish Community Relations Council — to maintain recognizable continuity, to point to the "national" component of the body, and to emphasize its community relations function. In the end, though, the choice was to rename NJCRAC the Jewish Council for Public Affairs. Not only was the name new but it also suggested a subtle but significant priority shift from involvement in community relations activities to attempting to impact on public policy — a shift which revealed itself in other ways as well.

In the days of NJCRAC, the organization annually produced something called a "Joint Program Plan for Community Relations," which was further described as a "Guide to Program Planning of the Constituent Organizations." Its propositions were reviewed in draft form by the member organizations and then refined and voted on at the annual plenums. Besides summarizing the consensus positions of the communities and the national organizations, these propositions recommended practical steps for action. In its new form, that product was renamed the "JCPA Agenda for Public Affairs." Though it still contained a series of propositions, the action principles were removed from them; instead, beginning with the publication for 1998-1999, a statement opening with such phrases as

"The JCPA supports" and enunciating policy positions was inserted to highlight the presentation of each proposition. Meanwhile, the JCPA began spending more time than it previously did on preparing resolutions to be issued to the general public.

In practice, the resolutions process denied communities and national organizations much opportunity to review proposed statements before the organization's annual plenum (let alone before the twice-annual meetings of the board of directors, for which no specific resolutions procedures were established). What was brought before the plenum, rather than being a statement drafted in an attempt to lay the groundwork for a consensus position, often originated with a national organization or a community which was likely to be partisan on one end of the spectrum or another. This was hardly the kind of system one would expect to see adopted by an organization aiming to bring communities together to ratify bottom-line points of shared concern. And indeed, in the first years in which the new procedures were in place, plenary meetings were at times marked by acrimonious difficulty in coming to agreement and by the tabling of resolutions when the majority felt it was inappropriate for the organization to even be looking at a given subject.

A graphic demonstration of the way the priorities of the organization shifted is provided by a comparison of its key publication over a twenty-year span. Though the sizes of the pages were no longer the same, their proportionality is revealing. *The Joint Program Plan for 1979-1980* devoted eleven pages to "Israel and the Middle East" and "Arab Economic Warfare," and another four to "Energy," which was then closely tied to U.S.-Middle East Policy. It added six pages on "Soviet Jewry," two pages on "Jews in Other Lands," and one page on "International Human Rights," for a total of twenty-four pages devoted to overseas issues. The JCPA *Agenda for Public Affairs 1999-2000* grouped all of these matters (except for energy, which was then part of a section called "The Environment and Jewish Life") together under the heading "Israel and Other International Concerns," which altogether filled only fourteen pages. In the domestic areas the contrast is similarly striking. In 1979-1980, three pages were devoted to "Individual Freedom and Jewish Security," four to "Church-State Relationships," two to "Jewish-Christian Relationships," and eight to "Social and Economic Justice," for a total of seventeen pages focused on the domestic agenda, plus two more on Holocaust-related matters. By 1999-2000, the section called "Jewish Security and the Bill of Rights," which absorbed church-state issues and interreligious relations as well as the Holocaust, had alone grown to thirteen pages. Meanwhile, the section then called "Equal Opportunity and Social Justice" had grown to fourteen pages and, accentuating its new significance, it had by then moved up to be at the top of the domestic topics. At the same time, the whole new section on "the Environment and Jewish Life" was added, with nine pages altogether.

If, to be consistent, one were to place energy concerns in the international area for both publications and the Holocaust were to be seen as a domestic concern in both cases, the numbers would line up as follows: 1979-1980, twenty-four pages for overseas issues and nineteen for domestic; 1999-2000, eighteen pages for overseas issues and thirty-two for domestic. To an extent this agenda shift reflects a change in world conditions, on the one hand, and in the priorities of the contemporary American Jewish community, on the other. But it could also be argued that the changes are too drastic to accurately reflect a widespread assessment of the needs and priorities of the overall community, certainly as maintained in a good many local JCRCs. Instead, this shift can be taken as a reflection of the sort of issues which certain forces within the JCPA wished to see the organization focus on in asserting itself as a policy-setting body.

Statements made in the late 1990s by the group's executive vice chairman, Lawrence Rubin, illustrate the attempt by elements within the JCPA to remake the organization primarily as a policy-making body focusing on a wide-ranging universalist domestic agenda. Rather than seeing consensus-respecting inclusion as the organization's greatest strength, Rubin declared to the annual plenum of 1999 that "controversy is not always bad, and consensus is not always desirable." Rather than reflecting on ways that a refined pro-Israel action and advocacy program might be part of the organization's current agenda, he limited his discussion of Israel to arguing that the JCPA had a "responsibility" to help Israelis better understand that American-style separation of church and state provides a desirable model for them. Elaborating on the "important issues" to which he felt the JCPA should be directing its attention in the coming years, he predicted that "questions related to the need for an independent counsel, or the importance of real campaign finance reform, or private behavior and public responsibility will rise to the top of the public policy agenda." Besides referring to "Freedom of Speech on the Internet," he went on to say, "Filling with civic values the naked public square, the matter of assisted suicide, expanded civil liberties for gays and lesbians, even cloning, present interesting and pressing public policy questions."[18] At that same plenum, while the organization listed hate crimes and the

Middle East peace process among four "priority public affairs concerns of the organized Jewish community" when preparing delegates for meetings with their congressional representatives, the other two issues it named, at a time when Soviet Jewry and other particularistic concerns still prevailed for others in the community, were public education and the "clean air problem of vehicle emissions."

The emphasis of the JCPA on policy issues, and the kinds of issues which it was choosing to act upon (and those it was not choosing) attracted criticism. On June 30, 1999, the president and executive vice president of the UJA-Federation of New York sent the chairman and executive vice chairman of the JCPA a letter saying that their volunteer leaders "increasingly view JCPA as 'out of touch' with the New York Jewish community." Shortly thereafter, the president of the Jewish Federation of Metropolitan Chicago wrote the same recipients, noting differences between the New York and Chicago federations regarding some of the specific policy issues on the JCPA's agenda but reiterating an ongoing concern in Chicago with the fact that "in taking public positions on policy issues, the JCPA does not always adequately reflect the range of attitudes held in Jewish communities around the country today, nor does it always function as a consensus-drive, bottom-up structure." That letter went on to say, "In our view the JCPA would fulfill its role better if, instead of focusing so much on the formulation of policy on an extended list of issues, it would do more to present itself as a community relations entity, functioning more extensively and effectively as the national resource and coordinating body for community relations councils and federations around the country."

Though these communications were sent privately, the issue became public when they were published by the *Forward*, a weekly paper known for playing up conflicts in Jewish organizational affairs, complete with a banner-headlined front-page story. Focusing on the New York letter, the *Forward* dealt with the subject in a political context which reflected its own ideological predilections, declaring, "A sea change in the political stance of American Jewry is being heralded by a newly disclosed letter written by the leaders of the community's largest charity, challenging the prevailing liberal orthodoxy that has obtained in the community since the 1960s and 1970s."[19]

While the New York letter expressed concerns "that JCPA's domestic legislative agenda ignores views held by many in our community about important issues," it itself did not lay this matter out in specific conservative versus liberal terms — and the Chicago letter did not even suggest that

that was the framework of its concerns. Nevertheless, once the *Forward's* interpretation was put forth, the battle lines seemed to be drawn. In subsequent issues of that paper, columnists and writers of letters to the editor followed suit. For example, Leonard Fein (a regular columnist but also an official of the Union of American Hebrew Congregations and a long-time advocate for "liberal" activity within the JCPA) wrote a piece the headline of which proclaimed, "That 1960s Consensus Is Not Dead Yet." He disputed views which he portrayed as proposing "that JCPA turn from its historically broad range of interests and its definitely liberal stance."[20]

A somewhat related reading of the letters was offered by J. J. Goldberg, journalist and author of *Jewish Power: Inside the American-Jewish Establishment,* who put his own spin on the topic. One story by Goldberg in The New York Jewish Week, with the headline "Family Feud," had a subheading which said, "Two big Jewish federations seek to rein in an outspoken Jewish advocacy group." A follow-up piece in the same publication asserted that what was driving Jewish community leaders nationwide was the desire to have "the community's resources focused on Jewish needs. They don't think that includes the environment or abortion rights. They want to maintain essential community services, like eldercare and Jewish rescue. Everything else should go to ensure Jewish identity in the next generation."[21]

Though many community leaders may indeed have been concerned that traditional areas of communal social welfare activity were at risk of damage through reduced funding and may have believed that Jewish identity should be a priority for the entire community, that did not necessarily make them advocates of wholesale abandonment of the community relations agenda. Furthermore, though those leaders may indeed have questioned whether the overall organized community must support abortion rights or make the environment one of the community's top priorities, members of the Jewish community with strong personal interests in these issues could readily associate themselves with any of a number of Jewish community organizations which advocate for them, without turning their backs on the unified community relations enterprise. In fact, for most of the critics of the JCPA, the problem was not, as some others chose to frame it, that the organization was too "liberal" *per se* in its choice of agenda items and in the positions it took on them, but that it often seemed to be going off the track as the unique coordinating body for the entire organized community in deciding how it should be spending its time, which issues it should be taking on, and how it arrived at positions regarding those issues.

The subject of public funding for parochial schools is illustrative. In an article in the December 1999 issue of *Commentary* magazine entitled "Who's Afraid of Jewish Day Schools?" Jack Wertheimer, provost of the Jewish Theological Seminary, was critical of the JCPA for resisting "every plan that might in some way bring government assistance to support the general-studies education offered by religious schools, including, as is often proposed today, in the form of direct subsidies to parents." In looking at a 1998 report prepared by the JCPA, Wertheimer referred to "its datedness, as if preserved in amber from the 1950s."[22]

That JCPA report was published after a year-long study from which one JCPA organization, the Orthodox Union, had dissented. Though the report itself said that "the JCPA received feedback from communities across the country, large, medium and small, that had examined the voucher issues locally within the last two years," it did not point out, as an earlier draft had, that of its 122 community members, only 28 had indicated that they had "examined the voucher issue within the last two years." Such results were hardly an overwhelming sign that the communities shared the JCPA's interest in treating this kind of topic in this fashion, nor that they had strong consensus-based feelings on it which they wished to have heard. While Chicago's JCRC, following the lead of the national body, did examine this topic, it reported that since there was no consensus on the vouchers issue in its community, it itself did not take a position. Instead of supporting either side in the debate, the Chicago JCRC forwarded the JCPA statements prepared by each of its constituent members who wished to provide a summary of their stands on the subject.

The kinds of positions taken by those on either side of the voucher question are instructive. On the one hand are members of the Jewish community who hold to the longstanding view that any softening whatsoever on church-state questions might endanger the wall of separation which has protected the religious freedom of American Jews. In a universalist fashion, many of those who hold this position fear that the creation of state-sponsored vouchers that could be used for parochial schools would weaken public school education. On the other side of the debate are those who claim that the constitutional dimensions of this issue are not all that clear and the Supreme Court has yet to offer a definitive ruling on the matter. Some of these advocates of vouchers say that with regard to education in inner-city communities, some members of those very communities favor vouchers as a device for improving educational opportunities. Above all, for the proponents of vouchers and those ready to take a new look at the subject, as for Wertheimer, there is a significant communal interest at stake in assisting parents to send their children to Jewish day schools.

Critics of the JCPA were thus suggesting that a national organization which is meant to embrace the entire community would be doing its job best if, instead of insisting on coming down on one side or the other of a controversial issue of this kind and rejecting the view of one section of the community or the other, it created a study which described the alternative positions held in the community, fairly reporting on the proportions of the community on each side but also acknowledging and exploring the developing trends in the area.

For many of its critics, a body like the JCPA was neither conceived of by its founders nor regarded by its constituents as an autonomous organization with independent members who come together to take positions on an open-ended number of issues of the day. It should not, therefore, approach all issues from any particular ideological point of view. For them, the JCPA is an organization of organizations which, when it deals with public policy issues, should focus on those in which the community has particular matters at stake and on which consensus exists or can be found. It is, they held, a body which should follow a process whereby representatives accountable to organizations and communities forge positions on those issues in the name of the overall community. The critics stressed that such an organization has the primary purpose of serving as a coordinating body which assists its constituents in programming to advance those communal interests, and they expressed the view that in recent years the action-centered aspect of the JCPA's role, though not entirely overlooked, had been slighted.

While JCRCs from communities like New York and Chicago actively played out their unhappiness with the JCPA (New York's by not attending plenums), two of the most powerful national agencies, the ADL and AJCommittee, mostly followed a passive route reflective of their perception that the JCPA is less of a force than it once was, increasingly marginalizing their involvement in JCPA affairs. The federation system, the original parent body, which continued to provide the bulk of the organization's funding, might have been expected to play a role with significant impact on the choice of direction for the JCPA. Instead, however, it was largely preoccupied with organizational restructuring of its own, as the Council of Jewish Federations underwent an extended and complicated merger period with the United Jewish Appeal and United Israel Appeal to form the United Jewish Communities. Still, in the summer and fall of 1999, disfavor with the JCPA also began to be seen coming from the federation world — witness the letter from the New York Federation — adding to pressure being put on the JCPA to modify its way of doing business.

In a post-ideological age, when the Jewish community was striving to steer its course in a changing world and changing community relations environment, the JCPA appeared to its critics to be out of step. While JCPA leadership began engaging in dialogue with some of the organization's critics and talking about making moves to respond to them as the 1990s drew to a close, that was not sufficient to quell all of the concerns of those critics. But if the JCPA was slow in responding to new realities and in playing the role of coordinator of communal activity that was looked for, communities in the field increasingly pushed the organization in those directions.

An example of this trend can be seen in the way the issue scheduled for year-long study in 1998 and 1999 played out. The original plan was to take a look at "Race, Public Policy, and Affirmative Action." Several CRCs then objected that there was little to be gained from entering into an extensive debate aimed at reasserting or modifying a position on affirmative action. A much more useful endeavor, they urged, would be to look at issues surrounding race relations in America today and to see what was being done around the country through action aimed at addressing these problems in a pragmatic way. Furthermore, said several of the communities, race relations today involve more than black and white relations. So the study, renamed *Race, Ethnicity, and Public Policy,* became a two-year project with on-the-ground considerations noted and with the complex racial mix in America today taken into account.

Somewhat similarly, the JCPA office was at first virtually oblivious to what quickly became a major agenda item in many JCRC offices in the 1990s: the need to assist survivors and to deal with other aspects of the swirl of issues surrounding Holocaust-era assets. With the subject achieving primacy in Chicago, New Jersey, Miami, and Los Angeles, JCRCs from those areas pushed the JCPA to give it appropriate attention, which the organization began to do. Although this attention came somewhat belatedly, once the JCPA did assume the role of coordinator, the organization was able to demonstrate the kind of resource function which it is in a position to play for the national community.

With the JCPA's difficulties having become public, a number of the issues at hand crystallized during the JCPA's annual plenum in February

2000. Delivering an address called *The Ghetto and the Globe,* Larry Rubin described the Internet as a worldwide phenomenon and complained that "even as worlds are opening around us, the organized Jewish world is turning inward." After noting that the priorities of the agency which he led had at first been "largely domestic" and then, after the Six-Day War, had become "increasingly international," Rubin asked, "What about now?" His answer was, "I believe that there continues to be a justice agenda in America." Though he later added that "the justice agenda demands our efforts to extend democracy to all corners of the world, for now that is where we live," the domestic thrust of his argument was clear.[23]

For Rubin and those in JCPA circles who shared his perspective, priority setting which begins by considering the community's particularist needs is a form of "ghettoization" which deserves to be regarded in a disparaging way. Ironically, though, in playing down international concerns and calling for a returned focus to the domestic social justice agenda, they, in a way, were the ones who were turning inward. Ignored by them was the fact that the Jewish community, even when coming at things from a subjective point of view, has provided wide-ranging leadership to the nation as a whole on a host of issues. Concern about the terrorist violence directed against Israel and Jews in Argentina and elsewhere around the world, for example, enabled the community to have useful insights as America itself became a direct target of the scourge of international terrorism in the early and mid-1990s. Similarly, communal responses to hate crimes, initially conceived of primarily because such acts were often being directed against Jews, have provided useful general models for addressing that problem as the country has increasingly focused on it. Furthermore, the Jewish community's still-resonating memories of the Holocaust enabled it to provide moral underpinning for international action when the ethnic cleansing in Kosovo, different but in a way reminiscent, unfolded. Indeed, the American Jewish community's interest in Israel and Jewish communities around the world has made it the primary backer of foreign aid overall and of the principle of foreign engagement for this nation, as government spokesmen have acknowledged. What begins with a particularist impulse may thus end up with universal impact.

When Rubin closed his plenum speech he announced that at the end of the year 2000 he would be leaving the JCPA. Though he was hardly the only one to take the kinds of positions that he espoused, the declaration of his departure was seen by many as providing the occasion for the organization to take a fresh look at itself at a significant moment.

In assuming the chairmanship of the organization at that time, Leonard Cole gave strong indication that he was prepared to lead it in doing just that. An article of his which appeared in *The Jewish Week* shortly thereafter further demonstrated sensitivity to the concerns of those calling for the setting of institutional priorities on the basis of a determination of communal interests.[24] At the same time, the United Jewish Communities initiated its own new look at its relationship with the JCPA.

In the year that has followed, a good deal has happened, but while the tensions between the JCPA and its critics have become less acute, the issues surrounding those tension have not yet been fully resolved. The Palestinians' turn to violence and their accompanying public opinion campaign have made Israel-related activities an unquestionable priority on the agenda for the community relations field, and the JCPA has played an important role in coordinating nationwide activities in that area. In that and other ways, under Cole's chairmanship and with a new executive, Hannah Rosenthal, the JCPA has become less wedded to a policy-centered, domestic-focused agenda than it had been under its previous leadership. Furthermore, the terrorist attacks on American of September 11, 2001 introduced new realities with an undefined but likely long-term impact on America's Jewish community and the community relations field. Still, as this chapter was being completed (in October 2001), the precise nature of the role to be played by the Jewish Council for Public Affairs in the years ahead and its relationship with its constituents and with the federation system remained uncertain.

Conclusion

At the turn of the new century, the fashion in which the Jewish community represented itself in the public square through its organizational entities was undergoing redefinition. On the one hand, community relations councils around the country continued to fulfill their historic role of combatting anti-Semitism and related threats to the security of the Jewish community and to join coalition partners in advancing contemporary aspects of the traditional civil rights and civil liberties agendas. On the other hand, they also found themselves focusing on priorities which reflected the evolution of the more particularist sort of agenda that first achieved prominence in the late 1960s, and they increasingly were framing and carrying out projects within the Jewish community itself. More and more, many of them were serving as the advocacy arm of the federations in their communities by helping to strengthen governmental support for those agencies' social welfare activities.

At a time when American Jewry has largely "made it" into the mainstream of American life, finding greater acceptance and opportunity, the community relations enterprise maintained a longstanding role by striving to protect the rights of all Americans and to expand overall tolerance. At the same time, however, the movement into the mainstream has come to be regarded in part as potentially threatening the future of the community. Many individuals increasingly seeing their identities tied up with their religious background and communal ties, and religion-based principles, in general, have become a more public matter in the country. Thus the community relations field, too, has found its role in advancing communal interests taking it into new territory.

In this context, the dialectical nature of Jewish communal affairs came to the surface in the national arena. The body newly named the Jewish Council for Public Affairs had increasingly assumed the shape of an entity tied to an earlier era's universalist approach while greatly focusing on the pronouncement of policy positions on a broad range of public affairs issues of the day. Meanwhile, a countervailing approach called for that body to be more committed to an evolving particularist agenda that more clearly identified itself as the vehicle of its collective constituent members, whom it represents and assists in carrying out their action-centered roles. The controversy surrounding the JCPA which emerged was an expression of differences between these answers to the question of what kind of community relations body the national Jewish community should have and how the community should be represented in the public square at that moment in its and the nation's history.

While this author's own perspective on these matters admittedly owes much to his experience with the federation-linked Chicago CRC as described in the initial section of this chapter, the conclusions drawn from an analysis of that operation offer useful insight into these broader issues. That experience suggests that the most effective and appropriate national body for the day would be one which serves as the community relations arm of the overall federation-linked system while maintaining its ties with its national member organizations. Focusing on community relations action and facilitating and coordinating such action as carried out by its constituents around the country, it would address significant needs by providing leadership, resources, models, and ideas to the national community relations enterprise in those priorities areas which have been of concern since CRCs began to be established and those which have emerged over the following decades. When it did take public policy positions, they would be on "bottom-line" matters where the community had a prevailing consensus and where the organization's constituents felt that there was a clear-cut communal interest. Thanks to the broad communal base of such an entity, its pronouncements on these issues would have strength and credibility. Individual CRCs, while empowering such an entity, would benefit from this kind of national structure while modifying their own agendas in tune with local circumstances.

A solution of this kind would blend organizational elements from an earlier time with current realities. Synthesizing aspects of the universalist approach to community relations issues of the past with the more particularist approach which emerged subsequently and which has continued to take shape, it would position the Jewish communality relations field to meet the problems of the present and future in a fashion in line with the organized community's assessment of its prevailing and emerging interests.

Given the various factors involved in dealing with institutional matters, one cannot be certain how these issues will indeed be resolved. But while the precise answer to the question of the structural way in which Jews will be represented in the American public square in the twenty-first century by the bodies which are the subjects of this essay remains open, it is clear that, to a great extent, the trend toward increasing emphasis on the "Jewishness" of Jewish community relations will remain intact.

NOTES

[1.] Daniel J. Elazar, "The Jewish Political Tradition in the English-Speaking World," unpublished manuscript.

[2.] Jerome A. Chanes, "The Voices of the American Jewish Community," *Survey of Jewish Affairs* 1989, William Frankel, ed. (Oxford: Basil Blackwell, 1989), 125.

[3.] R. M. MacIver, *Report on the Jewish Community Relations Agencies* (New York: National Community Relations Advisory Council, 1951), 99.

[4.] Jerold S. Auerbach is harshly critical of those segments of the Jewish community which, in his view, elevated and distorted the prophetic tradition in an attempt to be accepted by Christian Americans. "Severed from the Jewish covenantal tradition and grafted to Christian theology (and then to liberal politics), prophecy came to define enlightened Judaism," *Rabbis and Lawyers: The Journey from Torah to Constitution* (Bloomington: Indiana University Press, 1990), 99.

[5.] Peter Novick, *The Holocaust in American Life* (Boston: Houghton Mifflin, 1999), 148-51, and ff.

6. MacIver, *Report,* 101.

7. This and subsequent references to early Public Affairs Committee deliberations are taken from PAC minutes and related documents.

8. Novick, *Holocaust,* 133.

9. Mordecai Lee, "A Jewish 'March of Dimes'? Organization Theory and the Future of Jewish Community Relations Councils," *Jewish Political Studies Review,* 12:1-2 (Spring 2000).

10. Walter A. Lurie, entry on "NJCRAC" in *Jewish American Voluntary Organizations,* Michael N. Dobkowski, ed. (New York: Greenwood Press, 1986), 347-55.

11. Earl Raab in *The Turbulent Decades; Jewish Communal Services in America* 1958-78, Graenum Berger, ed., vol. 1 (New York: Conference of Jewish Communal Service, 1981), 537.

12. Gregg Ivers, *To Build a Wall: American Jews and the Separation of Church and State* (Charlottesville: University Press of Virginia, 1995), esp. chap 4, "Separation to the Fore," 100-45. See also J. J. Goldberg, *Jewish Power: Inside the American Jewish Establishment,* (Reading, Mass.: Perseus Press, 1996), 122-5. Goldberg covers several other developments reviewed in this chapter as well.

13. Raab, *Turbulent Decades,* 537-38.

14. Lurie, "NJCRAC," 348.

15. Albert D. Chernin, "Making Soviet Jews an Issue: A History," in *A Second Exodus: The American Movement to Free Soviet Jews,* Murray Friedman and Albert D. Chernin, eds. (Hanover, N.H.: Brandeis University Press, 1999), esp. 44-45 and 62-63.

16. Murray Friedman, "Jewish Public Policy: Its Unexamined Premises," *Journal of Jewish Service,* vol. 67, no.3 (Spring 1991): 175, 177-78.

17. Albert D. Chernin, "The Liberal Agenda: Is It Good or Bad for the Jews?" *Journal of Jewish Service,* vol. 67, no. 3 (Spring 1991): 166, 173.

18. Lawrence Rubin, "Y2B in Y2K: And If Not Now, When?" speech delivered February 21, 1999.

19. Ira Stoll, "End of Liberal Consensus Is Bruited by UJA-Federation," *Forward,* October 29, 1999, 1. The letters are reprinted on 9.

20. Leonard Fein, "That 1960s Consensus Is Not Dead Yet," *Forward,* November 5, 1999, 9.

21. J. J. Goldberg, *The Jewish Week,* November 5, 1999, and November 12. 1999.

22. Jack Wertheimer, "Who's Afraid of Jewish Day Schools?" *Commentary* (December 1999), 52.

23. Lawrence Rubin, "The Ghetto and the Globe," speech delivered February 27, 2000.

24. Leonard Cole, "Quick, Name a Jewish Issue," *The Jewish Week,* May 5, 2000.

GA 2006: One People, One Destiny

The Jerusalem Post, November 12, 2006

. . .

The General Assembly (GA), a four-day conference convened by United Jewish Communities: The Federations of North America, opens today in Los Angeles. The largest annual meeting of the organized Jewish community, the GA this year could be a watershed event for American Jews and Israelis alike.

Up until the war with Hezbollah, this GA was on track to follow a standard format, with the Israel-related components of the program accompanying fare relating to the day-in and day-out activities of the Federation world. But all that changed in late August as the GA was refocused around the theme "Together on the Front Line: One People, One Destiny." Dozens of Israel-related sessions were added to the program and Israeli leaders from the prime minister on down signed on as speakers.

Prompting this transformation was a recognition that Israel's war with Hezbollah was far more than a military flare-up. With Israel's civilian population under attack; with Iran developing a nuclear capability and its president declaring that the Holocaust never happened and that the State of Israel — founded to ensure Jewish survival — should itself be wiped off the map; and with Islamic radicalism and a new anti-Semitism on the rise globally, there was a heightened sense that we are in this together.

The conflict with Hezbollah had a visceral impact on American Jews, who responded with local rallies and solidarity missions, and have contributed $350 million to UJC's Israel Emergency Campaign. And the GA was seen as offering a means of moving the response to the next stage, providing an opportunity for the North American Jewish community to come together to better understand today's realities, to convey and enhance the centrality of its connection to Israel, and to commit itself to an action agenda that will address these concerns.

At the same time, with the Israel Emergency Campaign providing greatly needed assistance and receiving significant visibility in Israel, many Israelis have recognized that, in a world where they are increasingly isolated and vulnerable, there is something profoundly significant about the connections with their overseas brethren. They have been touched to realize that there is someone standing with them at a time of trial and need, someone with whom they have ties of kinship.

And so today, American Jews and Israelis come together in Los Angeles with a heightened recognition of the GA's importance and look forward to a program that is sure to be enlightening and inspiring. And there is something more at stake too. For this defining moment comes at a time when the Jewish people are not just affected by external circumstances but find ourselves at a significant moment in our shared history as well.

In some ways the Jews of Israel and the Jews outside Israel have been going in separate directions over recent years. This is not only the case in North America, where assimilation exerts a strong pull and where concerns with Jewish education and Jewish continuity, along with other local issues, have emerged as community priorities. It is also the case in Israel, where for some the sense of being "Israeli" has overwhelmed what it means to be Jewish, where attitudes triggered by classic Zionism's rejection of the Diaspora may have left a residue, and where, as a recent study has shown, the schools teach hardly anything at all about Diaspora Jewry and its vibrant communities.

Such a separation is bad for both of us. And if the situation is not addressed, things are likely to get even worse, especially given the fact that the younger generations from both sectors lack the personal memories that helped forge a common bond linking previous generations.

This is not to say that Israel and world Jewry have become totally detached from each other. In many ways it is precisely the Jewish Federations throughout North America that have most effectively advanced the functional Zionism of our time. They have established a range of projects and programs that have made personal connections between Americans and Israelis possible and have enabled us to perceive one another through a realistic, human lens while demonstrating that it is precisely through direct experiences in Israel that Jewish identity can be powerfully spurred in American Jewish youth. At the same time, many Israelis are increasingly recognizing that their ignorance and disconnect from Diaspora Jewry needs to be reversed.

But more needs to be done in both places, and the time is ripe for the framing of a vision and the forging of a program inspired by the ways the events of this past summer have resonated. Such an endeavor could meaningfully strengthen the sense of Jewish peoplehood in today's world, with Israel appropriately at the core, but with mutual familiarity and appreciation defining the relationship.

If the General Assembly beginning today can help bring that about, it will indeed be a watershed event.

Spreading the Word on Jewish Peoplehood

The Jewish Week, November 21, 2007

Reprinted in Peoplehood: A Sense of Belonging to a People
The Peoplehood Papers #2. Beit Hatfutsot,
Tel Aviv (Spring 2008), 9-11.

• • •

The subject of Jewish peoplehood is in the air, with attention now focused on what practical steps might be taken to ensure the continuity of the Jewish people at a time when that continuity is challenged by a number of factors. Those factors include high levels of assimilation, low birth rates and small numbers to start with.

Surely this is important work. All the same, at least as important is the development of an informed analysis, and, as the times seem to require, an articulate defense and appreciation of the concept of Jewish peoplehood.

This is a complex matter. The very idea of peoplehood — a unique and unfamiliar concept — is regarded by some as smacking of a narrow particularism that runs up against the fashionable universalism of the age. In the eyes of those who question its acceptability, the idea is associated with a primary evil of our time, racism. When linked to Zionist ideology, the concept of Jewish peoplehood is accused of being especially abhorrent and retrograde by post-nationalists who dominate much of the European intellectual scene and have a presence on American — and even Israeli — campuses.

Based in part on the biblical reference to a "chosen people," the religious dimension of Jewish peoplehood is made problematic when it is regarded as a selfish and unfair sense of superiority, an interpretation that has contributed to anti-Semitic stereotyping for centuries. Meanwhile, though at odds with the historic experiences and traditional beliefs of the Jewish people and both misleading and dangerous in its way, the contra-peoplehood notion that Judaism is merely a religion like any other religion and should see itself and be seen by others solely in that fashion is something that some might consider a natural formulation in today's world.

These challenges make it all the more difficult but also all the more essential to create a positive, informed study of Jewish peoplehood and to spread the word. Such an approach would help Jews — both in the Diaspora and in Israel —better understand the ties that bring them together, ties that are increasingly important in today's world. It would also help create a moral and intellectual bulwark against those who deny the legitimacy of the State of Israel, the practical expression of Jewish peoplehood today.

A project of this sort would call for research and an examination of ideas from biblical times through the modern era and for the framing of an argument regarding Jewish peoplehood that counters the postmodern challenges to the concept. Such an approach would show how the concept of Jewish peoplehood is rooted in the biblical text that describes how Jews first came together and conceived of themselves as a people while enslaved in the land of Egypt.

As the narrative continues, the Children of Israel, liberated and led by Moses, made their way to Mount Sinai, where they were "chosen" to keep God's commandments. After wending their way to the Promised Land, it was as a people that the Jews established sovereignty in that land, and as a people that they were exiled from it. In Babylon, they were strangers in a strange land once more and they remembered and yearned for Zion. After returning, they subsequently faced exile once more, this time for centuries.

The kind of approach I am thinking of would move from biblical narrative to historical review and show how it was as a people that, during the post-exile centuries, the Jews suffered persecution and faced genocide; as a people that they continued to recall the exhilaration of the exodus from Egypt and the glories of Jerusalem; and as a people that, inspired by Zionist ideology, they returned to the ancient land of their people, re-established sovereignty, and re-entered the history of nations. Finally, it is as a people that the Jews of the world retain and reinvigorate their sense of connection and the ties that bind them to one another.

There is of course much more to the story of the Jews. But in its basic form it is the story of a people — a people with the charge of being a light unto the nations, and a people striving to understand and shape its destiny in the contemporary world. It is a story that today bears telling and study if the steps being advanced to attempt to ensure Jewish continuity are to have a true and lasting impact.

Innovation and Tradition:
Finding the Middle Ground

The Jewish Week, May 15, 2012

• • •

An unfortunate local controversy involving the Jewish Federation of Metropolitan Chicago and the former leadership of the Newberger Hillel at the University of Chicago has attracted widespread attention. Some of the commentary has cast the issue as setting a stodgy, anachronistic establishment up against creative, exciting innovation ("Are We Overly Invested in Bricks and Mortar?" Editor's column, May 4). That formula is off the mark in this case, and it is a problematic way to look at communal dynamics in any event.

Chicago's federation is probably one of the most innovative institutions of its kind, with a long list of examples available to demonstrate that fact, especially in the areas of Jewish identity, community building and connection to Israel. Further, the federation has embraced the kinds of innovations that have been introduced at the Newberger Hillel while generously funding such breakthrough programs as Birthright Israel there and on other Illinois campuses.

These realities aside, it is important to stress that an either/or template that pits traditional institutions against innovative outsiders is a misleading oversimplification that leads to behavior detrimental to the well-being of the Jewish community.

To be an institution like a federation (or, let us say, a synagogue) does not necessarily mean being stuck in an old-fashioned, archaic framework. Institutions can and do change. In fact, if they do not change, they run the risk of becoming petrified and irrelevant. However, while adaptation may be a virtue and often is a necessary trait for maintaining continued relevance, and while we may feel that we are living in a rapidly changing world (a condition felt by citizens of the industrialized West for at least the last 200 years), there is much of value to be retained in the structure, methods and agendas of institutions that have proved their importance and centrality over time.

These are institutions that have helped individual Jews to lead meaningful lives enriched by the defining attributes of Jewish existence and to build strong communities rooted in Jewish values and the concept of Jewish peoplehood. Rather than weighing us down, such institutions have served as bulwarks against the vicissitudes of a changing, sometimes threatening world. While innovation and creativity are positive values in their own right, and while these days being a "change agent" is especially admired and encouraged, change merely for the sake of change is a questionable approach, calling to mind the old aphorism about throwing out the baby with the bath water.

And there is something else at stake in seeing Jewish institutional life via a zero sum lens, an approach that reflects and leads to the type of toxic thinking and rhetoric that is all too common in today's national political discourse. It is a polarizing approach, an approach that says my way or the highway, that I am right and you are wrong, and that there is no middle ground. Such polarization is harmful to the well-being of the Jewish community. And in fact, such choices do not have to be made. The best approach — in both the short term and the long term — lies in avoiding the extremes and embracing an effective synthesis.

Not all institutions from the past remain vital, of course, and those that have failed to evolve and no longer serve contemporary needs are indeed likely to fade away. Similarly, to secure a meaningful future the community needs to embrace fresh voices and fresh ways of seeing and doing things. Creative steps, and the people who take and advance them, need to be encouraged and welcomed.

But above all, we need to find ways to reconcile these two approaches, to let all flowers bloom. We need to support time-tested institutions that have sustained their ability to serve the community as well as new ways of doing things. We need to avoid automatically concluding that what has been around is bad and what is new is good — or vice versa. Instead, we need to find a way to merge what is good from the past with what is good in the present in order to ensure a strong and positive future for our community and our people.

Here in Chicago, as we work our way through current issues, leaders of this federation will continue to keep our eyes on the big picture, and we urge others in the national community to do so as well. And as thought leaders and commentators analyze these dynamics, let us hope that, instead of rooting for the survival of the most fashionable in a fight to the finish between the two poles of the organizational dialectic, they will demonstrate understanding of the need to move forward in a way that maintains a strong community — a community that is respectful of differences and alternative ways of doing things but at the same time is held together by a sense of a common past, common traditions, basic values and a shared destiny.

A Call to Forge a Zionist Narrative for Our Time
The Times of Israel, August 23, 2012

• • •

One hundred and ten years since Herzl's *Altneuland* was published, nearly 65 years since the founding of the modern State of Israel fulfilled its key prophecy, and some two decades since the notion of post-Zionism became fashionable, Zionist ideas are getting a new look in locales ranging from think tanks to education centers to the halls of academia. With Zionist concepts regarded as having continuing valence despite the fact that Israel has long since been established, and with the word "Zionism" being assertively kept in play despite the hostile bad-mouthing it has received in some quarters, the meaning and relevance of Zionism today is being studied and advanced. While much of this work is theoretical, there is practical application to be promoted as well.

Most simply, the basic Zionist concept enunciating the right of the Jewish people to national self-determination in their historic homeland merits being understood, if young Jews, and the world at large, are to understand what Israel is about and what makes it tick. This is especially the case at a time when the classic Zionist narrative that attached Jews to Israel and galvanized the world has lost much of its punch, and when the conditions that made the Zionist dream an imperative have faded into the mists of a history not widely known or cared about. With post-nation-alist, universalist concepts holding sway in many intellectual quarters, especially in Europe and much of the American university environment, and with Israel's enemies mounting a full-scale campaign denying Israel's right to exist, the need for giving Zionism an effective hearing becomes all the more important.

The terms of abuse that are currently attached to Israel and its Zionist underpinnings are not entirely original. They in part build on the United Nations' notorious "Zionism is racism" resolution of 1975. Today, however, joined with "apartheid" charges and Nazi analogies, the calumny at the core of that slogan has been incorporated into a wide-ranging, sometimes-blatant assault on Israel's very legitimacy.

With Israel's existence as a modern country based on a foundational idea, it is no wonder that, as Member of Knesset Einat Wilf has observed, the delegitimization of Israel would begin with the undermining of that idea. It is thus appropriate for today's scholarly and education-based considerations of the framing of a Zionism that is relevant for the 21st century to be joined by an approach with more operational purposes as well.

What is needed, I would posit, is the development and advancement of a Zionism for our times, a Zionism that is at once authentic, honest, and contemporary. By "authentic" I mean true to foundational Zionist principles. By "honest" I mean open to facts and complexities of a sort that earlier generations may have been unaware of or minimized. And by "contemporary" I mean reflecting the vibrancy, democratic ethos and diversity of today's Israel, rendered in a voice and idiom that speak to today's generations in a compelling fashion.

In today's postmodern world of narratives, it is necessary for this Zionism to be rendered both through discourse that sustains intellectual rigor and through a cogent, gripping narrative that captures the imagination with language and imagery that speak to the mind and the heart. Herzl knew the value of narrative in projecting his vision through what Shlomo Avineri has called "his great non-utopian novel," and writers like Leon Uris and Meyer Levin rendered the story of the establishment of the state through narrative as well. The time has come to dedicate attention to the framing of something in its way comparable for our time, however relatively humble in scale it may be and however vague the result may seem right now.

The ultimate purpose for approaching contemporary Zionism in this way now is to advance understanding of the basis of Israel's existence and to enhance a sense of personal connection with the state and its people. The practical goal of the exercise I am calling for is to rebut the mendacious, all-too-common demonization of Israel as an evil colonial power and of Zionism as a racist ideology, and to counter the misleading Palestinian narrative that is used to attract adherents to the delegitimization cause.

This isn't a simple matter, and the work I am talking about should both complement and benefit from the other contemporary work on Zionism that I referenced at the opening of this piece. But given the challenges that Israel faces from those with an ideological antipathy to Zionism and an abiding hatred for Israel as the nation-state of the Jewish people, it is work of the highest significance.

Reflections on Literature, Film, and Drama: Roth, Bellow, and Others

This section is made up of reviews and articles about books, plays, films, and authors. In all of those pieces, Jewish themes resonate in one way or another. The selections are presented in the order in which they were published except for the two pieces about Philip Roth, which appear together at the opening of the section, and the penultimate piece, which appears there for reasons explained in the overall Introduction.

There are personal and local angles in a number of these pieces, including the final one, which focuses on a work by Meyer Levin, a writer who was born, grew up, and began his career in Chicago. In a number of ways that article – which, as I write this, is awaiting its publication in Hebrew translation in an Israeli journal – serves as a sort of coda for the book as a whole, recapitulating several of its basic themes.

Looking at Roth Looking at Roth

JUF News, March 1989

• • •

Philip Roth's latest book, *The Facts: A Novelist's Autobiography*, (Farrar, Straus & Giroux, 1988), shows how far he has come, though the change is not as surprising as some might think.

It is a personal work and so invites a personal reaction. I first heard of Roth shortly after I entered the University of Chicago in February, 1959, when some older students said they had had him as a freshman English teacher a year or two before. I mentioned that to Roth late last summer, when I had the unexpected pleasure of meeting him. When I implied regret that I hadn't had that earlier classroom opportunity, he responded, "You didn't miss anything." Perhaps not. But for someone who grew up in West Rogers Park, even second-hand proximity to a soon-to-be-famous writer from a not-altogether-different background had been something special.

I remember with utter clarity the day a campus friend excitedly proclaimed that Roth's *Goodbye Columbus* had just won the National Book Award for fiction. Preparing to write this article, I opened up my copy of that book and discovered that I had saved the article from the *Sun-Times* of March 23, 1960, which reported on the award. In the yellowed clipping, Roth is described as "an alumnus of the University of Chicago and, at 27, the youngest author ever to win the award."

According to the judges, the novella and five short stories which comprise *Goodbye Columbus* depicted "with exhilarating freshness various aspects of American Jewish life in transition." But while Roth's literary gifts were winning him this early honor, his book's slashing treatment of materialistic nouveau-middle class Jews, often uncomfortable in their Jewishness, was winning him the enmity of a considerable segment of the Jewish community.

The chapter in *The Facts* called "All in the Family" focuses on this period in Roth's life, when he was accused "of being anti-Semitic and self-hating." He recounts an evening in 1962, when he spoke at Yeshiva University and members of the audience expressed deep hostility. "I realized that I was not just opposed but hated," Roth observes. In recent years, because of my professional role but also because of the greater awareness I have obtained, I have had frequent occasions to speak out against the dangers of perpetuating negative stereotypes of Jews and others – even when that stereotyping is done, as Roth has asserted, without malicious intent. I must confess, however, that as a youthful reader, I myself was more entertained than offended by Philip Roth, the *enfante terrible.*

I graduated from the U of C in 1962, the year of the Yeshiva University showdown when, in the words which end "All in the Family," Roth was "branded." Going elsewhere to do graduate work in English Literature, I found my literary interests headed into another century and another country. I didn't, however, leave Roth entirely behind. I remember reading what was to become one of the chapters in *Portnoy's Complaint* in *Partisan Review,* and my bookshelves continue to hold the April 1968 issue of *The New American Review* which contains "Civilization and its Discontents," another section-to-be of that scandalous novel.

By the time *Portnoy's Complaint* came out in book form, I was living and teaching in Israel – and, in fact, the edition of that book that I own is the one printed in England, which I remember purchasing in Steinmatsky's in downtown Tel-Aviv. Again there may have been extenuating circumstances which colored my "Jewish judgment" of this major work from Roth's early period, but here, too, I was more amused than disturbed. Indeed, reading the book, I was inclined to think (or perhaps wanted to think) that what Roth was belittling was not Jewishness but a form of American Jewish life – that it was the main character, not the author of the book, who was expressing "Jewish self-hate." I even wondered if *Portnoy's Complaint* could be regarded as a sort of "Zionist novel," with Portnoy's illness a product of his Diaspora condition and with the scenes set in Israel near the end of the book as perhaps opening the way to health and self-realization for Portnoy.

The possibility that Roth was somehow portraying ties with Israel as necessary for positive Jewish existence struck me again when I re-read "Eli, the Fanatic," one of the stories in *Goodbye Columbus.*

"Eli" revolves around the rattled reaction of middle-class suburban Jews to the opening of a yeshiva for Holocaust-surviving children on the outskirts of their community. Making matters even worse, the bearded, black-garbed teacher from the school has begun coming into town to make purchases. Eli Peck, an attorney, is selected to solve the problem. Unable to induce the headmaster to leave town, Eli decides to get the teacher to wear ordinary clothes, and sends him some of his own. To an extent that works, except that Eli, who has cracked up before and whose wife is about to give birth, has what his neighbors regard as a nervous breakdown. That's what they think when he starts to wear the clothes that the teacher discarded when Eli sent his own over, as Eli symbolically changes places with him.

Reading the story from an Israeli perspective, I saw in it a subtext which may or may not have been intended. When Eli comes home from his first meeting with the headmaster of the school, he sees a note from his wife and reflects that "scribblings on bits of paper had made history this past week." The period in question, the text tells us elsewhere, was the second week of May 1948 – which as it happens was when, in the midst of heavy fighting, the British mandate over Palestine was terminated, the state of Israel was proclaimed in a declaration signed by leaders of the new state and read by David Ben-Gurion, and the United States government recognized Israel.

Shortly after putting on the teacher's clothes, Eli imagines a phone conversation with a neighbor who says, "Eli, there's a Jew at your door." To which he answers, "That's me." Eli's ultimate fate is, at best, ambiguous. But if my sense of the subtext of the story is correct, then "Eli, the Fanatic" is not only mocking the empty, assimilated Jews of Woodenton for cutting themselves off from their past and its traditions; it is also indicting them for being oblivious to the emblem of Jewish rebirth in the post-Holocaust age and to a crucial source for Jewish vitality and identity in the future – the newly-established State of Israel.

In *The Facts,* after recounting the period of Portnoy's Complaint, Roth leaps forward to the present. For the purposes of this piece so can we, to see that Eli Peck is, in effect, reborn as Henry Zuckerman in *The Counterlife* (1986), Roth's most recent novel.

In a recent essay in the *New York Times* Book Review, Theodore Solotaroff describes Roth as one of a group of "American-Jewish writers on the edge once more." Saying that most of the authors who produced a flowering of American-Jewish literature in the 1960s have left behind the "marginality" which gave power to their work, becoming more American than Jewish, Solotaroff observes that "an unprecedented development in Jewish life is [now] creating a different kind of marginality. If Jewish leaders like Arthur Hertzberg and writers like Philip Roth are correct, and I think they are on to something very important, the new and increasingly tense margin of Jewish seriousness and conscience lies in the preoccupation with Israel."

Later in his essay, Solotaroff asserts that "as Philip Roth has shown in the brilliant second chapter of 'The Counterlife,' Israel is our counterlife." Solotaroff's reading of Roth dovetails with mine, and his enthusiastic praise for *The Counterlife* captures what I, too, felt when I read that novel while on a trip to Israel last year. It struck me as a virtuoso performance, dazzling in its treatment of the nature of Jewish identity, including the relationship of American Jews to Israel.

And now, with its touching and moving portrayal of a Jewish boy's relationships with his parents and community, comes *The Facts*, tenderly and beautifully evoking the very Jewish values which the early Roth was often seen as viciously belittling. The book provides a very different view of what it was like for a Jewish boy to come of age in the 1950s than the shocking satire one associates with Roth.

Roth himself clearly is conscious of all the contrast between the image of his earlier work and the tone of this recent text, and of the skepticism which that contrast might invite. Before a reader can finish the book and object that Roth is merely trying to give his "Jewish readers...what they've wanted to hear from you for three decades," Roth provides a final chapter to *The Facts* in which his fictional alter-ego, Nathan Zuckerman, makes those very charges.

The fact (in this realm of "facts") seems to be that while the current Roth must have been at least some part of the early one, and while aspects of the early Roth no doubt remain part of the current one, Philip Roth has earned the right to be regarded not as a hostile critic but as a sympathetic examiner of the Jewish condition. We should not be overly sentimental about the author of *The Facts,* but neither should we be overly cynical about his sincerity. The time has come to go beyond the stance of the writer of a recent article who, looking for a shorthand way to criticize Mike Wallace for a *60 Minutes* segment "bashing American Jewish support of Israel," calls Wallace "the Philip Roth of the airwaves."

Indeed, to appropriate the title of another one of Roth's early stories, he has become a veritable "defender of the faith," sensitive to anti-Semitism and going public to expose the irony of a portrayal of Franz Kafka as a German writer, not a Jew. In fact, over the years Roth's sense of himself seems to have drawn him closer to writers like Kafka and the Israeli novelist Aharon Appelfeld, each of whom came from a European assimilationist origin and moved toward greater Jewish self-identification.

Some uncanny similarities between Roth and Appelfeld can be seen in a "Talk with Aharon Appelfeld," a fascinating article written by Roth for the *New York Times* Book Review section last year. "It took me years to draw close to the Jew within me," Appelfeld, a Holocaust survivor, is quoted as saying. "I had to get rid of many prejudices within me and to meet many Jews in order to find myself in them. Anti-Semitism directed at oneself was an original Jewish creation...the Jewish ability to internalize any critical and condemnatory remark and castigate themselves is one of the marvels of human nature." Roth, whose fiction and whose fictionalized treatment of the facts of life derive so much of their dynamism, impact, and meaning from uses of the doppelganger (one's otherself), seems to find reflections of his own Jewish self in Appelfeld, the Holocaust-surviving, Israeli novelist.

A former *enfante terrible* and thorn in the side of his people, Roth, always gifted, now stands as one of the most important Jewish writers of our time. And whereas his puncturing satire emerged when the American Jewish community was relatively complacent, his current work appears while we, like him, are self-consciously struggling to answer the question of who we are.

The Plot Against America

JUF News, February 2005

• • •

As one of America's premier novelists for over four decades, Philip Roth has frequently touched on Jewish subjects. In his 1993 novel *Operation Shylock,* he put into the mouth of one of his characters a description of the global condition now often referred to as the new anti-Semitism. In the modern world, the character says, "the Jew has been perpetually on trial; still today the Jew is on trial, in the person of the Israeli." In this new novel Roth goes back in time to present a manifestation of the old anti-Semitism, imagining what might have happened had the isolationist celebrity pilot Charles Lindbergh been elected president in 1940.

It is an anti-Semitism in which Jews are scapegoated by Lindbergh and others for supposedly wanting to take America into war only to further their own tribal interests, and in which they are discriminated against by a hotel keeper in Washington D.C.. It is the genteel anti-Semitism of the white Anglo-Saxon Protestant power elite as well as the aggressive, populist anti-Semitism of the radio priest Father Coughlin; and it is the conspiracy-minded anti-Semitism of the industrialist Henry Ford, who in real life reprinted *The Protocols of the Learned Elders of Zion* and in this book is named secretary of the interior in Lindbergh's Cabinet.

The novel involves a public story describing how the condition of America's Jews increasingly worsens as Lindbergh brings Nazi-like policies to America while keeping the country out of the war with Germany. The radio commentator Walter Winchell exposes Lindbergh on the air and opposes him politically, and his own presidential campaign triggers anti-Semitic violence, which escalates after Winchell himself is assassinated by Nazi and Ku Klux Klan thugs. There is a further turn in the plot which makes matters still worse before precipitating the denouement that returns American life to the path it had been following.

Readers learn about all of this from the remembrances of a narrator who at the time was a child growing up in Newark, New Jersey. This makes the book not just a story about what would have happened had it happened, but also one about what things would have been like for a little Jewish boy had it happened. While positing an imagined set of circumstances embedded in an historic framework, the book projects a strong sense of the everyday reality of Jewish life in America at that time, rendering the nature of the people, of the social conditions in which they lived, of the impact of their immigrant origins, and of the way in which their Jewish identity was a given. Describing the Lindbergh years, the Philip Roth who narrates this book has much to say about their effect on his parents, his older brother, his cousin, his aunt, a friend, his neighbor downstairs, and others, and about their interactions with one another.

Writing in the *New York Times* Book Review section, Paul Berman has described ways that Sinclair Lewis's *It Can't Happen Here* and Nathanael West's *A Cool Million,* both written in the 1930s, prefigured this book's public narrative. I believe there are important precursors for the private narrative as well, such as works of Aharon Appelfeld, the Holocaust survivor and Israeli novelist to whom Roth has been connected in a number of ways, and even, though it may at first seem unlikely, Charles Dickens's David Copperfield.

Like Appelfeld and Dickens, Roth offers a first-person narrative in which a small boy faces childhood trauma. One difference is that both Appefeld and Dickens were presenting novelistic treatments of their own personal traumas, whereas for Roth, though the main character bears his own name, the trauma is imagined, like the swastika that his character dreams appears on the images of the national parks in his stamp collection. Furthermore, the Philip Roth in the novel does not himself suffer the worst of the childhood traumas encountered within it; that fate is reserved for his neighbor and sometimes double (whose clothes Philip wears when, like the young David Copperfield, he runs away from home).

There is as much power in this personal narrative as there is in the public one, and there are a number of places where they intersect — for example, when the unctuously egotistical rabbi who supports Lindbergh ends up marrying a sister of the fictional Philip Roth's mother. The novel's narrative proceeds with many digressions as Roth creates the texture of a living world filled with a range of individuals with their own passions and attributes. As Roth's dense periodic sentences keep us waiting to learn where they are headed and as they surprise us along the way, they replicate the structure of this novel and mirror its deepest insight into the affairs of humankind and the workings of history.

In a key passage in the book, the narrator says, "A new life began for me. I'd watched my father fall apart, and I would never return to the same childhood." That happened, he goes on to say, "because he was powerless to stop the unforeseen." And then he adds, "And as Lindbergh's election couldn't have made clearer to me, the unfolding of the unforeseen was everything. Turned wrong way round, the relentless unforeseen was what we school children studied as 'History,' harmless history, where everything unexpected in its own time is chronicled on the page as inevitable. The terror of the unforeseen is what the science of history hides, turning a disaster into an epic."

Besides reflecting the arcs of both the public and personal plots of this novel, that passage's take on reality has contemporary resonance as well. So today, post-9/11, there is a strong sense that what is unforeseen is lurking around the next corner. As Paul Berman pointed out in his *New York Times* review, as in the world of this novel, Jews have been blamed for supposedly propelling America into war only to satisfy their own tribal interests. And as in the world of the novel, so today there is a plot against America, this time coming from the radical Islamist perpetrators of 9/11, people with an animus not only against America but also against Jews.

In its opening sentence, the novel says, "Fear presides over these memories, a perpetual fear." Its final chapter is similarly titled "Perpetual Fear." Reversing the motto of post-Holocaust commitment to steadfastness, "Never Again," the central chapter of the novel is labeled "Never Before." As in the world of the novel, in today's world, Americans in general, and Jews in particular, must cope with the challenge of living in perpetual fear.

Dark as Roth's vision is, the developing stages of anti-Jewish behavior that he imagines having taken place in America are less malignant than what indeed happened in Germany under Hitler. With its strong democratic base and ingrained sense of tolerance, America is shown to have individuals ranging from public officials to humble Italian immigrants to Kentucky farmers ready to befriend and protect their Jewish citizens, neighbors and friends. What's more, Jews are considerably more accepted and secure in America today than they were in the 1940s.

Still, the close of the novel is disquieting. Though the Lindbergh era ends and America is spared a full-scale Holocaust, there is more of a sense of relief than a triumphant climax. Perhaps that is because in the real world the war against Hitler continued, with the full facts of what the Nazis and their henchmen did to the Jews of Europe remaining to be learned. In the personal narrative, while each of Philip's parents acts heroically to rescue their former neighbor, now an orphan and petrified with fear, and to bring him back from Kentucky despite the worst of the anti-Semitic violence, the impact of his shocked bewilderment and awful loss lingers.

The Plot Against America is richly rewarding as a reading experience, brilliantly written, utterly engrossing, touching in its personal portrayals, and wise in its perspectives. Yet it is also unsettling, not only in its view of what might have been the condition of Jewish life in America in the 1940s had history taken a different turn, but also in its implied sense of what the prevailing conditions are for Americans and Jews in the early years of the 21st century.

Lessons for Jews from the Rushdie Affair

JUF News, April 1989

• • •

If all the articles that have been written about the controversy surrounding Salman Rushdie's *The Satanic Verses* were published together, they
well might produce a book longer than the novel itself, and it is no thin
volume. Threaten authors with a denial of free expression and you're
looking for trouble.

Or so it would seem. Actually, however, it took the world's writers a while to get geared up when Rushdie's freedom of expression was
challenged and then a price put on his head. And that is only one of the
paradoxes and points of interest which have revealed themselves as the
Rushdie controversy has taken one turn after another over the past several
weeks.

For one thing, the first place in which *The Satanic Verses* was burned
for allegedly blaspheming Islam was not the Indian subcontinent or the
Middle East, as one might have expected, but the town of Bradford,
England – where Rushdie's Muslim fellow-immigrants from Pakistan
and India put the torch to it.

The event which first set off major alarm bells in America did,
however, take place in the Eastern part of the world, when a mob of
Pakistanis stormed the American Embassy in Karachi, presumably because of the forthcoming publication of the book in the United States.
Speaking of ironies, that happened to occur only a short time after the
U.S. State Department had criticized Israel for its response to the intifada.
But there was no censure of the Pakistanis who protected the embassy
against the stone throwers by shooting and killing some of them, no mention of a denial of human rights in this case.

Knowing a good thing when he sees it, Iran's Ayatollah Khomeini
entered the picture shortly thereafter to offer a multi-million dollar reward
for the murder of Rushdie, regarded by the Ayatollah and his followers as
an offender against Islam. That the Ayatollah, as well as the motivators
of the Pakistani mob, may have had political purposes for stirring up their
followers and promoting hostility against the West has not gone unno-
ticed. What has, I believe, been unmentioned is the fact that many of the

people crying out against a perceived insult to their religious sensibilities live in a part of the world where, even after the Holocaust, a printed work as vicious in its stimulation of religious bigotry as the notorious anti-Semitic forgery known as *The Protocols of the Learned Elders of Zion* has been widely published and disseminated.

It has been pointed out that in his book Rushdie disparages not only Muslims but the English, too – and that he has ironically been protected from the Ayatollah's threats by representatives of the very government he has criticized. As I write this, however, a British spokesman has observed that the book is unfriendly to his country as well, and the relationship between Rushdie and his protectors has gotten complicated.

The lineup of forces on this issue is interesting in a number of ways. One of the earliest and most powerful defenders of Rushdie was Christopher Hitchens, who, it has been pointed out, wrote an earlier article insisting that terrorism (which the Ayatollah certainly seems to be practicing) is merely "a cliché in search of a meaning." More recently, other writers throughout the world have come out en masse in support of Rushdie's (and their own) freedom of expression, outraged by the death threat against him and concerned with the implied challenge to the continued publication and sale of all books without obstacle.

One exception has been Roald Dahl, the English author best known in this country for books for young readers such as *Charlie and the Chocolate Factory.* Dahl has said, in effect, that Rushdie was asking for it. As it happens, Dahl is the fellow who five-and-a-half years ago was cited by the British writer Paul Johnson as producing "the most disgraceful item to appear in a respectable British publication for a long time." The work in question was an anti-Israel diatribe with an anti-Semitic stench, which was followed by an interview in which Dahl asserted that Jews were "cowards" in World War II and that, "even a stinker like Hitler didn't just pick on them for no reason."

Somehow, given that record, Dahl's current posture is not entirely surprising. At the same time, some conservative Christian religious spokesmen in this country have taken positions different from what might have been expected. Though members of that community only last summer were vociferously agitating against the movie *The Last Temptation of Christ* (with some of them stimulating anti-Semitism as they did so), they now wish to emphasize that nobody then put a "hit" on anybody, and they have come out strongly in condemnation of the violent threats made against Rushdie.

On the other hand, liberal Christian leaders, who might have been expected to place an emphasis on the protection of freedom of speech, have, instead, been more concerned with the need to understand and respect the hurt feelings of Muslims outraged by *The Satanic Verses*. An example of this point of view can be found in an opinion column by former President Jimmy Carter which appeared in *The New York Times* under the headline, "Rushdie's book is an insult." Bearing the sub-heading, "The cultural wound is difficult to heal," the article makes a distinction between Iranian fundamentalists and "most other Muslims." The fact that violent opposition to Rushdie has been endorsed by Muslims ranging from those in Bangkok, Thailand, who burned him in effigy, to Yusuf Islam, the former English singer Cat Stevens, does not necessarily contradict the observation that what is being expressed is alien to the beliefs and practices of most Muslims and to the true spirit of Islam. At the same time, however, it is abundantly clear that this is not merely a localized Iranian phenomenon.

Not to be kept out of things, the Soviets, benefitting from the timing of a visit to the Middle East by Foreign Minister Eduard A. Shevardnadze and perhaps seeing an opportunity too good to pass up, have attempted to set themselves up as middlemen. They have kept silent on the mobsterism of the Ayatollah. And — providing a new example for the dictionary definition of chutzpah — Yuri V. Dubinin, the Soviet Ambassador to the U.S. and spokesman for an atheistic government hardly known for its commitment to the cause of human rights, took the high road and announced that "religious feelings" constitute "a general human right," and the Rushdie affair "is something that reflects once more the importance of respect for all general human rights."

There, of course, could hardly be any form of international crisis without a Jewish angle, and one was introduced to this controversy when, from his hiding place, Rushdie produced a review of Philip Roth's latest book *The Facts* for *The London Observer*. In his work, which is subtitled *A Novelist's Autobiography*, Roth recounts his own early career, when his book, *Goodbye Columbus* provoked an attack on him from fellow Jews offended by his treatment of them. For all of the kinship which Rushdie might feel for Roth, however, a comparison of the responses of the Jewish community then and the Islamic community now is more instructive in regard to the differences than to the similarities. Roth's life, after all, was not threatened, nor to my knowledge was his book burned.

There is a lot to learn from the Rushdie affair. For one thing, it reminds us of how close emotional fanaticism is to the surface, even in our day and age. When people talk about what's been happening as a throw-back to some era in the dim and distant past, they are forgetting that the darkest moments in human history have come in our own century, and that perhaps the premier practitioners of the art of book-burning were Adolph Hitler's Nazis.

Furthermore, to the extent that Iranian rulers and Pakistani opposition leaders have been stimulating and focusing this emotionalism in an attempt to exploit it for their own political purpose, they have been demonstrating that the availability of such a recourse to demagogues everywhere is not to be taken lightly. Recent developments have graphically shown that once this kind of passion is turned loose, consequences are unlikely to be controllable. As Jews, we know we must continue to be concerned with the potential exploitation of racist and anti-Semitic feelings for political purposes – an activity not entirely alien to politics in our own city.

By putting a bounty on the head of Salman Rushdie and by leading his followers in threatening not only Rushdie but, in effect, anybody associated with his book, including publishers and booksellers, the Ayatollah Khomeini has introduced a new mode of international terrorist intimidation. And the apparent readiness of responsible figures in the Western world to capitulate to these threats, as evidenced in those days when it looked like some bookstores would not be carrying the book and when a number of people seemed unwilling to speak out in support of Rushdie, must also stimulate our concern. The reactions of the many authors who have rigorously protested this attempt to metaphorically hijack their freedom of expression is thus understandable – but it is not only writers whose rights are threatened. Principles basic to Western civilization are under attack.

Cartoonists have had a field day with this subject, and, indeed, the Ayatollah Khomeini almost seems to be a cartoonist's creation. But he is, in fact, not a caricature at all, and the reality of what he has done and the force that he both exerts and personifies has had a shocking effect. And the virus, it seems, is spreading. One news report tells us that Wole Soyinka, the Nigerian Nobel Prize-winning author, has come under attack from Muslims in his country for his defense of Rushdie. Another report tells us that the tomb of the great Italian poet Dante has been threatened unless his *Divine Comedy,* accused of treating Mohammed blasphemously, ceases to be published.

The depth of this response to Rushdie's book reminds us that the power of the printed word is to be taken seriously. Never mind that the overwhelming majority of those passionately protesting against *The Satanic Verses* have never read it, nor that it is "only" a work of fiction, and a dense and difficult one at that. They sincerely believe that its words can do harm.

And indeed, as Jews, we, too, know that language can not only hurt in what it says, but can provoke damaging responses. Our recognition of the power of language leads us to object in our way when we are the targets, and inclines us to be sympathetic when others' beliefs are vilified or they are harmfully stereotyped. But while Jews can understand the distress of offended Muslims, most today share the general Western response which firmly rejects dealing with the problem by censoring book publication and threatening writers, publishers, book sellers, and others.

Meanwhile, as these developments have been unfolding, those who care to pay attention have been provided with a clearer image than they might previously have had of what life is like in the part of the world where the State of Israel exists. Pakistanis demonstrating against Rushdie's novel in their country and Muslims demonstrating against it in New York have held up signs baselessly charging "Zionist" collusion in the original publication of the book. Ahmed Jibril, chief of the Popular Front for the Liberation of Palestine-General Command, a terrorist group linked with the Syrians, has reportedly jumped at the Ayatollah's offer and dispatched his followers to take care of Rushdie.

Islamic fundamentalists in the Gaza Strip were a major force behind the inception of the intifada there. And, in recent years, there has been a Muslim revival throughout the Middle East. Surely it is important to distinguish between Ayatollah Khomeini and his followers and other Muslims. But the power of a leader like the Ayatollah, and the possible pull of anti-Western hostility in the Islamic world demonstrated by the Rushdie affair, cannot be disputed. They render a reality which the Israelis must take acute cognizance of as they determine what kinds of risks they can take in making arrangements for a secure future.

The Rushdie affair, a tale almost too bizarre to have been imagined by the most creative of authors, thus plays itself out on the world stage – full of sound and fury, signifying much.

European Films Look Back at Nazi Era

JUF News, November 1992

• • •

While the collapse of Communism has been described as marking "the end of history," another way to look at it is a return to history – to unfinished business which characterized Eastern European affairs before the Communist era. Most notable has been a return to the expression of nationalist feelings, which in some instances, particularly in the former Yugoslavia and parts of the former Soviet Union, has involved conflict and even bloody violence.

Not unrelated to the resurgence of nationalist sentiment has been a resurfacing of anti-Semitism, a virulent disease of the continent controlled from the top by Communist regimes which used it when convenient. During the Communist decades, anti-Semitic feelings were often sustained in a relatively latent form among the populace below, where they are now being revived even as current governments strive to institute greater democracy and pluralism. Ironically, some of the countries where these developments are being played out have few remaining Jews, a result of the Holocaust which itself has never been fully come to grips with in most of the lands where it occurred.

This background is central to a number of fascinating and powerful recent European films.

Rediscovery of European culture's lost Jewish component is the indirect subject of the Czech film *Labyrinth*, which was shown at Spertus College in September. It tells the story of a German played by Maximilian Schell who goes to Prague to make a movie about Franz Kafka and finds that the key to understanding the author whose family members were murdered by the Nazis and whose books were banned by the Communists has to do with his Jewishness. Along the way, the Schell character learns about a medieval pogrom, about the Golem of Prague and the rabbi who created it, and more.

Discoveries of another kind are made by the central character in *Nasty Girl,* directed by Michael Verhoeven and released in 1990. She is a German student who selects as an essay topic the question of what her fellow villagers were doing during the war and who draws some shocking conclusions as to who collaborated with the Nazis. As her research efforts are sabotaged, as she and her family suffer vicious harassment, and as her conclusions are denied, the ongoing relevance of her quest becomes clear. The society we are shown is one in which the truth about awful deeds committed in the past lies buried, and in which villains are free and respected while justice remains undone.

Zentropa, a nightmarish 1991 film directed by Lars von Trier and set in post-war Germany, also suggests that the moral lessons of that period remain unlearned. This time, it is an American of German extraction, a variant on the classic "innocent abroad," who learns that Nazism remains alive and that unreconstructed Nazis retain positions of power – and also that naïve Americans may be guilty of complicity.

The original title of *Zentropa* was *Europa*, implying a broader and perhaps contemporary application of the film's point. Seen this way, *Zentropa* can be taken as a warning of the potential danger posed by a reunited Germany in today's Europe and commentary on America's responsibility for ensuring an avoidance of tragic results once more.

The reported reason for changing the film's title for its release in the U.S. was that it might have been confused with *Europa, Europa*, a popular film of the previous year which was set during the Holocaust. Directed by Agnieszka Holland, this is a story not of the discovery of facts pertaining to the Jewish experience in Europe by a non-Jew but of survival in that world by a Jewish boy. Incredibly enough, he remains alive by disguising himself as a Christian, even training with the Hitler Youth.

The doubling of the film's title resonates through much of it. The main character has two selves, one inner, one outer. He lives through the two ideologies which decimated so much of Europe this century – Communism and Nazism. There is the Europe of Christians and the Europe of Jews. There is the Europe of those who persecuted the Jews and the Europe of those who showed sympathy to the main character even when they realized he was Jewish, enabling him to survive.

While itself pointing toward Europe of the past, *Europa, Europa* prompts the question of what form the Europe of the future will take. A troubling possibility was suggested by the controversial fact that despite the film's popularity and support for it by a long and impressive list of Germans in the industry, the German film board failed to nominate it for an Academy Award. This prompted some to suggest that contemporary Germany, as if treating this film itself as a Nasty Girl of sorts, preferred not to acknowledge painful facts of the country's past.

In the last two months much notice has been given to the anti-refugee violence taking place in Germany, mainly in eastern sectors. Young toughs have taken to the streets flaunting the Nazi salute. In this time of social upheaval and economic distress, immigrants and not Jews are the visible scapegoats. There are few Jews left. Still, as though even dead Jews cannot be tolerated, Jewish cemeteries have been vandalized. And, as if in an attempt to both imitate and erase the past, monuments to the Holocaust have been torched and burned.

The German government, though still not to the satisfaction of all, has taken notice, and large anti-Nazi crowds have demonstrated on behalf of democratic values and tolerance. The compelling question of the day in Germany and elsewhere in central and eastern Europe is, on the one hand, the extent to which the past will be acknowledged and learned from, or on the other, the extent to which it will be returned to and repeated. It is a question artfully posed by contemporary European cinema.

Rodney King Is Center Stage
in Sellars' *Merchant*
The Forward, January 13, 1995

• • •

Peter Sellars, the man who made an opera out of the murder by terrorists of an American Jewish tourist, has turned his attention to
Shakespeare with equally controversial results. Mr. Sellars, whose adaptation of *The Merchant of Venice* opened at Chicago's Goodman Theatre and
then moved to Europe for a winter run, has said he would like to make a
film of the work to get it "in every high school in America."

The play, which Mr. Sellars wants to bring before American teen-
agers, is in fact an ideologically transformed version of Shakespeare's
drama. In Mr. Sellars' hands, Shakespeare's romantic comedy becomes
ponderous and moody, with suggestions of a homosexual relationship
between Antonio and Bassanio made explicit. He has shifted the setting from Renaissance Venice to today's Venice, California, with the
Antonio/Bassanio crowd played by Latinos, Portia and Nerissa by Asian-
Americans, and Shylock, Jessica and Tubal by Africans-Americans.

By casting black actors in the Jewish roles, and in effectively de-
Judaizing those characters, Mr. Sellars offers a parable about racism in
America today that has very little to do with Shakespeare's play and almost nothing to do with the Jewish dimension of *Merchant* so central to
its importance.

Mr. Sellars has said that the idea of drawing upon the contemporary
California scene for this play came to him during the discussions that followed the Los Angeles riots. Norman Frisch, another participant in those
talks and a frequent collaborator of Mr. Sellars, is cited in the Goodman
Theatre *Stagebill,* saying, "On the national media, the riots were being
portrayed as race riots; whereas in the city, one heard the violence discussed as an economic uprising." Videotapes of the Rodney King trial
and the disorders that followed it are shown on television monitors while
the courtroom scene is in progress during this production. The implicit
point is that both Shylock and King were unable to find the justice they
deserved, and the effect is to see this Shylock as a victim not of traditional
anti-Semitism but of contemporary racism. It is thus beyond the gimmick

of casting that Mr. Sellars transforms the most archetypal model of anti-Semitic stereotyping of them all into an African-American.

According to Mr. Sellars, "Four centuries ago, at the moment that modern capitalism was being invented, Shakespeare wrote a play that remains the most astute and shockingly frank analysis of the economic roots of racism that we have." Seen this way, Shylock is neither an emblem of evil, as Jews were regarded in the era that shaped Shakespeare's perspective, nor the villain of the play. This Shylock is rendered and made sympathetic not by a meaningful understanding of anti-Semitism past or present but by an ideological approach that strips away the character's Jewishness.

Mr. Sellars seems to have a thing with well-known Jewish victims. In a 1991 opera based on the 1985 Achille Lauro hijacking, during which Palestinians terrorists brutally killed Leon Klinghoffer, a wheelchair-bound American Jewish passenger, Mr. Sellars and his collaborators dissolved apparently clear-cut distinctions. As Samuel Lipman pointed out in *Commentary,* the whole episode is treated in the opera "as a matter of moral equivalence. One need look no further for evidence of this decision than the very title of the opera: 'The Death of Klinghoffer,' rather than 'The Murder of Klinghoffer.'"

If Mr. Sellars was capable of regarding the paralyzed, elderly Klinghoffer, slaughtered and thrown over the side of the cruise ship, with compromised compassion while offering a rationalization for Klinghoffer's assassins, there should be little surprise that he now seems to have scant regard for the Jewishness of Shylock and instead casts a representative victim of a different type of bigotry in the part. As ahistorical and muddled as that makes this production of *The Merchant of Venice,* his radical-chic approach ironically calls to mind the manner in which the followers of Louis Farrakhan also would deny Jews their identity and history of victimhood in claiming that status for themselves.

Lanzmann's Newest Film Probes the Soul of the Israel Defense Forces

JUF News, January 1995

•　•　•

It is a new, five-hour long documentary by the French director Claude Lanzmann. It has an early scene in which a cemetery is visited and the headstones of the Jews buried there, all of whom died young, are focused on. It deals with other Jewish suffering as well. It contains numerous references to experiences of the Holocaust, and it is in many ways a film about Jewish survivors. It can be taken as a sequel to Lanzmann's documentary about the Holocaust, called, simply, *Shoah.* It is, as its own one word title proclaims, about *Tsahal,* the acronym formed from the first letters of the words *Tzva Haganah Leyisrael,* the Israel Defense Forces.

As he did in *Shoah,* Lanzmann organized *Tsahal* by stitching together a series of contemporary interviews conducted by himself. Some of them are complete while others are dropped for a while and then picked up later. Some of the interviews deal with events taking place at the moment, with those interviewees often participating in meaningful current action. Many of the speakers in the other interviews describe events which took place in the past, and while presenting them, Lanzmann often fills the screen with visual shots of dramatic landscapes that are an appropriate match for what the individuals are talking about. No archival film footage of incidents which took place in the past is used. This becomes, then, a film about people (some well known, some not); about the institution which is the eponymous subject of the documentary; and in many ways, above all, about the nation which those people and that institution represent.

In a "positive" film about a powerful army, one might expect a good deal of glorification of arms and the man. But as much as this indeed can be taken as a paean to the Israeli army, and as noble as the soldiers who are portrayed may turn out to be, the characteristics which are most deeply explored and the virtues which are revealed are not what one might ordinarily associate with the military way of life.

The film opens with words superimposed on the screen that present the simple thesis that it is thanks to the Israeli Defense Forces that the State of Israel has continued to exist and that movement toward peace is possible. The first sounds we hear are tapes of radio messages from an IDF unit which, it turns out, had been trapped on the banks of the Suez Canal. The noises of battle are in the background, and we later learn from the person who did the taping about the disastrous fate suffered by that unit. The earliest exchanges in the film have to do with the fear felt while in combat. We meet a scarred veteran, most of whose comrades had been wiped out in action. Another veteran recalls the death in action of his brother.

The war which Lanzmann's early interviewees recall, which comes across as a defining experience for them and, by extension, their generation if not their nation, was not one of speedy triumph. It was the Yom Kippur War of October 1973, when Israel was caught by surprise and many casualties were suffered. One speaker tells of having been on his honeymoon when that war broke out and of how he returned as quickly as possible to rejoin his unit. It had, he discovered, been decimated in warfare on the Golan Heights. His commanding officer sent him there to try to remold the survivors into a fighting force, which he says he did by starting with a speech in which he suggested that the continuing existence of the State of Israel was in effect in their hands. This episode is in many ways a microcosm of the film, with a remnant of surviving Jews rising from the valley of the shadow of death to come together to protect their homeland and give their people new life.

Like Israel itself, Lanzmann's *Tsahal* is an answer to the Shoah. It is a vehicle of Jewish survival. It is, as its name indicates, a tool of defense, whose mode of behavior is forceful but at the same time deeply humane.

This is a film in which, as the American Civil War general said, war is regarded as hell (the word hell is even used twice by soldiers to describe their experiences and once by a Holocaust survivor to describe his), but in which the warriors maintain emotional connections. The veteran (now famous) who tells of his younger brother's death in the early days of the Yom Kippur War does so by recounting how their father, who had himself been serving in the Sinai, has been ordered to return home. He was certain that that meant that one of his three soldier sons had been killed, though he didn't yet know which one it was, and for the entire journey back, we are told, — with shots of the desolate desert he traversed shown as this is recounted — he wept.

The soldier who returned from his honeymoon to rejoin his unit tells how, from abroad, he phoned his father in Israel with instructions to get in touch with his commanding officer to say he was on his way back. References to, and visual images of, family ties permeate this film. And while the speakers often talk about their comrades in arms, they never use that kind of language, even when referring to those who are of higher, or lower, rank than themselves. Always, the words are "my friends."

Tsahal is shown as regarding the lives of its soldiers as precious. Retired General Israel Tal is interviewed at great length describing the principles behind the construction of the Merkava tank which he developed, in which much was done to protect the members of the crews.

A scene involving tank exercises leads to our first view of younger Israeli soldiers, who are also shown in scenes involving would-be pilots and paratroopers. We learn of the continued dedication of the new generation as they speak of choosing the most difficult of assignments and of fulfilling their destiny through military service. They come across as focused and proud, but also as sensitive young people.

All of that, and more, is developed in the three-hour first part of the documentary. It is mesmerizing in its presentation, profoundly moving in its content. And then comes part two, which includes a portrayal of the soldiers of Tsahal in a different kind of role and which ultimately moves to political considerations and issues.

There are scenes in this section in which the interviewer joins Israeli soldiers on patrol in Gaza and in which those soldiers speak of their efforts there in response to the intifada. Self-defense includes knowing how to drive through the town and, at times, shooting at stone-throwers, as was done two days before the interview by one of the soldiers we hear from.

Military action as portrayed here includes an elaborate screening of Arabs assembling early in the morning to leave Gaza to work in Israel. It includes checking every item in the luggage of Arabs crossing the bridge from Jordan to the West Bank, including that of a well-dressed professional who, with wife and child, is on his way to visit family in Gaza. Here, the army is dealing not with unseen and unprovoked would-be murderers of Jews but with civilians in plain clothes, people who can be regarded as somewhat demeaned by the situations which are shown. The Israeli soldiers engaged in this process – in contrast, for example, to those we see in the tank exercise – are more bored than stimulated. The unstated message of the film is that this is hardly an ennobling role for the members of Tsahal.

Such a perspective is carried even further by representatives of the Israeli left, such as the author David Grossman and a lawyer (himself one of the many children of survivors interviewed in the film) who is sharply critical of the Landau Commission report which gave Israeli interrogators the right to use appropriate "pressure," which he insists is "torture." They offer explicit censure of what they see as the evils of occupation.

At the same time, however, I believe it can be said that Lanzmann himself treats the soldiers of Tsahal sympathetically here as well. Watching the scenes involving military patrols in Gaza, I found myself wishing that this was how it had been done by network television or the Public Broadcasting System in their reports on the same subject which I remembered. This film tells us that the intifada put Israeli soldiers in true danger and that the rules of engagement which directed their response were reasonable. Interviews with Israeli reservists – including academics and scientists serving reserve duty in Gaza for the first time – show Israel's citizen army in a compassionate manner. At the same time, the Landau report is defended as a judicious, realistic response to the need to protect innocent civilians from terrorist violence while maintaining civilized norms.

As the film approaches its ending Lanzmann includes an extended interview with a West Bank settler. He is shown not as a wild-eyed fanatic but as an individual whose faith tells him of his people's right to that land and who describes the Arab-Jewish conflict in a rational manner imbued with skepticism as to Arab intentions.

Lanzmann's own role in the film seems to shift at the time of this interchange, during which he becomes less of a probing interviewer and more of a challenging interlocutor. But he has clearly chosen, and is willing to show, someone who can go head-to-head with him. In the end, while there is no meeting of the minds, there is a physical embrace which makes this too seem like something within the family.

Much of the film's politically-focused discussion may seem out of place, given its proclaimed topic. Lanzmann's implied point seems to be that, albeit through no fault of its own, the role of Tsahal has been in part redefined if not eroded. He, for one, it seems, would feel more comfortable if it could return to its traditional function – best of all, if it were only needed as a contingency force for acting out that combat role in a framework of peace.

Much of the filming for *Tsahal* seems to have been done before implementation of the September 1993 Declaration of Principles began. The Gaza patrol scenes have, to a great extent, become historic and not contemporary documentary footage, while the scenes of the crossing from Jordan are probably at least partly becoming so as well. But besides providing a perspective on recent history, those scenes, along with the discussion with the settler, raise issues which continue to be pertinent, particularly as difficulties in the peace process become increasingly manifest. (The fact that tear gas grenades were thrown in the two Paris theaters where Tsahal premiered in early November calls to mind some of those complexities.)

In many ways the forward-looking aspect of Lanzmann's message and much of the meaning of the film as a whole are brought together in the final spoken words, which come from Ehud Barak, Tsahal's chief-of-staff. We meet and hear from Barak earlier in the film as well, including via the description of a daring commando raid into Beirut against Palestinian terrorists which he planned and which he led disguised as a woman (a role, we are told, he was chosen for either because of his smooth cheeks or because he was shorter than his partner).

Barak, who emerges as the hero of this epic documentary, is both a fighter and a leader. He is also, we discover, an eloquent intellectual with a deep understanding of the history of his people and a sense of vision regarding their need to avoid extremes at either end of the spectrum to survive with their values intact. As his words bring this film about the Israel Defense Forces to a close we are shown the face of one of the young tank soldiers, a faint smile developing on his lips as he goes off into the distance, the future of his people.

Back to the Future:
An Israeli Novelist's Invitation to Discovery

A review of A Journey to the End of the Millennium
by A.B. Yehoshua
JUF News, November 1999

• • •

Though the turn of the millennium is not really a Jewish "thing," as the countdown proceeds, much of the world is turning its eyes toward Israel. It is there, as Israel's tourism ministry, anticipating loads of visitors, puts it, that everything began. And it is there that certain Christians, not only commemorating the birth of Jesus 2,000 years ago but also anticipating the apocalypse, believe that everything will shortly begin to come to an end.

When an Israeli novelist brings out a book called *A Journey to the End of the Millennium,* a reader thus might have certain expectations as to setting and subject. But such a reader of the latest work by A.B. Yehoshua would be disabused of those and other possible expectations.

Yehoshua is one of the most gifted of today's writers of fiction, in Israel or anywhere else. Reading *Mr. Mani,* which appeared in Hebrew in 1989 and then in English translation in 1992, I found myself utterly dazzled by the author's ability to expand on techniques developed by his modernistic predecessors as he gave the novel form new life. In writing his latest book, however, rather than looking forward Yehoshua looked backward, replicating one of the oldest of the types from which the genre of the novel developed.

Like such early works as Daniel Defoe's *Robinson Crusoe* and Jonathan Swift's *Gulliver's Travels* – and like Aphra Behn's *Oroonoko* before them – Yehoshua's book describes a visit to a strange land. As it turns out, the millennium whose end Yehoshua charts is not the one we are currently wrapping up, but the one that came to a close 1,000 years ago. In its content as well as its form there is thus something "old" as well as something unexpected about this book.

Like one of the most notable novels of discovery, Joseph Conrad's *Heart of Darkness* (written at the turn of the last century), Yehoshua's narrative is framed around river travel toward the center of a foreign continent. Though the Ministry of Tourism may have labeled Israel "the official destination of the millennium," this Israeli writer has chosen to set his novel abroad. And in one more twist, whereas Conrad portrayed travelers from the so-called civilization of Europe making their way by river into supposedly uncivilized Africa, it is Africa from which Yehoshua's travelers depart, and it is into the heart of Europe that they proceed.

Yehoshua's primary travelers are North African Jews from Tangiers who take the river Seine into Paris, then continue overland to the city of Worms, on the river Rhine. What they discover revolves in part around relations between Christians and Jews in that part of the world, and in part around the relations between Jews and Muslims, some of whom have participated in the trip from North Africa. But most of the book's action centers around the relationship between Jews and other Jews, particularly between the Sephardic Jews of the South and the Ashkenazi Jews of the North.

The plot of this novel is generated by the fact that its central character, a Tangiers-based merchant named Ben Attar, has a nephew and partner who has moved to Europe and whose new, Northern wife insists that the partnership be severed. In another twist, the issue at stake is one that contemporary readers might find uncomfortable if not downright bizarre – namely, the discovery that Ben Attar has two wives. But as the narrative is presented, rather than establishing a contrast between enlightened Northerners and benighted Southerners, it pits warmth, lightness, and life-enhancing energies of the South against the cold, dark, legalistic, rationalistic North.

Restricted neither by the traditionalism of his chosen form nor by the allegorical implications his plot outline suggests, Yehoshua propels his narrative forward through many twists and turns. This strange book of external and internal discovery, charting victory and defeat, triumph and tragedy, offers the reader delights and puzzles.

Before the action of this story of the past begins, there is a forward-looking prologue, presumably in the voice of the author, which begins by asking, "But will there be anyone to remember us in another thousand years?" Wondering whether a soul then will "Still feel the urge or the longing to travel back a thousand years and look for us, as you are looking for your heroes now," it goes on to say, "Surely we won't just be forgotten." In closing, however, it asks, "Or will some totally different cipher fuse and scramble everything that has gone so that our image can never again be intertwined as we imagine it to ourselves?"

In the final years of this millennium, Yehoshua has rendered a sense of what the end of the last one might have been like for some of our ancestors – though few of us, I suspect, would likely have pictured that earlier era as it is described in this book. On the other hand, it might be that he chose that earlier time and place from an urge to indirectly portray our current moment. In our time the Jewish world is struggling to reconcile differences of its own between two major centers of Jewish life, between Ashkenazim and Sephardim, between different forms of religious practice, between those called hawks and those called doves. One can only guess what kind of scorecard the readers of a thousand years from now might need to gain an understanding of us from reading Yehoshua's novel.

Or perhaps the point of it all is that, in fact, the more things change the more they are the same, that we really are not so different from the way we were 1,000 years ago. At the same time, the novel may suggest that the current moment needs to be put in perspective; that the cataclysmic importance many attach to the events of our day will fade as the world moves though the next millennium. Today's events will then be seen as far less significant in the broader scheme of things than many would have us think, while relatively overlooked developments will emerge as far more noteworthy.

In any event, as the countdown continues and the hype intensifies, there is a stimulating way to regard the current moment from a Jewish perspective, while simultaneously getting away from it all. That way beckons to readers to ready to join Ben Attar and the other characters in Yehoshua's imaginative novel on their journey to the end of the (last) millennium.

Remembering Saul Bellow
JUF News, May 2005

• • •

Saul Bellow, who died on April 5 at age 89, has received praise suitable for a Nobel Prize winner who was perhaps the greatest American novelist of the past half-century. Much of the commentary has focused on his longstanding ties to Chicago, and some of it has emphasized the importance of his Jewishness.

For me, Bellow's death has opened the floodgates of memory, bringing me back to a time when, as a 20-year-old undergraduate at the University of Chicago, I had the remarkable opportunity to be his student in a class on the modern novel.

Before coming as a "Celebrity in Residence" for that three-month quarter, Bellow had lived outside the city for most of the previous two decades. But his Chicago roots were intact. He and his family had moved to Chicago from Montreal when he was a child, and he had grown up in the Humboldt Park neighborhood. A graduate of Tuley High School, Bellow attended both the University of Chicago and Northwestern.

His breakthrough novel, *The Adventures of Augie March,* published in 1953, chronicled the coming of age of a Jewish young man in Chicago. I had studied it as the closing work in a class at Chicago taught by another notable American novelist, Ralph Ellison, who had preceded Bellow as a "Celebrity in Residence" there.

Reading a passage from Bellow's novel out loud, Ellison (who I've since learned was a good friend of Bellow's at the time) looked up at the class and, with a knowing look in his eye, asked us to identify the nature of Bellow's prose. Surprised by the absence of a response, he talked about the Yiddish qualities of the rhythms and digressions.

Close to the time when he produced *Augie March,* Bellow had demonstrated his grasp of Yiddish by translating Isaac Bashevis Singer's short story "Gimpel the Fool"–a step that did much to put Singer himself on the literary map.

I looked forward to Bellow's coming for a number of reasons. My father's family, with an Eastern European Jewish background similar to that of Bellow's, had also moved to the Humboldt Park neighborhood, in their case from western Canada, just one year before Bellow's family

did. Five of Bellow's novels had already been published, most recently
Henderson the Rain King, and he had already established himself as a major writer.

A teacher in the English department from whom I took several courses, Richard Stern, had talked enthusiastically about the novel Bellow was
working on at the time. Having read the manuscript, Stern predicted that
whenever that book, which came to be called *Herzog,* was released, that
would be the publishing event of the year.

When the class began, I found it and Bellow to be everything I was
anticipating and more. It met in Cobb Hall, where about 20 or so of us
sat around an oblong table. I can still picture him entering the room and
looking around, ready to sit down and talk with us. I vividly remember
the twinkle in his eye and his engaging smile. It struck me that he ex-
uded a unique "simpatico" quality, with an aura of what has come to be
called charisma.

Looking into the old class notebook I've saved in a now-mildewing
carton with a handful of other such relics from my academic past, I find
that one day, rather than taking notes, I spent a few minutes describing
"a middle-aged man's body, formerly slight and athletic, now spreading."
I see a reading list that went from Flaubert's *Madame Bovary* to Thomas
Mann's *Dr. Faustus.* In between were Dostoyevsky and Tolstoy, Thomas Hardy and Samuel Butler, James Joyce and D.H. Lawrence, William
Faulkner and Ernest Hemingway. They were writers who formed a literary tradition in which Bellow no doubt saw himself, though in his comments he rejected aspects of the modernism that they promulgated.

Over and over again, my notes show, Bellow's focus was on the creation of character and the use of language. He was preoccupied as well
with the role of the artist and the nature of art, and with the relationship
of modern fiction to both earlier literary traditions and contemporary
reality. A contemporary scholar might find it of particular interest to
note that, while teaching about D.H. Lawrence, Bellow talked of how the
"novel of 20th century becomes more personal–the writer trying to solve
in his book the problems he is trying to solve in his life."

Bellow approached literature by talking about the text itself, not
about what others had to say about it. He often referred us to other novels
rather than to criticism as a means of deepening our understanding and
appreciation for the works we were studying. In assigning the lone paper
required for the class (on the conception of the hero and the nature of
character in whatever novels we chose to write about), he recommended
that we look not at criticism but at essays written by the author or authors

in question.

The one external work that he did recommend and cite was *Mimesis: The Representation of Reality in Western Literature,* by Erich Auerbach. When a member of the class who appeared older than anybody else asked him the meaning of the book's title — something that would have been well known to any product of the Aristotelian environment on campus — Bellow looked up with a particularly active twinkle in his eye, implying that this was surely an "outsider" who somehow had gotten in there with the rest of us.

After the academic year, I was off to graduate school at the University of Minnesota, where Bellow himself had taught for a couple of stints during the previous decade. He was about to move back to the University of Chicago with a full-time appointment that he maintained for the next 30 years. The publication of *Herzog,* which came two years later, in 1964, was indeed a major literary event, as were the publications of his subsequent novels, many of them with Chicago as the setting.

While Bellow always resisted being pigeonholed as a Jewish writer (and belittled the frequent linking of himself with Bernard Malamud and Philip Roth as what he jokingly called "the Hart, Schaffner, and Marx of American literature"— using the name of a Chicago Jewish clothing manufacturer), his Jewishness continued to matter to him. He was, the records show, a donor to the Jewish United Fund annual campaign. As is revealed by his journalistic coverage of the Six Day War and a subsequent visit memorialized in "To Jerusalem and Back," he was significantly connected to Israel. And in 1988, when the vicious anti-Semitism of mayoral aide Steve Cokely (who accused Jewish doctors of deliberately spreading AIDS in the black community) surfaced, he spoke out forcefully in the *Chicago Tribune.*

Though Bellow left Chicago and lived "out East" during the final dozen years of his life, his Chicago roots were always basic to his identity and his art. That can also be said of his Jewishness, which informed not just the rhythms of his prose and the background of his characters. Auerbach's *Mimesis* begins by discussing texts from Homer and the Bible, representing the two traditions from which Bellow derived.

At the core of his work is a fusion of different, disparate modes: of the cerebral and the physical; of the sophisticated and the earthy; of the cultured and the everyday; of what, in our class, he labeled "low seriousness." (There is also the combination of "ebullience and gloominess" that the writer Paul Berman talked about while memorializing Bellow at a JUF community forum.) This anti-dualism, I would suggest, is not only a defining attribute of Bellow's work and of the ideas it contains, but is essential to the perspective on life and reality that Judaism has offered the world.

While in Lithuania a decade ago, I was speaking with a local Jewish writer who, upon learning that I was from Chicago, excitedly wanted to talk about Bellow. When I told him that I had once had Bellow as a teacher, it was as if I had said that I had personally been at Sinai and had studied with Moshe Rabbeinu himself.

As we celebrate the contributions that Jews have made to American life and culture in the 350 years that have passed since the first of us came to this land, high on that list stand the literary achievements of a gifted hometown writer, Saul Bellow.

Munich As a Post-Zionist Tale

JUF News, February 2006

• • •

Steven Spielberg shifted from black-and-white to color during the emotional coda to *Schindler's List*. It showed the Jews lucky enough to survive the Nazi Holocaust in Europe thanks to Oskar Schindler walking forth to the strains of "Jerusalem of Gold" (sung in Hebrew), then, years later, standing at Schindler's grave in Jerusalem while Itzhak Perlman's violin played the movie's theme. Spielberg's latest film, *Munich*, ends with similar heart-tugging music by John Williams. But its closing inverts the earlier one, as we see the Israeli hero of the film making his new home in Brooklyn — across the river from a Manhattan where, it being the early 1970s, the Twin Towers still stand.

Reminiscent in its way of the prevailing situation of *Schindler's List*, *Munich*, true to its title, begins with a scene taken from history when Jews — in this case members of Israel's Olympic team — were brutally massacred on European soil; indeed, in Germany itself. This time, however, the uniformed Germans are on the "right" side, though inept, and the perpetrators are Palestinian terrorists.

Much of what comes after the massacre is based not on history but on a book that drew upon a since-discredited source. The response to *Munich* has been mixed, with some of the criticism revolving around the film's deviations from fact. There are also disputes surrounding the subtext, which has to do with the application of the movie's "message" to America's current war on terror as well as to the war in Iraq. And for the Jewish community there is a serious concern surrounding the "moral equivalence" between the Palestinians, many of whom are treated with sympathy, and the Israelis, who respond to the Munich attack by creating a "hit" team to wipe out the Palestinian terror group's lead operatives in Europe.

Viewers begin seeing the movie from the point of view of the attacking Palestinians. Somewhat nervously and with the help of several easygoing Americans who think they are merely coming back from late-night carousing, they climb a fence to get into the Olympic Village. That fence climbing is echoed near the end of the film, when the Israelis are stalking the Palestinian mastermind of the Munich attack. Additional parallels between the two groups are implied in action and dialogue at various points throughout the film.

Spielberg has declared that he took daring steps in the film and that he wanted it to show the humanity on both sides. But he has also expressed offense that his commitment to Israel is being questioned by critics and Jewish community spokespeople. Indeed, though an armed PLO operative gets a chance to make the Palestinian case on screen, he is answered even as he is making it by Avner, the Israeli lead figure in the movie. And there are other times when the Israeli case is made as well. Similarly, though the Palestinians are not shown as the evil monsters the Nazis were in *Schindler's List,* one is never allowed to forget what their representatives did at Munich. The narrative is essentially about the Israelis, who are generally shown in a sympathetic fashion, as more justified in their use of violence than the Palestinians, with greater moral compunction about using it, and as more like "us" than the Palestinians are.

What is most problematic from a Jewish community point of view, I would suggest, is what happens to the main character in the movie's closing scenes and the light that sheds on aspects of what has gone before. It could be claimed that this film is just a spy thriller, and a rather conventional one at that, in which the hero, seeing his "handlers" in a new light, wonders if his mission was really worth it or if he was just being used, and ends up cynical, disillusioned, and guilt-stricken about things he has done. The trouble with that conclusion, though, is that the way Spielberg and Tony Kushner, who wrote the screenplay, have talked about the movie — its set-piece scenes and pointed declarations by its characters — indicates that it is clearly freighted with intended meaning. And the meaning that I believe emerges — especially, it seems, because of Kushner, who in 2002 proclaimed to a Chicago audience that "I am not a Zionist" — is a rendition of what has come to be known as post-Zionism.

As I have noted, this is not to say that the case for Israel is not made. For Spielberg, though, that case is just about exclusively linked to Jewish suffering in the Holocaust and the need for a homeland in light of that historic trauma. It is a point made most succinctly by Avner's mother, whose family was wiped out by the Nazis. By the end of the movie, though, that argument has very little valance for Avner, who paid the price of his father's dedication to the cause of establishing the state by growing up without a paternal presence, and who is living during a very different era.

Avner is torn between being like his father or being different from

him. His final decision is anticipated early on, when he says to his pregnant wife, "You are the only home I have had." Like his father, he still
goes off to serve the cause, but at the end he reverses himself and leaves
Israel to join his wife and child in Brooklyn, where he had moved them.

The decision to make that move, we sense, has not just personal but
symbolic meaning. It comes after Avner has returned to Israel at the end
of his assignment, torn by doubts over its pragmatic and moral justification and by a sense that, in carrying out their acts of violence, he and
his fellow team members have compromised civilized standards and have
violated basic Jewish values.

Spielberg is hardly the first creative figure to treat these kinds of
themes. In a way, it is as though Avner is choosing between emulating
the martyrs for the cause of Irish independence in William Butler Yeats'
"Easter 1916," whose hearts were "enchanted to a stone to trouble the
living stream" or being like the speaker in Matthew Arnold's "Dover
Beach," who, in a world which resembles "a darkling plain . . . where
ignorant armies clash by night," finds the only answer in saying to his
beloved, "let us be true to one another."

Though this film lacks the clarity and eloquence of those two great
poems, its issues are anticipated by them. But these issues appear in a
particular context charged with serious implications, and therein lies the
rub. That context is the Israel-Palestinian — and the wider Israel-Arab
— conflict. And more broadly it is the way in which, in acting out the
Zionist imperative, the Jewish people have returned to the stage of history after centuries of powerless exile.

In asserting the power of the Jewish people to determine their own
destiny in their ancient homeland, the Israelis have inevitably found themselves facing complex choices while struggling to remain uncorrupted. In
the film, Avner, having learned what maintaining a Jewish state requires
of him, ultimately chooses to be with his wife and child and to make a
private home, as opposed to being prepared to sacrifice himself to protect the Jewish people's homeland. The film shows Avner, who heard
some members of his team in Europe speculate that they might have been
violating Jewish values, implicitly conclude that only in America can he
stay true to those values. He invites his handler, who is in the States to
persuade him to return to Israel, to enable him to practice the hospitality
that goes all of the way back to Abraham by coming to his house for
dinner. The handler, who may seem merely piqued, probably understands
what is at stake and turns him down.

Looked at in this framework, an otherwise strange aspect of the film can be understood better. That has to do with the relationship Avner has with the family of Louis, the omniscient source he develops in Europe. For considerable cash, Louis provides him and his team with leads and assistance necessary to carry out their missions. Blindfolded, Avner is driven to meet with Louis' father, known as "Papa." This charismatic patriarch of a multi-generation family living in a near-paradisiacal setting in the French countryside conveys utter cynicism about all governments and explains how he and his family refuse to wittingly come to the assistance of anybody working on behalf of any sort of government. Near the film's end, Avner defies his handler by refusing to identify Louis and his father, thereby demonstrating greater loyalty to them than to his own country and associating himself with their brand of European post-nationalism. Near the very end of the film, it is implied that "Papa" cares more about Avner as a person than his handler does. Though Avner has previously told him that he has his own "Papa," in a sense this ambiguous figure ultimately becomes his spiritual father.

An instructive contrast to Spielberg's work can be seen in the films of Claude Lanzman, who attracted much attention for his Holocaust documentary, named, simply, *Shoah.* Less well known is *Tzahal,* a film about the Israel Defense Forces that came out a few years later. In it, Lanzman respectfully portrayed the army that the people of Israel created to ensure their post-Holocaust survival. (Interestingly, Ehud Barak, Chief of Staff during most of the time when *Tzahal* was made and in some ways that film's "hero," is portrayed in a scene in *Munich* where an Israel commando raid into Lebanon is shown.)

In Lanzman's universe, Jewish victimhood in Europe is followed by the assertion of Jewish sovereignty in Israel, maintained thanks to the principled use of force as necessary. In Spielberg's universe, too, there is Jewish victimhood in Europe. But for him, when Jews need to use force to protect themselves and their state, rather than being saved by a righteous gentile, things get so complicated that it seems hardly worth having the state. Whether or not that is what Spielberg really meant to say in *Munich,* that is at least suggested by the way things play out. And that, I believe, is what makes this film especially disquieting and problematic.

Words to Remember Him by:
Memories of Richard G. Stern

University of Chicago Magazine, March-April, 2013

• • •

A s the substantial obituary that appeared in *The New York Times* on January 24 indicated, Richard G. Stern was both a teacher of distinction at the University of Chicago and a notable author with a long and productive career. Though he never garnered a wide readership, he was highly praised by fellow writers. As his former colleague Philip Roth aptly told the *Times,* Stern was "an inspiring figure as a literature professor and an ace of great virtuosity as a novelist, short story writer, essayist and raconteur."

I had the privilege of being a student of Stern's back in his early years on campus. I took a couple of literature courses with him and enrolled in his signature creative writing class, where I really got to see him in action. I remember an exercise Stern had us do in class to hone our ability to choose the right word by together translating Charles Baudelaire.

Stern clearly loved words himself. He loved language. He loved writing. And he loved teaching. He was a big man with a big laugh, a great smile, and a wonderful glint in his eye. I remember how he spent one entire class session reading Flannery O'Connor's 1955 short story "The Life You Save May Be Your Own" to us. To this day I can hear the emphatic tone of his voice and can picture the energized gestures of his body as he came to the closing lines that describe how "fantastic raindrops, like tin-can tops, crashed over the rear of Mr. Shiftlet's car." And then, "Very quickly he stepped on the gas and with his stump sticking out the window he raced the gathering shower into Mobile."

I also remember clearly the day Stern walked into class, overflowing with enthusiasm, to tell us that he had just finished reading the manuscript of a friend's new novel. After giving us a sense of the novel's structure and basic plot, he predicted with certainty that the book's appearance would be the publishing event of the year, whenever that would be. The book was Saul Bellow's *Herzog,* and of course Stern was correct in his assessment.

Our final assignment for the course was to prepare our own pieces of

416 On the Front Lines in a Changing Jewish World

creative writing, from which he would select a "winner" to be published in the student literary journal of the time, called, I believe, the *Phoenix*. In my case the submission was a short story, and of all of the submissions from the class, mine was the one he picked. The manuscript was misplaced in the journal's offices and the story never appeared in print. But the fact that he had picked it remains a source of pride.

Stern's first novel, *Golk* (1960), was published during my undergraduate years at the University, as was his second, *Europe; or, Up and Down with Schreiber and Baggish* (1961). (I still have the copies of those books that I purchased and read as soon as they came out.) Replicating but by no means imitating the peregrinations of the eponymous heroes of the latter book, in the summer following graduation, I traveled abroad. Who should I bump into on the streets of Rome but Dick Stern himself. He couldn't have been friendlier. Whatever he was involved in at the moment, he said he would free himself up for the evening and invited me to join him at a well-known café.

It was a glorious evening, rich with conversation about books, writing, Rome, and life in general. I sensed it then, but as the years went by I came to appreciate even more, how gracious, warm, and forthcoming it was of him to spend that time with a wandering former student.

With a degree from the Committee on General Studies in the Humanities and a specialization in literature under my belt, thanks to the inspiration of Stern, Norman Maclean, and other U of C teachers, I headed off to do graduate work in English at the University of Minnesota. And I never forgot Stern's infectious affection for the written word.

Nearly a dozen years after graduation from the U of C and back in Hyde Park during a sabbatical from my own teaching, I visited Stern on campus. A couple of decades after that, when I was back living in Chicago with a new career as a Jewish communal professional, we briefly reconnected by mail. And then, when my class held its 45th reunion, he gave an *Un*Common Core session and afterward signed copies of his latest book, the short story collection *Almonds to Zhoof* (2005). After he inscribed mine "With Nostalgia," he, my wife, and I chatted about current writers. It was clear that he had retained an almost boyish delight in the discovery of literary talent.

The last piece of correspondence I have from him is an e-mail in which he talked about *Almonds to Zhoof* and the pleasure he had derived from the notice it had received in the *Forward,* where the reviewer had talked about Jewish elements in the work—something, he said, that had engaged him more and more in later years.

I found that striking. Unlike, say, his literary compatriots Roth (a handful of years younger) and Bellow (a number of years older), Stern had not imbued his earlier fiction with Jewish content, nor had he been known to present himself as a Jewish writer. While one's Jewishness was not as commonly worn on one's sleeve in the campus environment during those years when I had him as a teacher as it is in many cases today, he projected even less of that identity than others. Indeed, had I been asked as an undergraduate if I thought he was Jewish, I don't believe I would have said "yes" with any certainty. Perhaps his absence of a public profile in this area had something to do with his upbringing—unlike those other writers, whose ancestors came from Eastern Europe, his parents, a bit of research now has told me, were both German Jews, generally more assimilated in behavior. But in what he called "his autumnal days," he wrote me that he had "been thinking much about these matters." And aware of my own interests and involvements, he wanted me to know about that.

His message was a reply to one of mine in which I told him that I had recently been in Rome for a conference on Catholic-Jewish relations and that I had thought of our evening together there with appreciation for the graciousness that he had shown a young former student. He replied that, despite his ailments of the moment, he wished he would be able to visit Rome again himself "one last time."

I don't know if that time ever came for him. But I do know that the words of praise that his passing evoked from others, including those who knew him far better than I, were surely well deserved.

Jack Garfein: Strange, Wild, Triumphant

The Times of Israel, May 21, 2013

• • •

On the evenings of Sunday, May 26, and Monday, May 27, the Tel Aviv Cinematheque – to be followed by the Cinematheques in Haifa and Jerusalem on each of the following nights respectively – will be hosting a retrospective tribute for a cinema director whose entire corpus consists of two films, one of them from 1957 and the other from 1961. The director is Jack Garfein, now 82 years old, and limited though his directorial output may have been, not only are the films worthy of attention, but given the totality of Garfein's career and his history, the events promise to be extremely meaningful in a number of ways.

Garfein was born in a Czechoslovakian town in the Carpathian Mountains in 1930. His close-knit family was soon to be decimated by the Holocaust. After suffering the horrors of a series of death camps which he alone of his immediate family survived, Garfein came to New York, where an uncle of his had found refuge right before the war. And then, as he tells his story, he began a new life, with an opportunity to develop his theatrical gifts thanks in great part to the assistance of the United Jewish Appeal, for which he became a spokesman.

Trained at the Dramatic Workshop of the New School and then the famed Actors Studio, along with such luminaries of America's stage and cinema as James Dean, Marlon Brando, and Rod Steiger, Garfein had an early chance to make his name on Broadway, where he directed the 1953 play version of Calder Willingham's novel *End as a Man.* Recommended by Elia Kazan, he then also directed the film adaptation, renamed *The Strange One.* Produced by Sam Spiegel, its cast included Ben Gazzara, George Peppard, and Pat Hingle, all of them Actors Studio products making their screen debuts.

Four years later, Garfein directed Carroll Baker, to whom he was then married, in a film called *Something Wild,* with music by Aaron Copland. Failing to fit into the culture of the Hollywood movie studios, he saw his directorial career in film come to an abrupt end. But he continued to direct for the theater, including the works of such notable twentieth-century playwrights as O'Neill, Ionesco, Beckett, O'Casey, and Fugard.

Meanwhile, maintaining a distinguished career as acting coach and teacher, he first headed to Los Angeles to join with others in establishing the Actors Studio West, then moved on to found his own acting studio in Paris, where he continues to be an active force.

With his engaging personality, profound sensitivity, and lightning-quick mind, Garfein makes a striking impression. The novelist Henry Miller included a chapter about him in his 1978 book *My Bike and Other Friends,* in which he said, "What amazed me about him on our first meeting was the range of his knowledge and his mastery of English, a foreign language to him. When we meet the sparks fly. He is not only most affable, charming, exciting, but a great raconteur who holds you spell-bound."

Through all the years of effort and accomplishment, through all the occasions of working with stars and celebrities, writers and intellectuals, Garfein's early experience as a young Jewish boy from Central Europe whose life was ripped apart by the Holocaust has remained with him. A powerful documentary called *A Journey Back,* made for the Canadian Broadcasting System in 1987, which the Tel Aviv Cinematheque will also be screening, shows him revisiting his childhood home town and Auschwitz. In an interview I had the opportunity to do with him a year and a half ago, he reflected on the world today and spoke of what he called "constant anti-Semitism." "Sometimes it's hidden," he said, "but it's there. An unjust relationship to a people that has been going on for thousands of years. We have to have our eyes open."

I met Garfein after reading about him in *The New York Times* a little over two years ago, when that city's Film Forum offered a tribute similar to what he will be receiving in Israel, that one on the occasion of his 80th birthday. I was first drawn to the article by its references to *The Strange One,* which I had seen decades ago, not long after it had been released, and which I still remembered for its bold intensity. I had not seen *Something Wild* earlier, but when I recently did I had the strong feeling, as have others, that it – co-written by Garfein himself – was significantly influenced by his Holocaust trauma, which seems also to be reflected in *The Strange One* in some ways.

In the earlier film, set in a Southern military college, Gazzara plays a sadistic, cruelly manipulative cadet. In the later one, set in New York (which is shown in a series of hauntingly photographed scenes), Baker plays a young woman who struggles to deal with the effects of a violent rape. Though in different ways, both films grippingly explore the controlling imposition of power over others and the helplessness of victimization. And both have endings that capture the sense of ultimate hope that

Garfein has held to despite what life has brought him.

Besides the event in New York, Garfein has received retrospective tributes, like the one he will receive here especially thanks to the Tel Aviv Cinematheque, in London, Paris, Los Angeles, and at the Telluride Film Festival. But he says that having this now happen in Israel – which he calls "the soul of the Jewish people" – will mean the most to him.

Rediscovered by viewers and critics, his two films have continuing impact. Garfein himself will be present at all of the upcoming programs and available for question-and-answer sessions following the screenings of the films, when he will be joined by Foster Hirsch of Brooklyn College and the City University of New York, the author of over a dozen books on cinema.

There is good reason to anticipate that all of these evenings will provide experiences to be long remembered. And at a time when artists and intellectuals from around the world are being implored to boycott the Jewish state and some, like Stephen Hawking, are complying, there is surely nothing that would keep away this creative, principled man who is still proud of his father's role as a Zionist leader back in the Carpathian Mountains.

Utopia Deferred: A Powerful Look at the Divisions in Israel in the Decades after the Six-Day War

A Review of Like Dreamers by Yossi Klein Halevi
JUF News, October 2013

. . .

About one-third of the way through Yossi Klein Halevi's new book, *Like Dreamers: The Story of the Israeli Paratroopers Who Reunited Jerusalem and Divided a Nation* (Harper), there appears a paragraph which talks about the rise of rock music in Israel during the period following the Six-Day War of 1967. The creators of these songs, says the passage, "had been influenced by the rebellious music filtering in from the West, and yet most of them emerged from the army entertainment troupes, which sang patriotic songs to raise soldiers' morale. The result of those conflicting influences were anti-war songs more wistful than angry, at once mocking and rooted, an opposition from deep within the national self."

The paragraph can be seen as a microcosm of the total book. For one thing, there is the way that it sets up oppositions, in this case between patriotic and anti-war purposes and between a content that is both "mocking" of certain values and "rooted" in them. Beyond that is the dialectical way that the passage sees these conflicts resolved through the existence of a "national self," which synthesizes the collective and the individual. Carefully crafted, insightful, and focused on some of Halevi's central themes, the paragraph is typical of a great many passages interspersed within the book.

Like Dreamers takes its apt title from the 126th psalm, the "Shir Hama'alot" that Jews traditionally sing before the Grace after Meals on the Sabbath and holidays. Quoted in the book's introduction, the opening lines of that psalm say, "When the Lord returned the exiles of Zion, we were like dreamers." Building on the image, Halevi gives his book its shape by focusing on seven individuals who inherited the dreams of the early Zionists who enacted the modern return to the Land of Israel.

All of them raised with strong ideals and dreams of their own, these were young men who came of age in the years following the establishment of the State of Israel. Their joint involvement serving in the Paratrooper Brigade that conquered the Old City in the Six-Day War provides a dramatic opening for the book. At the same time, the treatment of that event sets in motion Halevi's dominant dialectic, which sees these paratroopers—and by extension large swaths of the Israeli population—belonging to different and at times opposing camps, and which then calls for a synthesis defined by Jewish unity and a national consensus.

The differences Halevi traces in establishing the divisions within Israel that form the subject of his book are especially between the secular and the religious members of Israeli society; between those who see Israel as the means for achieving Jewish normalcy and those tied to the concept of specialness; between those who see themselves primarily as Israeli and those who see themselves primarily as Jewish; and between those on the political left and those on the political right.

Of the seven paratroopers whom Halevi focuses on, four come from kibbutzim and three are Religious Zionists. Each in his own way is a fascinating personality, and Halevi — until recently Israel correspondent for *The New Republic* — writes in part as journalist, in part as historian, and in part with the gifts of a novelist, using language rich in meaning and lovely in its imagery and cadences. His characters are not just examples of typical Israelis, but complex individuals whose lives show us much about them and about the times they lived through and helped shape.

The Six-Day War was a turning point for each of these paratroopers as well as for the country. After it, in varying degrees and different ways, the kibbutzniks whom Halevi portrays drift away from the pure socialism of their parents, sometimes even leaving their kibbutzim while pursuing personal fulfillment, though for the most part the kinds of values with which they were imbued remain strong. Meanwhile, the paratroopers he writes of who come from a Religious Zionist background find their values and beliefs intensified by the results of the war.

All of this plays out in the course of the years and decades that follow, as many of these individuals not only hold to their own beliefs but criticize and challenge those of their former comrades in arms from the other side of the spectrum. The Religious Zionists become key figures in the Greater Land of Israel settlement movement, and two of the kibbutzniks become activists in the Peace Now movement (with a third of them becoming a severely radicalized revolutionary and the fourth becoming religious himself, in his own fashion).

Halevi portrays these characters and the contrasting ideas they hold with understanding and human sympathy. And as he shows them tempering their utopian dreams in light of the reality they experience, he himself, writing at the end about a 21st-century Israel in which the key opposing issues remain unresolved, posits no reconciliation of the countervailing forces he has shown, though that is what his dialectical impulse craves. Indeed, he ends the book with a scene that, while providing a frame for the book's overall narrative and a recapitulation of its basic themes, offers a beautiful, moving closing. This arrives through the sensibility of one of the book's central characters, who in the course of time has come to recognize that the ultimate redemption desired by Israel's earlier and later dreamers alike is not yet at hand.

A Look from the Left:
Underground to Palestine by I.F. Stone

The Book: An Online Review at The New Republic, February 14, 2012

• • •

In 1946, I.F. Stone, the celebrated left-wing journalist, became the first American reporter to travel with Jewish "displaced persons" (DPs) in Europe who were attempting to enter British Mandatory Palestine. With the British deeming such immigration illegal, the trip was perilous for these Holocaust survivors. Published first as a series of newspaper articles and then in book form as *Underground to Palestine,* Stone's recounting of his experiences is moving and dramatic in its descriptions of the painful fate that had been suffered by the people he joined, and of their subsequent resilience. Well worth reading today, the book offers a powerful eyewitness narrative in the period leading up to the establishment of the state of Israel. It is a narrative that shatters basic premises endorsed by people who today share Stone's political leanings but reject the legitimacy of Israel as the Jewish State.

Stone opened the book this way:

> This is a story of personal adventure. I was the first newspaperman to travel the Jewish underground in Europe and to arrive in Palestine on a so-called illegal boat. But this is more than the narrative of a journalistic escapade. I am an American and I am also and inescapably—the world being what it is—a Jew. I was born in the United States. My parents were born in Russia. Had they not emigrated at the turn of the century to America, I might have gone to the gas chambers in Eastern Europe. I might have been a DP, ragged and homeless like those with whom I traveled. I did not go to join them as a tourist in search of the picturesque, nor even as a newspaperman merely in search of a good story, but as a kinsman, fulfilling a moral obligation to my brothers. I wanted in my own way, as a journalist, to provide a picture of their trials and their aspirations in the hope that good people, Jewish and non-Jewish, might be moved to help them.

Reflecting on the conditions that the DPs confronted, Stone quickly concluded that there was no way that the Europe they were attempting to leave was a place where they might successfully rebuild their lives. Their families had been decimated; their homes had been destroyed; and the anti-Semitic hatred that drove the Holocaust remained widespread.

Recalling his first visit to Palestine the previous year, Stone wrote that "like most American Jews I was neither a Zionist nor an anti-Zionist." But he went on to say that "I fell in love with the place, with its vitality and its pioneering spirit. I understand the motivations behind the Return." And then, traveling with the DPs, he made clear that for him, as for those he was with, Zionist logic had become an imperative:

> The "pull" toward Palestine I heard expressed again and again, not only from the young *Chalutzim* on the train, but from older folk who would say, "I'm not a Zionist, I'm a Jew. That's enough. We have wandered enough. We have worked and struggled too long on the lands of other peoples. We must build a land of our own. *Mir mussen bauen a Yiddish land.* ('We must build a Jewish land.')

In describing Dutch youngsters whose parents had been killed by the Nazis, Stone observed, "They were not fleeing Holland—they were going to Palestine. They spoke of their native land with sad affection, but they were *Chalutzim,* Zionist pioneers bent on building a Jewish homeland."

Like the survivors with whom he was traveling, Stone repeatedly referred to the intended destination as *eretz,* or "the land"—shorthand for the Land of Israel. Those displaced persons were attempting the trip, as his narrative makes clear, not as European colonialists but as proud Jews who intended to rebuild their lives in the land of their forefathers. Their goal was to join the Zionist pioneers who had come before them in the preceding decades to together determine their collective future as a free Jewish people. Witness to their strength, Stone shared their pride. He dedicated his book to "Those Anonymous Heroes The *Schlichim* of the *Haganah*"—emissaries of the pre-state Jewish militia that was to evolve into the Israel Defense Forces—who organized the rescue that he reported on. "I must say I have never met a nobler group of human beings than the *Schlichim* I encountered abroad," Stone wrote.

Stone participated fully in the harrowing experiences of the DPs in crossing the Mediterranean. They faced harsh British officials, and the vessel they traveled in was hardly seaworthy. At one point, erroneously believing that their boat was already approaching its goal, they each received "illegal immigration certificates" stating that they "had been found qualified by the representatives of the Jewish Community of Palestine for repatriation to Eretz Israel." The certificates cited "four authorities for the Jewish community's action"—authorities based not only on the Jewish people's historic connection to the land as conveyed in ancient religious texts but also on modern legal documents and decisions.

> The first was from Ezekiel: 'And they shall abide in the lands that I have given unto Jacob my servant, wherein your fathers abode, and they shall abide therein, even they, and their children, and their children's children, forever.' The second was from Isaiah: 'With great mercies will I gather thee.' The third was *Lord Balfour's Declaration of 2 November 1917,* and the last was *The [League of Nations] Mandate for Palestine.*

As much as Stone linked himself with the other passengers during the trip from Europe, after their ship finally arrived at the Haifa harbor, he put on his uniform as an American military correspondent and separated himself from the quarantined new residents of what was to become the State of Israel.

In an Epilogue, Stone enlarged on the case for supporting the desires of the DPs:

> ...For most of them, Palestine is not merely the one possibility for a new life, is not merely a place of refuge, but the country to which they want to go....

> Is this so hard to understand? They have been kicked around as Jews and now they want to live as Jews. Over and over again, I heard it said: 'We want to build a Jewish country. ... We are tired of putting our sweat and blood into places where we are not welcome. ... We have wandered enough.' These Jews want the right to live as a people, to build as a people, to make their contribution to the world as a people. Are their national aspirations any less worthy of respect than those of any other oppressed people?

Ultimately presenting the formula he then preferred for reconciling the presence of both Jews and Arabs on the land, Stone declared, "I myself would like to see a bi-national Arab-Jewish state made of

Palestine and Trans-Jordan, the whole to be part of a Middle Eastern Semitic Federation." This was a position that some Zionists held then as well. But it was based on assumptions that proved to be unrealistic at the time, as the United Nations Special Committee on Palestine concluded after making its study visit in the summer of 1947. And it is an approach that has been shown to be all the more out of touch through the unfolding of events that have followed, as the Jewish and Palestinian national movements have sharply gone their separate ways. Indeed, most of those who today defy the United Nations's November 1947 Partition Plan, which called for the establishment of a Jewish as well as an Arab state in Mandatory Palestine, and who try to advance a so-called "One State Solution" can fairly be accused of in fact advocating the destruction of the State of Israel—a position drastically inconsistent with the spirit of Stone's commentary.

There is no little irony in the fact that those who embrace the ideological opposition to Israel's existence falsely accuse the country of being a colonial implant in the Middle East and see Zionism as nothing other than a European colonial enterprise. As Stone's eyewitness account makes clear, for the displaced persons who later became citizens of Israel, this was far from the truth. Rather than being agents of an imperial power based in Europe, they saw themselves as exiles returning to the homeland of their people. In fact, the true colonialists of the time were the officials of the British Empire who strove to keep those Jews out—however desperate their circumstances may have been—and who regarded and treated them as illegal immigrants.

Besides making their ideology-driven charge, contemporary opponents of Israel's existence who see its establishment as the original sin are also fond of endorsing the argument that while the Jews may have suffered at the hands of the Europeans, it was unjust for the Arab population of Palestine to have been expected to accept the dislocated survivors and the earlier Jewish refugees from Christian European oppression. That argument is countered in part by the evidence Stone presented. As his book demonstrates, many DPs were motivated by the pull of relocating in the Jewish homeland more than the push of getting out of Europe. Moreover, there were Jews on the land even before the Zionist pioneers began arriving from Europe in the late nineteenth century, and the population shifts of 1948 included not only the departure of Palestinian refugees but also the arrival of hundreds of thousands of Jews fleeing the Arab lands in which they had lived for centuries, who had their own strong sense of connection to the land of Israel.

In the years following his writing of this book, Stone's status as a diligent journalist and icon of the left was only to increase. This was especially so at the time of the Vietnam War when, particularly through hard-hitting reportage and commentary circulated in *I.F. Stone's Weekly,* he took on the establishment and unrelentingly made the strategic and moral case for withdrawal.

A graduate student at the time, I was an anti-war activist and a subscriber to that publication. Not only is a copy of *Underground to Palestine*—inherited from my parents—on my home bookshelves, but copies of the *Weekly* from 1967 through 1969 have been stored in a carton of "memorabilia" I stashed away in a crawlspace long ago, forgotten until I inadvertently came upon them after re-reading Stone's book a short time ago. A look at that newsletter now, starting with the issue published immediately after the Six Day War of June 1967, shows Stone to have been sympathetic to the plight of the Palestinian refugees; fearful that Israel would not use the opportunity of its victory to withdraw from territories it conquered during the '67 war in return for a quickly-established peace with its Arab neighbors that would improve the lot of those refugees; and critical of certain steps being taken (and others not being taken) by the Israeli government.

But despite his misgivings, Stone wrote then with a clear-eyed recognition that Israel was what he repeatedly, simply, referred to as "the Jewish State." While no longer advocating a bi-national state, Stone, who described the conflict as "a tragic quarrel of brothers," now believed that to resolve it "in some form or another ... must involve a Federated coexistence among Israel, the Palestinian Arabs, and the Jordanians." In the *Weekly* of June 19, 1967, dated just nine days after the end of the war, he wrote that "a return to the main idea of [the 1947 U.N. partition plan] may offer a way out for both sides," and he went on to note that "the original plan called for an Arab State and a Jewish State in Palestine west of the Jordan."

One can imagine how, if Stone were still writing today, he would be harshly critical of Israel for what he would probably describe as inadequately extending itself to make such a deal, and he most likely would be particularly sharp on the continued occupation of the West Bank. But being opposed to certain policies carried out since 1967—and even critical of some of those carried out previously—is very different from attempting to undo the events of 1948 that brought Israel into being as the modern nation-state of the Jewish people.

Today's left includes individuals and groups who are engaged in an enterprise of delegitimization that would deny Israel its right to exist. They are driven partly by an inaccurately applied anti-colonial ideology, partly by a selectively-applied belief in post-nationalism, partly by an acceptance of a maximalist application of the Palestinian narrative, and partly—one cannot help suspect about some of them—by a troubling though usually unacknowledged animosity to Israel and its supporters. I.F. Stone's *Underground to Palestine* provides a useful corrective and alternative to these perspectives, based on its revealing account of the situation prevailing in the period preceding independence. Stone, who was sympathetic to the suffering and legitimate aspirations of both sides, pointed the way to an approach which, rather than reinforcing the anti-Israel grievances and hatred that have helped keep the Israel-Palestinian conflict alive for all these decades, could instead play a part in finally resolving the conflict.

From Chicago to the Yishuv:
A Reading of Meyer Levin's
In Search: An Autobiography

Forthcoming in Hebrew translation in *Iyunim Bitkumat Israel:*
Studies in Israeli and Modern Jewish Society, 2014

. . .

*I*n Search: An Autobiography, by the Chicago-born writer Meyer Levin, was published in 1950. Levin was a prolific writer in various genres who, though relatively well known in his own time, is today probably best known – if remembered at all – for the "obsession" (his word) he developed regarding Anne Frank, her diary, and the dramatization of it. An inscribed copy of *The Old Bunch* – his 1937 novel – was on my parents' bookshelf, and I read it while still in my teens, relishing its portrayal of life in the Jewish community in Chicago – my hometown too – a couple of decades earlier. Levin was still fairly well known at that time, and in the 1970s, when I was teaching at Tel Aviv University and living in Nof Yam, I discovered that he had a home just across the Coastal Road, in Kfar Shmaryahu.

Decades passed and then, a couple of years ago, browsing in a used bookstore in another American Midwestern city, I came across a copy of *In Search.* I hastened to buy it and, starting to read it that night, I found it utterly engrossing. Called a "work of self-examination" in an introductory note, the book is a portrait of Levin as he saw himself before Anne Frank came into his life. But more than that, it is a book that I believe has much to tell us today through its depiction of one American Jew's connections with Jewish life in the Yishuv and then with Israel at the time of its founding.[1]

A Diaspora Sensibility

Proceeding with the attentiveness of an astute reporter, the language of a novelist, and the thoughtfulness of a person who knows he is in the middle of historic events, Levin rendered the details of a period of time when matters of great consequence were unfolding for the Jewish people. And he did that from the point of view of a Jew acutely aware of his Diaspora condition who recognized that the new reality of Jewish sovereignty in the Land of Israel would have a profound impact on Jewish identity, starting with his own.

The opening of *In Search* could hardly be more direct. "This is a book about being a Jew," Levin says. And then he adds, I suppose people are somewhat weary of the Jewish problem. The other day while breakfasting at a drugstore counter, I caught a snatch of conversation from the neighboring stools. '...there was a bunch of them there, carrying signs.' 'What were they kicking about now?' 'I don't know. Didn't we give them Israel...'" Early on, then, Levin both acknowledges that the world is getting tired of "the Jewish problem" and demonstrates that de-spite the recent revelations about the Holocaust and the establishment of Israel, Jews were still living in an environment of negative stereotyping and barely-hidden hostility.

"But the coming into being of Israel," Levin begins the next paragraph by saying, "has brought into focus many of our own inner problems, some of them appearing now as not so different from the problems of other people, and some of them unique – for every people has its unique aspects. And it has seemed to me a good time now to examine these problems in myself." And so, explicitly and specifically, the self-examination of himself as a Jew that he is about to undertake is carried out in the context of the creation of Israel.

That this self-examination is not done purely for personal reasons is made clear by Levin in the next paragraph, where he conveys his Diaspora sensibility. "I believe that in following out the sometimes conflicting elements of the Jewish question within myself, I may have served as such a testing agent for my own generation, and particularly for the American born," he says. "So I am telling my own story, not so much, I hope, out of a sense of self-importance as out of a feeling that the evidence I have picked up in seeking a solution of this problem can be of general use in bringing Jews to understand this part of themselves a little better, and bringing other people to understand us – and perhaps even themselves – a little better."

Levin's story about himself and his search involves his developing, defining, and reconciling the three strands of his identity – as a Jew, as an American, and as a writer. And for him, all of those categories are inextricably linked to Israel. As he says a couple of pages into the book, "I had since early manhood been passionately involved in the development of Jewish civilization in Palestine. Twenty years ago this had seemed a strange absorption for an American Jew, but now it appeared that I had not been on the wrong track. But now some of the questions took a new turn. What was my relationship to Israel? to America? to the world? More insistently than ever I had to ask myself, What am I? and, What am I doing here?" And then, a few paragraphs after that, he puts it this way: "I want to examine my way of life as a Jew born in America, seeking the full realization of his potentialities."

Ready, then, to start to tell his story, Levin makes a rather startling statement. "My dominant childhood memory is of fear and shame at being a Jew," he proclaims. Though America at the time was far more tolerant of differences than most of the European centers of Jewish life, and though Chicago had a sizable Jewish community, Levin still grew up in a climate imbued with its own anti-Semitism and with memories of life in Europe that significantly framed his perspective on the world around him and on himself. "Perhaps we knew there was something particularly inferior about being a Jew through all the tales we absorbed in childhood, of how the lives of our parents had been in the old country," he says. "We therefore knew that with our people, in no matter what country they lived, it has always been as it was with us – we were a despised people." If Levin's childhood fear was caused by anti-Semitism, making him a model figure in the classic template of the "Jewish problem" of his time, the accompanying "shame at being a Jew" that he describes was the result of his being born in America to immigrant Jewish parents.

Levin describes how in his own childhood he and his friends had been threatened by the Italian youths who outnumbered the Jews in his neighborhood on the near West Side of Chicago. Coming home from Hebrew class and gym one day, he found himself writing a short story that he in later years interpreted as meaning that "I was seeking an escape from my Jewishness in order to prove to the world that it was no crime. In the symbols of the fantasy, I wished for rebirth." Ultimately, his "rebirth" was to be not a form of escape from his Jewishness but a fulfillment of it, connected with Israel.

After graduating from the University of Chicago, Levin traveled to Europe with two of his classmates, stopping en route in New York, where he met with Elliòt Cohen at the *Menorah Journal*, a notable Jewish publication of the time. It was with one of those classmates that, visiting Vienna, Levin "for the first time…saw an approximation of an east-European ghetto." As threatened and uncomfortable as he had felt at times as a Jew in America, he came to recognize how much worse things were for Jews in Europe. "We were shocked and frightened at the misery, the lack of dignity, the hopelessness of the inhabitants," he writes.

When his friend went to the village which that young man's parents had come from, Levin "wandered over Italy and Greece, and finally went to Palestine." A decision portrayed here as made somewhat on a whim, it was to impact Levin for the rest of his life. "For a young American to have gone to Palestine in 1925 was itself strange," he reflects while describing that visit. "In those days Zionism was a question that had scarcely penetrated to Jews born in America. It was something dealt with in the Yiddish press, it was something that occupied the bearded ones from the old country....My own family, indeed, had no interest in the movement."

"I don't know what made me go to Palestine unless it was the curiosity of the young mind," he observes. But then, with youthful enthusiasm akin to that conveyed by William Wordsworth in "The Prelude," the "autographical poem" in which that English poet recalled visiting revolutionary France at about the same age, Levin says, "The experience of Palestine was electrifying. I felt like a discoverer. Here were Jews like early Americans, riding guard at night in vigilance against hostile natives, pioneering in the malarial marshes, and living in communal groups. And more powerfully than in earlier Greece, I was possessed by the physical beauty of the land, so deeply moved that I began to wonder whether my reactions were not instinct with racial memory."

While in Palestine, Levin reported on the opening of the Hebrew University for the *Menorah Journal.* And that event too had a great impact on him. "I was extremely excited by the ceremony of the founding of the Hebrew University. In the open-air theater hacked out of the side of Mt. Scopas [sic], looking down beyond the platform upon the awesome raw hills of the Judean wilderness that dropped away to the Dead Sea, I felt an overwhelming rightness of place."

When Levin left after a few weeks, it was in part to resist the pull of the location for him. "Though I knew I was not done with the land, my first impulse was to flee, to recontact America for fear of being seduced, of losing myself in a movement that perhaps was not meant for me – for wasn't it my destiny to become the great American novelist?"

But the Yishuv continued to exert its appeal, and after a couple of years in America spent writing two unpublished novels and doing other work, Levin "decided to go back to Palestine and try to live in one of the farm communes, perhaps eventually to write about that life." He ends up settling on Kibbutz Yagur, near Haifa.

It is a rich experience, but when he receives word of an offer to publish his two novels, he heads back to America and, in Chicago, works at the *Daily News*. Still, with "a sense of guilt at having left the colony with my self-experiment unfinished," he creates what he calls "a cross between a Bohemian and a Tel Aviv household." To accomplish that, he links up with Yitzhak Chizik, a member of a distinguished Yishuv family who was then a student at the University of Chicago. "A husky, tall fellow, boiling over with exuberance, [Chizik] was the first example of the new Palestinian Jew to appear in Chicago," Levin writes. Chizik moves into the apartment Levin was sharing with a number of others and, to pay his rent, teaches Levin Hebrew. In linking up with this charismatic first new Jew to have come to Chicago, Levin was forging a friendship that would last for decades. And then he decides to go back to Palestine for his third visit, and this time he returns to Yagur "on a different footing....I was a comrade."

The material I have summarized above, in which I have focused on Levin's early connections with the Yishuv rendered through his Diaspora perspective, covers only about one-tenth of the book as a whole. *In Search* is divided into three parts, and though the first section is called "America: The Self-Accused" and the nature of Jewish life in America is at its core, even here Levin's tightening ties to the Yishuv are of enormous importance. Indeed, the pages that follow where I left off describe the intensity of his experience at Yagur, which makes life there all the more attractive even as he continues to struggle against committing himself to living permanently in the Yishuv.

"What drew me here," he says, "was the seductive appeal of unity in one's life." Looking back from the vantage point of 1948/1949, when he wrote this book, he observes that "Here in Palestine – even before the Jewish community was a nation – I could live as a Jew in Jewish society, speaking our own tongue, raising wholly Jewish children....The logic of Jewish life in Palestine to me was irrefutable. Therefore the question stood before me: if you believe in it, why don't you do it?"

It is now 1929, and the Jews of Palestine are facing Arab rioting that includes the Hebron massacre. Levin leaves the kibbutz to report on some of that activity for the *Chicago Daily News,* but with the foreign correspondent John Gunther soon there to pick up the assignment, he then moves to Tel Aviv to write *Yehuda*, a novel about life at Yagur.[2]

With a stop in Europe, he next goes back to New York, does some work for the Jewish Telegraphic Agency, and is there when *Yehuda* is published. The book's sales are limited, to his disappointment. "I had hoped

Yehuda would reach the wider circles of my own generation, to whom Zionism was remote, and convey to them something of my own excitement about Palestine as a new force in our lives. But it failed to penetrate these circles."

After overseeing the publication of *The Golden Mountain,* a collection of Chassidic stories he had discovered in Europe, Levin returns to Chicago once more. While doing magazine and theater work there, he writes *The Old Bunch.* When it is published he says of his three most recent books, *"The Golden Mountain* was my connection with the traditional material in the past of my people, *The Old Bunch* represented my relationship to our present life, and *Yehuda* to what I consider the vital source of future Jewish culture."

Drawn to radical activity in Depression-era America, Levin discovers how different his Zionist leanings make him from his fellow political activists, who are critical of him for his support of Jewish life in the Yishuv. "It appeared to me that the communist line on Palestine was evolved out of abstractions, out of rulebook calculations by people who had no real contact with the Jews or Arabs in Palestine" he observes. Levin next heads off to Spain to report on the civil war there, and at the end of 1937 he is back in Palestine until a cable calls him back to the States to work on the new magazine he had been active in establishing. And then comes World War II, when he becomes a writer and filmmaker in the Office of War Information, first in the U.S., then overseas.

A low point for Levin at this stage of his development is again seen from a Diaspora point of view. It comes after he is involved in an incident while on his way to cover the liberation of Paris, goes to the wrong field censor, is accused of disobeying orders, and is sent back to London. Wondering "how it was that all my vaunted integration had dissolved," he says, "For all my labor in the last years to fit myself into the world pattern, I was still a little member of my clan, overanxious, self-centered, insecure, the eternal bright and troublesome Jew. As soon as I got into the world among the goyim, I messed up."

And then comes the climactic reversal which closes Part One:

> No one seemed to know what to do with me. Surely, I thought, it is because I didn't know in myself where I belonged. I hadn't been able to fit into "their" world. It was perhaps not yet the place for me. Though I had imagined, through my books, that I had worked out the Jewish equation for myself, I was still

unquiet. And now I saw a task for myself as a Jew.

For there was one story, in Europe, which I was peculiarly fitted to tell. It was the story of the fate of the Jews.

Getting himself named a news correspondent for the Overseas New Agency and then the Jewish Telegraphic Agency, Levin is on his way to Paris, where "there began a period when I felt that I functioned extremely well, as a human being who was doing what he was meant to do."

Europe As Exile

Part Two of the book is entitled "Europe: The Witnesses." If America is Diaspora, a place where, despite the occasional discomfort, there can be vibrant Jewish life of sorts, Europe is Exile, a place altogether inhospitable to Jewish existence. While Levin had previously recognized the virulence of anti-Semitism in Europe and its impact on that continent's Jews, what he comes to learn of the details of the Holocaust provides intense confirmation of that condition, as he reaffirms his sense that Jewish life in Europe was a condition of the past, and that only. Furthermore, as a witness to what the Holocaust had wrought, Levin has a profound personal experience that leads him inexorably to his next stage of self-discovery, helping him find his own place in the world, integrating his heretofore separate parts, and offering him creative fulfillment.

Telling "the day-to-day stories" he discovered in seeking out "the remnants of Israel" as well as "stories of fighting Jews," Levin produces a series of powerful narratives. Describing the "same dark sallow faces" he sees in sites "from Paris to Budapest," he says that "they inevitably appeared to me in terms of my people of the west side of Chicago, people of *The Old Bunch;* they were children of the same parents." And yet there is a difference, for "they all have death inside."

After some time has gone by, he and his photographer/jeep-mate come upon a branch of the Buchenwald death camp near the town of Ohrdruff and are shown a shed. Its door opened, they have their first view of what the Nazis had wrought:

There was a cordwood stack of stiff naked human bodies, a stack as high as we stood. The bodies were flat and yellow as lumber. A yellow disinfectant was scattered over the pile.

We had known. The world had vaguely heard. But until now no one of us had looked on this. Even this morning we had not imagined we would look on this. It was as though we had penetrated at last to the center of the black heart, to the very crawling inside of the vicious heart.

Levin has additional experiences of that sort, and then the war is finished. A rabbi chaplain with whom he crosses paths asks him if he could bring a Torah scroll back to the Jews of Cologne, and he agrees. "And as I drove through that smiling and evil land I asked myself, what was the Torah, literally, and what was the Torah to me?" Referencing what he regards as "the distortion in the American-born Jews of my generation, that rose from the intimidation that the immigrant parents felt in the fact of American life," he goes on to say, "The parents did not dare assert their Jewish culture before their children, whose avidity for American culture was so natural and powerful." For himself, though, matters are now different. As he says, "I had been in my own way recovering my link with my historic past, and restoring this element to its proportionate place in my life."

As he brings the Torah to the few remaining Jews in Cologne, he reaffirms his conclusions about the exilic condition of Europe, saying, "Yes, I knew I could go away and write a hopeful story, a symbolic story of the return of the Torah to the most ancient of Jewish communities, of the indestructibility of the Jewish community, of how it would rise here again." Instead he says, "But the truth was only desolation, the truth was only a handful of dazed survivors, each seeking a way to leave Germany, and this Torah they had wanted was wanted not to root them here, but to keep their faith in themselves alive, to remind them of their identity, for otherwise the world was unendurable. No, I had to write of the Jews of Cologne, of the Jews of Europe as they were: broken, finished. It was not for me to bear false witness."

Maintaining what is for him an important distinction, he says that, in contrast, "America was the antithesis of all this that had been sickness in Europe, America was in itself a unity of nations, a country where different peoples had learned to live together. America would never bring us to this." And so, he announces in ending Part Two, "I had done with the story of the Jews of Europe. I could go home."

Exodus To A New Life In "Their Own Country"

The title of Part Three of *In Search* is "Israel: The Released." The section begins with Levin's saying: "But I had not done. When I reached New

York I soon realized that the world outside Europe had little comprehension of the extent of the tragedy that had taken place nor of the tragedy that remained." Attempting to address that gap, he dedicates himself to helping the "broken and lonesome souls" he had seen end their exile and get to Palestine despite the quota the British had put in place and despite the uncaring sense he felt forthcoming from the other powers of the world. To further that effort, he "conceived the idea of filming the entire underground route from Poland to Palestine, so that the world might at least be able to see the reality, to see the poor thin remnant of survivors, and comprehend that they had to go to their own country, or else die." But then the Overseas News Agency asks him to cover the troubles developing in Palestine, and he is again on his way there, where he learns that "the war was not over; to us the British had replaced the Germans." Furthermore, the "British-tolerated Mufti factions" are stimulating violence against the Jews of the Yishuv.

A key moment during this visit occurs when he visits his friends in Yagur and celebrates Pesach with them. Reflecting on the new kind of observance he sees there, Levin elaborates on his view that if the Judaism of Europe is finished, the hope of a new Judaism exists not among the assimilated, embarrassed Jews of America he knows, but in places like this kibbutz in the Yishuv. "Where might the Jews have the daring to alter their traditional ritual if not here?" he asks. Describing a performance in which the Seder narrative is acted out accompanied by song and dance, with the ceremonial meal following, he adds: "Where, in two thousand years, had there been such a renewal of our way of worship?...Where had our national life given such a new form to the ancient content? It seemed to me that I was in the very center of the creative continuation of our culture. It was as though for an instant that the historic processes lay open before us, and I glimpsed the way things came to be, and I was awed as in watching the opening of a flower."

Thinking about the current situation as a whole, he concludes: "In this atmosphere of resistance, achievement, terror, construction, and undeclared war, I was trying to prepare the scenario for our film....I felt that the first big film about Palestine should be on the fundamental theme of this land – regeneration. It should be a positive story of what the county gave to those who came to it." And so he embarked on the creation of a film that would be called *My Father's House* (with a book based on the script to follow), about a child survivor who in coming to Palestine is "in search" of his father. A story of "rebirth" and "self-realization," it was in a way, as he came to realize when it was completed, "not only the child's story, and the story of the survivors, but my own story." And so, in the realm of nascent sovereignty, he sees the conditions for national and personal rebirth – for others and for himself. But history is still unfolding, and his own quest is not yet complete.

In the summer of 1947, both book and film were finished and Levin was ready to go to Europe to begin to make his next film, this one about the illegal immigration. "And in that other search, for a source…I wanted to reach Poland; I would begin the film there, in the sourceland of European Jewry. I had to go there, to touch Poland before I was free. Perhaps too, I had to re-enact for myself the exodus. Then my own journey would be rounded and complete."

The making of this film, to be called *The Illegals*, has enormous impact on Levin, and the anticipated stop in Poland, a return "to the old place" that had been "an obsession" with him, leaves him "released" – released from his personal roots there even as the Jews of Europe are released from their exile. Going back, he – and they – are able to go forward. And at the same time as he is filming the survivors heroically making their way to their new lives in Palestine, events of great consequence are transpiring. "For the partition of Palestine had been announced, and England had declared her intention of quitting the country in May."

For him the stop in Palestine that follows his arrival with the illegals is a short one which mostly revolves around concerns about making sure that the filming that had been done on the ship will not have been done in vain. Then it is back to Europe to work on the film and to try to address what he feels is a great need to "for once get the Jewish story before non-Jews." But he feels frustrated in his efforts by what he attributes to society's refusal "to look directly at the fact that it was capable of murdering six million people." So with statehood now declared, Levin asks the Overseas News Agency to send him to cover those developments. But, he is told, "they could not use me in Israel now because of my Jewish name. A gentile by-line, they felt, would receive wider acceptance in the American press." Left to devote all his energies to promotion of *The Illegals*, he is disappointed with the limited response the film receives. Sizing up the situation in a passage which can be taken as encapsulating his life to that time and the condition of the Jewish people at that point in history, he thinks:

> Unhappy as had been the result of the venture, as a personal experience the making of the film had been the richest and most rewarding event in my life. With it, I had come to the end of a

stage in my journey toward self-realization. I had at last been back to the beginning in Poland, and like every refugee I had seen for myself that all that connected my people to that place was gone. I had rounded out the task I had adopted for myself from the day I had entered the first concentration camp; I had told all I could find to tell, shown all there was to show. Now, like every Jew, I needed to come to a new understanding of myself in relation to Israel.

Coming To Grips With Sovereignty

Levin travels to what is now the sovereign Jewish state of Israel with Tereska Torres, whom he had known from her childhood and who had traveled and worked with him on *The Illegals,* in which she had a role. He had married her a short time before and he dedicates this book to her. Everything about this trip is out in the open. And for him and others aboard ship, there is a sense of great pride in sailing in an Israeli vessel and then entering Haifa harbor.

Observing the new reality around him, Levin quickly notices something else that is different about coming to Haifa this time. "There were no Arabs." "We had known, of course," he says, "And we had a prepared attitude on the question: their own people had caused them to evacuate." Nevertheless, as he sees a site which he knew as having been "a particularly nasty snipers village," now dynamited, on the way to Tel Aviv, he thinks, "Yet though our general justification on the Arab question was prepared in us, this sight gave us a strange guilty sensation of which we were not to rid ourselves, and this guilt must be carried, even if under the heading of the lesser injustice."

In Tel Aviv he discusses the moral complexities of the Arab situation with his old friend Yitzhak Chizik, then serving as the military commander of Jaffa. "The talk with Yitzhak reassured me; not that any solutions to our problems were good in themselves, but that there was a man, raised in this community, who was deeply concerned to do justice, and he was surely not alone."[3] Pages later, while passing a former Arab village where Jews now live, he would return to the topic, thinking, "History was harsh, it did not permit us to attain any ideal without the concomitant evil....It was a guilt, surely....Every people had such guilts in their history; we had to live with it. And perhaps it was not a great sin to have caused these Arabs to have removed to another Arab land, fifty miles away."

The visit includes attendance at a wedding, rich in symbolic meaning, of the only relative on Tereska's father's side who had survived the Holocaust in Poland, and then a stop at Ramat Naphtali, where the couple was to live. And where, thinking of himself, Levin wonders, "Was it imperative that a Jew now live in this land?"

This leads Levin into an extended reflection on Israel-Diaspora relations now that sovereignty has been established, and after a visit to Jerusalem, to speculation on the effect of the founding of Israel on the world's manner of viewing and treating the Jews. And now that the Jewish people have their state, he wonders, will the Jews of Israel and the Jews of the Diaspora grow closer to one another, as one people, or further apart, with different forms of Jewish life? A person with a foot in each world and an understanding of both, he observes how far apart the Jews in Israel and those in America, with their different experiences and perspectives, already are from each other. He captures the stereotypical judgments that each makes of the other, noting how for Americans "the tales of war prevalent abroad emphasized [the Israelis'] legendary qualities, rather than the reality," while for the Israelis, visiting Americans came across as "overpatronizing or overhumble."

He goes on to insist that they each need to get to know the others as they really are, and identifies his own role in that context.

On simplest terms, we needed to know each other, just as we needed to make our plain selves known to the outside world. In this was my task. It was also the work I had always been doing; it was the work I had still to do. My actual physical place of residence was of lesser importance, it would depend on the requirements and the opportunities of this work. It was appalling what small means there were for the two remaining Jewish populations to come to know each other....The average Israeli had only the most distorted idea of American Jewish life, and the American Jew had only the propaganda view of Israel....Only reality could close the gap.

For Levin, it is of enormous importance that the rift be reduced, and he ultimately sees it as his vocation to enhance the understanding that American Jews will have of Israelis. Looking forward prophetically and thinking of himself, he writes:

The forces of necessity would drive the two groups together, just as psychological factors tended now to drive them apart, and surely there would be many seeing the same needs that I had seen, for the Jews were still one people. They needed, just now, perhaps to be reminded of this truth. Indeed, my own coming and going between the two groups was not so much a sign of conflict, split in myself, as of their organic oneness.

And so for Levin, the search is finished. He has discovered his identity and integrated the strands of it, as Jew, as American, and as writer, with all of that tied to the state of Israel. And at the same time that that personal goal has been achieved, the search of the Jewish people has reached its fulfillment as well, with the establishment of a vibrant country, welcoming all Jews who need and wish to come there; providing opportunity for personal rebirth, especially for those who had suffered in the Holocaust; and offering national self-determination and sovereignty for the Jewish people.

At the same time, this is not an end, since rebirth means new birth and new life and all that goes with that. "The formation of the state of Israel is not, then, the end of the Jewish question," Levin says, "but a new basis upon which positive values can be erected. Our continuing Jewish culture will be related to living Israel rather than to a dying European Jewry. But it will be founded always on the historic memory of the folk, and it will contain, too, the admixture of every local community culture." And so, in moving through the tripartite, dialectical framework of this book, which goes from the Diaspora conditions of America backward to Exile in Europe and then forward to Sovereignty in Israel, Levin has traced the Jewish people's experience in the first half of the twentieth century and has offered a vision of the future.

Looking Forward

As ready for his own future as Levin may have thought he was, what awaited him was not something that he could altogether have foreseen or scripted. *The Diary of Anne Frank* was given to him in French translation by his wife just months following the publication of *In Search*, and reading it was to send him on an inspired but ultimately unhappy path. Within *In Search,* Levin had exhibited personality traits that included suspiciousness of others and disappointment that shaded into bitterness regarding the treatment of his literary efforts. But such traits became nearly overwhelming after he played a significant role in ensuring the *Diary's* translation into English and in advancing its initial reception and then saw the script he wrote for a dramatic version of that book rejected and replaced by a more universalizing and optimistic treatment. Meanwhile, though, in an act that reconciled and symbolized his ties to both America and Israel, Levin divided his residence between those two countries from the late '50s until his death in Israel in 1981.

Levin never intended *In Search* to be only about himself but also meant it to be about, and for, the Jewish people of his time. Today it serves as a record of that time – an era of great significance for the Jewish people when the children of immigrants came of age and took their places in a changing America; when the Jews of Europe suffered near-annihilation in the Nazi crucible; and when Zionists, refugees, and survivors made their ways into Palestine and created a country despite extreme challenges. Levin was a witness to all of that and a participant in much of it. He recognized that it was rare for an American Jew of his time to catch the Zionist "bug" the way he did, and he dedicated himself to writing about his experiences in the Yishuv in a manner that he hoped would broaden the American Jewish community's attachment to Israel. Though aspects of that era are now seen as more complex and in some ways problematic than they were by him or others then, his descriptions of subjects ranging from the early years of kibbutz life to the Arab riots of 1929 have an unmistakable eyewitness authenticity about them. Though much has changed since then – in Israel, Europe, and America alike – his observations about the developments of his time are rich with insights that have remained relevant to this day, while his personal reactions to Jewish life in the Yishuv and his views of its meaning to the Jewish people fore-shadowed responses that many American Jews would have years later.

As the decade of the '50s evolved, other American Jewish writers provided very different treatments of Israel and of coming of age in Chicago. "I am an American, Chicago-born – Chicago, that somber city – and go at things as I have taught myself, freestyle," opens Saul Bellow's *The Adventures of Augie March* (1953), with a very different tone than the opening of Levin's autobiographical *In Search*. And though Leon Uris' *Exodus* (1958) covered much of the same European and Israeli ground as *In Search* had, it did so in a less nuanced fashion, projecting stereotypical images of Israel and of the Israelis and becoming a bestseller. The American literary scene clearly had changed since the early years of Levin's career, when he had been frustrated in trying to obtain supporting publishers or a major audience for much of his work on Jewish subjects

– a situation that also applied to *In Search* itself, which he had to publish privately in France before it found a minor American publisher.[4]

But different as In Search was from much of what followed, as a work which conveyed the observations, reactions, and thoughts of an astute, involved American Jewish writer in the years leading up to and including the establishment of the State of Israel, it stands as a landmark publication. It opens a window onto an era not widely remembered as it was. It tells the moving story of its writer's engagement with the Yishuv, an engagement which gave his life meaning and had a profound impact on his sense of Jewish identity. And it offers a narrative of Zionist affirmation from a person not without awareness of the Other. Indeed, though much may have changed in Israel, in the American Jewish community, and in their interactions since 1950, the model of Levin's early life and the implications of his call for a reality-rooted, experience-based relationship between American Jews and Israelis can be said to be at least as resonant today as they were when this Chicago-born author wrote a book about himself and his people which revolves around the modes of Diaspora, Exile, and Sovereignty in dramatic fashion.

NOTES

[1] Meyer Levin, *In Search: An Autobiography* (Paris: Authors' Press, 1950).

The titles of the two most recent books on Levin, published in the late '90s, demonstrate the prism through which he is usually looked at these days. They are Lawrence Graver, *An Obsession with Anne Frank: Meyer Levin and the Diary* (Berkeley: University of California Press, 1995); and Ralph Melnick, *The Stolen Legacy of Anne Frank: Meyer Levin, Lillian Hellman, and the Staging of the Diary* (New Haven: Yale University Press, 1997). Graver regards *In Search* as an "imposing work of self-inquiry, confession, and explanation," p. 11.

The one earlier full-length study of Levin, in Twayne's United States Authors Series, is Steven J. Rubin, *Meyer Levin* (Boston: Twayne Publishers, 1982). The treatment of *In Search* appears on pp. 72-80. Rubin concludes that "Like all good autobiography, the book maintains a balance between individual awareness and historical truth, between self and the world" (p. 79).

[2] Though there no mention of *In Search* in Andrew Furman, *Israel Through the Jewish-American Imagination: A Survey of Jewish-American Literature on Israel, 1928-1995* (Albany: State University of New York Press, 1997), Furman does provide a chapter about Levin's early Yishuv-linked fiction, in which he calls *Yehuda,* published in 1931, "the first significant Zionist novel in America" (p. 26).

[3] Chizik, who would later change his last name to Horpi, went on to hold other administrative and diplomatic positions, including director general of the Ministry of Police and Is-

rael's Chargé d'Affaires in Liberia. As the Israeli consul, in 1958 he returned to Chicago, where he died suddenly. *The Settlers,* Levin's 1972 epic novel about the early years of the Yishuv, is dedicated "For Yitzhak, in promise, and in remembrance."

4. *In Search* was reprinted in paperback form by the American publisher Pocket Books in 1973, as discussed in Harold U. Ribalow, "A Conversation with Meyer Levin," Midstream (January 1978), pp. 39-43. Ribalow added the volume to The Old Bunch and Compulsion (1956) as the three books by Levin that "have become American-Jewish classics," but only the first two continued to be widely remembered in subsequent years.

A case for the influence of *In Search* on a major American Jewish writer has recently been argued in James Duban, "Written, Unwritten, and Vastly Rewritten: Meyer Levin's *In Search* and Philip Roth's "Defender of the Faith," *The Plot Against America,* and *Indignation," Philip Roth Studies,* 7-1 (Fall 2011), 171-186.

Postscript: Where To Now?

As is fitting in a time of uncertainty and change, as I write this in early spring 2014, much is up in the air in the world at large and regarding issues high on the Jewish communal agenda. As all of this plays out, there has developed what I believe to be a problematic polarization within the American Jewish community, especially about Israel, reflecting and in part influenced by the poisonous polarization that prevails within American politics today. With so much that is uncertain and with so much at stake, it is no surprise that there would be strong differences of opinion regarding the wisest course for Israel to follow and the directions that American policy might go. But I believe that some of what is happening goes beyond the pale, and that if the community cannot remain unified around bottom-line principles and if people and groups on one side of these issues or the other see all of those who might differ from them as maliciously motivated enemies, there will surely be negative repercussions of many kinds.

The sense of a unified community is breaking down in other ways too. In the age of the Internet, of personally directed funding, and of increasing decentralization, we have seen the decline of many traditional organizations and the rise of numerous start-ups, some of them making valuable contributions but others sometimes appearing to follow questionable or even counterproductive strategies. As I have argued elsewhere in this volume, it is not good for any organization to stagnate and merely rest upon its laurels, and there should be room and appreciation for new approaches. But it remains to be seen how well-served the community will be in the difficult years to come by an anti-establishment trend in which some organizations function with a limited sense of accountability and with diminished acceptance of the virtues of centrist, consensus-driven decision-making. Furthermore, the problem of maintaining community ties among younger generations is severe enough without having this kind of behavior added to the mix.

Lest this Postscript, and thus this volume, end on a negative note, I would emphasize that just as there is in America a centrifugal force which pulls many individuals away from the Jewish community and its institutions, so there is a strong centripetal force pulling others into the community's orbit. As is demonstrated by the success of the Birthright program and outreach steps being taken by Hillel Foundations on campus and by some Federations and others, including some of the newly-minted structures, Jewish identity and ties with Israel can have continuing value for younger members of the community, while connections with community can continue to have power. Thus, even as the community modulates its shape and nature, there is plenty to be hopeful about as the twenty-first century moves forward.

And finally, I end this Postscript as I began the Introduction, with a personal reflection. When my oldest grandson was given my father's first name as his middle name at his Brit Milah in the summer of 2006, I was touched by that traditional expression of connection and continuity. My father had been born almost exactly 100 years before, and while considering all that he had seen and experienced in his lifetime of 88 years, I wondered what awaited his great-grandson. Whatever it may turn out to be, I profoundly hope that for all of my grandchildren and their generation, the past of the Jewish people will continue to have meaning in the present while helping to forge a flourishing future.

Acknowledgments

• • •

Iam grateful to Steve Nasatir, President of the Jewish United Fund/ Jewish Federation of Metropolitan Chicago, for proposing to me that this book be put together and then for ensuring that whatever was necessary was done to bring the project to fruition. My debt to Steve goes well beyond the particularities connected with the publication of this volume, and I am grateful to him as well for bringing me on board as a member of the Federation team in the first place; for encouraging me to write the pieces collected here; for giving me a chance to play the many roles I have played at the Federation; for supporting me in those efforts; and for all along being, quite simply, an inspirational leader, a wonderful colleague, and a good friend.

I am grateful as well to Aaron Cohen, Ron Margolin, and Jay Tcath, close, long-standing colleagues, each of whom contributed to the creation of this volume in significant ways; to Jim Rosenberg, who helped shepherd the project along; and to my assistant, Connie Daniels, who played an important part in the production of many of these pieces in the first place and then did much to bring them together in this form.

There are others in the Chicago Federation and in the Jewish communal world in Chicago and beyond whose collegiality and friendship through the decades has meant much. And there are also friends, in the States and in Israel, with whom quite a number of these pieces were shared in their original draft form or shortly after publication and along with whom I have had the privilege of enjoying a fellowship of kindred spirits. Naming all of those people would make for a very long list, and I fear that while trying to cite them all I would inadvertently leave out somebody or other who deserves to be included. So I hope that everybody I am thinking of in this way who might read this realizes that I had them in mind, and I hope they all will forgive me for not identifying them individually.

There is one such person, however, who I cannot leave out, and that is Yossi Klein Halevi, who has touched me deeply with his friendship and his readiness to write the Preface for this book. Anybody who is familiar with the quality and importance of Yossi's own writings will recognize what a distinction it is to be able to include words of his in this volume.

Dearest of all are my family members. My children Daniel (and Jen), Joshua (and Dorian), and Abigail (and Matt) were helpful to me in various ways, first as I wrote these piece and then as I brought them together. Even more, they and their children have been a primary driving force for me through the years. I remember once saying to Steve Nasatir, as we reflected on our generation, that we were brought up believing that the purpose of our lives was to make our parents proud and our children happy. I don't know how to measure the extent to which I may have succeeded in fulfilling the latter goal. But to reverse the formula, I do know how proud my children and those with whom they have chosen to share their lives have made me, and how much happiness they have brought me. As for the grandchildren they have produced, who have brought me such enormous joy, I now realize that it is in many ways for them, and their generation, that the work I have done, which is reflected in the pieces in this book, will have whatever ultimate value it may obtain.

And now I come to Judy, my wife of half a century, with no words to conjure up to sufficiently convey the love and appreciation that I feel. She has guided me to probe and better understand the thoughts I have had and the beliefs I hold. She has been there with me through thick and thin, giving me the wisdom and the strength to face the challenges that life presents. She has brought me abiding joy, and the opportunity to link my life to hers has been the greatest good fortune I could have had. My gratitude to her is immeasurable.

About the Author

A Chicago native, Michael Kotzin is currently Senior Counselor to the President of the Jewish Federation of Metropolitan Chicago. He joined the staff of the Federation in 1988, and from 1999 until 2011 served as Executive Vice President. Before coming to the Federation he directed the Anti-Defamation League's Chicago office. He previously taught English Literature at Tel Aviv University for eleven years. The author of a book on the novels of Charles Dickens, he has published widely on literary topics and on issues high on the Jewish communal agenda.

Cover design: Ron Margolin
Book design: Susan Marx
Cover photos by Joel Fishman and Debbi Cooper